RUSSIAN COMMERCIAL LAW

Russian Commercial Law

by

Hiroshi Oda

Sir Ernest Satow Professor of Japanese Law,
University of London (University College),
Professor of College d'Europe (Brugge),
Attorney at Law (Japan)

Kluwer Law International

The Hague / London / New York

Library of Congress Cataloging-in-Publication Data

ISBN 90-411-1846-2

Published by Kluwer Law International,
P.O. Box 85889, 2508 CN The Hague, The Netherlands.

Sold and distributed in North, Central and South America
by Kluwer Law International,
101 Philip Drive, Norwell, MA 02061, U.S.A.
kluwerlaw@wkap.com

In all other countries, sold and distributed
by Kluwer Law International, Distribution Centre,
P.O. Box 322, 3300 AH Dordrecht, The Netherlands.

Layout and camera-ready copy:
Anne-Marie Krens – Oegstgeest – The Netherlands

Cover: SEUTTER, Georg Matthaus (circa 1750) IMPERIUM RUSSIAE MAGNA.
Copper engraving. Engraved by Tobias Conrad Lotter.
Little map of Northern Asia, from the Black Sea to Japan.
From the private collection of Hiroshi Oda

Printed on acid-free paper

PREFACE

'Law is like the handle of a horse cart; it lets you go everywhere you direct it.'

- an old Russian proverb -

I started my academic career as a specialist of Soviet law at the Law Faculty of the University of Tokyo some 25 years ago. Since then, things have changed considerably; the Soviet Union and almost the entire socialist world are now 'history', and a new discipline, Russian law, has emerged. People often ask me when they learn that I am a Russian law specialist whether law really exists in Russia. Many people believe from the anecdotal stories they hear that Russia is in a lawless state, and that whatever law there is in Russia remains only on paper.

If one looks into history, the pre-reform legal system, i.e. the system before 1864, was more in a state of chaos than a 'system'. With the emergence of constitutionalism, primarily led by lawyers in the late 19th century, the situation improved, but the development was stalled by the October Revolution. Under socialism, while the 'subjects' of the Soviet Union, i.e. the general public, were strictly bound by law, the Communist Party leadership was not. In fact, law was nothing more than a 'state discipline' imposed on the people by the political rulers. The situation has changed since *perestroika*. The present Constitution declares that Russia is a democratic law-governed state. As is presented in this book in detail, there have been remarkable legislative developments since 1990. There is a tangible legal system supported by a workable judiciary in Russia now. But still, there is no shortage of reports on the infringement of shareholders' rights and breaches of law by large companies, not to mention government officials. Obviously, a law-governed state cannot be created by the single stroke of a pen.

Some people explain the current situation of 'lawlessness' by resorting to the fact that it has been little more than a decade since the collapse of socialism. However, inexperience and lack of knowledge may explain errors, but not abuses.

Others, particularly Russians, refer to Russia's traditional 'legal nihilism'. In fact, the existence of a uniquely Russian 'legal nihilism' had already been pointed out in the early 20th century and in the late 1920s. The above proverb is often cited as an example of such a perception of law. However, as is the case with the myth of Japanese legal consciousness, such notions can be misleading. If one takes a closer look at this proverb, it is not the significance of law which is denied. Rather, it reflects the idea of the sheer instrumentalism of law combined with the denial of natural law. Such a view of law was further enhanced under socialism which ruthlessly used law as an instrument of consolidation and reinforcement of power.

Thus, it may be the case that neglect of law is not inherent in the Russian legal consciousness as is often contended, but rather, a different perception of law, an extreme legal instrumentalism, has prevailed in Russia. In fact, this may have been a truly realistic view of law in the absence of democracy. It is probably better than legal nihilism, since, at least, the usefulness of the law and the need for the observance of law are recognised. If this is the case, with a nascent democracy and a fairly developed legal system now in hand, there is some hope that Russia will gradually move towards becoming a law-governed state.

This book attempts to introduce the emerging system of commercial law in Russia to readers outside Russia. The core of this book is company law, but it extends to the entire area of commercial law. Although some books on Russian law have been published since the collapse of socialism, there are very few books focussing on commercial law, despite a high demand for such a book in the business world as well as in the world of academia.

The problem with research into Soviet law was that there was always a huge gap between the law in books and the law in action. At that time, most of us tried to pierce the veil of secrecy and get closer to reality by delving into archives, interviewing practitioners, visiting institutions etc. Now, there is not much secrecy surrounding Russian law, but there is still a tremendous gap between law and its implementation. The gap primarily comes from often inconsistent and contradictory laws as well as their ineffective implementation,

The method I adopted to fill this gap was to 'let the cases speak for themselves'. Unlike in the socialist period, court decisions play a major role in developing Russian law now. I went through numerous court decisions published in Russia and tried to explain how Russian law operates in reality by resorting to these cases. Admittedly, some of the decisions are of a questionable nature, but nevertheless, they give us an insight into the actual operation of law. These cases are supported by authoritative commentaries to the laws published recently. Another development is the Internet; websites of various agencies and institutions provide useful statistics which have been hitherto unavailable. Almost all the materials used in this book are from first hand sources.

I was fortunate to have been given an opportunity to be involved in various projects in Russia, including energy projects. Among other things, I have learned to look at the subject not only from the view point of an academic, which I continue to be, but also from the viewpoint of those who are the actual users of the legal system.

The preparation of this book has been supported and assisted by Herbert Smith, an international law firm based in London, where I have been working since 1997 as a consultant on Japanese and Russian law. I am grateful to the firm as a whole for its warm support for this undertaking, but specifically to Messrs Richard Bond, senior partner, Richard Fleck, Alan Jowett, who is responsible for the Herbert Smith's Moscow office, Sergei Baranchenkov, partner in Moscow, and Suren Gortsunyan also in Moscow. My special thanks go to Mr. Danila Logofet, a young and able Russian lawyer in the London office, who read the manuscript at an early stage and gave valuable comments from a Russian perspective.

I am also grateful to my senior colleagues in the 'Russian law fraternity', namely Emeritus Professors Andre Loeber (Kiel University), F.J.M. Feldbrugge (Leiden University) and Bernard Rudden (Brasenose College, Oxford). Bernard has kindly read part of the manuscript despite his busy schedule and commented on it.

As always, I am indebted to the Dean of the Law Faculty of University College London, Professor Jeffrey Jowell, who gave me his unfailing support throughout this work. I would also like to thank Ms. Lisa Goulding and Mr. William Long, both of University College, for editing the text and Mr. Long, particularly for preparing the index.

In the process of publication, Ms. A.-M.C. Krens has prepared a camera ready copy for the book. She had to cope with numerous changes at the last moment. Mr. Peter Buschman of Kluwer International has kindly arranged this book to be published promptly. Without their kind assistance, this book could not have been published in such a timely manner. I am grateful to them both for this.

Last, but not the least, I would like to thank my wife Midori for her warm support in writing this book. This book is dedicated to Midori and her parents.

London, March 2002

Hiroshi Oda

TABLE OF CONTENTS

LIST OF TABLES

ABBREVIATION OF RUSSIAN PERIODICALS

BVS RF	*Biuletten' verkhovnogo suda RF*
GiP	*Gosudarstvo i pravo*
KhiP	*Khoziaistvo i pravo*
NG	*Nezavisimaia gazeta*
PiE	*Pravo i ekonomika*
RG	*Rossiiskaia gazeta*
RIu	*Rossiskaia iustitsiia*
SU	*Sobranie uzakonenii i rasporiazhenii raboche-kreschainskogo pravitel'stva*
SZ RF	*Sobranie zakonov RF*
VE	*Voprosy ekonomiki*
VMU	*Vestnik moskovskogo niversiteta*
VSND RF i VS RF	*Vedomosti sobraniia narodnykh deputatove RF i Verkhovnogo soveta RF*
VVAS RF	*Vedomosti verkhovnogo arbitrazhnogo suda RF*
VVS RFSFR	*Vedomosti verkhovnogo soveta RFSFR*
VVS SSSR	*Vedomosti verkhovnogo soveta SSSR*
ZRP	*Zhurnal rosiiskogo prava*

* *Status juris*

Status juris of this book is December 31, 2001.

** Minimum wage

Minimum wage is often used as a basis of calculation in Russian law. The current minimum wage is set by the Law of June 2000 at 300 roubles (approximately 10 US Dollars) a month.

SOURCES OF LAW

1   THE CONCEPT OF THE LAW-GOVERNED STATE

The present Constitution of the Russian Federation, which was enacted in 1993, starts with the following provision (Art.1, para.1):

> The Russian Federation – Russia is a democratic federative law-governed state (*pravovoe gosudarstvo*) with a republican form of government.

The concept of the law-governed state originated as the *Rechtsstaat* in 19th century Germany and was introduced into Russia towards the end of that century. Some Russian proponents of this concept went further than their German counterparts and supported the introduction of a democratically elected parliament and the subordination of the Tsar to the laws enacted by the parliament. The Russian constitutional movement came close to fruition after the February Revolution in 1917, but the Bolshevik Revolution in October the same year thwarted all the hopes for the realisation of constitutionalism. The democratically elected constitutional assembly, in which the Bolsheviks were a minority, was disbanded by the Bolsheviks soon after the October Revolution.[1]

   Under the socialist regime, the concept of the law-governed state was totally rejected as a 'bourgeois ideology' which was against the dictatorship of the proletariat. It was eventually replaced by the concept of 'socialist legality'. Socialist legality was officially defined as the 'strict observance of law by administrative agencies, social organisations, government officials, and citizens'. This was totally different from the law-governed state in its concept as well as in reality, since i) the law was not enacted through a democratic procedure – to start with, there was no democratic election, ii) the law was subordinate to political expediency

---

[1]   On the development of this concept in Germany and Russia, see H.Oda, 'The Emergence of Pravovoe Gosudarstvo in Russia', *Review of Central and East European Law*, 1999 No.3, p.373ff.

determined by the Communist Party (CPSU) leadership, and iii) the CPSU leadership which actually ruled the country was not bound by any law. Furthermore, there was no independent court. It was not surprising that the coercive collectivisation of agriculture and the Great Terror in the 1930s were not regarded as breaches of socialist legality, but in fact, the implementation of it.

The concept of the law-governed state re-emerged in Russia in the 1980s in the course of *perestroika*. An extensive discussion on this concept began in 1987 in the CPSU official periodical, *Kommunist*. The 19th CPSU Conference, which was convened in 1988, adopted a resolution to create a 'socialist law-governed state'. Soon, the prefix 'socialist' disappeared.[2]

Since the collapse of socialism, new laws have replaced the laws enacted in the socialist period in almost all major branches of law. The Constitutional Court is in operation, and the courts in general have gained independence. As mentioned above, the Constitution has declared Russia to be a law-governed state.

Naturally, the mere fact that the concept has been enshrined in the present Constitution does not mean that Russia has become a genuine law-governed state. V.N.Kudriavtsev, who has been instrumental in reintroducing the concept of the law-governed state in the process of *perestroika*, pointed out in 1998 as follows:

> In reality, Russia in the past decades has become all too accustomed to the serious violation and flagrant neglect of the rights and lawful interests of individuals. Rectifying the present situation in several years is impossible, but it is our immediate task to consistently work towards that direction.[3]

At this stage, one can only say that, at least, the basic legal framework to create a genuine law-governed state is in place.

2   THE FEDERAL STRUCTURE

Russia is a federal state. It comprises 21 republics, 6 regions (*krais*), 49 provinces (*oblast's*), 1 autonomous province, 10 autonomous regions, and 2 cities of federal designation (articles 5 and 65 of the Constitution). These entities are 'constituent entities of the Russian Federation with equal rights' (Art.5, para.1). This means that these entities by no means form a hierarchical order; all these entities consti-tute the second layer of the structure of the Russian Federation. Thus, regions do not exist within the republic, or the provinces exist within the region; they

---

2   *Ibid.*, pp.412-415.
3   V.N.Kudriavtsev, 'Zakonnost': soderzhanie i sovremennoe sostoianie', *ZhRP*, 1998 No.1, p.7.

all exist in a parallel manner. Below these entities is the system of 'local self government' – the second layer of local governments. These are cities and towns (except Moscow and St.Petersburg which are 'cities of federal designation' and are constituent entities of the Federation), districts (counties), villages etc. They are not constituent entities of the Russian Federation as such, and are governed by the laws and statutes enacted by the constituent entities within the framework of the Federal Law on the General Principles of Organising Local Self-Government in the Russian Federation and by their own statutes (*ustavy*).[4]

The Constitution provides that the administrative structure of the constituent entities is determined by themselves independently in accordance with the fundamentals of the constitutional system of the Russian Federation and the general principles of the organisation of the representative and executive bodies of state power (Art.77, para.1).

A majority of republics are headed by a president, while some other republics have the title of the 'head of the republic', or 'chairman of the government'. In many cases, there is a separation of power; there is an executive body called the government or cabinet and a representative legislative body. Several republics have a state council as a form of government. As a legislative body, republics have a 'state assembly', 'state council', or 'legislative assembly' etc. Some republics have adopted a traditional name for their legislative body such as *Khural* in Buriatiia and Kalmykiia. The system of election also varies. On several occasions, the Federal Constitutional Court has ruled the electoral system of the republics to be against the Federal Constitution.[5]

The relationship between various bodies within the republic is often ill defined. For example, in the Fundamental Law of the Republic of Kalmykii, there is no provision on the government. In the Constitution of the Republic of Buriatiia, there are only four provisions on the government and one on the ministries and state committees. The relationship between the acts of these entities and federal acts is not defined at all.[6]

In the provinces and regions, there is a governor (*gubernator*), who is the highest official of the administration and who represents the province or region. The governor is elected by a direct election of the populace for a term of four years. The system of administration comprises the apparatus of the governor, departments, committees and territorial bodies of federal ministries. There is also a representative legislative body which is called *duma*, state *duma*, assembly of

---

4   *SZ RF*, 1995 No.35, item 3506.
5   M.V.Baglai ed., *Konstitutsionnoe pravo Rossiiskoi Federatsii*, second edition, Moscow 1999, pp.693-716.
6   Iu.A.Tikhomirov, *Kurs administrativnogo prava i protsessa*, Moscow 1998, pp.276-279.

deputies, etc. Again, the relationship between the executive and legislative branches as well as the governor varies.[7]

Cities like Moscow and St.Petersburg have a governor (formerly called the mayor), a city government and a legislative assembly. In Moscow, the governor is the highest official of the city and at the same time, the premier of the city government.

The long-awaited law which sets out the basic system of the legislative and executive bodies of the constituent entities was enacted in 1999.[8]

At the next level following the constituent entities of the Russian Federation, there is a system of 'local self-government'. The system comprises cities and towns (*gorod*s), districts (*raions, uezd*s), villages (including *volost's*), and rural settlements. These entities are called 'municipalities' (*munitsipal'nye obrazovanii*). The bodies of these entities are 'not part of the state system of administration' (Art.12). This system of local self-government is said to have originated from the system of local self-administration such as the *zemstvo* in the Tsarist period.[9]

The power of 'local self-government' is exercised by citizens by means of referenda, elections and other forms of the direct expression of their will and through elected and other organs of local self-government in urban and rural settlements and other territories (Art.130, para.2, Art.131, para.1). Bodies of local self-government independently manage municipal properties, formulate, approve, and implement the local budget, create local taxes and levies, implement the protection of public order and also resolve other questions of local significance (Art. 132, para.1). It is important to note that even at this level, the power to create taxes and levies is guaranteed by the Constitution. The list of taxes and levies which can be created by the local self-governments is provided by the Tax Code.

There is a Law on General Principles of Organising Local Self-Governments which gives further details on the system of local self-government.[10]

There have been intensive legislative activities, both at the federal level and the level of constituent entities since 1991. Between 1991 and 1998, at the Federal level, 1,504 laws (including the Constitution) and statutes (*ustavy*) were enacted, while there were 10,286 laws (including constitutions) and statutes, and 37,154 acts of the president and head of administration enacted at the level of the constituent entities.[11]

---

7   V.V.Lazarev ed., *Nauchno-prakticheskii kommentarii k Konstitutsii Rossiiskoi Federatsii*, second edition, Moscow 2001, pp.388-389.
8   *SZ RF*, 1999 No.42, item 5005.
9   Baglai ed., *supra*, p.724.
10 *SZ RF* 1995 No. 35, item 3506.
11 V.B.Isakov, 'Zakonodatel'stvo sub"ektov RF: ob"em, struktura, tendentsii razvitiia', *ZhRP*, 1999 No.12, p.63.

3   THE CONSTITUTION

The present Constitution of the Russian Federation was enacted in 1993. The history of Russian Constitution goes back to the early 19th century. The 1832 Digest of Laws of the Russian Empire (*Svod zakonov Rossiiskoi Imperii*; hereinafter, *Svod zakonov*) in its volume 1 contained the Fundamental Law (*osnovnoi zakon*) which set out the basic structure of the state. This was replaced by the Fundamental Law of 1906, which was modelled on the Prussian Constitution of 1850. The term 'constitution' was not used, since it was associated with constitutional monarchism, i.e. the idea of restraining the power of the monarch by a democratically enacted Constitution. The socialist constitutions, including the 1936 and 1977 USSR constitutions, had the term 'Fundamental Law' in brackets following the term 'Constitution'. The 1993 Constitution is the first Russian Constitution without it.

Unlike its predecessors, the present Constitution provides that the Constitution has 'supreme legal force and direct effect' (Art.15, para.1). Laws and other legal acts must not contradict the Constitution. In order to ensure the compatibility of laws and other legal acts with the Constitution, the Constitutional Court was founded in 1990. At present, the Constitutional Court operates on the basis of the 1994 Law on the Constitutional Court.[12]

The 'direct effect' of the Constitution means that without any enabling statute, the Constitution has an effect. Provisions of the Constitution can be directly invoked by the parties in court without any law. Under socialism, there were provisions in the Constitution, namely in the part of the basic rights of the people, which were not implemented due to the absence of corresponding laws. The Constitution itself could not be invoked to defend these rights, since its 'direct effect' had been denied. Therefore, these provisions merely had a symbolic meaning.

There are three different procedures for the amendment of the Constitution, depending on the object of the amendment. Chapters on the Foundation of the Constitutional System, human rights and freedoms, and constitutional amendments can be amended only by the Constitutional Assembly. The Assembly may adopt the amendment by two-thirds majority, or submit it to the nation-wide vote (Art.135). Amendments to the other parts of the Constitution, except for the provision on the composition of the Federation, are adopted in the same way as the federal constitutional laws (arts. 136 and 137: see below).

---

12   *SZ RF*, 1994 No.13, item 1447.

4   FEDERAL LAW

One of the basic components of *Rechtsstaat* is the supremacy of law (*verkhoven-stvo zakonov*), i.e. laws enacted by the democratic representative body have supremacy over other normative acts. In the Soviet period, with various bodies enacting binding norms while clear-cut rules as to the relationship between the different levels of norms were absent, the legislation was in a state of sheer chaos. In addition to the laws enacted by the Supreme Soviet, there were decrees of the Presidium of the Supreme Soviet, edicts of the Council of Ministers, and other normative acts. The arbitrary creation of norms (*normtvorchestvo*) by administrative agencies imposed problems. There were serious overlaps and contradictions between the numerous acts.

In the process of *perestroika*, the supremacy of law came to be acknowledged as the fundamental principle of the state. The present Constitution provides that the Constitution and federal laws have supremacy throughout the territory of the Russian Federation (Art. 4, para.2).

The legislative power in Russia is borne by the bi-cameral Federal Assembly (the Federation Council and the State Duma). The Federal Assembly enacts 'federal constitutional laws' and 'federal laws' in relation to the matters within the jurisdiction of the Federation. These laws have 'direct effect' throughout the territory of the Russian Federation (Art.76, para.1). Insofar as matters which fall within the exclusive jurisdiction of the Russian Federation are concerned, it is the federal constitutional laws and federal laws which are to regulate these matters.

Federal constitutional laws have a stronger legal effect than federal laws in that federal laws cannot contravene federal constitutional laws (Art.76, para.3). The legislative process for federal constitutional laws and federal laws differs. Federal laws are adopted by the State *Duma* by a simple majority and then sent to the Federation Council for consideration. If the Federation Council supports the law by a majority vote, or does not consider the law within 14 days, the law is deemed to have been approved by the Federation Council. If the Federation Council rejects the law, then both houses may set up a conciliation council to overcome the differences. Then, the law is subject to a second consideration by the State Duma. The State Duma may overcome the differences by a two-thirds majority vote of all members (Art.105). The law thus adopted is sent to the president within 5 days. The president is to sign the law within 14 days. If the president fails to sign the law within 14 days, and two-thirds of the total number of members of both houses nevertheless endorse it, the president is under an obligation to sign the law (Art.107).

In contrast, federal constitutional laws are adopted by a majority of three-quarters of the members of the Federation Council and two-thirds of the members of the State Duma. The Law is to be signed by the president and promulgated within 14 days (Art.108). Thus, federal constitutional law requires a qualified majority vote and is not subject to the presidential veto. Matters which are to be regulated by federal constitutional law are provided in the Constitution. These include; the admission to the Russian Federation and the creation of a new entity within the Russian Federation, changes to the constitutional status of the entities within the Russian Federation, the regime of martial law and the state of emergency, procedure for the activities of the government of the Russian Federation, and the court system. In fact, at present, there are only three federal constitutional laws; the Law on the Constitutional Court, the Law on Referendum, and the Law on the Commercial Court.

Under socialism, there were laws and other legal acts which were not published, i.e. laws 'not for publication' or 'for official use only'. This is not permitted any more. The Constitution provides that laws are subject to publication, and that unpublished laws shall not apply (Art. 15, para.3). The Law on the Publication and Taking of Effect of Federal Constitutional laws, Federal Laws and Acts of the Chambers of the Federal Assembly was enacted in 1995.[13] The date of the adoption of a federal law is the date on which the Duma adopted it in its final version, while for federal constitutional law, it is the date of adoption by the Federal Council (Art.2). The official date of publication is the date of their publication in the *Rossiskaia gazeta* (*RG*), or *Sobranie zakonov Rossiisskoi Federatsii* (*SZ RF*) (Art.3).[14]

5   LAW OF THE CONSTITUENT ENTITIES

Among the constituent entities, republics are entitled to have their own constitution and legislation. Other constituent entities may enact their statutes and legislation (Art.5, para.2).

With the spontaneous devolution which took place after *perestroika*, the constituent entities began enacting their own constitution, codes and statutes. According to a survey conducted by the Legal Department of the Duma, the areas covered by regional law-making activities were fundamentals of the constitutional system 15,7%, the problem of economic activities, 29,9%, finance and credit, 20,9%, labour and social policy, 8,6%, housing, 7%, and environmental protection, 6,7%. Legislation on economic activities included laws on enterprises and entre-

---

13   *SZ RF*, 1995 No.16, item 1881.
14   V.P.Malkov, 'Opublikovanie i vstuplenie v silu federal'nykh zakonov, inykh normativnykh aktov', *GiP*, 1995 No.5, p.26.

preneurial activities, laws on industry, laws on agriculture, and laws on transport and communication.[15]

However, these laws were often not compatible with the Federal Constitution. For example, laws of the Republic of Bashkortostan, Tatarstan, and Sakha (Iakutsiia), declared that the Republic was a sovereign state. The Law on International Treaties of the Sverdrovsk province provided for the power of the Province to conclude international treaties. In the area of taxation, these entities often exceeded the power granted to them.[16]

The Constitutional Court has not always been idle in ruling on the compatibility of the legislation of the constituent entities and the Federal Constitution. For example, in 1996, the Constitutional Court found the act of the City of Moscow, Moscow province, and Stavropol'skii region on the procedure of registering people who have a permanent residence in the territory to be unconstitutional.[17]

One of the reasons for such a chaotic situation was the absence of a clearly set order of priority between the federal law and the laws enacted by the constituent entities. The constitutional arrangement is that the order of priority depends on the matter which is being regulated.

Matters which fall within the exclusive federal jurisdiction are regulated by federal laws. Matters which are to be administered jointly by the Russian Federation and its constituent entities are to be regulated by federal laws as well as laws and other normative acts enacted by the constituent entities, but in accordance with federal laws (Art.76, para.2). On these matters, constituent entities are empowered to enact laws and other normative acts, but these acts cannot contravene federal laws. In the case of conflict, federal law prevails.

Regarding matters which are neither within the jurisdiction of the Russian Federation or the joint jurisdiction of the Russian Federation and its constituent entities, constituent entities have an inherent power of regulation, including enactment of laws and other normative acts (residual power). This means that constituent entities may enact laws and other normative acts independently and at its discretion in this area.[18]

Laws or other normative acts of the constituent entities may not contradict federal constitutional laws and federal laws in the areas of exclusive jurisdiction of the Federation or joint jurisdiction of the Federation and its constituent entities. In contrast, in the area left to the constituent entities, even if the laws and other

---

15 Isakov, *supra*, pp.71-72.
16 'Verkhovenstvo konstitutsii RF i federal'nykh zakonov – osnovnoi pravovoi printsip', *KhiP* 2000 No.1, pp.34-37.
17 Decision of the Constitutional Court, February 20, 1996; see B.N.Topornin ed., *Konstitutsiia Rossiiskoi Federatsii: nauchno-prakticheskii kommentarii*, Moscow 1997, p.450.
18 *Ibid.*, p.455.

normative acts enacted by the constituent entities are different from federal constitutional law or federal law, still these laws or normative acts prevail. However,
there is an important exception to this rule. These laws and other normative acts
which were enacted in these residual areas are not applicable in cases where they
are against the Federal Constitution, basic rights and freedom of the people,
universally accepted principles of international law, and international treaties
ratified by the Russian Federation (arts. 4 and 15).[19]

The demarcation of the competence of the Russian Federation and its constituent entities has always been a difficult matter. Before the enactment of the present
Federal Constitution, the Federal Treaty – in fact there were three separate agreements – was concluded. This was signed in 1992 by the representatives of the
Russian Federation and its constituent entities and was incorporated in the then
Constitution (originally of 1978). The Treaty was aimed at demarcating the
competence of the Russian Federation and its constituent entities. The Treaty is
still valid. The present Constitution provides that the demarcation of competence
between the Federation and its constituent entities is to be governed by the Constitution as well as the Federal Treaty and other treaties.[20]

The Constitution lists matters which fall within the exclusive jurisdiction of
the Russian Federation. These include the following (Art.71):

i)   the adoption and amendment of the Constitution of the Russian Federation and
      federal laws and the monitoring of compliance with them;
ii)   the federal structure and territory of the Russian Federation;
iii) the regulation and protection of human rights and freedoms, citizenship of the
      Russian Federation;
iv)   federal state property and its administration;
v)   the establishment of the legal basis of the single market; financial, currency, credit
      and customs regulation; federal economic service and banks;
vi)   federal energy systems, nuclear power generation, fissile materials, federal transport,
      means of communication, information and connections; activity in space;
vii) Russian Federation's foreign policy and international treaties, issues of war and
      peace;
viii) defence and security;
ix)   determination of the status and protection of state borders;
x)   the judicial system; the procuracy; legislation in the field of criminal law, criminal
      procedure and criminal enforcement law, amnesty and pardon; legislation in the
      field of civil law, civil procedure and law of commercial court procedure; the legal
      relation of intellectual property;

---

19   *Ibid.*, p.456.
20   A.R.Paramonov and L.Ia.Poluian, 'Federativnyi dogovor', in A.Ia.Sukharev ed., *Rossiskaia iuridi-
     cheskaia entsiklopediia*, Moscow 1999, pp.3067-3069.

xi)   adoption of the federal law on conflict of laws.

Matters which fall within the joint jurisdiction of the Russian Federation and its constituent entities include the following (Art.72):

i)   issues relating to the ownership, use and disposal of land, subsoil, water and other natural resources;
ii)   demarcation of state ownership;
iii) the use of natural environment; environmental protection and the ensuring of ecological safety;
iv)   the establishment of general principles of taxation and levying of duties in the Russian Federation;
v)   administrative, administrative-procedural, labour, family, housing, land, water and forestry legislation and legislation on subsoil and on environment;
vi)   personnel of judicial and law enforcement agencies; advocates and notaries;
vii) the establishment of the general principles for the organisation of a system of agencies of state power and local self-government.

In relation to the matters which fall within the exclusive jurisdiction of the Russian Federation and the joint jurisdiction of the Federation and its constituent entities, federal administrative agencies may establish their territorial agency in the territory of the constituent entities and appoint their officials. These territorial agencies of the Federal government form a single system of administration jointly with the administrative agencies of the entities (Art.77, para.2 of the Constitution).

This concept of joint jurisdiction in Russia is apparently an outcome of a compromise between federal and regional power which failed to solve the problem 'once and for all' at the time of the enactment of the Constitution. Exclusive jurisdiction and joint jurisdiction sometimes overlap. For example, protection of human rights is listed as an exclusive jurisdiction of the Russian Federation as well as a joint jurisdiction of the Russian Federation and its constituent entities. This provision is not only general and vague, but it does not always coincide with the provisions in the other part of the Constitution. For example, in the area of land law, possession, problems of use and disposal of land fall within the joint jurisdiction of the Federation and the constituent entities (Art.72, para.1). On the other hand, another provision of the Constitution provides that the condition and procedure of the use of land are to be determined on the basis of federal law (Art.36, para.3). Furthermore, there is also a provision to the effect that the establishment of a single market is a matter which falls within the exclusive competence of the Federation (Art.71).

Since the demarcation of competence in the present Constitution was not clear enough, the president has concluded agreements with the heads of the constituent entities. In 1999, there were around 30 of them. There are specific matters covered by the agreements, such as property relations, problems related to fuel and energy complexes, and budgetary relations.[21]

With the adoption of the 1999 Law on the Fundamental Principles and Procedure of Demarcating the Competence of the Agencies of State Power of the Russian Federation and the Constituent Entities, the matter has become clearer. Since the majority of the legal acts in the area of joint jurisdiction were enacted before this Law came into force, there is an enormous task of aligning the existing laws and legal acts with this new Law.[22]

6   PRESIDENTIAL DECREES

At the federal level, in addition to laws enacted by the representative body, some other bodies enact binding rules. In fact, in Russian terminology, laws, presidential decrees, and edicts of the government (cabinet) of the Russian Federation are put in the same category as 'legal acts (*pravovye akty*)'.[23] Another concept, 'normative acts', in addition to these, covers acts of ministries and other federal administrative agencies.[24] By the same token 'Legislation (*zakonodatel'stvo*) in Russian includes not only acts of the legislature, but also edicts of the government. Between 1995 and 2000, while around 1,000 federal laws were adopted, there were 800 presidential decrees and 2,000 edicts of the government.[25]

The president is the head of state in Russia (Art.80, para.1) and is elected for four years' term by direct election of the citizens (Art.81, para.1). The president is empowered to issue decrees (*ukazy*) and orders (*rasporiazheniia*) (Art.90, para.1). Although it is binding in the same way as decrees, the latter normally does not have a normative character; it addresses individual matters.[26] President Yel'tsin heavily resorted to presidential decrees in the early 1990s. Of the legislation enacted at the federal level between 1991-1998, presidential decrees accounted for 14,4%, while laws accounted for 1,7%. In fact, in 1991, presidential decrees accounted for 28,5%.[27] In the earlier period after the collapse of socialism, in many areas, relevant federal laws were absent, while the legislative process

---

21   Baglai ed., *supra*, p.323.
22   Lazarev ed., *supra*, pp.344-345.
23   M.I.Braginskii ed., *Nauchno-prakticheskii komentarii k chasti pervoi grazhdanskogo kodeksa Rossiiskoi Federatsii*, second edition, Moscow 1999, pp.43-44.
24   *Ibid.*, p.45.
25   A.Makovskii and A.Silkina, 'Novyi klassifikator pravovykh aktov', *RIu*, 2000 No.5, p.7.
26   Topornin ed., *supra*, p.505.
27   Isakov, *supra*, pp.63-65.

was slow for various reasons. Therefore, the president utilised his power to issue presidential decrees in an extensive way. A commentator reminisces that the President had 'radically changed many essential aspects of social relations in the country' by resorting to presidential decrees.[28] The percentage of presidential decrees among the legislation has been in constant decline. In 1998, it dropped to 8,5%.[29]

Presidential decrees and orders may not contradict the Constitution and the federal laws (Art.90, para.2). Federal laws in this context include both federal constitutional laws and federal laws. However, 'many of the presidential decrees were not perfect, some of them not totally coincided with the constitutional norms and previous legislation, some of them were contested in the parliament chambers and the constitutional court'.[30] The Constitutional Court has the power to review the constitutionality of presidential decrees. On some occasions such as the sending of military forces to Chechniia, the Constitutional Court acknowledged the constitutionality of the relevant presidential decree, while there were other cases where a presidential decree was found unconstitutional, such as the decree establishing a new ministry by combining the Ministry of State Security and the Ministry of Internal Affairs.[31]

The priority between the presidential decree and legal acts of the constituent entities is decided by analogy with the relationship between federal laws and the legal acts of the subjects.

7   EDICTS OF THE GOVERNMENT

Executive power in Russia is exercised by the government (*pravitel'stvo*), which is the Russian equivalent of a cabinet (Art.110). The head of the government – the Prime Minister – is appointed by the President with the consent of the State Duma (Art.111, para.1). The Prime Minister proposes candidates of ministers to the President who is empowered to appoint and dismiss them (Art.112, para.2). The President has the right to chair the sessions of the government.

The government is empowered to enact edicts (*postanovlenie*) on the basis of, and in implementation of the Federal Constitution, federal laws, presidential decrees of a normative nature and for their implementation (Art.115, para.2). In contrast to presidential decrees which the President issues on the basis of his

---

28   Topornin ed., *supra*, pp.505-506.
29   Isakov, *supra*, p.65.
30   *Ibid.*
31   Topornin ed., *supra*, p.507.

inherent power, it is clear from this provision that government edicts derive their power from the Constitution, federal laws, and even presidential decrees. What is more, if an edict of the government is against the Federal Constitution, federal laws, or presidential decree, the President is empowered to revoke it (Art.115, para.2).

Federal ministries are established by presidential decrees and regulated by the respective statute either in the form of an edict of the government or a presidential decree. According to the Federal Constitutional Law on the Government of Russia of 1997, ministries are subordinated to the government and are responsible to the government for performing the entrusted tasks. Within their power, ministries issue instructions, circulars and other subordinate acts (*podzakonnye acty*).

8   ACTS OF LOCAL SELF-GOVERNMENTS

The system of local self-government (municipalities) falls within the joint jurisdiction of the Russian Federation and the constituent entities (Art.72). Under this provision, the above-mentioned Federal Law on the General Principles of the Organising of Local Self-Government was enacted in 1995. Within the framework of this Law, which is fairly general, each constituent entity regulates the problems of local self-government within its jurisdiction. Therefore, the structure of local self-government varies from place to place.[32] As a rule, there is a representative body and an executive body. Representative bodies are called duma, assembly, *sovet*, etc. The executive body is organised under the head of administration. In most places, the head of administration is elected by the populace.[33]

Local self-governments have a representative body which enact their fundamental statute (*ustav*) and other normative legal acts.[34] Local self-governments are empowered to enact such acts via a representative body, or by direct referendum on matters of local significance, based upon the interest of the inhabitants, their historical traditions and other local traditions. This includes the creation of taxes and levies, the maintenance of law and order in the locality and the registration of inhabitants. Acts of some constituent entities and local self-governments involving these matters were contested at the Constitutional Court.[35]

---

32   Lazarev ed., *supra*, p.624.
33   Baglai ed., *supra*, pp.729-730.
34   I.V.Vydrin and A.N.Kokotov, *Munitsipal'noe pravo Rossii*, Moscow 2001, pp.178-182.
35   Lazarev ed., *supra*, p.632.

9   COURT JUDGMENTS

Precedents are not binding on the courts in the same way as in Anglo-American jurisdictions. Under the current system, judicial precedents are not regarded as a source of law in the sense that contravention of precedents is not a ground for appeal or any other means of reviewing the judgment by superior courts. In fact, precedents are not referred to in the judgments at all.

If one compares the entry of 'judicial precedents (*pretsedent*)' in legal encyclopaedia published in 1984 and 1999, there is not much difference. In both publications, court precedents are primarily treated as alien institutions. The only difference is that in the 1999 Encyclopaedia, there is a brief reference to Tsarist Russia and the contemporary period, but there is no substantive discussion as to the status of court precedents as a source of law.[36]

The fact that Russian law is part of the Civil Law system does not necessarily mean that judicial precedents have not been regarded as a source of law in Russia. In fact, in many Civil Law jurisdictions, judicial precedents are considered to be a source of law. As a leading expert on comparative law has pointed out, matters are not really very different between Anglo-American jurisdiction and Civil Law countries:

> It is true that there is never any legal rule which compels a judge to follow the decisions of a higher court, but the reality is different. In practice a judgment of the Court of Cassation or of the *Bundesgerichtshof* in Germany can count on being followed by lower courts just as much as a judgment of an appeal court in England or in the United States.[37]

In the Tsarist period, there were different views on the status of precedents. Some people acknowledged that court precedents qualified as a source of law, despite some reservations, such as 'supplementary'. Others totally denied this.[38] In the socialist period, court precedents were not regarded as a source of law. It was only natural that under a system where political power was highly centralised, law creation by lower court judges could not be tolerated. It was also noted that

---

36   R.O.Khalfina, 'Pretsedent' in A.Ia.Sukharev ed., *Iuridicheskii entsiklpedicheskii slovar'*, Moscow 1984, p.296. V.V.Boitsova and L.V.Boitsov, 'Pretsedent sudebnyi', in A.Ia.Sukharev ed., *Rossiiskaia iuridicheskaia entsiklopediia*, Moscow 1999, pp.2385-2394.

37   K.Zweigert and H.Kötz, *An Introduction to Comparative Law*, third edition, Oxford 1998, pp.261-263.

38   V.V.Boitsova and L.V.Boitsov, *supra*, p.2387.

the system of judge made law gives opportunities to the ruling class to contradict provisions of the existing legislation in the capitalist world.[39]

Under socialism judges were supposed to apply the law in a mechanical way without exercising any discretion. There was no room for free interpretation of the statutes by judges. In fact this has been a tradition since the Tsarist period. The Fundamental Law dictated the judges to apply laws in a 'mechanical manner'.[40] However, since provisions of the law tend to be fairly general and abstract, it was technically impossible to restrain judges from interpreting the law and at the same time, let them apply the law to specific circumstances. The solution was to concentrate the power of interpretation to the Supreme Court, more specifically to the Plenum of the USSR Supreme Court which comprised the President and the justices as well as chief justices of the constituent republics. It goes without saying that the Plenum was under strict control of the CPSU. Thus, the court, even under socialism, had some power to interpret the law, not only to mechanically apply it, but such power was not given to lower courts.

The device used by the Plenum of the Supreme Court was its 'guiding explanations'. Guiding explanations were issued in various areas of law from time to time. Also publications entitled 'Sudebnaia praktika (court practice)' edited by the Supreme Court were published occasionaly to give guidance to lower court judges. Therefore, some people acknowledge that judicial precedents were 'de facto source of law' even under socialism. However, such views remained in the minority.[41]

This system of 'guidance' by the Supreme Court still remains in Russia, but in a slightly different format. They take the form of the decisions of the plenum of either the Supreme Court, the Supreme Commercial Court, or the joint plenum of both. The Supreme Commercial Court also publishes a 'review (obzor) of the court practice' covering various areas and take the form of a an 'information letter'. They are published in the official periodicals of the court – Vestnik verkhovnogo arbitrazhnogo suda RF and the Biulleten' verkhovnogo suda RF. In addition, the former publishes around 40-50 cases a month, and the latter, around 10 cases, which is quite different from the practice in the socialist period when even judgments of principal significance were not always published. There is a view which regards the publication of the higher courts on specific cases as another form of 'guidance'.[42]

---

39   Khalfina, supra, p.296.
40   N.M.Korkunov, Lektsii po obshchei teorii prava, eighth edition, St.Petersburg, 1909, p.306.
41   M.N.M.Marchenko, 'Iabliaetsia li sudebnaia praktika istochnikom rossiiskogo prava', ZhRP, 2000 No.12, p.12.
42   G.T.Ermoshchin, 'Problemy obespecheniia nezabisimosti sudebnoi vlasti', in Iu.A.Tikhomirov ed., Sudebnaia reforma v Rossii, Moscow 2001, pp.28-29.

Usually, decisions of the plenum take the form of compilations of rules. Thus, the joint decision No.6/8 of the plenum of both courts entitled 'Some problems on the application of Part One of the Civil Code of the Russian Federation', which comprises more than 50 items, provides as follows:

> 3. In accordance with the Federal Constitution, civil legislation falls within the jurisdiction of the Russian Federation (Article 3, para.1 of the Civil Code). Provisions of civil law of the constituent entities of the Russian Federation, before the Federal Constitution has taken effect, can be applied by the courts in settling disputes, if they do not contradict the Federal Constitution and the Code.

> 19. The list of activities which juridical persons may conduct only on the basis of a license is determined by law (Article 49, para.1, subpara.3). On this matter, the court should bear in mind that after the entering into force of the Civil Code, types of activities which are subject to license can be established only by law.[43]

In contrast, 'review of court practice' is more specific. Usually, it is a compilation of a summary of cases. A rule, e.g. 'a party to a foreign trade sales contract is exempted from liability of non-performance only if he proves that the non-performance was caused by an impediment beyond his control', is derived from a summary of a case decided by the Supreme Commercial Court in the review of court practice in this area. Thus, there is no doubt that judgments of the Supreme Commercial Court and Supreme Court of the Russian Federation are meant to 'guide' the lower courts.

A commentary on the Code of Civil Procedure published in 1999, referring to the fact that erroneous interpretation of the law by the court is a ground of appeal, states as follows:

> If the court does not have the possibility of utilising the result of the official interpretation of the Supreme Court of the Russian Federation of one or another provision of substantive law, the court may interpret it in a wrong way. Therefore, such circumstances may serve as a ground for quashing such a judgment. It should be noted that if there is a decision of the Plenum of the Supreme Court of the Russian Federation on the problem which is being examined by the court, in order to avoid the possibility of having the judgment quashed, the court should utilise the rules set out in the given decision. If the conclusion of the court is based upon the interpretation of the norm of substantive law by the Supreme Court of the Russian Federation, the possibility of having the judgment quashed on the ground of erroneous interpretation is excluded.[44]

---

43   *VVAS RF*, 1996 No.9, pp. 6,10.
44   A.P.Ryzhakov and D.A.Sergeeve, *Postateinyi kommentarii k grazhdanskomu protsessual'nomu kodeksu RSFSR*, Moscow 1999, p.523.

The judicial system in Russia has undergone significant changes since *perestroika*. The independence of judges, which has been only on paper, is increasingly gaining substance. The authority of the court is being strengthened which is demonstrated e.g. by the expansion of court jurisdiction. After all, acknowledging judicial precedents as a source of law is about granting power to create law to the courts. With the progress of the reform, discussions on the status of judicial precedents have started to take place.

The vice president of the Supreme Court pointed out in 1997 as follows:

> With the taking of effect of the new Federal Constitution and the increased role of the court in society and the state, also in court practice, emerged new, extremely important functions of the court.... despite significant renovation of legislation and adoption of a number of laws, there are many vacuums in the legal system and many contradictions emerged. Overcoming these problems is more complicated than before and is one of the most difficult tasks of court practice. On several occasions, judgments of the Supreme Court have become sources of law.[45]

He also commented elsewhere that at present, courts are often forced into having to create law, otherwise, 'their activities would not only be ineffective, but result in the opposite of what society legitimately expects of them; they will not defend rights, but will facilitate their violations'.[46] There are others who claim that 'the courts, at present, are simply under an obligation to create law'.[47]

It is premature to say that judicial precedents have officially become a source of law in Russia. Although some arguments against it, based upon e.g. the separation of power, tradition of the Civil Law system, are not necessarily persuasive, still there is some hesitation to officially allow judges to create law. While some support the idea by referring to the lack of specialised knowledge on the part of the members of the legislature, others are against it:

> Among our judges, there are still not a small number of lawyers with a low level of qualification. Granting each of them the right to create law means to bury legality.....At present, in Russia, a 'war of laws' is going on. Allowing the creation of laws by the court and the expanding of the discretion of judges will reinforce this negative process.[48]

---

45   V.M.Zhuikov, 'Rol' sudebnoi praktiki v pravoprimenitel'nom protsesse', Zhuikov ed., *Sudebnaia praktika po grazhdanskim delam 1993-1996*, Moscow 1997, p.6.
46   Marchenko, *supra*, p.17.
47   Quoted in I.L.Petrukhin, 'Problema sudebnoi vlasti v sovremennoi Rossii', *GiP*, 2000 No.7, p.19.
48   *Ibid.*

There are views which acknowledge that the Constitutional Court, by reviewing the constitutionality of normative acts, creates law, and therefore, their judgments are sources of law. But this is naturally a totally different matter.

10   CUSTOM

Custom and Customary law were regarded as something backward and to be overcome in the socialist period. 'Socialist states actively fought against customs which reflected ignorance, inequality, the exploited status of women and other remnants of exploiting forms'.[49] Besides, under socialism, the political leadership could not tolerate norms to emerge outside their control. An exception was commercial custom which was referred to in the Civil Code and other civil legislation. Commercial custom in this context meant international commercial custom, mainly those terms covered in Incoterms, which were worked out by the UN, and also international custom referred to in Comecon – the Council for Mutual Economic Cooperation – General Conditions of Supply as well as some international arbitration treaties. Naturally, a socialist regime never recognises rules which emerged spontaneously without the involvement of the rulers. Commercial custom was applicable only when it was sanctioned by the state.[50]

The present Civil Code provides that commercial custom (*obychai delovogo oborota*) is a rule of behaviour not provided by legislation, but existing and widely applied in any area of entrepreneurial activities, regardless of whether it is fixed in any document or not (Art.5, para.1). It is important to note that unlike before, such custom does not have to be 'sanctioned' by the government.

Commercial custom is applied only when there is no applicable contract or mandatory provision of the law (Art.5, para.2). Commercial custom is not only a source of law, but is one of the factors which should be considered when interpreting contracts (Art.431). Commercial custom is referred to in various provisions of the Civil Code (arts. 311,312,314. 474,478 etc.). .

11   INTERNATIONAL TREATIES

The Civil Code provides that generally recognised principles and rules of international law as well as the treaties of the Russian Federation are the a part of the

---

49   R.O.Khalfina, *'Obychnoe pravo', 'Obychai' in* A.Iu.Sukharev ed., *Iuridicheskii entsikolopedicheskii slovar'*, Moscow 1984, pp.208-209.

50   *Ibid.*, p.209.

Russian legal system (Art.7, para.1). The same provision can be found in the Constitution. If an international treaty contains a rule which is against Russian law, the international treaty prevails (The Constitution, Art.15, para.4).

Principles and rules of international law must be recognised as such by the Russian Federation in order to be a 'constituent part' of the Russian legal system and bind the state as well as state agencies and officials.[51] Such principles and rules are found in the United Nations Charter, declarations and resolutions of the UN, documents and statements of international organisations and conferences as well as in the judgments of the International Court of Justice.[52]

Concerning international treaties, the Law on International Treaties of the Russian Federation was enacted in 1995. According to this Law, international treaties denote inter-state, inter-governmental, and inter-agency agreements in the form of treaties, conventions, agreements, protocols, exchanges of letters and notes.[53] Russia is a signatory to the Vienna Convention on the Law of Treaties.

Generally, principles and rules of international law and international treaties are applicable to civil law relations in a direct way, i.e. without an enabling legislation (the Civil Code, Art.7, para.2). A potential problem is the situation where there is a conflict between an international treaty and Russian law. The Constitution has an explicit provision addressing such a situation; provisions of the international treaty has priority to the provisions of the laws of the Russian Federation (Art.15, para.4). Those who apply law are not only empowered to, but are under an obligation, to apply international treaties on such occasions, and the people are entitled to quote the rules of international law in order to defend their rights.[54]

On the other hand, this provision does not directly refer to a situation where there is a conflict between an international treaty and the Constitution. There is a view that in such cases, the Constitution is understood to prevail, because of the supremacy of the Constitution within the Russian legal system, of which international treaties became a constituent part.[55]

International treaties concluded by the USSR have been, in principle, inherited by the Russian Federation, unless these treaties were declared to have lost effect. Such treaties which lost effect were published in the official gazette between 1989-1991.[56]

---

51   Lazarev ed., *supra*, p.101.
52   O.N.Sadikov ed., *Kommentarii k Grazhdanskomu Kodeksu Rossiiskoi Federatsii*, enlarged edition, Moscow 1999, p.21.
53   *SZ RF*, 1995 No.29, item 2757.
54   Lazarev, *supra*, p.101.
55   *Ibid.*, p.102.
56   Sadikov ed., *supra*, p.21.

2

THE SYSTEM OF SETTLING DISPUTES – INSTITUTIONS

1   THE COURTS

1)   Historical Background

The modern court system in Russia emerged as a result of the Great Judicial Reform of 1864. The pre-Reform state of affairs could best be characterised as sheer lawlessness and chaos. The court system was organised in such a way that different lines of courts adjudicated cases involving people from different classes. In civil procedure, there could be 16 instances and 30 different procedures.[1] There was no independence of the courts while judges were corrupt and susceptible to pressure from outside. 'Our courts have got all the shortcomings which Western European courts used to have when the inquisitorial system prevailed'.[2] I.S.Aksakov, a renowned philosopher, remarked in 1884; 'Old courts! Simply thinking of them, your hair stands on end and your flesh begins to creep.'[3]

In 1864, a new Statute on Court Organisation was enacted together with the rules of criminal and civil procedure. The reformed system was modelled entirely on the Western European system which existed at that time; there was a clear discontinuity with the indigenous Russian system. Laws of France, Switzerland, Belgium, Germany, and Austria as well as England were studied. There are different views as to the origin of institutions introduced by the Reform. One observer pointed out that 'the most liberal foreign institutions' served as a model. More specifically, the French system had a major influence, although some German and English elements could be seen.[4] At that time, the German judicial system

---

1   I.V.Gessen, *Sudebnaia reforma*, St.Petersburg 1905, p.65.
2   *Ibid.*, p.28.
3   *Ibid.*, p.29.
4   F.Kaiser, *Die russische Justizreform von 1864*, Leiden 1972, pp.407-412. See also S.Kucherov, *Courts, Lawyers and Trials under the Last Three Tsars*, Westport (Conn.), 1974 (reprint of the 1953 publication), pp.21-106.

was in the process of modernisation under the influence of French law, and therefore, it was no wonder that the French system was preferred. Although this system was formally abolished by the October Revolution, traits of the continental judicial system and procedure still remain to this day.

One of the first decrees which the Bolsheviks enacted was the Decree on Courts by which the Tsarist Russian courts were abolished and a new system of people's court was set up. This system is the immediate predecessor to the current ordinary court system. Commercial courts did not exist as part of the judiciary under socialism. The most important feature of the people's court was the 'democratic principle' in that the judges were all elected by the populace, but for the time being, by the executive committee of local soviets. In addition, people's assessors, who were laymen chosen from among the general public, sat with the judge in court. This system was consolidated in 1922 by the Law on Court Organisation.[5] While at the initial stage, this system existed only in the RSFSR, after the Soviet Union was founded, the USSR Supreme Court was established in 1923.

Under the socialist regime, particularly since the consolidation of power by Stalin in the late 1920s, the independence of the court remained only on paper. First, the election of judges came to be reduced to a formality. The position of a judge was on the *nomenklatura*, a list which contains positions which require the approval of CPSU organisations. Judges were nominated by the local CPSU organisation and the election, which allowed only one candidate for one seat, was merely a ceremony. Besides, without a CPSU membership, it was impossible to be nominated as a judge. Second, judges were under pressure from various sources in handling the cases, namely the local CPSU organisations and local government officials. Third, the Procuracy was empowered with 'judicial supervision', i.e. supervision over the legality of court judgments.

In general, the prestige of the court was extremely low under socialism. Judges were not even required to have had higher legal education. CPSU organisations which nominated judges were lower in rank than those nominating procurators.

In 1987, when the creation of the 'law-governed state' (*pravovoe gosudarstvo*) came on the agenda, one of the first issues raised was the revamping of the court system and the increasing of the prestige of the court. In 1989, the Law on the Status of Judges was enacted in order to strengthen the independence of judges and to shield them from undue pressure.[6] Changes were introduced in the system of electing judges; a new system of appointment of judges by the local legislative

---

5   *SU RSFSR*, 1917 No.4, item 50. For the formation of the judicial system in Russia, see J.Hazard, *Settling Disputes in the Soviet Society*, New York 1960.
6   *VSND SSSR i VS SSSR*, 1989 No.9, item 223.

body upon recommendation by the 'qualification committee', comprising judges, was introduced in the same year. However, these changes proved to be insufficient. As one commentator put it, the 1989 Law was still prepared 'in the best tradition of law creation at the time of developed socialism'.[7] Therefore, after the collapse of the socialist regime, these laws were replaced by new laws.[8]

Currently, in order to ensure the independence of judges, in addition to the provisions of the Constitution, the Law on the Status of Judges of 1992[9] , the Statute on the Qualification Committee for Judges of 1993[10] as well as the Law on the State Protection of Judges and Officials of Law Protection and Control Agencies of 1995[11] are in force. These laws apply to ordinary court judges as well as to commercial court judges.

The 1993 Constitution provides that judicial power is exercised only by the court, through constitutional, civil, administrative, and criminal proceedings (Art.118). The basic law which determines the court structure and the basic system of recruitment of judges is the Law on Court Organisation of the Russian Federation of 1996.[12]

There are two systems of court which deal with civil and commercial disputes: the ordinary court system and the commercial court system. The Law on Court Organisation covers both the ordinary court system and the commercial court system. As for procedural law, each system has a separate law. The procedure for the commercial court is set by the Code of Commercial Court Procedure (hereinafter, 'ComPC'). The ordinary court procedure is determined by the Code of Civil Procedure (hereinafter, 'CivPC').

There is also the Constitutional Court of the Russian Federation which has jurisdiction over the compatibility of the federal laws, normative acts of the President, both houses of the Parliament, and the cabinet, as well as the constitution and laws of the constituent entities of the Russian Federation with the Constitution of the Russian Federation. It was only towards the end of socialism that an embryonic form of constitutional review emerged. In 1990, the Committee on Constitutional Supervision started operation, later to develop into a constitu-

---

7   V.Savitskii, *Organizasiia sudebnoi vlasti v Rossiskoi Federatsii*, Moscow 1996, p.17.

8   For details of the reform since *perestroika*, see P.H.Solomon Jr. and T.S.Foglesong, *Courts and Transition in Russia: the Challenge of Judicial Reform*, Boulder 2000.

9   *VSND RF i VS RF,* 1992 No.30, item 1792.

10   *Ibid.,* 1993 No.24, item 856.

11   *SZ RF,* 1995 No.17, item 1455.

12   *Ibid.,* 1997 No.1, item 1.

tional court.[13] There is a separate Law on the Constitutional Court which was enacted in 1994.[14]

2)   Commercial Courts

Commercial courts are called *'arbitrazhnyi sud'* in Russian. However, the name is more historical than a reflection of the true nature of the institution. It should not be confused with arbitration institutions such as the International Arbitration Court of the Russian Chamber of Commerce and other arbitration institutions which are called *treteiskii sud* in Russian. In fact, at the time of preparing the 1992 Law on Arbitration Courts, some people proposed that instead of the traditional *'arbitrazh'*, the court should be called an economic court as was the case in the Tsarist period.[15]

In the Tsarist period, commercial courts were set up in St.Petersburg, Moscow and other cities in the 1830s. The system was basically German.[16] There was a Statute on the Procedure at the Commercial Court and brief Rules on Commercial Bankruptcy. Institutionwise, the Great Judicial Reform of 1864 did not affect the commercial courts, but in addition to the above-mentioned statute, the general Statute on Civil Procedure came to be applied. The 1913 edition of the *Svod zakonov* introduced the Statute on the Procedure of the Commercial Court.[17] Part one of the Statute covered the organisation of the courts, while part two accommodated provisions on the procedure, and part three dealt with commercial bankruptcy. Commercial courts continued operation until they were abolished by the Decree on Courts in 1917.

After the October Revolution, already in the early 1920s, the necessity for setting up a specialised body to deal with disputes between the emerging state enterprises in the socialist sector was felt. After all, it was not practical to leave disputes between socialist enterprises to the court which was staffed with ostensibly elected judges without sufficient expertise in economic matters. By 1924, a system of arbitration commissions which handled proprietary disputes between state and cooperative enterprises had been established. Incidentally, even at the time of the New Economic Policy in the 1920s, private enterprises did not benefit from the system; they had to go to ordinary courts, instead of the arbitration commission.

---

13   R.Sharlet, 'Russia's Second Constitutional Court: Politics, Law, and Stability', V.E.Bonnell and
      G.W.Breslauer eds., *Russia in the New Century: Stability or Disorder?*, New York 2001, p.59ff.
14   *SZ RF*, 1994 No.13, item 1447.
15   M.Treushnikov, *Arbitrazhnyi protess*, Moscow 1995, p.6.
16   L.Schultz, *Russische Rechtsgeschichte*, Lahr 1957, S.217.
17   *Svod zakonov Rossiiskoi Imperii*, 1913 edition, vol.XI, part 2.

After the introduction of the Planned Economy, arbitration commissions were transformed into the system of *gosarbitrazh* – state arbitration organisation in 1931.[18]

Gosarbitrazh institutions were subordinated to the Council of Ministers of the USSR and the equivalent body at the lower level, down to the regional executive committees. They were designed to settle economic disputes between entities in the socialist sector in order to 'ensure strengthening of planning and contractual discipline and economic accounting'. Separate procedural rules to civil procedure were applicable in the proceedings. A significant difference of these rules from the ordinary court system was that there was no lay element in *gosarbitrazh*; the case was settled by an arbitrator and representatives of both parties, as in commercial arbitration.

In fact, the primary purpose of *gosarbitrazh* was to ensure that the disputes were settled so that the state economic plan was appropriately carried out by state enterprises in a timely manner. *Gosarbitrazh* had a duty to 'actively interfere with the activities of state enterprises in implementing economic plans and enforcing contractual obligations'.[19] For this purpose, not only disputes arising from contracts, but pre-contractual disputes – disputes concerning the formation of contracts – fell within the jurisdiction of *gosarbitrazh*. The right of the parties to dispose of their rights was severely limited. Regardless of the intention of the parties, their superior agencies could bring the case to *gosarbitrazh*. *Gosarbitrazh* were even empowered to initiate the proceedings *ex officio*. The parties were not entitled to freely accept the claim or withdraw the claim.[20]

There have been discussions concerning the legal nature of *gosarbitrazh* since its inception. Some people regarded *gosarbitrazh* as a specialised court, while others considered it to be an administrative agency.[21] One cannot deny that *gosarbitrazh* was an administrative agency; it was subordinated to the Council of Ministers of the USSR and had no independence. Although they were bound by statute laws, the Law on *Gosarbitrazh* of 1970 provided that *gosarbitrazh* handled 'economic disputes on the basis of laws as well as decisions of the Council of Ministers and other legal acts and *in accordance with the State Economic Plan*'.[22] The present author agrees with Professor D.A.Loeber, who pointed out that

---

18   T.Abova, *Arbitrazhnyi protsess v SSSR*, Moscow 1985, pp.8-11.
19   *Ibid.*, pp.9-10.
20   *Ibid.*, p.84.
21   S.Kucherov, *The Organs of Soviet Administration of Justice: Their History and Operation'*, Leiden 1970, pp.140-153.
22   *VVS SSSR*,1979 No.49, item 844. Article 4.

gosarbitrazh was an administrative agency though it acted, to a considerable extent, in a judicial manner.[23]

This system underwent a radical change after the collapse of socialism in 1990. In 1991, the Law on Commercial Courts (*arbitrazhnyi sud*) was enacted, followed by the Law on Commercial Court Procedure of 1992. By virtue of these laws, *gosarbitrazh* was transformed into a system of commercial courts.[24] The 1993 Constitution contains a provision on the Supreme Commercial Court; it is the highest court in settling economic disputes and other cases assigned to the commercial court (Art.126). The Law on the Court System of 1996 refers to commercial courts as part of the unified court system (Arts.3 and 4).

Commercial courts enjoy independence in the same way as ordinary courts. While *gosarbitrazh* had arbitrators, the commercial court now has judges who are qualified in the same manner as ordinary court judges. Commercial courts do not have the power to initiate the proceedings *ex officio* any more. In the light of the coming into force of Part One of the Civil Code and other developments, the 1992 laws, which still had a legacy of socialism, were replaced by the Law on Commercial Courts and the Law on Commercial Court Procedure in 1995.[25] The new commercial court started operation in April 1992.

The basic level of commercial courts comprises 'federal commercial courts of the constituent entities of the Russian Federation', i.e. commercial courts of the republics, regions (provinces), cities with federal status, and autonomous provinces and regions. There are 82 such courts. These courts handle cases as the first instance court. It is important to note that appeals against the first instance judgments are handled by the same court.

The second level of the commercial courts are the federal territorial courts, which were apparently modelled after the US Federal Circuit Courts. There are 10 such courts which handle cases as an instance of cassation in relation to the courts within the jurisdiction. The system of cassation on Russia is different from the original French system, in that in Russia, it is a system of remedy against the judgments of the first instance court and also the appellate instance *which have already taken effect* (see *infra*).

The third and the highest level of commercial court is the Supreme Commercial Court of the Russian Federation. The Supreme Commercial Court comprises the Plenum, the Presidium, the Department of Civil Cases, and the Department of

---

23   D.A.Loeber, 'Law and Contract Performance in the Soviet Union', in W.R.LaFave, *Law in the Soviet Society*, Urbana 1965, pp.131-132.

24   K.Pistor, 'Supply and Demand for Contract Enforcement in Russia: Courts, Arbitration and Private Enforcement', *Review of Central and East European Law* 1996 No.1, pp.69-70.

25   *SZ RF*, 1995 No.18, item 1589; No.19, item 1710.

Administrative Cases. The Plenum is composed of all judges of the Supreme Administrative Court. Members of the Parliament, the president of the Supreme Court, the president of the Constitutional Court, as well as the Procurator-General are entitled to attend the Plenum session. One of the most important functions of the Plenum is to issue 'explanatory guidelines' addressed to lower courts. The Supreme Commercial Court also has a Presidium which comprises the President, deputies and the heads of the department. The Presidium, among other things, reviews cases by way of supervision.

In 1999, commercial courts newly accepted a total of 581,729 cases. These cases are divided into cases arising from civil law relations and administrative law relations. Among the former, the largest portion comprises claims concerning non-performance or inadequate performance of obligations. The publication of the breakdown of cases for the year 2000 is delayed. According to the latest report, the total number of cases which reached the commercial court in 2000 was 634,363.[26] This is a significant increase from 1999.

The 581,729 cases accepted by the commercial court in 1999 include cases included the following:

Table 1 Cases Accepted by the Commercial Court

conclusion of, changes to, and rescission of contracts	6,085
recognition of contracts as void	5,376
non-performance or inadequate performance of contracts	379,870
recognition of the right to ownership	1,410
retrieval of property from an unlawful possessor	2,238
reorganisation and liquidation of juridical persons	74,371
securities	3,484
protection of business reputation	248
protection of intellectual property	227
violation of environmental law	3,531
compensation of extra-contractual damage	4,929
use of land	2,507

---

26 'Ob itogakh raboty arbitrazhnykh sudov v 2000 godu', *VVAS RF*, 2001, No.5, p.10.

bankruptcy (completed cases)	5.959
application of tax law	85,334

(*VVAS RF,* 2000, No.3, pp.6-8)

The commercial court handles a substantial number of cases involving the application of tax law. The number of such cases has increased by three times from 1998 to 1999. The total number was 85,334 in 1999. This includes cases of collection of arrears and fines involving tax other compulsory payments from individuals and organizations by the Ministry of Taxes and Levies.[27]

Although the number is relatively small, 'socially the most significant' cases are bankruptcy cases. There was a sharp increase in the number of bankruptcy cases; in 1999, there were 15,583 applications for bankruptcy, whereas this number reached 19,000 in 2000, of which 80% involved the bankruptcy of companies and entrepreneurs.[28]

It should be noted that the commercial court handled around 1,281 cases involving foreign companies in 2000. In 707 cases, the foreign party won the case.[29]

Until recently, international commercial arbitration in a third country was the preferred method of dispute settlement where foreign companies were involved. The significant number of such cases handled by Russian courts may be due firstly to the increase in the number of disputes in the newly developed market economy, but also may partly be attributed to the growing confidence in the Russian commercial court system on the part of foreign companies.

3)   Ordinary Courts (Courts of General Jurisdiction)

The structure of the ordinary court system is provided by the Law on Court Organisation of 1996 as well as the Law on Court Organisation of the RSFSR of 1981 (with subsequent amendments).[30]

---

27   *Rlu,* 2000 No.5, p.52.
28   *Rlu,* 1999 No.5, pp.57-58; 'Rabota arbitrazhnykh sudov Rossiskoi Federatsii v 2000 godu', [www.akdi.ru/vas/rabota]; *VVAS RF,* 2001 No.5, pp.11-12.
29   *VVAS RF,* 2001, No.5, p.14.
30   *SZ RF,* 1997 No.1, item 1.

The basic level of the ordinary court system is the district court. District courts handle cases as first instance courts. There are 2,440 district courts.[31] In some areas, such as in Moscow, inter-district courts were formed recently. In relation to the newly introduced system of justices of peace, district courts are higher instance courts.

The second level of courts are supreme courts of the subjects of the Russian Federation as well as regional (provincial) courts, courts of cities with federal status, and courts of autonomous provinces and regions. Currently, there are 87 such courts.[32] These courts handle cases as second instance courts of the judgments of district courts. In some cases, such as cases involving state secrets, these courts handle cases as a first instance court. They are also empowered to review cases in a supervisory procedure and cases reopened on newly found circumstances.

The Supreme Court of the Russian Federation is the highest court within the system of ordinary courts, i.e. in relation to the supreme courts of the subjects of the Russian Federation as well as regional (provincial) courts, courts of cities with federal status, courts of autonomous provinces and regions, and military tribunals. It also acts as a first instance court in some limited cases, and as a second instance court in cases where supreme courts of the subjects of the Russian Federation as well as regional (provincial) courts, courts of cities with federal status, courts of autonomous provinces and regions handled the case as the first instance court. The Supreme Court also reviews cases in a supervisory procedure and cases reopened on newly found circumstances.

The Supreme Court has a Plenum, Presidium, Civil and Criminal Departments and Court Administration Department. The Plenum is composed of all judges of the Supreme Court plus the Procurator General and other officials. The issuing of 'explanatory guidance' is its most important function. The Presidium comprises the President, deputies, heads of the departments. It reviews cases by way of supervision.

Unlike its predecessor under socialism, the Supreme Court does not have a special statute as yet.

According to the 1999 statistics, ordinary courts accepted a total of 5,100,400 civil cases. These include the following:

---

31   V.I.Radchenko, 'Sudebnaia reforma v Rossii', *ZhRP*, 1999 No.1, p.70.
32   *Ibid.*, p.70.

Table 2 Cases Accepted by the Ordinary Courts

marriage-family cases	941,300
employment disputes	951,500
claims of compensation for death or serious injury of a breadwinner	36,500
housing disputes	197,600
land disputes *1998 figures	11,200
consumer claims on goods and services	31,600
claims on protection of honour, dignity and business reputation	11,300
cases arising from administrative law relations, including: · actions against unlawful acts of government officials · actions for the recognition of legal acts as unlawful · actions against violations of tax law	331,900 140,700 3,170 84.500
Other cases of litigious nature (including disputes involving contracts)	2,309,400

(*RIu*, 2000, No.7, pp.58-59)

4)   Jurisdiction of the Ordinary Court and Commercial Court

The demarcation of competence between the ordinary court and the commercial court has been confusing from the beginning. The commercial court handles 'economic disputes arising from civil, administrative and other legal relations, between juridical persons, physical persons who perform entrepreneurial activities without forming a juridical person and are licensed as an individual entrepreneur (ComPC Art.22). 'Disputes arising from civil law relations' means disputes regulated by civil law which is embodied in the Civil Code. The Civil Code has a provision which determines the scope of 'civil law relations' (Art.2).

The ComPC has a non-exhaustive list of economic disputes which are to be handled by the commercial court. These include (Art.22):

i)   differences concerning contracts whose conclusion is mandated by law or where parties have agreed to the jurisdiction of the commercial court;

ii)   amendments to or rescission of a contract;

iii)   non-performance or inadequate performance of contracts;

iv)   recognition of the ownership to property;

v)   recovery claim by the titleholder vis a vis an unlawful possessor of a property;

vi)   infringement of the right of the titleholder and other lawful possessors not related to the deprivation of possession;

vii)   payment of compensation;

viii)   protection of honour, dignity and business reputation;

ix)   appeals against rejection or failure of state registration within the period provided by law.

This list is not exclusive. By virtue of the Law on Insolvency, insolvency cases fall within the jurisdiction of the commercial court. Bankruptcy of individual entrepreneurs is also included. It should be noted that here, the requirement that both parties be juridical persons (entrepreneurs) is dropped. Thus, creditors, not only juridical persons, but physical persons, not explicitly limited to entrepreneurs, are entitled to initiate the proceedings.[33]

On the other hand, CivPC provides that ordinary court has competence over 'civil, family, labour, and *kolkhoz* related cases' (Art.25). Experts agree that the provision of the CivPC which determines the competence of the ordinary court has 'become hopelessly obsolete' and contradicts the Constitution and the laws', although it is formally still in force.[34]

The problem was that although the competence of the commercial court was fairly clear from the ComPC, the corresponding provision in the CivPC was not amended after the commercial court came into operation. There was no legal basis to exclude those disputes listed in the ComPC from the competence of the ordinary court. For example, disputes between juridical persons in general could be handled both by the commercial court and the ordinary court. Another example could be found in cases involving foreign companies. The Commercial court has jurisdiction over cases involving foreign organisations, organisations with foreign investment, international organisations, foreign citizens and citizens without nationality who perform entrepreneurial activities, insofar as there is no international agreement which provides otherwise (ComPC Art.22, para.6). However, the CivPC also provides that ordinary courts have jurisdiction over cases involving foreign citizens, juridical persons and organisations (Art.25, subpara.4). The Supreme Court ack-

---

33   Supreme Commercial Court ed., *Kommentarii k arbitrazhnomu protesseual'nomu kodeksu Rossiiskoi Federatsii*, Moscow 1999, p.63.

34   Shakarian ed., *Grazhdanskoe protsessual'noe pravoe Rossii*, Moscow 1999, p.129.

nowledged in 1996 that disputes involving foreign companies and organisations fall within the competence of both courts.[35] Thus, there was an overlap of competence between the commercial court and the ordinary court.

A further example is the jurisdiction over administrative cases. The commercial court also handles administrative cases. In addition to the traditionally limited categories of administrative cases, since the late 1980s, courts obtained jurisdiction over cases where citizens had their rights or freedoms infringed by unlawful actions on the part of state agencies including local government agencies and their officials. Actions in this context include decisions of either an official or a collective body.[36] The problem is that this Law failed to indicate to which court such cases should be brought. The commercial court has jurisdiction over claims for recognition of invalidity of non-normative acts of state agencies and local self-government agencies which are against the laws and other normative acts and which infringe upon rights and lawful interests of organisations and citizens (ComPC Art.22). However, ordinary courts also have jurisdiction in such cases.

There have been proposals for the introduction of the system of administrative courts for some years.[37] As part of the package of judicial reform bills prepared by the government in 2001, a bill on the Law on Administrative Courts prepared by the Supreme Court was submitted to the Parliament.

On general demarcation of jurisdiction between both courts, the joint decision of the Plenum of the Supreme Court of the Russian Federation and the Plenum of the Supreme Commercial Court of the Russian Federation was issued in 1992, which, *inter alia*, stated that when the law does not clearly demarcate the boundary of competence of the courts, the jurisdiction should be determined primarily by whether both parties were juridical persons, or either of them was a non-juridical person. In the latter case, ordinary courts has jurisdiction.

The current understanding is that the competence of courts should be determined by way of exclusion, i.e. the ComPC is first applied, and the ordinary court handles cases which do not fall within the competence of the commercial court as determined by ComPC.[38]

However, this solution is not really convincing. For example, the Law on Joint-Stock Companies provides for various remedies, including those contesting the validity of the resolution of the general shareholders' meeting and the executive

---

35 Decision of the Civil Division of the Supreme Court, November 28,1996 in A.P.Ryzhakov and D.A.Sergeev eds., *Postateinyi kommentarii: Grazhdanskii protsessual'nyi kodeks RSFSR*, Moscow 1999, p.75.

36 Law on Appeal to Court of Actions and Decisions which infringe upon Rights and Freedom of Citizens, *VSND RF i VSRF*, 1993 No.19, item 685.

37 V.Kriazhkov and Iu.Starilov, 'Administrativnye sudy: kakimi im byt'?', *RIu*, 2001, No.1, pp.18-20;

38 M.Shakarian, *supra*, p.130; Ryzhakov and Sergeev, *supra*, pp.64-65.

board. On the other hand, the procedural law is silent on the jurisdiction in such cases. The joint decision of the Supreme Court and the Supreme Commercial Court acknowledges that this kind of claim should be handled by the commercial court as well as the ordinary court. Also in a shareholder's action, i.e. an action of a shareholder *vis à vis* members of the board or executive body, it is understood that both courts have jurisdiction. In such cases, according to a Russian specialist, if the defendant is an officer, i.e. a physical person, the case will be considered by the ordinary court. If the defendant is a body within the company and the plaintiff-shareholder is a juridical person, the case falls within the competence of the commercial court.[39] This is an odd arrangement; the subject matter is the same, but depending on the parties, the case is heard by different courts. If the *raison d'être* of a commercial court is to have commercial cases handled by specialist judges subject to special procedural rules, certainly, these cases should be handled solely by the commercial court.

The merger of the commercial court and ordinary court systems has been proposed, but there seems to be a strong resistance, and the forthcoming judicial reform has failed to accommodate this proposal.

5)   Jurisdiction of Russian Courts over Transnational Disputes

The Commercial Procedural Code has a provision on the competence of the commercial court in cases involving foreign persons, while the CivPC merely refers to other USSR laws (Art.434). This part of the Code has not been amended since the 1960s, and therefore, the ComPC contains the latest rules. According to the ComPC, Russian commercial courts have jurisdiction over cases where the defendant-juridical person is located in Russia, or the defendant-physical person is a resident in Russia (Art.212). The location of juridical persons and the domicile of physical persons are determined by provisions of the Civil Code. The domicile of a physical person is the place where this person permanently or primarily lives. The location of a juridical person is the place where it is registered (Art.20).

The rule that in domestic litigation, claims emerging from activities of a subdivision of a juridical person has to be initiated at the place of this subdivision is applicable to international litigation as well. This means that, according to the Supreme Commercial Court, if there is a dispute involving a branch of a foreign juridical person in Russia, the foreign plaintiff has no choice but to initiate the

---

39   Iu.Mateleva, *Pravovoe ppolozhenie aktionera v aktionernom obshchestve*, Moscow 1999, p.175.

proceedings in Russia.[40] Thus, the Russian commercial court has jurisdiction in the following cases:

i)   where a branch or a representative office of the foreign juridical person is located in the Russian Federation;
ii) when the defendant has property in the territory of the Russian Federation;
iii) where the dispute arises from a contract in which the place of performance is in the Russian Federation;
iv) in cases of compensation of damage where the incident which serves as the basis of the claim took place in the Russian Federation;
v)   where the claim is based upon unjust enrichment which took place in the Russian Federation;
vi) in cases involving the protection of honour, dignity and business reputation where the plaintiff is located in the Russian Federation;
vii) where there is an agreement between the Russian entity and foreign persons on jurisdiction.

In 2000, the commercial court handled 1,281 cases where one of the parties was a foreign company. Foreign companies were successful in 707 cases.[41]

6)   Independence of the Courts

Since *perestroika*, the Russian court system has undergone significant changes. The independence of the court has been reinforced by law and their prestige is gradually increasing.

Whether or not the courts have successfully gained authority is questionable. Disrespect of the court is reported from time to time. In November 1999 in St.Petersburg, a group of armed and masked members of the 'special division' of the Ministry of Internal Affairs forced their way into the court room and snatched a person who was standing trial. The conference of judges of St.Petersburg adopted a resolution criticising the Ministry and demanding that measures be taken by the Procurator-General.[42] In 2000, it was reported that there were 22 incidents of injury of judges and 18 incidents of arson on the court building.[43]

---

40 Supreme Commercial Court ed., *Kommentarii....* , *supra*, P.469.
41 *VVAS RF*, 2001 No.5, p.14.
42 *RIu*, 2000 No.2,p.2.
43 *Ibid.*, p.6.

There are also cases where 'local pressure', which used to be common under socialism, is inflicted upon judges. The head of administration of the Volgograd province was reported to have asked the commercial court as well as the ordinary court in the capital to suspend or postpone the procedure and enforcement of some categories of cases in relation to the 'extraordinary situation' in the region.[44] A commercial court judge, who reportedly 'ran afoul of the local governor', was disqualified by the qualification committee in Primorskii Region.[45]

There have been some cases where the independence of the court or the capability of the court was questioned by foreign investors. One case involved a company called Sidanco, which was the fifth largest oil company in Russia. In 1998, a bankruptcy petition was filed for Sidanco's three subsidiaries, followed by a petition for Sidanco itself the next year. BP-Amoco held 10% of Sidanco's shares and there were foreign creditors such as US Export-Import Bank and EBRD as well as German banks. The bankruptcy procedure was handled by local commercial courts, but on various occasions, these courts failed to supervise the activities of administrators in an appropriate way, but sided with another oil company which was a competitor of Sidanco. At one stage, Sidanco had to file a petition for the transfer of the case to another court.[46] What was more, the Supreme Commercial Court itself succumbed to political pressure and changed its position within a month.

Another case involved a 'de-privatisation' of a privatised state enterprise. The company was privatised in 1993 with foreign investment, but in 1999, the commercial court of St.Petersburg ruled that the documents which served as a basis of privatisation were illegal and that foreign investors must return the property to the state. It was alleged that the Ministry of State Property joined with workers to oust foreign investors by seeking weaknesses in the privatisation documents.[47]

The poor financial state of the court is also regarded as a threat to the independence of the court. In 1998, despite the constitutional guarantee of the finance of courts, the Ministry of Finance substantially cut the allocation of budget to the courts. The Constitutional Court found this to be against the Constitution, but the situation was not rectified. Local courts were forced to ask for resources from the local government as well as 'commercial organisations'.[48]

---

44 'Verkhovenstvo konstitutsii RF i federal'nykh zakonov – osnovnoi pravovoi printsip'. *KhiP* 2000 No.1, p.38.
45 *RFE/RL Newsline*, September 22, 2000.
46 *Project Finance International*, June 2, June 16, October 6, December 1, 1999; *New York Times*, November 24, 1999; *Eastern European Energy*, September issue 1999, pp.11-12.
47 *Wall Street Journal*, October 12, 1999.
48 *RIu*, 1999 No.1, p.3. See also G.T.Ermoshchin, 'Problemy obespecheniia nezavisimosti sudebnoi vlasti', in Iu.A.Tokhomirov et al eds., *Sudebnaia reforma v Rossii*, Moscow 2001, p.23.

2   INTERNATIONAL COMMERCIAL ARBITRATION INSTITUTIONS

Russia has had two international arbitration institutions since the 1930s; The Foreign Trade Arbitration Commission of the USSR Chamber of Commerce and the USSR Maritime Arbitration Commission. The former was renamed the International Commercial Arbitration Court in 1988 on the occasion of the enactment of the new arbitration rules.

Occasionally, people cast doubt on the neutrality of the Soviet arbitration institutions. However, overall, these arbitration institutions maintained their credibility throughout the socialist period.[49] On the other hand, there were some inconveniences, such as the mandatory use of Russian language and the limited choice of arbitrators. In a majority of East-West joint-ventures and major projects, Stockholm, and not Moscow, was chosen as the venue of arbitration.[50]

A new Law on International Commercial Arbitration was enacted in Russia on July 7, 1993 based upon the UNCITRAL model law. This Law is applicable to commercial arbitration, including ad hoc arbitration, handled in Russia.

The present International Commercial Arbitration Court is attached to the Chamber of Commerce of the Russian Federation, which is a non-profit organisation. Although it is called a 'court', it is an arbitration institution, and should not be confused with the 'arbitration court', which is in fact a commercial court in Russia as mentioned above. The International Commercial Arbitration Court handles the following cases upon agreement of the parties (Art.1, para.2):

i)   civil law disputes which emerge in the process of foreign trade and other foreign economic cooperation in which at least one of the parties is a foreign commercial organisation;
ii) disputes between companies with foreign participation, international organisations established in Russia as well as disputes between these bodies and Russian juridical persons.

The International Commercial Arbitration Court handles around 500 cases every year. More than two-thirds of the foreign parties are from the United States, Western Europe and Asian countries.

If there is an arbitration clause or agreement, unless the said clause or agreement is void, or has been terminated, Russian courts must terminate the procedure and refer the case to arbitration:

---

49   See the case involving an Israeli company and a Soviet foreign trade organisation in 1958 at the time of the war in the Middle East, M.M.Boguslavskii, *Mezhdunarodnoe chastnoe pravo*, third edition, Moscow 1999, pp.140-141.
50   V.Viechtbauer, 'Arbitration in Russia', *Stanford Journal of International Law*, 1993, pp.371-374.

A Russian company brought an action to the commercial court against a French trading company for payment of compensation. Despite repeated notices in accordance with international treaties, the defendant failed to turn up in court, but instead, submitted a written objection to the jurisdiction of the court, referring to the clause in the contract which provided for an ad hoc arbitration. Russian and France are signatories to the European Convention on International Commercial Arbitration of 1961. The Convention acknowledges ad hoc arbitration and provides for the procedure of setting up an ad hoc tribunal.

Under such circumstances, the Supreme Commercial Court ruled that the court must decide on its jurisdiction by taking into account the Convention and national law. According to Article 87, para.2 of the ComPC, the commercial court must leave the case without examination, if there is an agreement between the parties to refer the dispute to arbitration and the possibility of referring the case to arbitration has not been exhausted, and further, if the party which objects to court jurisdiction, no later than its first response in relation to the substance of the case, petitions for the transfer of the dispute to arbitration. In this particular case, the possibility of arbitration has not been exhausted, and the opposing party had expressed its desire to have the case handled by international arbitration. Therefore, the Court ruled that the parties should take measures to have the case settled by ad hoc arbitration.[51]

The Law on International Commercial Arbitration expressly acknowledges that the parties are free to choose the applicable law (Art.28, para.1). From the time of its predecessor under socialism, the International Commercial Arbitration Court had applied foreign laws chosen by the parties.

The parties may appeal to the court against the arbitral award on limited grounds, but only within three months after the award has been granted (Art.34, para.3).

The ComPC and the CivPC both provide that arbitral awards serve as a basis for enforcement in the same way as court judgments.

In cases where arbitration took place outside Russia, the problem of enforcement arises, despite the fact that Russia is a signatory to the New York Convention on the Enforcement of Foreign Arbitral Awards.

The 1993 Law provides that arbitral awards are binding, regardless of the country from which the award has emanated, and can be enforced in Russia by applying to the 'competent court'(Art.35, para.1). Grounds for the refusal of recognition and enforcement are listed as follows (Art.36):

i)   one of the parties did not have capacity to act, or the arbitration agreement was void;

---

51   'Obzor sudebno-arbitrazhnoi praktiki razresheniia sporov po delam s uchastiem inostrannykh lits', informatsionnoe pís'mo, *VVAS RF*, 1998 No.4, p.52.

ii)   the party against which the award is to be enforced was not duly informed of the appointment of the arbitrator, of the arbitration proceedings, or for other reasons, was unable to present his case;

iii) the award was granted on a case which was not covered by the arbitration agreement;

iv)   the composition of the arbitration panel or the arbitration procedure did not coincide with the agreement or law;

v)   the award is yet to be final, was revoked, or its enforcement was suspended by the court of the country where the award was granted;

vi)   the subject matter of arbitration is unable to be dealt by arbitration by Russian law;

vii) recognition and enforcement of the award are against the public policy of the Russian Federation.

The 1993 Law does not specify which court, i.e. ordinary court or commercial court, has jurisdiction on enforcement. The Law merely provides that petitions should be presented to the 'competent court'. On this matter, the decree of the Presidium of the USSR Soviet of June 21,1988 is still in force. This decree primarily addresses the enforcement of foreign judgments, but acknowledges the applicability of most provisions to foreign arbitral awards.

The decree provides that petition for enforcement is heard in open court with the respondent being notified of the date and place of the hearing. The court, after hearing the explanation of the respondent and reviewing the documents presented by the claimant, decides whether enforcement should be allowed. Although there is no explicit provision to this effect, arbitral awards are enforced in Russia without the court reviewing the case on its merit.

According to the 1988 decree, enforcement falls within the jurisdiction of the higher ordinary courts, i.e. the Supreme Court, provincial and regional courts as well as the city courts of the *locus rei sitaei* of the respondent. However, this decree had been enacted at the time when there was no commercial court. So far, ordinary courts have been exercising jurisdiction over such cases, but since 1995, when the new Law on Commercial Court Procedure was enacted, commercial courts also assert jurisdiction in these cases. The forthcoming amendment to the ComPC is expected to grant the commercial court an exclusive jurisdiction over such cases, but there is understandably a strong resistance from the ordinary court.[52]

There are some cases where foreign arbitral awards have been enforced in Russia. In an earlier case, the Moscow City Court acknowledged enforcement

---

52   B.Karabel'nikov, 'Problemy ispolneniia reshenii mezhdunarodnykh arbitrazhei v Rossiiskoi Federatsii', in Tikhomirov et al eds., *supra*, p.150.

of an award rendered in London on the basis of the New York Convention and the 1988 decree. The decision of the court was not appealed. In another case, the Moscow City Court enforced an award rendered in Stockholm.[53] In a more recent case, another Stockholm award has been enforced in St.Petersburg. In this case, the case reached the Supreme Court which made a dubious ruling, but the City Court of St.Petersburg, after the case had been referred back, acknowledged the enforcement.[54]

However, 'many Russian courts, as before, do not understand that their power is limited by the New York Convention, and that they are not entitled to review the arbitral award on its merit'.[55]

The ground which Russian respondents often resort to when objecting to enforcement is public policy. In the above-cited case in St.Petersburg, the Russian party claimed that the requirement of the Soviet law of two parties signing a contract was part of the public policy and that the enforcement of a loan agreement which was signed by only one person was against public policy.

Concerning public policy, the following decision of the Supreme Court is relevant:

> In accordance with the award of the International Commercial Arbitration Court of the Russian Chamber of Commerce, Russian factory Izmeritel' came under an obligation to pay Omegatekh Elektroniks GmbH 197,119 US Dollars plus interest and costs. Izmeritel' brought an action at the Moscow City Court, requesting the court to annul the award of the arbitration on the ground that there had been no contract between the parties; there was no genuine copy of the contract; there was no arbitration agreement; the award was based upon forged documents.
>
> The Moscow City Court, on August 19, 1998, acknowledged the claim of the plaintiff and quashed the arbitral award on the ground that at the arbitration, the liability of Izmeritel' had not been sufficiently proved, and that enforcement of this award was against public policy.
>
> The defendant appealed, and the Supreme Court ruled in favour of Omegatekh. Referring to Art.34, para.2 of the Law on International Commercial Arbitration, the Supreme Court found that the Moscow City Court had erred in applying this provision by annulling the award on the ground that the International Commercial Arbitration Court accepted a Xerox copy of a contract as evidence. This is not a ground for annulling an award. The Supreme Court also found the reference to public order by the Moscow City Court was wrong. According to the Supreme Court, 'public order' of the Russian

---

53 K.Hober, 'Enforcing Foreign Arbitral Awards in Russia', *Russia and Commonwealth Business Law Report*, August 16, 1995, pp.8-10.

54 A.Mouranov and N.Toupikina-Holm, 'Enforcement in Russia: Chronology of a Loan Recovery', *Stockholm Arbitration Report*, 1999:2, pp.138-172.

55 Karabel'nikov, *supra*, p.156.

Federation was not the same as the substance of national legislation of the Russian Federation, since application of foreign law is also allowed under the Law on International Commercial Arbitration (Art.28), and therefore, a discrepancy between Russian Law and foreign law does not necessarily serve as a ground for annulling an award for being against public order. The Supreme Court proceeded to point out that public order should be understood as the 'basis of the social system of the Russian Federation'. The defence of public order should be available only when the application of foreign law would entail a result which is not permissible from the viewpoint of Russian legal consciousness.[56]

A Russian commentator acknowledged that there was a risk of the concept of public policy being broadly interpreted. She pointed out that the Russian concept of public policy was in the process of formulation, and that the concept was likely to include the 'basis system of anti-monopoly legislation, privatisation, fundamental legal basis of commerce, bankruptcy, large (town-forming) enterprises etc.[57] It is proposed that rules concerning the application public policy should be made clear by law.[58]

3   THE PROCURACY

The office of the procurators was created by Peter the Great in the early 19th century. The primary task of the procurators was to oversee the administration on behalf of the Tsar. After the Judicial Reform in 1864, the function of general supervision over the administration was regarded to be obsolete and was abolished. Criminal prosecution was made the procurators' main function.

The Procuracy – the office of procurators – was abolished altogether by the October Revolution, but was restored in 1922 on the initiative of Lenin. However, the Procuracy which was restored was not the Procuracy of the post-Judicial Reform period, but of the period of Peter the Great. The Procuracy was entrusted with the task of overseeing the administration on behalf of the rulers – the CPSU. Although it operated as a prosecuting agency, their main area of activities was the 'general supervision', i.e. supervision of the observance of legality by administrative agencies. In the process of *perestroika*, there were calls for the abolition

---

56   Decision of the Civil Law Division of the Supreme Court, September 25, 1998. [www.akdi.ru]
57   N.Pavlova, 'Nekotorye osnovaniia otkaza v priznanii i privedenii v ispolnenie arbitrazhnykh reshenii', *VVAS RF*, 1999 No.3, pp.22-23.
58   Karabel'nikov, *supra*, p.155.

of the Procuracy, but eventually, the Procuracy has survived the changes, despite some setbacks.[59]

In the area of commercial law, the Procuracy is important in that i) the Procuracy is empowered to initiate an action in order to defend the interests of the state and the society, and ii) the Procuracy lodges protests together with the presidents of the court against judgments of the court and thus trigger the supervisory procedure in civil cases. Concerning i), in 2000, procurators initiated the procedure in the commercial court in 8,437 cases. 72% of the claims by the procurators were satisfied.[60]

Sometimes, procurators are overzealous in defending the interests of the region:

A procurator brought an action against the government of a constituent entity of the Russian Federation, requesting the court to recognise the order of the local government to extend privileges to a joint venture between Russian and foreign enterprises as void, since it was against the interest of the region. The joint venture was formed by a foreign company (40% stake) and two Russian companies. Originally, the rate of the payment for the use of sub-soil was set at 10%, and the rate of profit tax was 32%. The foreign company invested 40 million US dollars.

Then, after one year of the commencement of business, the tax law and the Law on Sub-Soil were amended and also a new export duties introduced. The foreign company asked the government of the constituent entity of the Russian Federation to decrease the fiscal burden to the original level. This was accepted, and an order of the government to the effect to exempt the joint venture from export duties for three years and to reduce the royalty to 5%. This was contested by the procurator.

The government of the constituent entity of the Russian Federation argued that this was in accordance with the Foreign Investment Law of the RFSFR and the Foreign Investment Law of the Russian Federation of 1999 which has a grandfather clause, protecting investors from the worsening of terms of investment. The commercial court found this argument to be justifiable and dismissed the claim of the procurator.[61]

---

59   H.Oda, 'The Re-Emergence of *Pravovoe Gosudarstvo* and the Russian Procuracy', paper presented at the VI ICCEES World Congress, Tampere, 2000.

60   *VVAS RF* 2001 No.5, p.14.

61   'Obzor praktiki razresheniia arbitrazhnymi sudami sporov sviazanykh s zashchitoi inostrannykh investorov', informatsionnoe pis'mo, VAS RF, January 18, 2001, item.8 [Inforis].

4   LEGAL PROFESSIONS

1)   Judges

As of January 1, 2000, there were 2,354 commercial court judges.[62] In the same year, in ordinary courts, there were 16,742 positions for judges at the district court level. There were 3,223 judges at higher courts.[63]

The Constitution provides that a Russian citizen over the age of 25, who has had a higher legal education and experience in the legal profession for a minimum of 5 years may become a judge (Art.119). The Law on the Status of Judges of 1992 provides for additional requirements. Thus, the candidate is required to pass an examination and receive the recommendation of the qualification committee (Art.4). Qualification committees are formed at various levels of higher courts including the commercial court. The highest is the Supreme Qualification Committee, members of which are elected by the All Russian Congress of Judges. For judges of the higher courts, there are further requirements. The minimum age is 30, and for the Supreme Court and the Supreme Commercial Court judges, the minimum age is 35, and 10 years experience in the legal profession is required (Art.4).

Many judges had started their career in the socialist period. Under socialism, judges, as CPSU members, were directly subordinated to the local CPSU organisations. 'Judges were regarded as second grade bureaucrats'. After the collapse of socialism, changes were slow to take place.[64] In 1992, the then Minister of Justice reported that 98% of judges were former communists.[65] Even after the adoption of the Law on the Status of Judges in 1992, people are said to believe that 'many things remain without changes to the better – people come across arbitrariness, boorishness of judges, their hunger for profits, lies and lack of ethics'.[66] The President of the Supreme Court acknowledged that 'corruption, abuse of power by judges do exist, alas, but there is nothing we can do about it.'[67] According to the chairman of the Supreme Qualification Committee, in 1999, 95 judges were dismissed. Grounds for dismissal ranged from falsification of court documents to serious violation of procedural norms and even appearance

---

62   *VVAS RF*, 2000 No.4, p.12.
63   *RIu*, 2000 No.3, p.3.
64   Radchenko, *supra*, p.55.
65   Iu.Stetsovskii, *Sudebnaia vlast'*, Moscow 1999, p.102.
66   *Ibid.*, p.92.
67   *Ibid.*

in court in an intoxicated state.[68] In 2000, two senior judges –presidents of higher courts – were dismissed for 'compromising acts'.[69]

While judges adopted their ethical code in 1993,[70] not every judge follows the code. In a case where a judge falsified a document on the destruction of a weapon – evidence in criminal procedure – the qualification committee found that the judge had committed an offence and discredited the judiciary, but nevertheless, merely reprimanded him, considering his long service and the fact that this was his first offence.[71]

2)   Attorneys

The profession of *advokat* – attorneys emerged in Russia as a result of the Great Judicial Reform of 1864. A majority of these advocates practised on their own without being a member of a law firm or consultancy. The first legal consultancy was established in St.Petersburg in 1870. It was only in three major cities, St.Petersburg, Moscow and Khar'kov, that an association of advocates – *kollegiia* – was allowed to be established. In fact, advocates practising in these cities enjoyed the privilege of being 'above the hierarchical ladder'. However, even those *kollegiia* of three major cities were supervised by the intermediate court, *sudebnaia palata*. There were various restrictions on the membership. Jewish people were not allowed to become a full member; they were not even allowed to practice as an attorney; they had to work as assistants. Women were not allowed to practise law until the February Revolution.[72] During the constitutional movement in the early 20th century and in the period leading to the February Revolution, advocates played a major role in the democratic movement, many of them being members of the Constitutional Democratic Party. They were often persecuted by the Tsarist government. S.Kucherov, who himself was an advocate before the October Revolution, quoted the chairman of the lawyers' guild:[73]

> With the greatest efforts, often forgetting their own interests, our colleagues in all corners of Russia fulfilled their modest but great office – *the office of the defence of the individual against the onslaught of the state.*

---

68   *RIu*, 2000 No.5, p.3.
69   *VVAS RF*, 2001 No.5, p.18.
70   *Ibid.*, 1993 No.23, p.31.
71   Stetsovskii, *supra*, p.105.
72   M.Iu.Barshchevskii, *Organizatsiia i deiatel'nost' advokatury v Rossii*, Moscow 1997, p.12.
73   Kucherov, *supra*, p.312.

Probably because of this, immediately after the October Revolution, the *kollegiia* of advocates was abolished together with the Tsarist courts and the Procuracy. Although the profession itself was not abolished, the number of advocates declined from 13,000 in 1917 to 659 in 1921. In 1922, at the beginning of the New Economic Policy, the Statute on the Advocates was enacted. The practice of advocates in the traditional way was tolerated during this period, but then, being labelled as 'juridical *kulaks*', they were collectivised into a Soviet type *kollegiia*s in the 1930s. Advocates were allowed to practice only as a member of the legal consultation bureau run by the respective *kollegiia* in the area. The *kollegiia*s had almost no autonomy at all. They were strictly controlled by the Ministry of Justice, and ultimately by the CPSU. In political trials, those advocates who were issued a special permit by the Presidium of the *kollegiia* in consultation with the KGB were allowed to take part.

The judicial reform which gradually took place since the time of *perestroika* did not first affect the advocates. The reform focussed on the courts and to a lesser extent, the Procuracy. Since 1990, work has been going on for the enactment of the new Law on Advocates. However, the parties involved – members of the *advokatura*, practising attorneys, local government, and the Ministry of Justice – have failed to reach a consensus, and therefore, the 1980 Statute on Advocates is still in force.

Although legislative reform has been slow, major changes have taken place in practice. While the system of state supervision provided by the 1980 Statute still has not been formally abolished, the Ministry of Justice has reluctantly given up their supervisory power in favour of the *kollegiia*s. Now *kollegiia*s have power to decide on issues such as entry, training, remuneration, and creation of new offices.[74] The system of payment for legal services has changed from a fixed fee system set by the Ministry of Justice to the system of fees negotiated with the clients. Another important development was the establishment of the Union of Advocates of the USSR in 1989, which was the first independent union under socialism.

Already under Gorbachev, a new form of legal business – 'legal cooperatives' which were *de facto* private law firms were allowed to be set up. In the late 1980s, the Ministry of Justice, in order to ensure that legal services are available to small and medium-sized businesses, authorised 'parallel *kollegiia*s' to be set up in regions where *kollegiia*s already existed. Furthermore, law offices and bureaux were allowed to operate within the framework of the *kollegiia*s.[75] Local governments

---

74 P.Jordan, 'The Russian Advokatura (Bar) and the State in the 1990s', *Europe-Asia Studies*, 1998 No.5, p.769-770.
75 The then Minister of Justice cited in Barshchevskii, *supra*, p.199.

often supported the creation of the 'parallels' in their territory. Indeed, some of them have close links with the local government. In addition to the traditional friction between the Ministry of Justice and traditional *kollegiia*s, there are now conflicts between the traditional and parallel *kollegiia*s.[76]

Also in the early 1990s, the Ministry of Justice permitted private law firms to be formed outside the purview of the *kollegiia*s. These were the successors of the legal cooperatives which emerged under Gorbachev. Since the term 'advocate' denotes those screened and accepted by a *kollegiia* of one type or another under the 1980 Statute, members of these law firms cannot be called advocates, but simply lawyers or attorneys. Instead of concentrating on litigation like the Soviet advocates, members of these law firms primarily focussed on non-contentious corporate work.[77]

The number of advocates has substantially increased. In mid-1997, there were 26,500 advocates organised in over 100 traditional *kollegiia*s (19,000-2000 members) and 40 parallel *kollegiia*s (7,000 members).[78]

One of the problems was that there was no formal requirement as to the qualification to become members of the new *kollegiia*s as well as the newly set up law firms. This was rectified when, in April 1995, the government enacted a decree on the licensing by the Ministry of Justice of providing paid legal advice. Members of the *kollegiia*s were exempted from the licensing requirement. By early 1997, the Ministry and local justice organs had issued approximately 8,000 licenses of which half were issued to members of private law firms.[79] However, this decree was abolished and at present, there is no licensing system for attorneys working in the private law firms.

Even with the traditional *kollegiia*s, the requirement for qualification is not so high. The candidate must have had a higher legal education and two year's experience in the legal profession. 'Legal profession' in this context includes senior officers of the police, espionage and counter-espionage, and the head or experts in the legal department central and local administrative agencies, trade unions and enterprises.[80]

Since 1990, many drafts of the Law on Advocates have been prepared by various entities including the Ministry of Justice, the President, and the advocates. A presidential draft, which allegedly was a compromise between the drafts prepared by the Ministry of Justice, working group of academics, and the Federal

---

76   *Ibid.*, pp.33-34.
77   Jordan, *supra*, p.773.
78   *Ibid.*, pp.771-772.
79   *Ibid.*, p.773.
80   Circular Letter of the Ministry of Justice, October 10, 1995.

Union of Advocates respectively, was submitted to the Duma in 1995. In this draft, the *kollegia* was defined as an independent non-commercial organisation for providing qualified legal advice to citizens and juridical persons. *Kollegia*s were given full autonomy; acceptance to the *kollegia* and its membership as well as exclusion and disciplinary measures were to be decided solely by the *kollegia*s. Advocates were allowed to form legal bureaux, firms, and cabinets within the *kollegiia* in addition to the traditional legal consultation bureaux. The qualification required to become an advocate was the higher legal education and two years' practice of legal profession. If the candidate had less than two years' experience, an apprenticeship at the *kollegiia* between one and two years was required.[81]

The draft has undergone numerous changes and the variant which was submitted in February 1999 is said to be based upon the idea of 'state regulation of the activities of *advokatura*', for which it is criticised particularly by attorneys from the parallel *kollegiia*s as destroying '7 years existence of Russian *advokatura* on the basis of democratic principles' and a return to the 'administrative-command system' under socialism.[82] One advocate singled out the differences between the interested parties to be the organisational structure of the *kollegiia* (non-profit organisation or profit-making organisation?), the procedure for creating and liquidating *kollegiia*s, the number of *kollegiia*s in each subject of Federation, mechanism of self-administration, and the mutual relationship between the *advokatura* and the state. The Ministry of Justice has turned into a strong opponent of the autonomy of the *advokatura*. Officials now maintain that state control over the *advokatura* should be reinforced, and even proposes to have a committee of judges and procurators under the aegis of the Ministry to license advocates. 'Parallel' *kollegiia*s are also to be abolished.[83]

The new Law on the *advokatura* is part of the package of the bills for judicial reform in 2001 and is expected to be enacted soon.

3)   Notary Public

The profession of notary public dates back to the 19th century. They were government officials – officials of the 8th rank. This system of notary public as a state institution continued under socialism. One of the primary tasks of the notary public

---

81   Barashchevskii, *supra*, pp.54-56.
82   'Zakonoproekt ob advokature protivorechit Konstitutsii Rossii i zdravomu smyslu', *RIu* 1999 No.4, p.1.
83   'V.Smirnov, 'Zakon ob advokature nado priniiat' nezamedlitel'no', *RIu* 1999 No.5, pp.12-13. See also Jordan, *supra*, pp.776-777.

at that time was to check the legality of contracts concluded by the state enterprises. It was another device for the state to keep control over these enterprises.

After the collapse of socialism, significant changes took place. First of all, the scope of the activities of the notary public has become narrower; part of their activities came to be replaced by the system of registration of transactions involving immovables. Second, organisationwise, private practice was allowed to the notaries (Art.8). At present, there are state notaries public and notaries public in private practice. It is mandatory for a notary public in private practice to be a member of the chamber (*palata*) of notaries (Art.56).

The legal basis for the activity of the notary public is the Fundamental Principles of the Legislation on Notary Public of 1993.[84] According to this Law, the task of the notary public is to defend the right and legitimate interests of individuals and juridical persons by performing, *inter alia*, the following acts in the name of the Russian Federation (arts.1 and 35):

i) notarisation of transactions;
ii) authentication of copies of documents and excerpts;
iii) authentication of the translation of documents;
iv) confirmation of the time of presentation of a document;
v) accepting of money and securities as a deposit;
vi) preparation of enforcement documents;
vii) protesting bills of exchange;
viii) presentation of cheques for payment and confirmation of the failure of payment;
ix) presenting maritime protests;
x) preservation of evidence.

A notary public is licensed by the Ministry of Justice. It is required to have finished a high legal education, must go through at least one year of apprenticeship, and pass a state examination (Art.2).

In cases where the law mandates a transaction to be notarised, the remuneration of the notaries public in private practice is calculated in accordance with the Law on State Duties (*poshlina*). Otherwise, they are free to negotiate the amount of remuneration with the client.[85]

---

84   *VSND RF i VS RF*, 1993 No.10, item 357.
85   V.S.Repin, *Kommentarii k osnovam zakonodatel'stva Rossiiskoi Federatsii o notariate*, Moscow 1999, pp.45-50.

3

BASIC PRINCIPLES AND RULES OF PRIVATE LAW

1   HISTORICAL BACKGROUND

The first attempt at enacting a systematic code in Russia was the *Ulozhenie* (Code) of 1649. Primary sources of this Code are said to be the indigenous law of Russia, which included the *Sudebniki* of 1497and 1550, but mostly customary law with some influence of Byzantine law and Lithuanian law. It comprised 25 chapters with 967 provisions including some chapters on civil law – mainly property relations.[1] Successive tsars, including Peter the Great and Ekaterina II, attempted to enact a new *Ulozhenie*, but all these attempts failed.

In the late 18th century, another commission was set up to prepare the laws. There seem to have been two different schools of thought. One aimed at the enactment of a new *Ulozhenie*, while the other sought the codification of the existing law. M.M.Speranskii, who was an active member of this commission, actually prepared a draft of part one of the Civil Code (persons) and submitted it to the State Council. This was followed by parts two (property) and three (contracts) in 1810. There was a very strong influence from the French Code civil. However, the draft code was met with opposition; the State Council was not convinced that the new Code should be modelled on the Code civil.[2] After Speranskii was banished, it was decided that instead of borrowing from foreign codes, they should turn afresh to the investigation of law in the past, based upon the idea that the 'laws which survived the years would best serve the state'.[3] The 1649 *ulozehnie* as well as separate legislation which had been enacted since then were compiled, first organised in a chronological way in the Complete Collection of

---

1   'Ulozehnie', in F.A.Brokgauz et al eds., *Entsiklopedicheskii slovar'*, vol 34-a, St.Petersburg 1902, p.685.
2   A.N.Filippov, *Uchebnik istorii russkago prava, chast' 1*, 4th edition, Iur'ev 1912, pp.561-567; 'Ulozhenie grazhdanskoe', in F.A.Brokgauz et al eds., *Entsiklopedicheskii slovar'*, vol 34-a, St.Petersburg 1902, p.692.
3   Fillipov, *ibid.,* p.567.

Laws (*Polnoe sobranie zakonov*) and then in a more systematic way. After his return from exile in Siberia in 1823, Speranskii was instrumental in this enormous undertaking, which finally culminated in the 15 volume *Svod zakonov* of 1832. In fact, the idea of Speranskii was that the *Svod zakonov* was only a first step in the future enactment of the new Code, which was not only a codification of the existing law. Even in the process of preparing the *Svod zakonov*, Speranskii often exceeded his humble role as a person compiling and systematising existing law and became, occasionally and unintentionally, 'the genuine creator of many of our legal norms, particularly in the area of civil law'.[4]

The first part of Volume 10 of the *Svod zakonov* was devoted to civil law. Since the total 15 volumes were revised in 1842 and 1857, there have been two editions of Volume 10; 1887 and 1900.[5] Russian Civil Law as incorporated in the *Svod zakonov* was primarily based upon the 1649 Code with the addition of various laws enacted at different times. It was arranged in a way similar to the Code civil. Speranskii was familiar with Roman law, French law, Prussian law as well as Austrian law, and actually used the concepts and definitions of foreign laws in the process of compiling and editing the then existing laws. However, despite the efforts of Speranskii, the fact remained that the law was obsolete, inconsistent, full of loopholes, and casuistic. The Law lacked the fundamental 'guiding ideas'. In fact, it was hoped that the problems which were left unsolved in the *Svod zakonov* would be solved in the future *ulozhenie*.[6]

Shortcomings of the civil law part of the *Svod zakonov* were recognised in the 19th century; in 1869, a commission for the preparation of rules on contracts and obligation was established, followed by a commission for the preparation of the Civil Code (*grazhdanskoe ulozhenie*) which was set up in 1882. By 1903, five volumes of the draft Civil Code had been published.[7] The draft Code was not entirely different from the existing Russian law. Basic principles of Russian law were preserved, insofar as they were not obsolete or failed to match the needs of modern times. In order to fill the gaps in the existing law, first of all, the practice of the Russian higher courts was taken into account. In principle, the commission is said not to have accepted foreign law directly. However, the Code

---

4   *Ibid.*, pp.573-574.
5   L.Schultz, *Russische Rechtsgeschichte*, Lahr 1951, S.218-219.
6   'Ulozhenie grazhdaonskoe', *supra*, p.692.
7   A.M.Guliaev, *Russkoe grazhdanskoe pravo*, St.Petersburg 1907, p.5. In fact, in the Russian Empire, there was no unified system of civil law. In the early 20th century, in addition to the *Svod zakonov*, there were the Civil Code of the Kingdom of Poland based upon Code civil, civil codes of the Baltic states, Belarus and the Kingdom of Finland. *Ibid.*, p.3. See also *Grazhdanskoe ulozhenie; proekt visochashche uchrezhdeniie Redaktsionnaia Kommisiia po sostavleniiu grazhdanskogo ulozheniia*, St.Petersburg 1905.

civil had much influence, since it was actually being applied in Poland which, at that time, was part of the Russian Empire. Also the commission studied the German *Bürgerliches Gesetzbuch* (BGB), which had been translated into Russian shortly after its enactment, as well as the Austrian Civil Code, the Swiss Code, and the Californian Law.[8] In October 1913, part of the draft Code on the Law of Obligations was submitted to the Duma, but failed to be approved, due to the First World War.[9] Thus, civil law provisions accommodated in the *Svod zakonov* remained in force until the October Revolution of 1917.

After the October Revolution, in 1922, the Civil Code of the RSFSR was enacted.[10] This was at the time of the New Economic Policy, when a market economy controlled from the 'commanding heights' by Bolsheviks was allowed to operate. As A.Goikhbarg, the principal author of the Code, remarked in 1923, 'until the October Revolution, there was almost, or absolutely, no theoretical work which, in a systematic way, developed and described the legal structure which was to emerge after the overthrowing of the capital' in detail.[11] It was not surprising that the draft Civil Code of the Tsarist period was extensively studied. Many provisions were taken from the draft Code, but the number of provisions was reduced from some 1,500 provisions to 431.[12] It took only four months for Goikhbarg to prepare the draft. The structure of the Code closely resembled the European codes such as the BGB and the Swiss Code. However, there were some significant differences. Firstly, the part on family law was left out of the Code. There was a separate law – the Family and Marriage Code of 1918. At that time, civil law was thought to 'wither away', and only Family and Marriage Law would remain under socialism.[13] Secondly, the Land Law was separated – the Land Code, which was part of the administrative law. This was due to the nationalisation of land.

Although the 1922 Code was designed to give stability to the economy and commerce, it did not give any protection to pre-Revolutionary rights. Nor were the newly-acquired private rights secure. This was at the time when Lenin made the famous remark – 'we do not recognise anything private'. Goikhbarg even went further and stated as follows:[14]

---

8   W.von Seeler, *Der Entwurf des Russischen Zivilgestzbuches*, Berlin 1911, S.10-11.
9   Schultz, *supra*, S.223.
10   *SU RSFSR*, 1922 No.71, item 904.
11   A.Goikhbarg, *Khoziaistvennoe pravo R.S.F.S.R.*, vol.1, Moscow 1923, p.5.
12   V.Gsovski, *Soviet Civil Law*, Ann Arbor 1948, pp.24-25.
13   M.V.Antokol'skaia, *Semeinoe pravo*, Moscow 1999, p.64.
14   Goikhbarg, *supra*.

Laissez faire, laissez passer are by no means the principle of the 20th century. This principle is even less applicable in our country, when a predominant part of economic activities is concentrated in the hands of the state agencies, and private persons and their associations are allowed limited participation in economic activities.

The basic idea was to exclude individualism as much as possible from the Code. The theory of A.Duguit, a French legal philosopher, contributed a theoretical basis. Individual rights were subordinated to the interests of the state. Article 1 of the Code proclaimed that private rights were protected insofar as they were exercised in accordance with their social and economic purpose. Article 30 explicitly provided that transactions directed against the interest of the state were void. One observer commented that the Bolsheviks chose to go in the direction of state capitalism.

The period of the New Economic Policy ended in 1928 and under the planned economy, the drive for industrialisation began. With the demise of the market economy, some lawyers envisaged the demise of civil law as well. Their view was that civil law was based upon the exchange of goods, but now that the economic plan was to replace such relations, civil law should also be replaced by economic law. Economic law, according to E.B.Pashukanis, a prominent proponent of this view, was not really law, but administrative command, which was a transitional form of law towards its ultimate withering away. However, this view went too far towards the left at a time when the communist leadership was trying to tighten control over the nation by strengthening law and order in the early 1930s. Pashukanis was criticised for his 'leftist deviation' and was executed in 1938. Nevertheless, the view that an economic code was needed in addition to the Civil Code survived the socialist period and can still be encountered.

The 1922 Civil Code remained in force until the 1960s, although the relationship between state enterprises came to be regulated not by civil law, but by the Law on Enterprise and other laws which were part of the administrative law. In 1961, the Fundamental Principles of the Civil Law of the USSR were enacted, followed by the civil codes of constituent republics.[15] There was not much difference between the 1922 Code and the codes in the 1960s. One conspicuous difference was that the 1960s codes contained provisions which consolidated the role of the state as an 'organiser of civil law relations' and 'ensured the primacy of plans over contracts'.[16]

---

15   *SZ SSSR* 1961 No.19, item 685.
16   Forword, in M.I.Braginskii ed., *Kommentarii chasti pervoi grazhdanskogo kodeksa Rossiiskoi Federatsii dliae predprinimatelei*, first edition, Moscow 1996, pp.7-8.

With the transition to the market economy, these laws were naturally found to be unsuitable. In the very last year of the existence of the USSR, the Fundamental Principles of the Civil Legislation of the USSR was enacted. This was a total break from the civil law under socialism; it was orientated towards the market economy, although in a primitive form. Even after the collapse of the USSR, part of this law is still in force. In the area of civil law, the USSR Law on Ownership of 1990 was also a breakthrough, since it acknowledged, for the first time since 1922, diverse forms of ownership, including private and collective ownership.

Preparation for a new Civil Code started in the early 1990s. As was the case with the reforms before the October Revolution, the law of various jurisdictions including the BGB, the Uniform Commercial Code, and even the legislation of Quebec were extensively studied. In addition, indigenous laws including the draft Civil Code of the Tsarist period and the 1922 Code were studied. In the end, the Dutch Civil Code served as a basis for the new Civil Code as a whole, although the influence of laws from other jurisdictions can be found in various parts of the Code. The primary reason for the choice of the Dutch Code was because, together with the Italian Civil Code, the Dutch Code was the latest Civil Code to be enacted in Europe. The Dutch government sent advisors to Russia to assist in the preparation of the Code.

The First Part of the Civil Code was signed by the President on November 30, 1994 and came into force on January 1, 1995. The Second Part was adopted one year later and came into effect on March 1, 1996. The Third Part was enacted in November 2001, and is expected to come into effect on January 1, 2002.

2   THE CIVIL CODE AS THE PRIMARY SOURCE OF PRIVATE LAW

1)   The Unification of Civil and Commercial Laws

The Civil Code is the fundamental legislation of Russian private law. This is supported by the fact that first, the Code encompasses both the civil law and commercial law, and second, it has priority to all other laws in the area of private law.

The structure of the Civil Code is in line with the *Pandekten* system:[17]

---

17   This is more in line with the German BGB. The Dutch Code is organised in eight parts, but does not have a general part; it starts with Book One, 'persons'.

Part One

Section One General Part
    Sub-Section One Basic Provisions
    Sub-Section Two Persons
    Sub-Section Three Objects of Civil Rights
    Sub-Section Four Juristic Acts and Agency
    Sub-Section Five Periods of Time and Prescription

Section Two Property Rights and other Real Rights
    [No Subsections: chapter numbers are consecutive from Section One]
    Chapter 13 Contents of Right of Ownership
    Chapter 14 Acquisition of Right of Ownership
    Chapter 15 Termination of Right of Ownership
    Chapter 16 Right of Joint Ownership
    Chapter 17 Right of Ownership and other Real Rights over Land
    Chapter 18 Right of Ownership and other Real Rights over Living Quarters
    Chapter 19 Right of Economic Administration and Operational Management
    Chapter 20 Protection of Right of Ownership and other Real Rights

Section Three General Part of the Law of Obligations

    Sub-Section One General Rules of Obligations
    Sub-Section Two General Rules on Contracts

Part Two covers specific contracts and obligations arising from unlawful acts and unjust enrichment. Part Three accommodates the Law of Inheritance and rules on International Private Law.

As can be seen from the above structure, as far as parts one and two are concerned, the Russian Civil Code is very much in line with the Continental civil codes.

One of the primary characteristics of the Russian Civil Code is that it accommodates not only civil law, but also commercial law as well. There is no separate Commercial Code. Among the former socialist countries, Hungary takes a similar approach.

Traditionally, Russian civil statutes have always contained commercial law provisions. G.F.Shershenevich, who was a leading expert on commercial law in the Tsarist period, pointed out that in Russia, there has always been an idea of 'unity (*edinstvo*) of private law'. It was the intention of Speranskii when compiling *Svod zakonov* to accommodate everything which, in the West, was divided into

Civil and Commercial law.[18] The 1887 edition of *Svod zakonov*, in addition to Volume X which contained the Civil Law, incorporated Statute on Commerce (*Ustav torgovyi*), in Volume XI, part 2. Towards the end of the Tsarist period, this Statute came to accommodate provisions on commercial contracts as well as merchant shipping. There were some provisions on various types of companies, including two provisions on joint stock companies.[19] However, the position of the law was not clear. Civil Law as contained in Volume X still accommodated provisions on commercial companies (primarily from the 1837 Company Statute) as well as commercial contracts such as insurance in Book Four (obligations arising from contracts).[20]

The draft Civil Code was clearly based upon the unified system. Book Five of the draft Code (Law of Obligations) which was submitted to the Duma contained provisions on commercial contracts such as contracts of storage, carriage, carrying out of works, commission, and insurance. It also had a fairly extensive chapter on commercial companies including joint-stock companies.[21] The 1922 RSFSR Civil Code, despite its affinity with the German BGB in various aspects, inherited this 'unity of private law'. The 1991 Fundamental Principles of Civil Legislation of the USSR followed this, and so does the present Civil Code.

In the early 1990s, when the enactment of a new civil code came on the agenda, some people proposed to separate commercial law from civil law.[22] However, in the end, the Civil Code maintained the system of the 'unity of private law'. There were several reasons for this. Firstly, this was true to the Russian legislative tradition as we have seen above. Secondly, the two latest civil codes in Europe, Dutch and Italian, had adopted this system. Thirdly, there was a strong antipathy against those proponents of the concept of 'economic law' as separate from civil law, continuing from the time of socialism. Dualism of civil and commercial law was seen to be associated with this school of thought.[23]

Article 2 of the present Civil Code provides as follows:

> Civil law determines the legal status of the participants of civil commerce (*oborot*), the basis for the emergence and manner of exercising the right of ownership and other real rights, exclusive rights on the results of intellectual activities (intellectual property),

---

18   G.F.Sheshenevich, *Uchebnik torgovago prava*, seventh edition, Moscow 1914, pp.14-15.

19   A.A.Dobrovol'skii et al eds., *Ustav torgovyi*, fourth edition, St.Petersburg 1914.

20   D.A.Nosenko ed., *Ustav torgovyi*, St.Petersburg 1909.

21   V.E.Gertsenberg and I.S.Pereterskii, *Obiaszatel'stvennoe pravo, Proekt*, St.Petersburg 1914.

22   V.V.Chankin,'Torgovoe pravo: sovremennye tendentsii', *GiP* 1993 No.2, pp.57-64; A.G.Bykov, 'Predprinimatel'sloe pravo; problemy formrirovaniia i razvitiia', *VMU, seria pravo*, 1993 No.6, pp.4-5.

23   E.A.Sukhanov, 'O proekte novogo grazhdanskogo kodeksa Rossii', *VMU, seria pravo*, 1993 No.5, p.5.

regulates contracts and other obligations, other proprietary rights as well as personal
non-proprietary rights related to them, based upon the equality, autonomy of will, and
proprietary independence of its participants.

Then, it goes further and confirms that civil law is applicable to 'entrepreneurial
relations':

> Civil law regulates the relationship between persons who perform entrepreneurial
> activities, or the relationship in which they participate, based upon the premise that
> entrepreneurial activities mean independent activities performed at the person's own
> risk and aimed at the systematic receiving of profit from the use of property, sale of
> goods, performance of work and providing of service by those who are registered as
> such by procedure established by law.

The Code seems to avoid the term 'commercial (*torgovyi*)' and instead, uses the
term 'entrepreneurial' (*predprinimatel'skyi*). However, various works on commercial law (*torgovoe pravo*) are still being published.[24]

2)   The Primacy of the Civil Code over other Laws on 'Civil Law Relations'

The Code provides that civil law comprises the Civil Code and other federal laws
adopted in accordance with it. Civil law in this context includes other federal laws
(but not presidential decrees or governmental edicts).[25]

These laws include the following:

General Part

    Law on Joint Stock Companies,
    Law on Limited Liability Companies,
    Law on Non-Commercial Organisations,
    Law on Religious Organisations,
    Law on Social Organisations,
    Law on Production Cooperatives,
    Law on Bankruptcy,
    Law on the Civil Status.

---

24   M.M.Lassolov, *Kommercheskoe pravo*, Moscow 2001; Iu.E.Bulatotskii and V.A.Iazeev, *Kommerches-
      koe (Torgovoe) pravo*, Moscow 2002.
25   M.I.Braginskii ed., *Nauchno-prakticheskii kommentarii k chasti pervoi grazhdanskogo kodeksa
      Rossiiskoi Federatsii*, second edition, Moscow 1999, p.43.

Property Law

> Land Code,
> Law on the Payment for Land,
> Law on Subsoil,
> Law on Registration of Real Property and Related Transactions,
> Water Code,
> Forest Code,
> Housing Code,

Law on Obligations

> Law on Pledge (*zalog*),
> Law on Hypothec,
> Law on Leasing (*lizing*),
> Law on the Protection of the Rights of Consumers,
> Law on Bills of Exchange and Promissory Notes,
> Law on Currency Regulation and Control.

The Civil Code has a special status, as the very basis of private law, in relation to these laws. The Civil Code explicitly provides that 'norms of civil law contained in other laws should coincide with the present Code' (Art.3, para.2). This principle of the 'primacy of the Civil Code' is a significant exception to general rules that new law breaks the old law and special law has priority to general law.[26] Under socialism, the legislature attempted to 'eliminate defects of economic legislation' by enacting an enormous number of laws and regulations which were not always properly coordinated. The intention of the present legislature is to avoid contradictions between various laws covering the same area by giving primacy to the Civil Code which is 'unified, logically consistent, and free from internal contradiction'.[27] The only exceptions to this rule are provisions which have a clause 'unless the law provides otherwise'. This is understood to give priority to laws other than the Code.[28]

However, this often creates confusion. For example, company law is part of the civil law. Therefore, the Civil Code has priority to the Law on Joint Stock Companies and Law on Limited Liability Companies. These laws have been enacted after the Civil Code, and have more detailed provisions. Nevertheless, in cases of contradiction, the Civil Code prevails. Thus, the scope of the books

---

26 *Ibid.,* p.42.
27 M.I.Braginskii and V.V.Vitrianskii, *Dogovornoe pravo, obshchie polozheniia*, Moscow 1997, p.41.
28 *Ibid.,* p.42.

of accounts to which shareholders are granted access differs between the Civil Code and the Law on Joint Stock Companies, but the Civil Code is decisive.

There are still a number of laws to which the Civil code refers, but which have not been adopted. These include the following:[29]

> Law on State Ownership and Organisation of its Management,
> Law on the Compensation for Damage caused by the Agencies of Investigation, Preliminary Investigation, Procuracy, and the Court,
> Law on Management by Entrustment of Securities,
> Law on Bills of Exchange and Promissory Notes,
> Law on Investment Funds,
> Law on State and Municipal Land.

3   BASIC PRINCIPLES OF RUSSIAN PRIVATE LAW

Book One of the Civil Code is the General Part of the Code. It sets out basic principles and rules of civil and commercial law.

Article 1 of the Code lists various principles of civil law. These are:

i)   equality of the participants in the relationship regulated by civil law;
ii)   inviolability of property;
iii)   freedom of contracts;
iv)   prohibition of arbitrary interference with private individuals;
v)   recognition of the necessity of the uninhibited exercise of civil law rights;
vi)   ensurance of restoration of infringed rights and court protection.

These principles are better understood when contrasted with the system under socialism, where the state played a predominant role in the economy.

The equality principle primarily means that entities participating in civil circulation shall be treated in an equal manner regardless of their form of ownership, i.e. whether they are owned by the state, municipality or by private capital. The USSR Law on Ownership of 1990 provided, for the first time since the October Revolution, that ownership rights of the state, local government, state enterprises, private enterprises and individuals should be protected equally. The present Constitution guarantees that 'private, state, municipal and other forms of ownership are recognised and protected in an equal manner' (Art.8, para.2). This was certainly

---

29   'Zakonoproektnye prioritety Pravitel'stva Rossii, Predlozheniia IZiSP', *ZhRP*, 2000, No.2, p.12.

not the case under socialism; interest of the state always had precedence over rights of individuals. It should be added that in contrast with the 1964 Civil Code, individuals are now allowed to be involved in entrepreneurial activities. These people, and their association in the form of commercial organisations, must be treated equally with state and municipal enterprises in civil law relations.

Inviolability of property is also a constitutional principle. The Constitution provides as follows (Art.35, para.3):

> No person shall be deprived of his property except by a judgment of the court. Compulsory alienation of property for the needs of the state shall be carried out only with prior and equivalent compensation.

This rule is also incorporated in the Law on Foreign Investment in the following way (Art.8, para.1):

> Property of foreign investors or commercial organisations with foreign investment is not subject to compulsory withdrawal, including nationalisation, or requisition, except in cases and on the grounds established by a federal law or an international treaty.

The Civil Code has a provision to the effect that requisition of property for the interests of society should be allowed by the decision of a state agency in cases of epidemics, natural disasters and other circumstances of emergency based upon the manner and terms provided by law, with payment (Art.242, para.1).

Concerning the uninhibited exercise of civil law rights, again, this is a constitutional right (Art.34). The relevant provision of the Civil Code provides as follows (Art.1, para.2):

> Individuals (physical persons) and juridical persons shall obtain and exercise their civil law rights by their will and in their own interest. They shall be free in establishing their rights and duties on the basis of a contract and to determine any terms of the contract which are not against the law.

> Civil law rights may be restricted on the basis of federal law but only to the extent that it is necessary for the purpose of the protection of the constitutional system, morals, health, rights and lawful interests of other persons as well as ensuring the defence and security of the State.

[Freedom of contract will be discussed in Chapter 6]

The Civil Code prohibits abuse of rights, anti-competitive acts and abuse of a dominant position in the market (Art.10):

Use of civil law rights by citizens and juridical persons solely with the intention of causing harm to another person, and abuse of rights in other forms are impermissible.

Civil law rights shall not be used for the purpose of restricting competition or for the abuse of a dominant position in the market.

The first half of this provision is explained to have originated from *chikane* in Roman law. An example is creating noise in a flat in order to force the neighbour out of the adjacent flat. One commentary quotes a novel of Gogol', in which a farmer plants goose wheat on his land (which is perfectly in exercise of his right) solely for the purpose of causing inconvenience to his neighbour. As an example of 'other forms of abuse of rights', the commentary quotes pollution of the environment by an enterprise:[30]

A foreign trading firm brought an action to the commercial court against a Russian commercial bank, claiming payment of a large amount of money based upon a bank guarantee issued by this bank for securing a foreign trade transaction. The trading firm (the beneficiary) based its claim on the fact that the principal had failed to supply the products as agreed in the contract. The bank (the guarantor) refused payment, since, in their view, the basic obligation had been performed in a way satisfactory for the beneficiary.

In fact, in the foreign trade contract for the supply of goods, it was agreed that the seller provided a pledge for the performance. The seller actually provided two ships as collateral to the buyer. According to the contract, in case of non-performance of the obligation on the part of the seller, the buyer was to obtain the right to have the claim satisfied from the sale of the ships. This part of the contract was governed by foreign law. The buyer paid the price when he received the collaterals. At the same time, parties to the foreign trade contract approached the commercial bank and asked the bank to issue a bank guarantee for the supply of goods under this contract. In this instance, neither the parties or the beneficiary disclosed to the bank that the foreign trade contract contained a clause on pledge and that the collateral had been provided. The bank issued a guarantee. Then, the seller failed to supply the goods.

The beneficiary argued that if the guarantor becomes aware that the basic obligation has been fully or partly performed, he is under an obligation to notify the beneficiary without delay. The bank argued that the beneficiary deceived the bank because the latter failed to inform the bank that the claim of the foreign party to the contract had actually been performed by the sale of the pledged collateral. The bank claimed that this was an abuse of right on the part of the beneficiary.

The court acknowledged that the beneficiary had actually had the claim satisfied from the sale of collaterals abroad, and therefore, there was no ground for claim on

---

30   Braginskii ed., *Nauchno-prakticheskii kommentarii......supra*, pp.63-64.

the part of the beneficiary. The court found the claim to be an abuse of rights as provided by Article 10 of the Civil Code.[31]

In such cases of abuse of rights, the court and the arbitration tribunal may refuse protection to civil law rights.

It should be noted that restrictions on civil law rights can only be effected by federal law (see also Constitution, Art.55, para.3). This means that these rights cannot be restricted by a presidential decree or edicts of the government.

The Civil Code lists various means of protecting civil law rights and restoring infringed rights by court (Art.12). These include:

i) recognition of rights;
ii) restoration of the *status quo ante* and termination of acts which infringe the right or creates threat of infringement;
iii) recognition of contested acts as void;
iv) recognition of acts of the state and municipal agencies as void;
v) self defence of rights;
vi) compulsory performance of obligation in kind;
vii) compensation for damage;
viii) composition of penalty for delay;
ix) compensation for moral damage;
x) termination or alteration of legal relations;
xi) non-application (by the court) of the act of state agencies and agencies of local self administration which are against the law.

The content of this provision is more or less the same as the 1964 Code. Two of them – ix) compensation for moral damage [see Chapter 10] and v) self-defence – are new. Self-defence is allowed, but its means has to be equivalent to the violation of rights and should not exceed the scope of acts necessary for the elimination of violation (Art.14).

Court protection of these rights is now universally available. The court has the power to review the compatibility of the acts of state agencies and agencies of local self administration with the law and other legal acts and if it finds them to be incompatible, recognise them as void (Art.13). The Law on Complaints to the Court for Acts and Decisions which Violate Rights and interests of Citizens of 1993 provides for the procedure.[32]

---

31 'Obzor sudebno-arbitrazhnoi praktiki razresheniia sporov po delam s uchastiem inostrannykh lits', informatsionnoe pis'mo, VAS RF, February 16, 1998, item 3, in *Spory pri ispolnenii denezhnykh obiazatel'stv i osushchestvlenii raschetov; sbornik dokumentov,* Moscow 2000, pp.60-61.
32 *VSND RF i VS RF,* 1993, No.19, item 685.

4   PARTICIPANTS OF CIVIL LAW RELATIONS

1)   Individuals

The Civil Code applies to individuals (physical persons; often referred to by the Code as 'citizens', following the conventional usage) as well as juridical persons.

Individuals acquire civil law capacity, i.e. the capacity to be a subject of rights and obligations, at the time of birth (Art.17). The capacity to act, i.e the capacity to obtain and exercise civil law rights, to create civil law rights and obligations and to perform them by his or her own act, is acquired by individuals at the age of 18 (Art.21).

The Constitution guarantees that every person has the right to unrestricted use of his property and assets for entrepreneurial and other activities not prohibited by law (Art.34, para.1). This is reflected in the Civil Code in the following way (Art,23, para.1):

> Individuals have the right to participate in entrepreneurial activities without forming a juridical person from the moment of registration as an individual entrepreneur.

Individuals may invest in companies and become shareholders, participants (in the case of limited liability companies) etc., but if they are to perform business as an individual without forming a juridical person, then they must be registered. The Law on Registration of Juridical Persons was enacted in 2001.[33] Provisions of the Civil Code applicable to activities of commercial organisations are, as a rule, also applicable to individual entrepreneurs (Art.23, para.3).

2)   Juridical Persons

(1)   Types of Juridical Persons

A juridical person is defined as an organisation which holds certain assets under its ownership, economic management, or operational administration, is liable for its obligations with these assets, and can, in its own name, acquire and exercise proprietary and personal non-proprietary rights, assume obligations, and be a plaintiff and defendant in court (Art.48, para.1).

Juridical persons can be classified in the following way:

---

33   *RG,* August 10, 2001.

Non-Commercial Organisations (pursuit of profits not as the primary goal)

Consumers' cooperatives[34]
Social and religious Organisations[35]
Foundations (*fond*)
Institutions (*uchrezhdenie*)
Associations and Federations of juridical persons

Commercial Organisations (pursuit of profit as the basic goal)

Commercial companies and partnerships

Full partnerships
Limited partnerships
Companies with supplementary liability
Companies with limited liability
Joint stock companies

Production cooperatives
State and municipal unitary enterprises
Unitary enterprises based upon the right of economic management
Unitary enterprises based upon the right of operational administration (*kazennoe predpriiatie*) [treasury enterprises]

Among the non-commercial organisations, the original intention of the legislature seems to have been that *fond*s correspond to foundations (*Stiftung*) in other jurisdictions. *Fond*s, for the purpose of the Civil Code, are non-commercial organisations without members and set up by individuals and/or juridical persons on the basis of proprietary contributions for social, charity, cultural, educational and other socially useful purposes (Art.118, para.1). However, in practice, 'with the absence of a strict division between commercial and non-commercial organisations, many *fond*s are actively involved in entrepreneurial activities which this juridical construction had not envisaged'.[36]

An institution (*uchrezhdenie*) is an organisation which is set up and financed entirely or partly by the owner of the property for the performance of administrative, social-cultural and other functions (Art.120, para.1). They can be set up by private entities as well as government entities, but the 'predominant category of

---

34 *VSND RF i VS RF,* 1992 No.30, item 1788; *SZ RF* 1997 No.28, item 33036.
35 Law on Social Organisations (*SZ RF,* 1995 No.21, item 1930); Law on the Freedom of Conscience and Religious Organisations (*SZ RF,* 1997 No.39, item 4665).
36 Braginskii ed., *Kommentarii chasti pervoi grazhdanskogo kodeksa....., supra,* p.149.

them is governmental'.[37] In fact, these are 'remnants of the previous economic system' and are mostly government or municipal agencies.[38] Institutions do not have the title over the assets allocated to them; the title remains with the owner/ founder. On the other hand, the owner/founder bears supplementary liability for the debts of the institution (Art.120, para.2).

The Law on Non-Commercial Organisations, which provides slightly more detail, was enacted in 1996.[39]

Concerning commercial organisations see Chapter 4.

Production cooperatives are associations of individuals who are not entrepreneurs, established for the purpose of production or other commercial purposes. Members contribute their labour and/or assets. They bear supplementary liability for the debt of the cooperative (Art.107, paras. 1 and 2). This form of organisation has long been known in Russia as *artel'*. It was revived in 1988 as a vehicle of private investment hitherto unknown under socialism, dropped in the 1990 Law on Enterprises and Entrepreneurial Activities of the USSR, but restored in the Civil Code.

Enterprises which are directly owned by the Russian Federation or its constituent entities – former state enterprises which have not been privatised – are called unitary enterprises. They have juridical personality separate from the state or constituent entities of the Russian Federation. Their difference from other commercial organisations is that they do not have ownership over the assets which are allocated to them; the Russian Federation or its constituent entities have the title to their assets (Art.113).

There are two types of unitary enterprise: one is a unitary enterprise based upon the right of economic management and the other on the operational administration. Unitary enterprises based upon the right of economic management are not entitled to sell, lease, pledge, contribute or otherwise dispose of the immovables which had been allocated to them without the consent of the owner. Other assets can be disposed of unless prohibited by law or other legal acts (Art.295).

Unitary enterprises based on the right of operational administration is called federal treasury enterprises (*federal'noe kazennoe predpriiatie*). They are all state (federal) enterprises, not enterprises owned by the constituent entities of the Russian Federation. They have the right to possess, use and dispose of the assets allocated to them at their discretion within the scope of law in accordance with

---

37   O.N.Sadikov., *Kommentarii k grazhdanskomu kodeksu Rossiskoi Federatsii, chasti pervoi*, first edition, Moscow 1997, p.161.
38   Braginskii ed., *Nauchno-prakticheskii komenntarii...*, *supra*, pp.212-213..
39   *SZ RF* 1996 No.3, item 145.

the goal of their activities, instructions by the owner, and the purpose of the property (Art.296, para.1) but cannot dispose of any assets without the consent of the state (Art.294, para.1). The number of this type of unitary enterprises is relatively small. They are limited to state enterprises in the defence industry and enterprises attached to penitentiary institutions.[40]

In unitary enterprises based upon the right of economic management, the owner is not liable for the debt of the enterprise, except in cases where its bankruptcy was caused by the owner (Arts.114, para.8). In contrast, the state bears supplementary liability for the debts of unitary enterprises with the right of operational administration (Art.115, para.5). The difference comes from the fact that the scope of power of such enterprises is narrower, and therefore, there is a necessity to protect third parties who entered into a transaction with them.[41]

(2)   Civil Law Capacity of Juridical Persons

The Civil Code provides that juridical persons may have civil law rights in accordance with the purposes provided in their founding documents and are liable in relation to these activities (Art,49, para.1).

The 1964 Civil Code had adopted a rather strict approach to *ultra vires*. Under socialism, state enterprises had to be kept under close supervision of the state. There was a case where a cooperative whose registered purpose was to 'satisfy the needs of citizens' sold computers to various organisations. The court found the sale to be void as *ultra vires*.[42] The present Code still provides that juristic acts effected by juridical persons against their purposes are void. On the other hand, it is not mandatory for commercial organisations to register their specific purposes of activities any more. Commercial organisations, except for unitary enterprises, may have civil law rights and assume obligations necessary for performing all kinds of activities not prohibited by law (Art.49, para.1). Naturally, commercial organisations may restrict the scope of their activities. However, the construction of the provision is different from the socialist period in that 1), only the juridical person itself, its founders, or state agencies which supervise the juridical person is entitled to claim that an act was *ultra vires* and that 2), the act can be found void only if the opposite party had known or could have known that the act was *ultra vires* (Art.173).

Certain categories of businesses, e.g. exploration and development of sub-soil as well as banking and insurance businesses, require a special license. The list

---

40   Braginskii ed., *Nauchno-prakticheskii komenntarii...*, *supra*, p.204.
41   Braginskii ed., *Kommentarii chasti pervoi grazhdanskogo kodeksa....*, *supra*, p.145.
42   *Ibid.*, pp.78-79..

of activities subject to license is provided by the Law on Licensing of Specific Activities.[43]

Juridical persons acquire legal capacity by registration. Juridical persons are subject to state registration with the Ministry of Justice (Art.51). There is a unified state registrer of juridical persons.

The Civil Code also contains provisions on the managing bodies of juridical persons, their names and locations, liability, reorganisation (merger, split, conversion etc.), liquidation and bankruptcy [see Chapter 4, Company Law].

3)   The State as a Participant of Civil Law Relations

The Russian Federation, constituent entities of the Russian Federation (constituent republics, regions, provinces, cities of federal designation, autonomous regions and provinces as well as specially designated cities), and municipalities (entities of local self government) may be a party in civil law relations, i.e. they may 'acquire and exercise proprietary rights and personal non-proprietary rights and assume obligations, and be a party to litigation' (Arts. 124 and 125). In such cases, they act not as subjects of prerogative power, but as entities with an equal status as individuals and juridical persons. They have the same status as commercial and non-commercial organisations and individuals and therefore, civil law provisions are applicable, unless the law provides otherwise or a different treatment emanates from the special character of the subject.

These entities are liable for their obligations arising from the property which belongs to them under their ownership. The attachment of natural resources which they own, including land, is allowed in cases provided by law (Art.126, para.1). The Russian Federation is not liable for the debt of the other entities, and *visa versa*. This effectively means that each entity at various levels has its own account (*kazna*). The Russian Federation and its constituent entities are, in principle, not liable for the obligation of entities, such as state or municipal enterprises which they have created.[44] Indeed, this has been the norm under socialism, although the state never let state enterprises default.

An exception to this rule is 'unitary enterprises based upon the right of operational administration' which are directly under the control of the Russian Federation. In such cases, the State bears subsidiary (supplementary) liability, i.e. if the enterprise cannot pay, then the Russian Federation will pay (Art.115, para.5).

---

43   *SZ RF*,1998 No.39, item 4857.
44   Sadikov ed., *Kommentarii k grazhdanskomu kodeksu Rossiskoi Federatsii, chasti pervoi*, enlarged edition, Moscow 1999, p.263.

Another example is government institutions – under the Law on Non-Commercial Organisations, the government bears subsidiary liability for the debt of these institutions (Art.9, para.2).

Concerning the liability of the State and other entities in civil law relations with foreign elements, i.e. with the participation of a foreign government, juridical persons, or individuals, the Civil Code refers to the forthcoming Law on Immunity of the State and its assets (Art.127). This Law is yet to be enacted.

Russia has for many years maintained the absolute principle of sovereign immunity. This meant that even when the State was acting not as a subject of prerogative power performing public functions, but as engaged in commercial activities, still, it was entitled to sovereign immunity, although in practice, the Russian State has, in the past, waived sovereign immunity by subjecting itself to international arbitration in various treaties. This doctrine of absolute sovereignty is being superseded by the 'restrictive doctrine' or 'functional theory' of immunity, which does not allow immunity from foreign jurisdictions when the state is involved in commercial activities. The US and UK statutes on sovereign immunity as well as the European Convention of State Immunity have taken this position. The United Nations International Law Commission has prepared a draft treaty to the same effect. It is now more or less accepted by the Russians that the restrictive doctrine is the commonly adopted approach in other countries. The draft Russian Law on Sovereign Immunity is said to take the same line as this draft treaty.

5   OBJECTS OF CIVIL LAW RIGHTS

The Civil Code lists 'things including money and securities as well as other property including property rights, works and services, information, results of intellectual activities including exclusive rights on them (intellectual property), and non-material values' as objects of civil law rights (Art.128).

Things can be divided into immovables and movables. Immovables denote pieces of land, fields of sub-soil, demarcated sections of water, and other things firmly attached to the land. The latter includes multi-year plants, buildings and structures. In addition, aircraft, ocean going ships, inland water ships, and satellites are treated as immovables. An enterprise in its entirety as a 'proprietary complex' is also regarded as an immovable (Art.132). Things which are not immovables, including money and securities, are movables.

Ownership rights and other real rights over immovables, restriction on such rights, emergence, as well as assignment and termination of such rights are subject to state registration on a unified state register (Art.131). The Law on the State Registration of Immovables and Related Transactions was enacted in 1998.[45]

It is important to note that enterprises are now made an object of civil law rights. Enterprises are regarded as proprietary complexes used for performing entrepreneurial activities. They can be objects of sale, pledges, leases, and other transactions related to the establishment, assignment or termination of real rights (Art.132, para.2). Enterprises in this context not only means specific forms of commercial organisations such as unitary enterprises, but is much broader and means companies as a 'going concern *(predpriiatie na khodu)*'.[46]

Currency valuables are also 'things'. These include foreign currencies, securities denominated in foreign currencies, precious metal and stones except for jewellery. The Law on Control of Foreign Currency Transactions regulates transactions on foreign currency (Art.141).[47]

Securities also fall within the category of 'things'. The Civil Code has a separate chapter on securities. Under socialism, available securities were limited to government bonds, bearer's savings books etc. Cheques were also used for settlement of payment between juridical persons. With the transition to the market economy, the scope of securities has significantly broadened. The Code defines a security as a document which certifies in an established form and by following mandatory requirements, proprietary rights, the exercise or assignment of which is possible only by its presentation (Art.142). The Code lists the following securities (Art.143):

i)   government bonds;
ii)   corporate bonds;
iii)   promissory notes *(veksel')*;
iv)   cheques;
v)   certificates of deposit and savings;
vi)   bearer's bank account book;
vii)   bills of lading;
viii) shares;
ix)   privatisation securities;
x)   other documents designated as securities by law.

The Civil Code only accommodates basic provisions on securities. Details are left to other laws such as the Law on the Securities Market, the Statute on Bills

---

45   *SZ RF*, 1997, No.30, item 3594.
46   Braginskii ed., *Nauchno-prakticheskii kommentarii....*, *supra*, p.240.
47   *VSND RF i VS RF*, 1992, No.45, item 2542.

of Exchange and Promissory Notes, the Law on Joint-Stock Companies etc. Bills of lading are covered by the Merchant Shipping Code.

The Civil Code also has a provision on 'non-documentary securities', i.e. securities without documentary embodiment, which 'developed countries, including Western European countries, began to accommodate from the early 1980s'.[48] In cases provided by law or by procedure established by law, licensed persons may fixate rights in bearers' or non-bearer's securities including those in a non-documentary form (with the assistance of 'electronic-computing technology' etc.). Persons who are responsible for fixating rights in this form are under an obligation to issue a document certifying the rights on request of the right-holder (Art.149, para.1). Under the Law on Joint Stock Companies the issue of shares 'without documents' is allowed.[49] The Law on the Securities Market also allows the issue of nominal securities in a 'non-documentary form'.[50]

Concerning intellectual property, it has been a tradition since 1922 to incorporate this in the Civil Code. The 1990 Fundamental Principles of Civil Legislation of the USSR contained some provisions on intellectual property, which are still valid insofar as they do not contradict special laws and international treaties. There are various special laws enacted since 1990 in this area. These are:

i)   Patent Law,
ii)   Copyright Law,
iii)   Trademark Law,
iv)   Law on Semiconductor Topography,
v)   Law on the Protection of Computer Programmes.

There are discussions as to whether some of these laws should be incorporated in the Part Four of the present Civil Code.

'Information', referred to as an object of civil law relations in the Civil Code, denotes business and commercial secrets. The Code provides that information is a business or commercial secret if it has existing or potential commercial value providing that it is unknown to a third party, there is no legitimate free access to the information, and the holder of the information has adopted measures to protect its confidentiality. Those who, by unlawful means, obtain information which comprises a business or commercial secret, are liable for compensation (Art.139).

---

48   Braginskii ed., *Nauchno-prakticheskii komenntarii...*, *supra*, pp.258-259.
49   G.S.Shapkina ed., *Postateinyi kommentarii k federal'nomu zakonu 'Ob Aktionernom Obshchestve*, second edition, Moscow 2000, p.85.
50   *SZ RF* 1996, No.17, item 1918; Braginskii, *Nauchno-prakticheskii komenntarii...*, *supra*, p.259.

Concerning 'non-material values', the Code lists 'life and health, personal dignity, honour and good name, business reputation, inviolability of personal life, personal and family secrets, the right to free movement, choice of the place of stay and residence, the right of a name, an author's moral rights, and other personal non-proprietary rights and other nonmaterial value which belong to physical persons by birth or by law and which are inalienable (Art.150, para.1).

6   JURISTIC ACTS

1)   General

The Russian Civil Code belongs to the Civil Law system which developed out of the French Code civil. One of the fundamental concepts in this system is the concept of juristic acts (*acte juridique*, *Rechtsgeschäft*). The concept was already known in the Tsarist period. In a book published in 1907, A.M.Guliaev defined juristic act (*iuridicheskie akty*) as an expression of will which is aimed at causing specific legal effects. According to the author, juridical acts comprise two factors: will and its expression.[51] The concept was retained under socialism, but under a different name – transaction (*sdelka*). The present Civil Code continues to use the term *sdelka*. *Sdelka* (hereinafter, 'juristic act') is defined, in an identical way to the 1964 Code, as an act of a physical person or juridical person directed at establishment, alteration, or termination of civil law rights or obligations (Art.153). It is an intentional act; it has a legal meaning only when it is externally expressed in an objective manner.[52] It is common for the civil codes to provide for basic rules concerning the form and validity of juristic acts in the general part.

Juristic acts can be either unilateral, bilateral, or multilateral. Examples of unilateral juristic acts are the waiver of ownership rights (Art.236) and the granting of a power of attorney (Art.185). Bilateral and multilateral juristic acts are basically contracts.

2)   Form of Juristic Acts

Under the socialist civil law, there were strict requirements on the form of juristic acts. Notarisation was required on various occasions to enable the state to supervise transactions between state enterprises. Non-compliance with the requirements made

---

51   A.M.Guliaev, *supra*, pp.62-63.
52   Sadikov ed., *Kommentarii…*, first edition, *supra*, p.200.

these juristic acts absolutely void. Since 1990, there have been significant changes. The formality of juristic acts became less stringent.

Juristic acts may be effected orally or in writing. As a rule, juristic acts which, by law or by the agreement of parties, are not required to be in writing, can be effected orally (Art.159, para.1). Juristic acts which may be effected orally are also deemed to have been effected, if, from the behaviour of the person, his intention to effect the juristic act is apparent. On the other hand, silence is regarded as an expression of will only when so provided by law or the agreement of the parties (Art.158).

Juristic acts in a written form can be in a simple written form or in a notarised form. The following juristic acts are required to be in writing (some acts may need notarisation as well):

i) juristic acts between juridical persons or between a juridical person and a physical person;
ii) juristic acts between physical persons with the amount not less than 10 times the minimum monthly wage and other instances provided by law.

If a juristic act was not effected in writing although written form is required, the effect is that the parties will be deprived of the possibility of referring to witness statements in order to prove that the given juristic act has taken place and with specific terms in case of disputes. Only written evidence, tangible evidence and expert opinion can be cited. As a rule, juristic acts which fail to comply with the requirement of written form are not void, unless it is expressly provided by law or stated in the agreement between the parties. However, foreign trade transactions always have to be in writing, and the non-fulfilment of this requirement results in the transaction being void (Art.162).

Some juristic acts have to be notarised. Notarisation is necessary when the law so provides, or when it is required by agreement of the parties. The Civil Code requires notarisation in the following instances (Art.163):

i) power of attorney for performance of juristic acts which require notarisation;
ii) delegation of power of attorney;
iii) agreements on hypothec, as well as pledges on movables for securing an obligation subject to notarisation;
iv) assignment of claims and assumption of debts based on juristic acts which require notarisation.

Non-fulfilment of the requirement for notarisation of juristic acts deprives such acts of any effect and makes them void. Failure to register has the same effect only when so provided by law (Art.165, para.1). For example, failure to register a hypothec makes it void.

Juristic acts involving land and other immovables must be registered (Art.164).

3)   Defective Juristic Acts

Juristic acts are based upon the expression of will by the parties in civil law relations. A corollary is that if the expression of will is defective in one way or another, it affects the validity of the act. Juristic acts can be voidable, or void in such cases. A juristic act can be found to have no effect in cases provided by the Civil Code. In cases where the act is void (*nishtozhnyi*), the act does not have effect even without the recognition to that effect by the court. An action by an interested party is not needed, although in order to have the effect of voidness applied, i.e. to restore the *status quo ante*, a court action is needed. In contrast, the effect of voidable (*osporimyi*) juristic acts can only be denied on the initiative of interested parties.[53] This distinction did not exist in the 1964 Civil Code. Under socialist law, defective juristic acts were, in principle, void. This is understandable, since in voidable acts, it is left to the party whether or not to take an action to void the act. This could not be tolerated under socialism.

The new arrangement in the present Civil Code is based on the Civil law system, but is said to be closer to French Law (relative voidness and absolute voidness) than German Law.[54]

Void juristic acts include: juristic acts against the law or other legal acts, acts against public order and morals, mock and sham juristic acts, acts effected by persons without capacity to act, and acts effected by those under the age of 14. Voidable acts include acts effected by a person between the age of 14 and 18, juristic acts of a juridical person in excess of its legal capacity, those effected by a person with limited capacity to act, as well as acts effected by mistake and acts effected under duress, violence, threat etc.

There is no time limit in asking the court to recognise a certain juristic act to be void. This is because the act is regarded to have been void from the beginning even without the involvement of the court. However, an action for applying the consequences of voidness can be initiated only within 10 years of the day when the performance of the act had started. Concerning voidable acts, actions for voiding such acts must be brought to court within one year of the termination

---

53   Sadikov ed., *Kommentarii...*, enlarged edition, *supra*, p.356.
54   A.Solotych, 'Das neue russische ZGB aus rechtsvergleichender Sicht', in F-C.Schroeder ed., *Die neuen Kodifikationen in Russland*, second edition, Berlin 1999, p.35.

of the violence or threat under which the act has been effected, or the day from which the plaintiff became aware, or should have become aware of the grounds for voiding the act (Art.181).

4)   Primary Categories of Void Juristic Acts

(1)   *Juristic Acts against the Law or other Legal Acts*

Juristic acts which do not comply with the requirement of laws or other legal acts are void, unless such law or legal act provide that they are voidable or provides for other consequences (Art.168). For example, creditors are not allowed to require of the debtor that the title to the collateral be transferred to the creditor in case of default of the debtor (Art.349, para.1). Such an agreement is against the law, and is void.[55] In the following case, the problem of whether the object of the pledge was transferable as required by law was at issue:

> Sberbank of Russia brought an action against Pakamar Bank, claiming that the contract of pledge concluded between them was void. The pledged object was the amount credited to the corresponding account. The Supreme Commercial Court found this contract to be void by virtue of Article 168, since the amount credited to the corresponding account was not transferable, while the Civil Code required that the collateral should be transferable.[56]

Article 168 is based upon the presumption that everybody knows the law. Therefore, as a rule, 'the absence of fault on the part of the party does not mean that the act is not void'.[57]

(2)   *Juristic Acts effected whose Aims conflict with the Fundaments of Law and Order and Morals*

Acts deliberately counter to the fundaments of legal order and morals are void (Art.169). This is based upon fault (*vina*), i.e. the act has to be intentional. This is in fact the equivalent of a public policy provision. It is not designed to deal with a mere breach of law; it is intended to cover those acts which intend to

---

55   Joint Decision of the Plenum of the Supreme Court and the Supreme Commercial Court, No.6/8, July 1 1996, in V.Zhurakovskii and V.Kalinin, *Kommentarii i primenenie zakonodatel'stva arbitrazhnymi sudami Rossiskoi Federatsii*, Moscow 2000, p.42.
56   Decision of the Presidium of the Supreme Commercial Court, July 2, 1996, *VVAS RF* 1996 No.10.
57   Sadikov ed., *Kommentarii…*, enlarged edition, *supra*, p.359.

contradict the *fundaments of legal order*. Mere breaches of law are covered by
the preceding provision (Art.168). One of the possible elements of this kind of
act is whether the act is punishable as a criminal offence, but this is not a prerequisite.[58] An act with 'anti-social character' may qualify for the application
of this provision:

> An open joint stock company, Voucher Investment Fund 'Initsiativa', extended a loan
> to another company. It was agreed with the borrower that the interest would be paid
> by privatisation vouchers which had been distributed to the general public to enable
> them to take part in privatisation. According to a presidential decree, privatisation
> vouchers were to be used solely for the privatisation of state and municipal enterprises.
> The contract was against this requirement. What was more, the contract 'intentionally
> infringed the right of citizens to receive income from privatisation'. The contract was
> therefore regarded by the Supreme Commercial Court to have an 'anti-social character'
> and was found to be void under Article 169.[59]

Other examples quoted in commentaries include juristic acts against the state
monopoly on certain kinds of activities which restrict the legal capacity of persons
or the right of ownership, or acts with the intention to create the monopolistic
position of a juridical person in the market.[60]

The major difference between articles 168 (acts against the law) and 169 (acts
against public policy and morals) is the effect of the acts. In the former, the
general rule applies, and the parties are under an obligation to return those benefits
received in relation to the transaction. In the latter case, if both parties acted with
intention, all they have received from the already performed transaction will be
confiscated by the state (Art.169). The outcome can be rather harsh.

The Supreme Commercial Court is rather cautious in applying Article 169
too liberally:

> Mosbiznesbank brought an action to the Moscow City Commercial Court against a
> limited liability company 'Edel'veis' for payment of 64,467,605 roubles of interest on
> a loan. The first instance court acknowledged this claim, but at the appellate instance,
> the court rejected the claim and the amount the parties received from the loan contract
> was confiscated and transferred to the federal budget, since the contract was 'against
> the basis of legal order' for violation of foreign exchange legislation.

---

58   Braginskii ed., *Nauchno-prakiticheskii komenntarii...*, *supra*, p.289.
59   Decision of the Presidium of the Supreme Commercial Court, November 12, 1998, *VVAS RF*, 1997
     No.2, pp.46-47.
60   Sadikov ed., *Kommentarii...*, first edition, *supra*, p.215.

Upon protest by the deputy president of the Supreme Commercial Court, the Supreme Commercial Court quashed the judgment of the appellate instance on the following grounds.

The contract for loan was intended to finance the import of grain from Kazakhstan. The plaintiff purchased US dollars for Edel'weis and transferred this to a Kazakh bank which served an intermediary company, 'Kustanai'. Edel'weis then repaid the capital to the plaintiff, but interest was not paid. Thus, the plaintiff had duly performed its obligation under the contract of loan and was entitled to a payment of interest by the defendant. The purchase of foreign currency and its payment to the Kazakh bank was outside the scope of the contract of loan and is separate, and therefore does not affect the contract of loan. The appellate instance was found to have erred in combining the contract of loan and the currency transaction and confiscating all that parties have received.[61]

By the same token, a contract of substitute performance has been addressed:

The State Tax Inspectorate of a district in the City of Cheliabinsk initiated an action at the Commercial Court of Cheriabinsk Province claiming that the contract of substitute performance concluded by a limited liability company 'Spetsstroi' and Cheriabinvestbank – a joint stock company (Investment bank) was void. The first instance court rejected the claim, but the appellate instance court found the said contract to be void on the ground that the transaction was effected with the intentional purpose against the fundaments of legal order and ethics, since it was against the procedure for settling payment by companies in arrears of tax payments. A total of 47,749,540 roubles was confiscated from both parties.

The Supreme Commercial Court did not accept the protest lodged by a deputy president of the Court in full and found that the contract was indeed void for the violation of the presidential decree. However, the Court ruled that the contract should be declared void under Article 168 for the violation of law or other legal acts, and not by Article 169. Therefore, the confiscation of the above amount from both parties was found to be in error.[62]

(3)   Juristic acts against the Requirement of Form and Registration

[See above 6-2]

---

61   Decision of the Presidium of the Supreme Commercial Court, April 18, 2000 [Garant].

62   Decision of the Presidium of the Supreme Commercial Court, March 10, 1998 [Garant]. In fact, there were three cases initiated by the same State Tax Inspectorate which resulted in the same conclusion by the Supreme Commercial Court (December 9, 1997, October 21, 1997).

(4)   Mock and sham juristic acts

Mock juristic acts (*mnimaia sdelka*) are those acts effected solely for appearance without the intention of creating the corresponding legal consequences. Sham juristic acts denote those acts which are effected in order to conceal another act (*pritvornaia sdelka*).

   Both kinds of juristic acts are void. In the case of sham acts, relevant rules applicable to the act which the parties genuinely intended to effect will be applied (Art.170). An example of the latter is a contract of gratuitous lease of a vehicle instead of sale in order to avoid paying state fees (*poshlina*). Although the lease contract is void, provisions on sale are still applicable.

   This provision may be applicable in cases involving atypical security rights. The Civil Code has stringent provisions on the enforcement of real security rights. A practice has developed in which the parties agree to transfer the title to the collateral to the creditor and have it returned to the debtor once the debt is repaid. Since the parties do not really intend to transfer the title to the collateral, and the intention is to conceal the pledge transaction, there is a possibility that this will be regarded to be a sham act. The same applies to the use of specific performance (*ostupnoe*) [see Chapter 7 Means of Securing Obligations].

5)   Primary Categories of Voidable Juristic Acts

(1)   Acts of Juridical Persons beyond their Capacity

Acts of juridical persons in contradiction to the purposes restricted by their founding documents or acts which were effected without license when license was required are voidable (Art.173). As mentioned above, *ultra vires* acts of any organisation were void under socialism. Under the present Code, these acts are merely voidable, i.e. can be recognised by the court based upon the action by the juridical person itself, its founders (members), or state controlling or supervisory agencies. However, this is only possible when the opposite party to the transaction had known or should have known that the act was *ultra vires* or effected without license. In this way, a bona fide third party is protected.

   A specialised investment fund for privatisation initiated an action in court for the recognition of the contract for the sale of shares to be void and for the application of the outcome of voidness. The court of first instance found that the Fund had no license for such activities and recognised the sale contract to be void under Article 173. The court of cassation instance overturned this judgment, but the Supreme Commercial Court quashed this judgment and found the contract of sale to be void.[63]

(2)   Juristic Acts in Excess of the granted Power

If the power of a person to effect a juristic act is limited by a contract, or in cases of organs of a juridical person, restricted by a founding document in comparison with the power of attorney, law, or what is regarded as apparent under the circumstances where the act was effected, and the person exceeded such limits, the act is voidable, i.e. can be recognised by the court as void in favour of the person in whose interest the restriction was set. This is possible only when it is proven that the opposite party had known or should have known that the act was in excess of power (Art.174). Thus, in this provision as well as in the preceding provision, the Code is designed to strike a balance between the interest of the person who is represented and a bona fide party which entered into a transaction:

> An open joint stock company brought an action against a bank claiming that the contract of pledge concluded with the bank was void. In this case, the general director of the company presented a resolution of the shareholders' meeting authorising the transaction and an excerpt of the share register which showed that he held 56,6% of the shares. These documents turned out to be falsified. The Supreme Commercial Court ruled that from the appearance, there was no ground for the bank to suspect the authenticity of the document, and ruled in favour of the bank.[64]

(3)   Juristic Acts effected by Mistake

Juristic acts effected by a mistake which has an essential significance are voidable. The court may recognise it as void at the suit of the person who acted under the influence of a mistake. Essential mistake in this context means errors concerning the nature of the transaction, or the identity or other qualities of the object of the transaction which significantly reduce the possibility of its use in accordance with its purpose. A mistake concerning the motive of the act does not have essential significance (Art.178, para.1). Mistakes concerning law are not considered either.

The party, by whose action the juristic act was recognised by the court as void, is entitled to compensation if it is proved that the mistake had occurred by fault

---

63   'Obzor praktiki razresheniia sporov po sdelkam, sviazannym s razmesheniem i obrashcheniem aktsii', informatsionnoe pis'mo VAS RF, April 21, 1998, *VVAS RF* 1998 No.6, item 2.
64   Decision of the Presidium of the Supreme Commercial Court, February 11, 1997, *VVAS RF*, 1997 No.5, pp.102-103.

of the opposite party. Otherwise, the mistaken party must compensate the other for any reliance loss (*ibid.*, para.2).

(4)   *Juristic Acts effected under Fraud, Duress, Threat, by an Agreement in Bad Faith between the Agent of the Party with the Opposite Party, or by Combination of Harsh Circumstances*

The common thread among these acts is that one of the parties has been deprived of the possibility of expressing his will and actioning on his interest in an appropriate way.[65] There is also an element of 'blameworthiness (*uprechnost'*)' in the o   p   -
posite party. These acts are voidable at the suit of the victim (Art.179, para.1). If such acts are found to be void by the court, the opposite party must return to the victim the property which has been received from the victim. The property which the victim has received is to be transferred to the state (*ibid.*, para.2).

    Acts effected under the combination of harsh circumstances are denoted as *kabal'naia sdelka* – a predatory transaction. It is defined as an agreement concluded under difficult circumstances in conditions more extremely unfavourable to one party than those available to the opposite party. This existed under socialism, and is claimed to be unique to Russian Law, but the German BGB has a similar provision.[66]

    There are three requirements for a predatory act to be voided; it was effected i) under difficult circumstances, ii) under extremely unfavourable conditions, and iii) against the will of the person involved.[67]

6)   Representation and Power of Attorney

Juristic acts do not have to be effected personally; they can be effected through a representative (agent) in the name of the principal. The power of the agent may be based upon a power of attorney, law, or decisions granting such power by state or municipal agencies (Art.182, para.1). In addition to the provisions in Part One, General Part of the Civil Code, Part Two of the Code has a chapter on agency contracts [see Chapter 9 Individual Contracts]. While the term 'representation' and 'representative' are used in Part One, in Part Two, the term 'agency' and 'agent' are used. There does not seem to be any rationale for this distinction.

---

65   Sadikov ed., *Kommentarii...*, enlarged edition, *supra*, p.373.
66   Solotych, *supra*, p.36. See BGB Art.138, para.2.
67   Braginskii ed., *Nauchno-prakticheskii komenntarii...*, *supra*, p.294.

An agent may not represent the principal in relation to himself. Nor may an agent effect a transaction with a person whom he simultaneously represents, except in cases of commercial representation (*ibid.*, para.3).

The Code has a special provision on commercial representation. Commercial agents are those who, on a continuous basis and independently, represent entrepreneurs and conclude contracts in the name of the entrepreneur in entrepreneurial activities (Art.184, para.1). Commercial agents are allowed to represent various parties simultaneously in the same transaction, but with the consent of all parties (*ibid.*,para.2). Commercial representation is based upon a written contract which specifies the power of the agent; if such a power is not specified, the agent acts on the basis of a power of attorney (*ibid.*, para.3). Commercial agents are under an obligation to maintain confidentiality of information on commercial transactions to which they became privy even after a given assignment has been performed (*ibid.*, para.3).

As a rule, juristic acts effected by a person who is not empowered to act in the name of another person or in excess of the granted power do not have any effect in relation to the principal. Such an act is deemed to have been effected in the name and interest of the person who acted as an agent, unless the other person (principal) later directly ratifies this act. Ratification makes the act valid in relation to the principal from the moment of the effecting of the act (Art.183).

In order to authorise another person to act in one's name, a power of attorney is needed. Power of attorney is an authorisation issued to another person for representation before a third party. It needs to be in writing. Power of attorney for effecting juristic acts which require notarisation also requires notarisation (Art.185, paras. 1 and 2).

Power of attorney in the name of a juridical person is to be issued with the signature of the general director or other persons empowered to do so by the founding document and with the seal of the organisation attached to it (*ibid.*, para.5). Power of attorney for the purpose of receiving or granting money and other proprietary valuables in the name of juridical persons founded on the basis of state or municipal ownership must also have the signature of the senior accounting officer of the organisation (*ibid.*).

The term of a power of attorney may not exceed three years. If the period of validity is not specified, it is valid for one year after its execution. Notarised power of attorney for use abroad is valid until the person who issued it cancels it (Art.186).

The person who was granted a power of attorney must personally effect the act which he was empowered to do. This person may delegate this power if he is empowered to do so by the power of attorney, or was compelled to do so due to the force of circumstances for the interest of protecting the interests of the person who issued the power of attorney (Art.187, para.1). The delegated power of attorney must be notarised (*ibid.*, para.3). The person who delegated the power must inform the issuer of the power of attorney of the fact of delegation, and give necessary information on the person who has been delegated the power. Failure to perform this obligation entails the liability of the person who delegated the power for the act of the person who was delegated the power in the same way as this person (*ibid.*, para.2).

A power of attorney expires on the following grounds (Art.188, para.1):

i)   expiry of the term of the power of attorney;

ii)   rescission of the power of attorney by the issuer;

iii)   refusal of the person who was issued the power of attorney;

iv)   termination of the juridical person in whose name the power of attorney was issued;

v)   termination of the juridical person to whom the power of attorney was issued;

vi)   death, declaration of incapacity, limited capacity, or disappearance of the issuer (physical person);

vii)   death, declaration of incapacity, limited capacity, or disappearance of the person to whom the power of attorney was issued (physical person).

The issuer may, at any time, rescind the power of attorney or its delegation (*ibid.*, para.2).

7   PERIODS OF TIME AND LIMITATION PERIODS

1)   Periods of Time

Periods of time established by law and other legal acts, juristic acts, or designated by the court are determined by calendar date or by flow of years, months, days or hours. Periods of time can also be set by an incident which will definitely happen (Art.190). The period starts flowing on the next calendar day or occurrence of the incident which determines the start of the term (Art.191).

Periods counted by years expire on the fixed month and date of the last year. Periods counted by months expire on the fixed date of the last month. If the period counted by months ends in a month in which there is no corresponding date, the period expires on the last day of that month (Art.182). If the period expires on a non-working day, the date of expiry is the closest working day after this day (Art.193). If the period is fixed for performing a certain act, the act must be performed by the 24th hour of the day. However, if such an act is to be performed by an organisation, the period expires at the time when this organisation, in accordance with established rules, finishes its operation. Written declaration and notification given to an organisation before the 24th hour of the last day of the period are deemed to have been given within the term (Art.194).

2)   Limitation Periods

A limitation period is the period for litigation for the protection of rights by a person whose right has been infringed. The general period of limitation is three years (arts.195 and 196). There are some provisions which provide for a special period of limitation in the Code as well as in other laws, e.g. the Law on the Protection of Consumers.

The claim of the person whose right was infringed will be heard by the court regardless of the expiry of the period of prescription for action. Prescription is applied only upon the petition of the party before the court renders the judgment. In such cases, the court dismisses the case (Art.199).

The limitation period starts, as a rule, from the day when a person became aware of, or should have become aware of the infringement of his rights. For obligations with a fixed time of performance, the limitation period starts from the time the period for performance ends. For obligations in which the time of performance is not determined, or obligations which become due on request, the period starts at the time the right of the creditor to require performance emerges (Art.200, paras. 1 and 2).

The flow of the period of prescription is suspended in the following circumstances (Art.202, paras. 1& 2):

i)   presentation of the claim to court was hindered by extraordinary and insurmountable circumstances under the given conditions;
ii)   the plaintiff or the defendant was in military service;
iii)   moratorium by the Russian Government based on law;
iv)   suspension of the law or legal act which regulates the performance of the obligation.

These circumstances must have emerged or continued in the last six months of the period.

The flow of the limitation period is interrupted by the initiation of litigation or performance of an act by the obligee which demonstrates the recognition of the obligation (Art.203).

If the court, in exceptional cases, acknowledges that there was a justifiable ground related to the personal circumstances of the plaintiff for the lapse of the period for prescription being unnoticed (serious illness, helpless situation, illiteracy etc.), the right of a physical person should be protected, i.e. the period of prescription is not applied (Art.205).

The period of prescription for an action is not applied in the following cases (Art.208):

i)   claim for the protection of personal non-proprietary rights and other things of non-material value;

ii) claim of the depositor against the bank to return the deposit;

iii) claim for compensation for damage caused to the life or health of an individual; however, for claims made after three years, the compensation shall only cover the preceding three years;

iv) claim of the owner or other possessor of a property concerning removal of all violations of his rights, regardless of whether this individual was dispossessed or not (Art.304).

4

COMPANY LAW

1   HISTORY OF RUSSIAN COMPANY LAW

It was in the late 18th century that a company akin to a joint-stock company called the Russian-American Company was founded in Russia. Some more companies followed, and in 1836, the Statute on Stock Companies (*aktsionernaia kompaniia*) was enacted. It was the intention of Speranskii, when compiling *Svod zakonov*, to combine the civil and commercial codes, but for technical reasons, some of the commercial provisions had to be separated from the civil law. In the later editions of *Svod zakonov*, the part on civil law in volume X part 1 contained provisions on companies (*tovarishchestvo*) including joint stock companies. Most of them came from the 1836 Statute. The Statute on Commerce (*ustav torgovyi*), which was accommodated in volume XI part 2 of the *Svod zakonov,* also had some provisions on commercial companies such as full partnership, limited partnership, limited liability companies and joint-stock companies.[1] This was obviously insufficient, and attempts were made to modernise company law. The draft Civil Code (*grazhdansko ulozhenie*) of 1905 accommodated company law provisions in Book V – law of obligations. Some 160 provisions were allocated to joint stock companies.[2] However, these attempts to enact a commercial code or a new law on joint-stock companies failed, and therefore, the 1836 Statute served as the basic law on joint-stock companies until the October Revolution.[3]

After the Revolution, the Civil Code of the RSFSR was enacted in 1922.[4] This was the beginning of the New Economic Policy, the period in which the Bolsheviks pursued a policy of mixed economy – socialist and market. The 1922 Code,

---

1   D.Nosenko ed., *Ustav torgovyi*, 5th edition, St.Petersburg, 1909. G.F.Shershenebich, *Uchebnik torgovago prava*, 7th edition, Moscow 1914, pp.20-23.

2   *Grazhdanskoe ulozhenie; proekt vysochaishche uchrezhdennoi redaktsionnaia kommisia po sostavleniiu grazdanskogo ulozheniia*, St.Petersburg 1905.

3   G.Shershenevich, *Uchebnik torgovago prava*, Moscow 1914, pp.128-129.

4   *SU RSFSR*, 1922 No.71, item 904.

which was close to the draft Civil Code prepared earlier in the century, incorporated provisions on commercial companies including limited liability companies and joint-stock companies.[5] In 1927, a separate statute on joint stock companies was enacted.[6] However, the government abandoned the New Economic Policy in 1928 and embarked on the course of 'socialist industrialisation' which made commercial companies based upon private capital totally redundant. In fact, under a system in which means of production was to be solely owned by the state, it was an anathema to socialism to allow 'accumulation of private capital'. Even small private entrepreneurial activities were banned under the threat of criminal penalties.

It was only in 1988 that a limited scope of private entrepreneurial activity was legalised. The newly enacted Law on Co-operatives allowed individuals to form and invest in co-operatives and perform entrepreneurial activities as long as the size of business remained small and others were not employed.[7] Cooperatives were allowed to operate outside the state economic plan and to determine the price of the product by themselves. It was a monumental piece of legislation allowing de facto companies to be set up by individuals. By 1990, there were around 210,000 co-operatives, but with the liberalisation of various forms of companies, they were converted into companies and the number declined.

In the socialist period, there were no commercial companies; instead, there were state enterprises which were solely owned by the state.[8] In place of company law, there was the Law on State Enterprises which was part of administrative law. This Law regulated the vertical relationship between the ministries and enterprises rather than the horizontal relationship between the enterprises. Under the planned economy, state enterprises conducted business in strict conformity with the state economic plan. The autonomy of these enterprises was severely limited, although they were granted juridical personality and had a separate balance sheet. In the absence of the market, prices were determined by the state economic plan. State enterprises did not have power to dispose of their income and make investments. They did not even have the power to conclude a contract unless so mandated by the plan. It was only towards the end of socialism that state enterprises came to be granted some autonomy.

Following the USSR Law on Ownership of March 6, 1990, which significantly expanded the scope of private ownership, the USSR Law on Enterprises was enacted

---

5   An English translation can be found in Gsovski, *Soviet Civil Law*, vol.2, Ann Arbour 1949.
6   *SZ SSSR*, 1927 No.49, item 499.
7   *VVS SSSR* 1988 No.22, item 355.
8   Some foreign trade organisations and other entities were joint-stock companies, but the state was the sole shareholder.

on June 4, the same year.[9] This Law referred to joint stock companies and other forms of commercial companies based upon 'collective ownership' without going into much detail. The next year, on May 31, the USSR Fundamental Principles of Civil Legislation was enacted. This Law, for the first time in the history of Soviet law, accommodated provisions on various commercial organisations, including joint-stock companies and limited liability companies.[10]

At the RSFSR level, the Law on Ownership and the Law on Enterprises and Entrepreneurial Activities were enacted on December 24 and 25, 1990 respectively.[11] The former allowed ownership of 'enterprises and property complexes' by individuals. This latter Law was the first piece of legislation which can be characterised as company law. In a way similar to the 1922 Civil Code, it listed full and limited partnerships, limited liability companies and joint-stock companies as basic types of companies. However, there was some confusion; the legislature seemed to have failed to distinguish between limited liability companies and closed type joint-stock company. On the same day, the RSFSR Statute on Joint Stock Companies was enacted.

As a result of these legislative developments, companies owned by private capital mushroomed in Russia. This was accelerated by the privatisation of state enterprises, in which state enterprises were converted into joint-stock companies.

However, it was only by the enactment of the present Civil Code (Part One) on October 21, 1994, that a detailed regulation on companies emerged.[12] As the Civil Code was based upon the unified system, i.e. civil and commercial laws were combined in the Code, it contained fairly detailed provisions on companies in the part dealing with juridical persons.

Regulations contained in the Civil Code were still insufficient until the Law on Joint-Stock Companies was enacted on November 24, 1995.[13] This was followed by the Law on Limited Liability Companies of February 8, 1998.[14]

There were proposals to amend the Law on Joint-Stock Companies, particularly in order to curb abuses by the management, and a bill was submitted to the Duma in 1999. However, due to some pressure from large companies resisting introduction of 'constraints' on corporate governance, the adoption has been delayed. It was only in August 2001 that a fairly substantial amendment was introduced. The changes will take effect from January 2002.

---

9   *VVS SSSR,* 1990 No.25, item 460.
10   *VSND SSSR i VS SSSR,* 1991 No.26, item 766.
11   *VSND RSFSR i VS RSFSR,* 1990 No.30, item 418.
12   *SZ RF,* 1994 No.32, item 3301.
13   *SZ RF,* 1996, No.1, item 1.
14   *SZ RF,* 1998 No.7, item 785.

The 2001 amendment was a major step towards the improvement in corporate governance. A foreign observer rather prematurely commented as follows:

> Corporate governance .... has receded as an issue because of changes in both legislation and management attitudes.[15]

Blatant breaches of the rights of shareholders by the management may have decreased in number, but certainly, there is still more room for improvement.

2   PRIVATISATION OF STATE ENTERPRISES

In present day Russia, a majority of companies are either former state enterprises which have been privatised or companies which have been spun-off by state enterprises in the process of privatisation. Many of the co-operatives established after 1988 were later transformed into companies. In addition to those companies, there are 'unitary enterprises' – state enterprises, which have not been privatised yet, or are not planned to be privatised.[16]

In a market economy, private enterprises – companies, not state enterprises – play a major role. Naturally, a sizeable private sector cannot develop in a short time span from scratch. In a country which had almost no private sector (except the 'second economy'), in order to create a market economy, the capital has to be transferred from the existing state sector to the private sector. Towards the end of socialism, the enormous state sector which had developed over the decades in Russia was not sustainable any more. In order to alleviate the burden on the budget and to generate income, privatisation of state enterprises was needed.

However, before the official privatisation process began, privatisation of state enterprises in Russia had already started in a spontaneous way after the enactment of the 1988 Law on Co-operatives. As one Russian author put it, 'the process of 'allocation' of state property got under way long before the adoption of official decisions on privatisation'.[17] State enterprises set up co-operatives to avoid state interference with their business activities. This was understandable, since it was much more profitable to sell their products through co-operatives which were not bound by the state plan. What was more, profits could be distributed among the members without having to surrender them to the state. Thus, there was a large-

---

15 *Petroleum Review*, February 2002, p.15.
16 Russian Academy of Science, Institute of Economy in Transition ed., *Russian Economy -1999, Annual Report*, Moscow 2000, p.158.
17 A.Letenko and D.Lvov, 'Problems of Ownership and Privatization in Russia', in J.Prokopenko ed., *Privatization: Lessons from Russia and China, ILO Working Paper*, Geneva 1998, p.21.

scale erosion of state property – unofficial transfer of assets from state enterprises to cooperatives.

In 1989 the USSR Fundamental Principles of Leases was enacted.[18] Together with the Law on Cooperatives, this was a breakthrough against the principle of the state monopoly of means of production. The Law allowed non-gratuitous lease of various means of production by state enterprises to juridical persons as well as natural persons. Lessees were even granted the right to purchase the assets, including enterprises. Soon afterwards, the USSR Law on Enterprises allowed state enterprises to spin off part of the enterprise as a separate, non-state enterprise.[19]

In practice, the process was grossly abused by insiders, i.e. officials of sectoral ministries and the management of state enterprises as well as the employees. Government officials and the management colluded to transfer part of the state enterprise to newly set up companies whose founders were those officials and executives. These companies leased and eventually purchased the assets of the state enterprise at a low price. Such insider privatisation was dubbed '*nomenklatura privatisation*'.[20] Russian economists reminisced ten years later;

> …with the collapse of the state control over enterprises, on the one hand, and the absence of the legal basis for private ownership on the other hand, the seizure and maintenance of control were effected by forceful methods with the connivance of the criminal network and bribery of state and party officials traditionally responsible for the control of enterprises.[21]

The formal legal basis for privatisation was created by the RSFSR Law on Privatisation of July 1991 (replaced by a new Law in 1997). The Law provided for four methods of privatisation: tender, auction, public offer of shares, and lease buy out. This Law gave significant privileges to employees. Then, in July 1992, a presidential decree introduced the system of voucher privatisation modelled on the Polish scheme. Vouchers distributed among citizens free of charge could be used for the purchase of shares of enterprises being privatised. On the other hand, one-third of state enterprises were exempted from this privatisation programme.

According to the State Privatisation Programme of 1992, there were three alternative methods of privatisation:

---

18 *VVS SSSR*, 1989, No.25, item 481.
19 *VVS SSSR*, 1990, No.25, item 460.
20 J.Tedstrom, 'Russia; Progress Report on Industrial Privatization', *RFE/RL Research Report*, 1992 No.17, pp.46-48.
21 A.Radygin and I.Sidorov, 'Rossiiskaia korporativnaia ekonomika: sto let odinochestva?', *VE*, 2000, No.5, p.47.

  i)   25% free distribution of shares to employees, a further 10% sale to employees
          with a 30% discount and 5% sale to the management. Remaining shares to be
          sold by voucher auction or tender;

 ii)   51% of shares sold to employees at nominal value. Remaining shares to be sold
          by voucher auction and/or tender;

iii)   a group of employees are entrusted with the implementation of privatisation. They
          purchase 20% of shares and are given further 20% voting rights. Remaining shares
          to be sold by voucher auction or tender.

Naturally, the second alternative was the most popular. As many as 77% of state
enterprises which took part in this scheme opted for the second variant.[22] In fact,
there were few incentives for state enterprises to sell their shares for vouchers,
since it did not bring any income and there was a risk of losing control to outsiders. The average proportion of shares sold for vouchers was a mere 21%.[23]
In a well-known car company Zil, 12% of shares were distributed free of charge
to employees. A further 12.5% were sold to employees at a discount price. 50%
of the shares were offered to the public, of which 30% were sold by auction in
exchange for vouchers.[24]

   As the result of this 'voucher privatisation', which took place between 1992
and 1994, and of a fairly successful small privatisation, i.e. privatisation of the
small scale retail sector, in 1995, the number of companies in the private sector
exceeded the number of state enterprises for the first time.[25] According to the
statistics of the Ministry of State Property, as of January 1, 2000, there were
130,000 privatised companies. This was 58,9% of the number of state enterprises
before privatisation. Over 60% of GDP was produced in the non-state sector. On
the other hand, there was a sizeable state holding of shares including 7,000-8,000
unsold companies and 2,500 companies in which the state held more than 25%
of the shares. It held 'golden shares' in 580 companies in November 1999. As
of November 1999, there are 13,786 state and municipal enterprises.[26]

   As of January 1, 2000, in terms of number, 4,8% of enterprises were state
enterprises; another 6,4% account for municipal enterprises. 74,4% of the enterprises are in the private sector.[27] While in 1992, 62.9% of employees worked

---

22   P.Rutland, 'Privatisation in Russia: One Step Forward: Two Steps Back?', *Europe-Asia Studies*,
     1994 No.7, p.1113.
23   *Ibid.*, p.1116.
24   *EiZh*, 1993 No.11, p.10.
25   A.Radygin, 'Privatizatsionnyi protsess v Rossii v 1995 g.', *VE*, 1996 No.4, p.5.
26   Letenko and Lvov, *supra*, p.59; Institute of Economy in Transition, *supra*, pp.153,158.
27   Goskomstat ed., *Rossiia v tifrakh*, Moscow 2000, p.157.

for state enterprises and organisations, this fell to 44.7% in 1994, and 38.3% in 1998. In 1998, 41.8% of workers were employed by the private sector.[28]

However, even in the process of formal privatisation, abuses were rampant; 'most of the privatisation activities seemed to be of dubious legality'.[29] Most breaches of law occurred at the stage of creation, reorganisation or liquidation of enterprises. There were cases where State Property Committee officials were lobbied for decisions infringing the property interest of the state or competitors. Managers of state enterprises 'parachuted' to privatised companies, often with their contribution to the share capital in the form of 'intellectual property' highly overvalued.[30]

There was a general lack of transparency in the process. After the completion of the voucher privatisation, in 1995, the government introduced a 'loans-for-shares' scheme in which the government accepted loans from the public and in return, offered shares in major state enterprises. Shares of some 15 major state enterprises were offered by auction in this scheme. In practice, this process was seriously flawed and benefited a small number of financiers only. In 1999, in the auction of 9% of the shares of a large oil company, an off-shore company based in Cyprus won the bid at a price only 5,000 US dollars higher than the starting price. Another off-shore company bid for 1,000 US dollars higher. 'Self-acquisition' of the company was suspected.[31]

In the privatisation process, foreign investors were allowed to take part with some restrictions. According to the 1993 presidential decree, for privatisation of the defence industry, oil and gas companies, transport and communication companies etc., special permission of the government is required for foreign investors to acquire an interest. The 1997 Privatisation Law has a list of properties which can only be privatised with the exclusion of foreign physical and juridical persons as well as Russian resident companies with the participation of these persons. There was confusion when a law enacted in 1998 addressing the disposal of government held shares in energy companies set a limit on the holding of shares by foreign shareholders at 25%. In fact, in some of the companies, the holding of shares by foreign investors had already exceeded 30%, and in 1999, it further went up to 33%.[32]

The privatisation process has slowed down in recent years. This is not only because a majority of palatable enterprises have been already privatised. 'Genuine

---

28 S.Clarke and V.Kabalina, 'Employment in the New Private Sector in Russia', *Post-Communist Economies*, 1999 No.4, p.425.
29 Rutland, *supra*, p.1113.
30 Letenko and Lvov, *supra*, p.24.
31 Institute of Economy in Transition, *supra*, pp.154-155.
32 *Ibid.*, p.149.

outsiders' and 'bona fide investors' are apprehensive of various problems including the possibility of 'deprivatisation'. Since a significant number of cases of privatisation have been conducted in breach of the law, there is always a possibility of the contract being nullified and the assets being ordered to be returned on the initiative of the Procuracy:

> A deputy procurator of St.Petersburg initiated an action 'for the protection of state and public interest' at the Commercial Court of St.Petersburg and Leningrad Province against the Property Fund of St.Petersburg, a US company, and other entities. The deputy procurator asked the court to declare void the sale of shares of the state enterprise 'Leninets' by an auction based upon privatisation vouchers of September 13, 1994 and order the shares to be returned to the Property Fund.
>
> The first instance court and the appellate instance court dismissed the claim, but the court of the cassation instance accepted the claim of the deputy procurator. The court found that the auction was against the State Programme of Privatisation of State and Municipal Enterprises approved by a presidential decree which placed restrictions on foreign companies taking part in the privatisation process. The enterprise 'Leninets' supplied more than 30% of its products to the military and therefore, foreign investors should not have been allowed to take part in its privatisation. The court ordered the US company to return the shares to the property fund, but refused reimbursement of the vouchers to the US company, since at the time of the judgment, privatisation vouchers had no value. Besides, vouchers were eventually received by the State, and the property fund was not in a position to reimburse privatisation vouchers. Thus, the US company had the shares taken away, but failed to receive any compensation.
>
> Upon protest, the Supreme Commercial Court upheld the judgment of the court of cassation instance in that the auction was void. However, the Court modified the judgment to the extent that the Property Fund was ordered to return the nominal value of the vouchers, 50 million roubles, to the US company by applying Art.167, para.2 of the Civil Code.[33]

In this case, the US company eventually managed to retrieve the investment. But this is not always the case. The problem here is that there is no mechanism to protect the bona fide party from the nullification of the transaction by the court. There is a 10 year period of prescription for action, but this is regarded as being too long.

---

33   Decision of the Presidium of the Supreme Commercial Court, September 16, 1997, *VVAS RF* 1998
No.2, pp.55-56.

3   STRUCTURE OF CORPORATE OWNERSHIP IN RUSSIA

A conspicuous characteristic of corporate ownership in Russia, particularly in privatised companies, is the dominance of insiders. The scheme of the 1992 Privatisation Programme itself was designed in favour of employees. In the privatised companies, between 1992-1993, 48% of the shares belonged to employees, 19% to the management, and 20% to the state.[34] However, according to a survey by the State Property Committee, by 1994, the percentage of workers collectives holding more than 50% shares of a company went down by 20% to 63%, while joint stock companies in which the management held more than 10% shares went up to 20%.[35]

A survey of 100 joint stock companies conducted in the mid-1990s showed that 60% of companies had 'outsider' shareholders. The average share of large outside shareholders was over 25%. On the other hand, managers held over 40% shares in privatised companies (former state enterprises), while in ordinary companies, their share was around 17%.[36] Since 1995, an increase of the portion of shares held by outsiders can be seen (35,2% to 42,4%), while the share of insiders fell from 54,8% to 42,4%. Among insiders, shares held by employees fell from 43,6% to 31,5%.[37] The increase in the share of outsiders is attributed to the need for external financing.

There was a further decrease of insiders and increase of outsiders since the 1998 financial crisis. The share of insiders fell from 55-60% in 1996 to 30-35% in 2000, while the share of outsiders increased from 30-35% to 50-55% in the same period.[38] This is said to have been caused by the 'post-crisis concentration of ownership' and the fall in the officially registered management stake.[39] However, it is not clear whether there was a genuine shift of control from the management to outsiders, or the management still holds control via insiders.[40]

---

34   Murav'ev and Savul'kin, 'Korporativnoe upravlenie i ego vliianie na provedenie privatizirovannykh predpviiatii', *VE* 1998, No. 1, pp.86-87.

35   Letenko and Lvov, *supra*, p.29.

36   E.Gubin, *Upravlenie i korporativnyi kontrol' v aktsionernom obshchestve*, Moscow 1999, p.102.

37   R.Kapeliushinikov, 'Krupneishie i dominiruiushchie sobstvenniki v rossiiskoi promyshlennosti', *VE*, 2000, No.1, p.102.

38   A.Radygin, 'Sobstvennost' i integratsionnye protsessy v korporativnom sektore', *VE* 2001 No.5, p.27.

39   A.Radygin and S.Arkhipov, 'Ownership Structure and Financial Position of Firms in Russia: Empirical Analysis', *Russian Economic Trends*, 2001 Issue 2, p.20.

40   Radygin, *supra*, p.27.

Table 3 The Structure of Shareholding in Russian Companies

Catergory of Shareholders	1995	1997	1999	2001 (forecast)
Insiders Total	54,8	52,1	46,2	45,54
Managers	11,2	15,1	14,7	18,2
Employees	43,6	37,0	31,5	27,2
Outsiders Total	35,2	38,8	42,4	44,9
Non-Financial	25,9	28,5	32,0	31,9
Financial	9,3	10,3	10,4	13,0
State	9,1	7,4	7,1	6,4
Others	0,9	1,7	4,3	3,2
Total	100%	100%	100%	100%

(R.Kapeliushinikov, 'Krupneishie i dominiruiushchie sobstvenniki v rossiiskoi promyshlennosti', *VE*, 2000, No.1, p.102)

Since 1994, large business conglomerates which are termed financial industrial groups emerged and gained power. There is a Law on Financial Industrial Groups of November 30, 1995.[41] In mid-1997, there were 70 such groups which integrated more than 1,000 industrial companies and 90 financial institutions.[42] In a financial industrial group, companies combine their resources on the basis of an agreement to create a group for economic integration, realisation of various projects and a programme for the increase of revenues, competitiveness, efficiency, and expansion of market shares. Member companies are industrial companies and banks and other financial institutions. The group has a core company, normally an 'investment institution', which is empowered to act on behalf of the member companies. The Law provides that member companies are jointly and severally liable for the debt of the core company.

However, since the 1998 financial crisis, 'the rule of the game has changed'.[43] These financial industrial groups seem to have been replaced by a new type of concentration of economic power. Some financial groups, such as Onexim and Menatep groups, actually collapsed in the financial crisis. Now, instead of financial

---

41   *SZ RF*, 1995 No. 49, item 4697.
42   E.Utkin and M.Eskindarov, *Finansovo-promyshlennyie gruppy*, Moscow 1998, p.7.
43   H-H. Schröder, 'El'tsin and the Oligarchs: The Role of Financial Groups in Russian Politics Between 1993 and July 1998', *Eurape-Asia Studies*, 1999.

industrial groups, companies are organised as a holding company group. A large number of holding company groups have developed in the energy and metal sectors. In the oil industry, Lukoil and Surgutneftegaz, as 'vertically integrated companies', have expanded significantly in the late 1990s. Such vertical integration can also be seen in the regions as well.[44]

4   TYPES OF COMPANIES

The Civil Code is the basic law which accommodates provisions on companies. Chapter Four, Part One of the Civil Code covers juridical persons. The Chapter begins with basic provisions on juridical persons, followed by a sub-chapter on commercial partnerships and companies, and then by sub-chapters on production cooperatives, state and municipal unitary enterprises, and non-commercial organisations. There are separate laws on joint stock companies, limited liability companies, and non-commercial organisations.

Commercial partnerships and companies are defined in the Code as 'commercial organisations with a capital divided into participatory shares (shares) of the founders (members). Commercial partnerships can be set up as full partnerships (corresponding to the German *einfache Gesellschaft*) and limited partnerships (*Komanditgesellschaft*). Commercial companies can be established as joint stock companies, limited liability companies, or companies with additional liability (Art.66). It is important to note that not only commercial companies, but commercial partnerships have juridical personality.

In a full partnership, partners are liable for the debts of the partnership in cases where the assets of the partnership are insufficient to cover the debts, i.e. partners bear unlimited liability. In a limited partnership, one or several partners who conduct entrepreneurial activities in the name of the partnership bear unlimited liability, while other partners are liable to the extent of their capital contribution. Since these two forms of commercial organisations involve unlimited liability, they are seldom utilised by foreign investors.

Among commercial companies, the company with subsidiary liability is perhaps unfamiliar to most people. This exists in the Hungarian Company Act of 1988 (amended in 1997) which served as one of the models of Russian company law. It is a variation of limited liability companies. When the assets of the company are not sufficient to cover the debt, participants in this type of company are liable

---

44   Institute of Economy in Transition, *supra*, p.147.

in a subsidiary way up to a fixed amount determined by the articles of incorporation in proportion to their participatory share.

In reality, it is the joint stock companies and limited liability companies that are the most common forms of companies in Russia.

Joint stock companies are defined in the Civil Code as companies whose capital is divided into a fixed number of shares. Shareholders are not liable for the debt of the company and bear the risk of loss only within the amount of their contribution (Art.96). There are two types of joint stock companies; open and closed. In open joint stock companies, shareholders are entitled to transfer shares freely without the consent of other shareholders. Open joint stock companies may publicly offer and sell shares. Joint stock companies whose shares are distributed only among founders or other pre-determined persons are closed joint stock companies. Their shares may not be offered to the public or to an unspecified scope of people. Shareholders of closed joint stock companies have pre-emptive rights to purchase shares sold by other shareholders (Art.97). The number of shareholders in closed joint stock companies may not exceed fifty (Law on Joint Stock Companies, Art.7, para.3).

The Civil Code defines a limited liability company as a company which is established by one or several persons whose capital is divided into participatory shares held by the members in accordance with the ratio (percentage or quota) determined by the articles of incorporation (Art.87, para.1). This is in contrast with joint stock companies in which the capital is 'divided into a fixed number of shares' (Art.96, para.1). Participants (holders of the participatory share) are not liable for the debt of the company and bear the risk of loss only within the amount of their contribution (Art.87).

Differences between joint stock companies and limited liability companies are as follows:

Table 4 Comparison of Joint Stock Companies and Limited Liability Comapnies

	Limited Liability Companies	Joint Stock Companies
Sources of Law	The Civil Code and the Law on Limited Liability Companies	The Civil Code and the Law on Joint Stock Companies
Minimum Capital	100 times minimum wage.	1,000 times minimum capital for open joint stock companies and 100 times for closed joint stock companies.

	Limited Liability Companies	Joint Stock Companies
Management Structure	Participants' meeting, board of directors (optional), collective or single executive body.	Shareholders' meeting, board of directors, single executive body or single executive body plus collective executive body (companies with less than 50 shareholders can dispense with the board).
Transfer of Shares (participatory share)	Transfer to a third party subject to restrictions.	In closed joint stock companies, transfer to a third party subject to restrictions.
Withdrawal from the Company	Possible without the consent of other members; contribution to be paid back.	Redemption of contribution not possible.
Expulsion of Members	Expulsion from the company possible by a 10% participant.	Not possible.
Audit	Audit committee not mandatory; audit by an independent professional auditor not mandatory.	Audit committee not mandatory with some exceptions; audit by an auditor.
Issuing of Bonds	Possible up to the amount of the capital or of the guarantee provided by a third party.	Possible; also convertible bonds can be issued.
Disclosure	Public disclosure not required except when bonds are issued.	Annual accounts to be published (open joint stock companies).

There are no definitive statistics as to the number of both types of companies. It is reported that limited liability companies are much more popular than joint stock companies. In July 1996, there were 228,911 limited liability companies, while there were only 39,740 closed joint stock companies.[45] In total, 30,800 joint stock companies were set up between 1992-1999.[46] There is also a survey data on the form of enterprises in four cities, according to which 83,9% of the

---

45   K.Holloch, 'Das neue russische Wirtschaftrecht, insbesondere das Gesellschaftsrecht', in F-C.Schroeder ed., *Die Neuen Kodifikationen in Russland*, second edition, 1999 Berlin, p.60.
46   Goskomstat ed., *Rossiia v tsifrakh*, Moscow 2000, p.168.

joint stock companies are privatised former state enterprises, while 67% of the limited liability companies are newly set up private companies.[47]

5   COMMON RULES ON JOINT STOCK COMPANIES AND LIMITED LIABILITY COMPANIES

1)   Liability of Shareholders (Participants)

In both types of companies, the risk of shareholders (participants) is limited to their contribution. However, the Civil Code has a couple of provisions which seem to set an exception to this principle. Thus, Article 56, para.3 provides as follows:

> If bankruptcy of a juridical person was caused by founders (members)......, or other persons who have the right to give binding instructions to the juridical person or in other ways have a possibility of determining its activities, in cases where the assets of the juridical person are insufficient, these persons shall be subjected to subsidiary liability on its obligation.

In fact, the 1990 USSR Fundamental Principles of Civil Legislation had a similar provision, but it was applicable only when the act of the relevant person was unlawful. The Civil Code has dropped the requirement of unlawfulness.

As a result of criticisms from foreign investors, the Law on Joint Stock Companies subsequently added a provision pertinent to this provision (Art,3, para.3):

> Bankruptcy of a company is regarded as caused by an act (omission) of its shareholders or other persons who have the right to give binding instructions to the company, or in other ways have a possibility of determining its activities, only when they utilised such a right and/or potential for the purpose of the performance of an act by the company, knowing that it would result in the bankruptcy of the company.

Furthermore, the Civil Code provides for the liability of the parent company (Article 105, para.2):

> The parent company which has the right to give binding instructions, including those by a contract, is liable jointly and severally with the subsidiary for the transaction concluded in implementation of such an instruction.

---

47   Clarke and Kabalina, *supra*, p.430.

In cases of bankruptcy of the subsidiary by fault of the parent company, the parent company bears additional liability for the debt of the subsidiary.

These provisions are reproduced in the Law on Joint Stock Companies and the Law on Limited Liability Companies.

A joint decision of the Supreme Court and Supreme Commercial Court of April 2, 1997 on Joint Stock Companies further provides that shareholders of the subsidiary are entitled to pursue liability of the parent company for losses incurred by the subsidiary on general grounds in cases where the parent company was at fault.

A parent company is defined in the Civil Code as a company which, by virtue of an overwhelming (*preobladaiushchie*) participation in the capital, by agreement concluded between the parties, or in other ways, is capable of determining a decision which is adopted by another company (Art.105). This provision is repeated in the Law on Joint Stock Companies (Art.6).

'Overwhelming participation' does not necessarily mean a 50% or more stake. In fact, there is no fixed percentage set by the law. A commentary suggests that the percentage is not always decisive. Depending on the number and the spread of shareholders of the company, even a 10-15% stake may be regarded as a definitive influence.[48] It should be added that the Joint Stock Company Law also refers to 'affiliated companies', which are defined as those companies in which another company has more than 20% voting rights (Art.6, para.3).

As is the case with Article 56 of the Civil Code, the Law on Joint Stock Companies introduced a provision which limits the application of this provision. Thus, the Law provides as follows (Article 6, para.3):

Bankruptcy of a subsidiary is regarded to be caused by the fault of the parent company, when the parent company utilised the above right and/or potential for the purpose of the performance of an act by the company, knowing that it would result in the bankruptcy of the company.

The Law on Limited Liability Companies, which was enacted after the Law on Joint Stock Companies does not have the equivalents of such limiting provisions. The above-mentioned joint decision, however, stressed that in such cases, the fault on the part of the parent company is required.[49] This joint decision referred to

---

48   M.Iu.Tikhomirov ed., *Kommentarii k federal'nomu zakonu ob aktsionernykh obshchestvakh,* second edition, Moscow 1999, p.47.

49   Joint Decision of the Plenum of the Supreme Court and Supreme Commercial Court, No.4/8, April 2, 1997, item 12, in V.Zhurakovskii and V.Kalinin, *Kommentarii i primenenie zakondatel'stva arbitrazhnymi sudami rossiskoi federatsii,* Moscow 2000, p.54.

Article 401 of the Civil Code which provides for the principle of fault in liability under the Law of Obligations as the basis of this interpretation.

It is important to note that there have been no reported cases where these provisions have actually been applied.

2)   Registration

Whereas in the Tsarist period, companies could be set up only with a concession of the government, now, registration is the only requirement. All juridical persons are subject to state registration and are deemed to be established by registration (Civil Code Art.51).

For the establishment of a company with foreign participation, Foreign Investment Law provides that such companies may be set up in accordance with provisions of the Civil Code and other laws (Art.20). Foreign investors are allowed to make investments in Russia in any form which is not prohibited by legislation (Art.6). As exceptions, investments which endanger the basis of the constitutional regime, ethics, health, rights and lawful interests of citizens, national defence and public security can be restricted (Art.4, para.2). There are some other restrictions such as the registration found in the Aviation Code, which sets the maximum level of foreign participation at 49% in airline companies and requires that the top management be a Russian national.[50]

The Foreign Investment Law lists additional documents needed for the registration of companies with foreign participation, i.e. excerpts from the commercial register of the home country of the foreign investor and a comfort letter from the bank dealing with the foreign investor.

The actual process of registration was common in both joint stock companies and limited liability companies. There was confusion as to the body which registers companies. Local governments began setting up their own 'registration chambers', such as the Moscow Registration Chamber established in 1991. The Civil Code provides that juridical persons are to be registered by the Ministry of Justice in accordance with the Law on State Registration of Juridical Persons. However, this Law was not enacted until 2001, and therefore, until then, 'existing procedure' was applied. Thus, state registration of companies in which foreign investment did not exceed 100,000 roubles was effected by the local government, except for oil and gas production companies and refining companies as well as coal mining companies. The State Registration Chamber had jurisdiction over companies in

---

50   G.S.Shapkina ed., *Postateinyi kommentarii k federal'nomu zakonu 'Ob aktsionernykh obshchestvakh'*, second edition, Moscow 2000, p.83.

the above-mentioned industries, and companies in which foreign investment exceeded 100,000 roubles.[51]

The State Registration Chamber was established by government in 1994. The Chamber operated on the basis of a statute enacted by the Ministry of Economy.[52] By the Decision of the Government of September 5, 1998, the Chamber was transferred to the Ministry of Justice.[53] For the registration of joint-stock companies with foreign participation, there was a special instruction which set out the procedures including the documents required.[54]

The long-awaited Law on the State Registration of Juridical Persons was enacted on August 8, 2001.[55] The Law is to take effect from July 2002.

The Law covers not only the registration of commercial companies, but all juridical persons including non-commercial organisations. Registration is handled by the Ministry of Justice. The register contains the following information (Art.5, para.1):

i)   full and abbreviated name of the company;
ii)   organisational and legal form;
iii)   address of the permanent management body of the company;
iv)   means of establishment (founding or restructuring);
v)   information on the founders;
vi)   copy of the articles of incorporation;
vii)   information on the succession of rights (for companies which have been created as a result of restructuring);
viii)   means of terminating the activities of the company (restructuring or liquidation);
ix)   share capital as indicated in the articles of incorporation;
x)   name and positions of persons who, without power of attorney, are entitled to act on behalf of the company, passport number etc. and identification number as a tax payer if this applies;
xi)   information on the licence which the company holds.

Information contained in the Register is open to and accessible by the general public, except for the passport number and identification number as a tax payer (Art.6, para.1).

---

51   A.Kramarenko, 'Poriadok gosudarstvennoi registratsii kommercheskikh organizatsii s inostrannymi investitsiiami', *PiE*, 1999 No.10, pp.12-17.
52   *SZ RF* 1994 No.8, item 866.
53   *RG*, September 16, 1998.
54   See S.Mogilevskii, *Aktsionernoe obshchestvo*, Moscow 1998, p.49.
55   *RG*, August 10, 2001.

Documents required for registration are as follows (Art.13):

i)   application form for registration;
ii)   resolution, or agreement to establish a company;
iii)   articles of incorporation (original, or a notarised copy);
iv)   excerpt from a register of foreign juridical persons of the respective country or proof of a similar nature of the status of the foreign founder of the company;
v)   receipt of the payment of the registration fee;

Application is to be made at the registration office of the location of the company's permanent management body (Art.13, para.1). Registration is to be made within 6 working days of the application (Art.8, para.1).

6   JOINT STOCK COMPANIES

1)   Procedure of Establishment

Physical persons as well as juridical persons can be founders of a joint-stock company. The number of founders is not limited, but for closed joint stock companies, the number may not exceed fifty. Companies can be founded by a single person, but this single person may not be another commercial organisation with a single founder. Founders (promoters) bear joint and several liability for the debt related to the establishment and state registration of the company. The company is liable for the founders' debt related to the company's establishment, only when the company has subsequently approved the founders' act at the shareholders' meeting (Law on Joint Stock Companies Art.10).

Joint stock companies may also be founded by conversion from another type of company, merger, spin-off and division.

Companies are established on the basis of a decision of the founders which determines *inter alia*, the procedure for the joint activities regarding the establishment of the company, the amount of capital, the categories and types of shares to be issued, the amount and method of its payment, and the obligations of shareholders. When approving the articles of incorporation and the value of contribution in the form of securities, things as well as proprietary rights and other rights, the decision of founders must be made by a unanimous vote. Members of the management bodies must be elected by a three-quarters majority (Art.9).

In the process of establishment, the full amount of contribution has to be paid for by subscribers within a period less than a year determined by the articles of incorporation; but at least 50% has to be paid in before registration (Art.34, para.1).

Founders elect (appoint) executive bodies of the company, and if there is in kind contribution, confirm its value.

Shares (initial offer as well as subsequent offers) can be paid in by money as well as 'securities, other things or proprietary rights and other rights which have monetary value' (Art.34, para.2). Although this provision seemingly allows the contribution of intellectual property rights, the joint decision of the Plenum of the Supreme Commercial Court and the Supreme Court of the Russian Federation denies this. Only the right to use these rights under license can be contributed. Presumably, this is intended to ensure that the contribution can be objectively valued.[56] In kind contribution at the time of establishment is to be valued by agreement of the founders. Payment in kind for additional issue of shares is to be valued by the board of directors in accordance with Art.77 of the Law (see *infra*). In such cases, an independent valuer has to be brought in (Art.34). Previously, this requirement was applicable only in cases where the payment exceeded 200 times the minimum wage, but this threshold was removed by the 2001 amendment. Decisions to approve the articles of incorporation and to confirm the value of in-kind contribution should be made unanimously (Art.11).

2)   Articles of Incorporation

Joint stock companies operate on the basis of articles of incorporation. The Civil Code has general provisions on articles of incorporation for juridical persons. The Law on Joint Stock companies provides for mandatory items of the articles of incorporation for joint stock companies (Art.11):

i)   full and abridged name of the company;
ii)   location of the company;
iii)   type of the company (closed or open);
iv)   total amount, nominal value, category of shares and types of preferential shares issued by the company;
v)   rights of shareholders of each category of shares;
vi)   share capital of the company;
vii)   structure and competence of the company management and the procedure of adopting decisions;
viii) procedure of preparation and conducting of general shareholders' meeting including the list of matters which require qualified majority or unanimous vote;
ix)   information concerning branches and representative offices;

---

56   Joint decision of the Plenum of the Supreme Commercial Court and the Supreme Court, July 1, 1996 No.6/8, item 17, in Zhurakovskii and Kalinin, *supra*, p.33.

x)   other information provided by the present Law.

Articles of incorporation may include other items which are not against the law. In the light of the past history of Soviet civil codes which were strict on *ultra vires*, conspicuous omissions from this list as provided in the Law on Joint Stock Companies are the purpose of the company and the scope of its activities. The Law on Joint Stock Companies does not list the purposes of the company as mandatory for articles of incorporation. The Civil Code provides that the name, location, procedure of administration, and other matters required by the law on the respective type of juridical person are mandatory in the articles of incorporation. The purposes of commercial organisations are a mandatory component of the articles of incorporation only when required by law (Art.52, para.2).

Changes to the articles of incorporation must be approved by the shareholders' meeting. As a rule, such changes require three quarters of the votes present at the meeting (Art.49, para.4).

3)   The Capital and Shares

(1)   The Capital

The share capital (*ustavnyi kapital*) comprises the total amount of nominal value of shares acquired by shareholders. The capital determines the minimum amount of assets which serve as 'a security for the interests of creditors' (Art.25). The minimum amount of capital for joint stock companies is set at 1,000 times the minimum monthly wage (approximately 3,500 USD) for open type joint stock companies and 100 times for closed type joint stock companies (Art.26).

The capital can be increased by increasing the nominal value of shares or issuing additional shares. Increase of capital by raising the nominal value of the share is effected by a resolution of the shareholders' meeting. Increase of capital by issuing of additional shares is effected either by a resolution of the general shareholders' meeting or a decision of the board of directors. In the latter case, a unanimous vote is required (Art.28, paras. 1 and 2). Previously, although there was no explicit provision, it was understood to be possible for the company to increase capital out of the received profit, although there is an opposing view.[57] The 2001 amendment introduced a provision to the effect that (i) increase of capital by issuing additional shares can also be effected from the company's assets, and

---

57   M.Tikhomirov ed., *supra*, p.150. Iu.A.Meteleva, *Pravovoe polozhenie aktionera v aktsionernom obshchestve*, Moscow 1999, p.110.

(ii) increase of capital by increasing the nominal value of the shares can only be effected out of the company's assets. In the case of (i), the issued shares must be distributed to all existing shareholders (*ibid.,* para.5).

If the power to approve the additional issue of shares lies with the general shareholders' meeting, then the resolution to increase the number of declared shares can be adopted at the same time (*ibid.,* para.3).

The additional issue of shares has often been abused by the incumbent management to dilute the share of existing shareholders:

> Novolipetskii Metallurgical Kombinat is regarded as a leading company in the field. Around 60% of the shares are consolidated in a company founded by the chairman of the board of directors and 34% belonged to an offshore company TWG. Norilisk Nickel, which is under the holding company *Interros*, acquired 9% of the shares. The board of the Kombinat decided to issue additional shares which would double the capital and proposed this at the extraordinary shareholders' meeting. Such a new share issue was ostensibly needed to repay the Kombinat's debt to one of its shareholders. *Interros* claims that there was no legitimate board meeting to propose this to the shareholders' meeting because the quorum was not met.[58]

In fact, as a Russian specialist pointed out, dilution of shares by additional shares has become the most popular way of changing the corporate structure and violating shareholders' rights.[59] In 1998, as a result of an additional issue of shares by Saianskii Aliuminievyi Zavod, the foreign investors' share fell from 37,8% to 15%, and the share of the State Property Fund from 15% to 6,15%. In another case, the share of a bank was reduced to one-sixth. The Bank brought the case to the court which annulled the additional issue.[60]

Even in cases where the decision to issue additional shares falls under the competence of the general shareholders' meeting, there were still many cases where increase of capital by the additional issue of shares took place without informing shareholders:

> In a company called A.Liur'ka Saturn, two days before the shareholders' meeting, there was an official notice in the press regarding the additional issue of shares (9 million shares), as a result of which the capital was to be increased by 10 times. Although the agenda of the shareholders' meeting included the additional issue of shares, in fact, shareholders were asked by the board to vote on a matter which had already been decided and publicised.[61]

---

58   *Izvestiia,* May 30, 2000.
59   E.Torkanovskii, 'Predela aktsionernoi sobstvennosti', *KhiP,* 1999 No.4, p.32.
60   *Ibid.*
61   Mateleva, *supra,* pp.134-135.

Additional shares are often issued and offered to a closed group of people. Even if it is supposed to be a public offer, the company requires that the payment be made in kind, which most existing shareholders are unable to do, and thus turns the offer to a *de facto* closed offer. In one case, the additional issue of shares by Joint Stock Company Nost was found void because of the disproportionate distribution of newly issued shares among the shareholders.[62] After the 1998 financial crisis, it is reported that the number of closed offers of shares doubled, while the number of public offers has decreased to one-seventh. This is said to demonstrate the process of the 'consolidation of shareholders' assets'.[63]

If the issuing of additional shares was left to the competence of the general shareholders' meeting, the resolution could be adopted by a simple majority. The 1999 Law on the Protection of the Rights of Shareholders introduced a requirement of a two-thirds majority vote of shareholders in cases of closed offers.

The 2001 amendment has introduced some changes in order to prevent abuses. Firstly, in cases where the board of directors has the power to make a decision to issue additional shares, a unanimous vote is required. In cases where the power to approve increase of capital belongs to the general shareholders' meeting, a mere majority vote is still sufficient. However, important exceptions are that for additional issues of shares and securities convertible to shares by closed offer, a qualified majority of the shareholders' meeting is now required. Additional issues of shares by public offer require a qualified majority, but only if the number exceeds 25% of the number of already issued shares (Art.39, para.3 and 4).

Secondly, existing shareholders are to be granted a right of pre-emption to purchase the newly issued shares or securities convertible to shares. Previously, only shareholders of closed joint stock companies were granted such a right; for open joint stock companies, this was not mandatory:

> Open joint stock company Transneft brought an action against a closed joint stock company Natsional'noe perestrakhovochnoe obshchestvo, asking the court to declare void the decision of its board of June 10, 1998 on the additional issue of shares by a closed offer.
>
> The Commercial Court of the City of Moscow rejected the claim; this was supported at the appellate instance. At the instance of cassation, part of the original judgment which had held valid the offer of shares to a UK company, Holbrook Insurance Brokers Limited, was quashed.
>
> Upon protest, the Supreme Commercial Court revoked the decision of the cassation instance. The Court found that the board had lawfully adopted the decision, including

---

62   Torkanovskii, *supra*, p.33.
63   Institute of Economy in Transition, *supra*, p.151.

the allocation of shares to the UK company, without having an actual meeting and that the allegation of the plaintiff that there was no board decision was groundless.

By the articles of incorporation, shareholders had been given a right of pre-emption to subscribe to newly issued shares. The plaintiff argued that the new shares were also offered to a third party, the UK company, who was not a shareholder and therefore, infringed the right of the plaintiff as a shareholder. However, the Court referred to the provision of the Law on Joint Stock Company which provided that shares of a closed joint stock company could be distributed among other persons whose scope is determined in advance. At the shareholders' meeting of April 27, 1998, the UK company in question had been chosen as a potential investor. Furthermore, the plaintiff had been offered the opportunity to exercise its right of pre-emption, but failed to do so, and did not oppose the acquisition of shares by other shareholders and third parties. The plaintiff even offered to sell shares to the above firm. At the subsequent general shareholders' meeting of the defendant company, a resolution was passed to the effect that the new shares be allocated to the above UK firm.

The Court upheld the decision of the first instance and appellate instance court which had found that the plaintiff's rights had not been infringed.[64]

As a rule, the price of shares to be issued is to be determined by the board of directors in accordance with Article 77, i.e. it is to be based upon market value. In cases where the shareholders exercise their rights of pre-emption, the price can be lower, but not below 90% of the market value (Art.36).

The capital can be decreased by the reduction of the nominal value of the shares or the reduction of the number of shares. Purchasing by the company of its own shares is one of the alternative ways of effecting the latter. Decrease of capital can also be effected by redemption of shares insofar as the articles of incorporation provide for this. The decisions to decrease the capital and to change the articles of incorporation have to be adopted by the shareholders' meeting (Art.29). Creditors must be informed; they are entitled to terminate the obligation or accelerate the maturity of the claim within thirty days of the notice (Art.30).

(2)   Shares

Joint stock companies may issue both ordinary shares and preference shares. Preference shares may not exceed 25% of the capital. Securities convertible to shares can also be issued (Art.25, para.2).

In the articles of incorporation, the total number as well as the nominal value of the issued shares must be indicated. In the articles of incorporation, the company

---

64   Decision of the Presidium of the Supreme Commercial Court, March 21, 2000, *VVAS RF*, 2000, No.6, pp.60-61.

may set a ceiling to the number of shares a single shareholder may hold and their total nominal value, as well as the maximum number of votes to be granted to a single shareholder (Art.11, para.3). This was supposedly meant to prevent concentration of excess power in a small number of shareholders.[65] The ceiling can be very low. Thus, in the oil and gas upstream company Surgutneftegaz, the maximum a single shareholder can hold is set at 1% by the articles of incorporation. In Nizhneenergo, it is 0.5%. In this way, 'undesirable outsiders' can be prevented from holding significant block of shares.[66]

It should be noted that at the time of establishment, all shares must be allocated among the founders; no public offer of shares is allowed at this stage (Art.25, para.2). In the articles of incorporation, it is possible to determine the number of shares which the company may subsequently issue, their nominal value and the category as well as the rights granted to the holders of these shares. Without such entry, the company is not entitled to issue additional shares (declared shares; Art.27, para.1). The resolution which determines the number of declared shares, if not already determined by the articles of incorporation, requires the qualified majority (three-quarters) vote of those who attend the meeting (Art.49, para.1, subpara.5). Additional shares can be issued only within this limit (Art.28, para.3).

All shares have to be registered shares; bearer shares are not permitted (Art.25). Preference shares can be issued. In the articles of incorporation, it is necessary to provide for the amount of dividend and/or amount to be paid in case of liquidation for preference shares. These amounts can be determined as a fixed sum or percentage of the nominal value. There can be several types of preference shares including cumulative preference shares (Art.32, para.2).

In order for the shareholders to exercise their rights, it is necessary that the shares be registered. The company is under an obligation to ensure the compilation and keeping of the register from the time of company registration (Art.44, para.2). Companies may entrust the keeping of the register to a 'professional participant of the securities market'. Companies which have more than 50 shareholders with voting rights must entrust the compilation and maintenance of the register to a such a registrar licensed by the Federal Securities Commission (*ibid.*, para.3). However, this does not relieve the responsibility of the company to compile and maintain the register (*ibid.*, para. 4).

The entry into the register should be effected within three days of the presentation of the necessary documents. Refusal to register is not allowed except for circumstances provided by law. The administrator of the register is obliged to

---

65   G.S.Shapkina ed., *supra*, p.53.
66   Gubin, *supra*, pp.113-114.

notify the reason of refusal to the applicant within five days of the filing of the application. The refusal and failure to register can be contested in court (Art.45).[67]

Issuing of shares and other securities is regulated by the Law on the Securities Market of 1996.[68] The agency in charge of the implementation of this Law is primarily the Federal Commission on the Securities Market. The Law provides for the licensing regime of the 'professional participants in the securities market', such as brokerage, dealing, clearing, deposits and trading. In order to issue securities, when the decision to do so has been adopted, the issuer is required to register the securities issue. If the securities are offered to an unspecified scope of investors, to a group of specified people whose number exceeds 500, or if the amount of issue exceeds 50,000 times the amount of the minimum wage, a prospectus must be prepared and registered (Law on the Securities Market, Art.19). In such cases, there is a requirement for the disclosure of relevant information (Art.23).

Disclosure is effected by providing investors information on the securities and their financial-commercial activities by a quarterly securities report and publicising material facts on an ad hoc basis (Art.30).

Unlawful issue of securities can be suspended. If the issue has been completed, it is void, and the issued securities must be retrieved by the issuer and the payment must be reimbursed to the investors (Art.26).

The problem is that this Law has not been effective enough. There is no effective sanction for the breach of disclosure requirements. The State Programme for the Protection of the Rights of Investors 1998-1999 has pointed out as follows:

> Insider trading and manipulation of prices in the securities market are regulated in an extremely lax manner. The regulation of transactions with affiliated persons is at an early stage. Regulators do not have sufficient power to ensure the implementation of the law.[69]

The Law on the Protection of the Legal Interests of Investors in the Securities Market of 1999[70] granted a power to impose fines of up to 10,000 times the minimum wage, to the Federal Commission on the Securities Market, but this is obviously insufficient.

---

67 See also the Law on the Securities Market of April 22, 1996, Article 8.
68 *SZ RF*, 1996 No.17, item 1918.
69 M.K.Treushnikov ed., *Formy zashchity prav investorov v sfere rynka tsennykh bumag*, Moscow 2000, p.294.
70 *SZ* 1999 No.10, item 1163.

(3)   Some Regulations on the Acquisition of Shares

There are some regulations on the acquisition of substantial amounts of shares by the Law on Joint Stock Companies (Art.80):[71]

    i)   A person intending to acquire 30% or more of the issued ordinary shares by himself or together with affiliated persons must notify the company of his intention in writing not earlier than 90 days but not later than 30 days before the purchase, provided that the company has more than 1,000 holders of ordinary shares.

    ii)   A person who has acquired 30% or more of the issued ordinary shares of a company with more than 1,000 holders of ordinary shares by himself or together with affiliated persons is under an obligation to offer to purchase the shares of the shareholders, as well as securities convertible to shares, at market price, but not lower than the average price for the last 6 months preceding the date of the acquisition of those shares, within 30 days of their acquisition.

By virtue of the Law on Competition and Restrictions on Monopolistic Activities of March 22, 1991, with the exception of the founders, the prior approval of, or a posterior notification to the Anti-Monopoly Agency is required for an acquisition of more than 20% of the voting shares. Prior approval is required when the total amount of assets of the acquirer and the issuer exceeds 100,000 times the minimum monthly wage. If the total amount exceeds 50,000 times the minimum monthly wage, a posterior notification is needed.

The Law on the Central Bank provides that if a person or a group of persons acquires more than 5% of the shares of a credit institution, the Central Bank has to be notified, and if the amount exceeds 29%, the central bank's prior approval is needed.

Companies which have acquired more than 20% of the shares of a joint stock company are under an obligation to publicise the fact without delay.

(4)   Bonds and other Securities

Joint stock companies may issue bonds and other securities by the decision of the board of directors. Bonds and other securities convertible to shares can be issued by the decision of the board of directors or the general shareholders' meeting, depending on the articles of incorporation (Art.33, paras. 1 and 2). The total nominal value of the issued bonds and securities may not exceed the capital, or the largest security provided to a third party by the company for the flotation

---

[71]   In general, see A.Bushev and O.Skvortsov, *Aktsionernoe pravo*, Moscow 1997, pp.44-52.

of bonds. Bonds can be secured or non-secured. Non-secured bonds can be issued by companies not earlier than their third year in existence, and on the condition that by then, two annual balance sheets were duly approved (*ibid.*, para.3).

(5)   Acquisition of the company's own shares

Acquisition by the company of its own shares is subject to restrictions. Companies may acquire its own shares in order to reduce the capital by a resolution of the shareholders' meeting, insofar as the articles of incorporation provide for this. These shares have to be redeemed once they are acquired (Art.72, paras.1 and 3). Companies may also acquire its own shares by the decision of the board of directors, unless otherwise provided by law or articles of incorporation. However, this is not possible if the nominal value of the shares which are in circulation is less than 90% of the share capital (*ibid.*, para.2). Shares acquired by the decision of the board must be sold within one year of acquisition; otherwise, the general shareholders' meeting must adopt a resolution to reduce the capital by redeeming the shares or increase the nominal value of remaining shares and thus maintain the amount of capital (*ibid.*, para.3).

The decision of the company to acquire its own shares must specify the types and the amount of shares to be acquired, the price of acquisition, the manner and date of payment, and the period during which shares will be acquired. This period has to be more than 30 days. Once the decision to acquire shares has been adopted, every shareholder is entitled to sell the shares to the company and the company is under obligation to purchase them. If the total amount of shares requested by the shareholders to be purchased exceeds the number of shares which the company may acquire, shares are purchased in proportion to the amount each shareholder has requested to be purchased (*ibid.*, para.4).

However, companies may not acquire their own shares in the following cases (Art.73):

i)   when the capital has not been fully paid in;
ii)   when, at the time of acquisition, there is a symptom of insolvency or where such a symptom will emerge upon acquisition;
iii) when, at the time of acquisition, net assets are less than the capital, the reserve fund and the difference between the liquidation value of preferential shares and the nominal value.

(6)   Dividends

Dividends are paid out from the net profit of the current year. Dividends for preference shares may be paid out of a specific fund designated for this purpose

(Art.42, paras. 1 and 2). The decision to pay an annual dividend, including the amount and the method of payment, is adopted by a general shareholders' meeting. The amount of an annual dividend may not exceed the amount recommended by the board of directors (*ibid.*, para.3).

Dividends may not be paid until the capital has been fully paid in, and the company has purchased all the shares from shareholders when they exercise their appraisal rights (Art.43, para.1). Also in cases where there is a symptom of insolvency on the day of the adoption of the resolution, or if, as a result of the dividend payment, there will be a symptom of insolvency, such a resolution cannot be adopted. The same applies when, on the day of payment, the net value of assets is less than the capital, the reserve fund, and the difference between the liquidation value and the nominal value of preferential shares combined. The actual payment cannot be made either, if such circumstances exist on the day of payment (*ibid.*, paras.1 and 4).

In reality, far from all Russian companies pay dividends, primarily because of low profitability or emergence of loss. Companies which have a high liquidity and income are very limited. It is reported that there are companies which manipulate circumstances in order to make no profit, e.g. by transfer pricing, and therefore, pay no tax or dividend, and accumulate the profit elsewhere by using various schemes including off-shore companies. Profit from such a scheme goes only to the shareholder which has a controlling stake in the company. Others are not privy to this 'extra-dividend income'.[72]

4)   Shareholders' rights

(1)   Basic Rules

The basic provision of the Law on Joint Stock Companies on shareholders' rights provides as follows (Art.31):

> Each ordinary share of the company grants the shareholder – possessor of the share – the same range of rights.
> The shareholder-possessor of ordinary shares, in accordance with the present Federal Law and the articles of incorporation, may take part in the general shareholders' meeting with the right to vote on all matters within the competence of the meeting, and has the right to receive dividends and the right to receive part of the assets in case of liquidation.

---

72   Mateleva, *supra*, p.72.

However, a commentary to the Law on Joint Stock Companies described the actual state of the protection of shareholders' rights as follows:

> The practice of application of the Law on Joint Stock Companies has demonstrated that in reality, in large joint stock companies which are banks, insurance companies, and investment funds....... and in companies established as a result of privatisation, it has become a rule to fend off a majority of shareholders from participating in the management of the respective organisation. Infringement of the proprietary rights of the shareholders of these organisations is not rare.[73]

Since Russian companies tend to be dominated by insiders, the management often ignores the shareholders' rights in order to maintain control over the company. A survey in Russia shows that the dominating role in the management as well as in the distribution of the profits was played by the top executives of these companies; second came the 'higher management (*administratsiia*)'. It was pointed out that 'all these things such as registrars of shares acting in bad faith, flagrant breach of laws (which themselves are 'super liberal' for the management), manipulation of the procedure for the general shareholders' meeting, allow us to talk about the dominance of the top executives'.[74]

Foreign investors have been concerned about the flagrant violations of shareholders' rights by major Russian companies. OECD has been making efforts to facilitate improvements in this area. In 2000, it arranged a symposium with the participation of officials from the Federal Commission on the Securities Market. A White Paper on Russian corporate governance is being prepared. The Federal Commission is working on a code of corporate conduct in line with the OECD Code of Corporate Behaviour. In the meantime, some organisations have conducted research on the state of corporate governance in Russia. According to these surveys, typical breaches include:[75]

i)   unlawful refusal of share registration;
ii)   preventing shareholders from taking part and voting in the shareholders' meeting;
iii) dilution of shares of existing shareholders by the issuing of additional shares;
iv)   asset-stripping by transfer pricing and other means, by holding companies;
v)   conflict of interests and abuses of power by directors and the members of the executive bodies.

---

73   Tikhomirov ed., *supra*, p.11.
74   G.Klein, 'Upravlenie korporativnymi predpriiatiiami v perekhodnoi ekonomike', *VE* !999 No.8, p.68.
75   Institute of Corporate Law and Corporate Governance ed., *Corporate Governance in Russia*, Moscow 2000, pp.5-9; C.Sprenger, 'Corporate Governance in Russia', *European Economic Trends*, 2000, No.2, pp.7-8; A.Ledeneva, *Unwritten rules: How Russia really works*, London 2001, pp.17-31.

Arbitrary refusal of registration was rampant and presidential decrees had to be issued to address the problem:

> Irkutsk Mebel' brought an action against a company, Primorsk, for the refusal to include the plaintiff in the shareholders' register. A voucher investment fund, 'Vozrozhdenie' acquired 2,400 shares of Primorsk at a share auction. The shares were sold to a company called 'Rossiia' and then to the plaintiff, Irkutsk Mebel'. Primorsk refused the registration of shares held by the plaintiff, arguing that since Rossiia had not been registered as a shareholder, it therefore had no power to assign the shares to the plaintiff. Lower courts upheld the argument of the defendant, but the Supreme Commercial Court quashed the lower court's decision. Primorsk was under an obligation to register the plaintiff, since documents supporting the title to the shares had been presented, and no request for further documents had been made, but nevertheless, Primorsk failed to register the plaintiff within three days as required by the statute.[76]

The Law on the Protection of Rights and Legal Interest of Investors in the Securities Market of 1999 introduced fines for breaches of regulations on the registration of shares. In practice, in order to manipulate the register and eliminate 'undesirable' shareholders, manipulation of the register often takes place:

> Management company Sibirskii Variant brought an action against Kirovskii Shinnyi Zavod and the registrar of its shares, the Kirov branch of the Sberegatel'nyi Bank, asking the court to declare void the contract of sale of shares of the defendant company of March 25, 1997. The plaintiff was a shareholder of the defendant company until, under this agreement, the shares were sold to the defendant company. The plaintiff argued that this transaction was void, since the general director of the defendant company signed this agreement on behalf of the plaintiff as well as the defendant. Furthermore, the purchase of its own shares by the defendant company was effected against the Law on Joint Stock Companies. The first instance court dismissed the claim. This was supported at the appellate instance. Upon protest, the Supreme Commercial Court quashed the decision of the lower court, found the transaction to be void, and ordered the plaintiff company to be restored in the register.[77]

The independence of share registrars is said to be still problematic.[78] In another case, the Supreme Commercial Court found a removal from the share register

---

76   Decision of the Presidium of the Supreme Commercial Court, June 18, 1996 (cited in Bushev et al., *supra*, pp.135-137).

77   Decision of the Presidium of the Supreme Commercial Court, January 27, 1998 (cited in Gubin, *supra*, pp.178-179). .

78   Sprenger, *supra*, p.9.

by the registrar – a bank – without the entrustment and instruction of the share-holder, void.[79]

Shareholders have the right to take part in the management of the company. One of the most basic rights in this respect is the right to take part in the share-holders' meeting and vote. In reality, in Russia, it is not uncommon that even the right to participate in the shareholders' meeting is restricted or denied to some shareholders. Shareholders were often denied participation in the general share-holders' meeting out of purely technical reasons such as the failure to present their passport. In some companies, employee shareholders, who left the job, were not allowed to take part in the shareholders' meeting.[80]

It is not rare for a general shareholders' meeting to be held without the know-ledge of a significant number of shareholders:

A resolution to liquidate the company was taken at the shareholders' meeting of a closed joint stock company with foreign participation. A foreign investor, who held 49% of the shares, brought an action, asking the court to declare the resolution void, since this foreign shareholder had not been notified of the shareholders' meeting and the resolution adopted there. The first instance court and the court of the appellate instance dismissed the claim on the ground that a representative of the foreign company was present at the meeting, and that the power of attorney had been properly prepared. However, the court of the cassation instance quashed the judgment and reversed it to the lower court. The court found that the information on the share holders' meeting and its agenda were not properly sent to the foreign company but instead, were sent to a company represent-ing this foreign company in Moscow in the name of a Russian individual. On the other hand, the articles of incorporation of the joint venture provided that a resolution of liquidation should be made with explicit agreement of the parties and should be notarised. At the shareholders' meeting, a Russian individual, who merely had the power to perform 'commercial and representative functions', was present. This person did not have the power to represent the foreign company in liquidating the joint venture.[81]

Various irregularities involving shareholders' meetings are reported:

Russia's second largest oil company, Yukos, voted to cause a 194% share dilution of its subsidiary Yugeskneftegaz and also voted to seize oil revenues and assets belonging to this company. The largest minority shareholder of Yugeskneftegaz was barred from voting at the extraordinary shareholders' meeting. After minority shareholders were denied entry, the shareholder's meeting, dominated by Yukos, approved the massive

---

79   Decision of the Presidium of the Supreme Commercial Court, November 17, 1998 [Garant].

80   Institute of Corporate Law and Corporate Governance ed., *supra*, pp.5-6.

81   'Obzor praktiki razresheniia arbitrazhnymi sudami sporov sviazanykh s zashchitoi inostrannykh investorov', informatsionnoe pis'mo VAS RF, January 18,2001, item 8 [Inforis].

additional share issue in a closed subscription to unknown companies for promissory notes which had not been independently valued.[82]

Commercial bank Baltvneshtorgbank brought an action at the commercial court against a closed joint stock company Panikora to have the resolution of the general shareholders' meeting of July 27, 1998, and clause 3.1 of the articles of incorporation, declared void. Clause 3.1 contained information that A.N.Parikov was a shareholder who held 946 shares which comprised 70% of the shares. The plaintiff bank argued that the actual owner of the shares was the Bank, and not Parikov. The general shareholders' meeting of July 27, 1998, which appointed L.V.Parikova as a general director and approved the new version of the articles of incorporation, was held without the participation of the Bank. Votes based upon the shares of the Bank were exercised unlawfully by another person. The provincial commercial court acknowledged the claim. Upon protest, the Supreme Commercial Court reversed the judgment and referred the case to a new hearing. The Supreme Commercial Court did acknowledge that the shares in question did not belong to A.N.Parikov, and that the Bank had the title to them, and therefore, the articles of incorporation and the resolution of the general shareholders' meeting of July 27, 1998 were void. The Supreme Court, however, reversed the judgment, since A.N.Parikov, whose rights were affected by the procedure and who had a registered right on the disputed shares, had not been part of this procedure.[83]

Concerning shareholders'meetings, shareholders also have the following rights:

i)   the right to become acquainted with the agenda before the shareholders' meeting (Art.52, para.3);

ii)   The right to have an issue added to the agenda (*ibid.*, para.1)

iii) The right to demand an extraordinary shareholders' meeting (1% of the shares required) (Art.55, para.1)

The rights of shareholders to take part in the management of the company also include the right to elect and be elected to the board of directors and the audit committee.

In order to exercise their rights, shareholders need to have access to information. The Law on Joint Stock Companies provides for the following rights:

i)   shareholders with 1% or more shares may inspect the list of persons who are entitled to take part in the shareholders' meeting (Art.51, para.4);

ii)   the right to have access to documents as provided in Article 89 (Art.91).

---

82   *Alexander's Gas and Oil Companies*, April 28, 1999.
83   Decision of the Presidium of the Supreme Commercial Court, *VVAS RF*, 2000 No.12, pp.42-43.

Documents available for inspection include documents of significance such as the documents which certify the right of ownership of the company over the assets on the balance sheet, the internal rules of the company, documents of account, the protocol of the general shareholders' meeting, the board of directors, the audit committee and the collective executive body, and opinions of the audit committee and auditors as well as state and municipal financial control agencies (Art.89). By the 2001 amendment, access to documents of account and protocol of the corporate bodies was restricted to shareholders with 25% or more of shares (Art.91, para.1).

In practice, companies are often reluctant to disclose information to the shareholders. The problem is that there is no sanction against companies which fail to comply with the requirements, although this is regarded as a 'serious violation of shareholder's rights'.[84]

At Gazprom, representatives of minority shareholders raised the issue of the relationship of Gazprom with a company group called Itera (a group of more than 100 companies) and Stroitransgaz. The basic criticism was that the Gazprom management had transferred assets from Gazprom to companies affiliated with them. However, information on the affiliation of the Gazprom management with the Itera group was not made available to the shareholders.[85]

Before the 2001 amendment, companies were under an obligation to disclose, *inter alia*, a list of persons affiliated with the company along with the number and type of shares which belonged to this person. This requirement has been dropped by the amendment.

(2)   Remedies available to Shareholders

Shareholders have the right to take measures to rectify unlawful actions of the company and its bodies. Shareholders' rights in this context include:

i)   the right to contest the validity of a resolution of the general shareholders' meeting which is against the law, other legal acts as well as the articles of incorporation, provided that the shareholder voted against the resolution or was absent at the meeting, and that the resolution infringes the right and lawful interest of the shareholder (Art.49, para.8);

---

84   G.S.Shapkina ed., *supra*, p.259.
85   Radygin, *supra,* p.30.

   ii)   the right to contest the lawfulness of a resolution of the meeting of the board
          of directors and the executive bodies;
   iii)   the right to a shareholder's action (Art.71)

Concerning i), there is a conspicuous omission in the provisions on the procedure of corporate litigation. If, for instance, the validity of the resolution of the general shareholders' meeting was denied, the effect of the decision should have an effect not only between the parties, but on everybody. Otherwise, there will be a number of actions involving the same resolution but resulting in different conclusions. The possibility of other shareholders joining in the action has to be addressed at the same time. These provisions are completely missing. The same applies to the shareholder's action (see *infra*). By the 2001 amendment, a requirement that the action must be initiated within 6 months after the shareholder became aware, or should have become aware of the resolution, was introduced (Art.49, para.8).

Furthermore, the jurisdiction of such cases – whether it is the commercial court or the ordinary court, which has jurisdiction – is not clear:

> Closed joint stock company Russkii Khrom brought an action to the commercial court as one of the shareholders, asking the court to declare void the decision of an open joint stock company, Mostvormet, of June 6, 1997 to issue securities. There was a letter of the Federal Commission on the Securities Market which supported the view of the plaintiff that this decision was against the Law on Joint Stock Companies. However, the Commercial Court of the City of Moscow terminated the procedure on the ground that the action may involve the interests of other shareholders, who are physical persons, and that therefore, the commercial court did not have jurisdiction. The court of appellate instance upheld this decision. It was only when the case reached the Supreme Commercial Court that the jurisdiction of the commercial court on this matter was acknowledged. However, it is not clear what would happen if another shareholder brings an action in the ordinary court.[86]

Regarding ii), there is no explicit provision in the Law on Joint Stock Companies (unlike in the Law on Limited Liability Companies) to this effect. However, the joint decision of the Plenum of the Supreme Commercial Court and the Supreme Court of the Russian Federation provides that shareholders may contest the validity of the decisions of the board of directors and executive bodies in all circumstances where the decision is against the law and infringes the rights and lawful interests of the shareholder.[87]

---

86   Decision of the Presidium of the Supreme Commercial Court, August 3, 1999 [Garant],

87   Joint Decision, April 2, 1997, *supra*, item 10, in Zhurakovskii and Kalinin, *supra*, p.53.

The court is entitled to maintain the effect of the contested resolution by taking into account various circumstances; if the vote of the shareholder/plaintiff would not have influenced the resolution, the breach was not essential, and the resolution did not cause damage to the company (*ibid.*):

> A shareholder who held 12% of the shares of Uralstal' konstruktsiia brought an action against the company in the commercial court, asking the court to declare void the resolution of the shareholders' meeting which took place without his participation. The shareholder was not informed of the date or agenda of the shareholders' meeting. These facts were ascertained by the court. However, the court found the resolution to be valid, because the procedural flaw could not have influenced the outcome.[88]

The protection by the court may not be timely:

> A closed joint stock company, Andreevskii Torgovyi Dom, brought an action against another closed joint stock company LDM, in which the plaintiff is a shareholder, claiming that the resolution of the general shareholders' meeting was adopted without its participation, and therefore, should be declared void. The defendant company argued that the plaintiff was not a shareholder, since the transfer of shares to the plaintiff which took place in 1992 was invalid. In fact, the plaintiff had taken part in the general shareholders' meeting for several years, without any objection from the company until the general shareholders' meeting in question. The commercial court of first instance found the resolution to be void, since there was a breach of the shareholder's rights. In the appellate instance, the judgment was reversed – the court ruled that the plaintiff was not a shareholder of the company. This was supported by the cassation instance. Finally, upon a protest from the first deputy president of the Supreme Commercial Court, the Supreme Commercial Court quashed the judgment of the appellate instance and upheld the judgement of the first instance court.[89]

(3)   Transfer of Shares and Appraisal Rights

Shareholders have the right to withdraw from the company by assigning shares. Shareholders of both open and closed type joint stock companies enjoy this right, although there are some differences. While in open joint stock companies, there is no restriction, in closed joint stock companies, other shareholders have a right of pre-emption to purchase shares offered for sale by a shareholder. Terms of the

---

88   Mateleva, *supra*, p.159.
89   Decision of the Presidium of the Supreme Commercial Court, April 22, 1997 (cited in Gubin, *supra*, pp.173-175).

sale will be the same as the terms between the seller and a third party (Civil Code Art.97).[90]

Shareholders also have the right to require the company to purchase their shares (an appraisal right) in the following cases (ComC Art.75, para.1):

i) Reorganisation of the company, or effecting of major transactions which require the approval of the shareholders meeting, in which the shareholder voted against the reorganisation or major transaction, was absent;

ii) Changes, supplements to the articles of incorporation, or the adoption of new articles of incorporation, which the shareholder voted against, or did not attend the shareholders' meeting

The company is under an obligation to inform shareholders of their right to have their shares purchased by the company, as well as the price and the methods of exercising their right. Shares are purchased at the price determined by the board of directors, but not lower than their market value which is determined by an independent valuer without taking into account the changes caused by the incidents which gave rise to the appraisal right (*ibid.,* para.3).

5)   Structure of the Management

(1)   General Shareholders' Meeting

The highest body of the company is the general shareholders' meeting (Art.47, para.1). The annual shareholders' meeting takes place once a year, more than 2 months, but no later than 6 months after the end of the financial year. At the annual meeting, members of the board of directors and the audit committee are elected, the auditor is confirmed, and the annual report as well as other documents submitted by the board are examined.

The exclusive competence of the general shareholders' meeting includes (Art.48, para.1):

i)   changes and supplements to the articles of incorporation or adoption of new articles of incorporation;

ii)   reorganisation of the company;

iii) liquidation of the company, appointment of the liquidation committee and approval of the interim and final liquidation account;

---

90   O.Sadikov ed., *Kommentarii k grazhdanskomu kodeksu RF, chasti pervoi,* first edition, Moscow 1997, p.132.

iv)   determination of the number of members of the board of directors, election of the members and the early termination of their power;

v)   determination of the number, nominal value and types of declared shares;

vi)   increase of capital by raising the nominal value or issuing additional shares; in the latter case, only if it is not entrusted to the board of directors by articles of incorporation;

vii)   decrease of capital;

viii)   formation of the executive body and early termination of its power, provided that this power is not delegated to the board of directors by articles of incorporation;

ix)   election of the members of the audit committee and the early termination of its power, unless the power does not belong to the board of directors under the articles of incorporation;

x)   approval of the auditor;

xi)   approval of the annual report, balance sheet, profit and loss report, and the proposal of the distribution of profits and loss;

xii)   division and consolidation of shares;

xiii)   approval of transactions with interested parties;

xiv)   approval of major transactions in cases provided by articles 79 and 83;

xv)   approval of acquisition of own shares by the company;

xvi)   approval of participation in a holding company group, financial industrial group, associations etc;

xvii)   adoption of internal rules which regulate the activities of corporate bodies.

Exclusive competence in this context means that these issues cannot be delegated to the executive body. The same applies to delegation to the board of directors, except that the increase of capital by issuing new shares can be delegated to the board (Art.48, para.2).

While the resolution, as a rule, is adopted by a simple majority, items i) – iii), v), and xiv) have to be adopted by a qualified majority – three quarters of those present (Art.49, para.4).

Previously, the notice of the meeting could be effected either by sending shareholders a written notice or by publication of information. Sometimes, the notice was published in a regional newspaper which no one but those who lived there had access to. Under the 2001 amendment, in principle, each shareholder has to be sent a notice by registered mail, but only insofar as the articles of incorporation do not provide otherwise. When the notice is published in the media, the medium has to be accessible to all (Art.52, para.1).

Materials to be sent to shareholders include the annual report of accounting including the opinion of the audit committee and auditor, a draft resolution of the meeting, as well as information on candidates for the board and the audit committee (*ibid.*, para.3).

Although it is rather unusual in other jurisdictions, the resolution of the shareholders' meeting does not have to be taken by holding an actual meeting (*zaochnoe golosovanie*) (Art.50). Reportedly, this has been practised since joint stock companies came into existence in the post-socialist period.

An extraordinary shareholders' meeting can be convened by the decision of the board of directors on its own initiative, by request of the audit committee, auditor, or a shareholder with more than 10% shares. Extraordinary meetings by the request of the audit committee, auditor, or a shareholder have to be convened within 40 days of the request. The decision to convene or not to convene the meeting must be taken within 5 days of the request (Art.55, paras. 1 and 6). The board may refuse the convocation of a meeting on the following grounds (*ibid.,* para.6):

i)   the procedure for submitting the request was not followed;

ii)   the shareholder did not hold 10% of the shares;

iii) none of the issues proposed to be discussed at the meeting fell within the competence of the shareholders' meeting or they were against the law.

The quorum for the general shareholders' meeting is shareholders representing more than 50% of issued shares (Art.58, para.1). Shareholders who are on the list of shareholders are entitled to take part in the general shareholders' meeting. The list is compiled on the basis of the shareholders' register at the time determined by the board of directors. This date cannot be earlier than the decision of the board to convene the general shareholders' meeting, and cannot be more than 60 days ahead of the meeting (Art.51, para.1).

Shareholders may take part in the shareholders' meeting personally, or through a representative. Shareholders are free to select the representative; this right cannot be restricted by the articles of incorporation. However, in some companies such as Gazprom, the articles of incorporation provide that representatives can only be other shareholders or officers of the company.[91]

In principle, one voting share is entitled to one vote. A significant exception is that under the articles of incorporation, it is possible to limit the maximum number of votes given to a single shareholder (Art.11, para.3). Incidentally, similar provisions can be found in German and French law.

---

91   Tikhomirov, *supra*, p.262.

(2)   *Management Bodies: Board of directors and executive bodies*

(i)   *An overview*

Generally, the systems of corporate governance in the industrialised world can be divided into two types; a single tier system and a two tier system. In a single tier system, the management of the business and its supervision are both entrusted to a single body, i.e. the board of directors. In contrast, in a two tier system, these functions are separated; there is a board of directors which manages the business, and a supervisory board, which supervises the activities of the board of directors. In Anglo-American jurisdictions, the single tier system is adopted, while the two tier system is found in the Civil Law countries. However, the system varies from country to country. US companies are supposed to be in the single tier group, but in fact, boards of directors in the United States tend to perform more supervisory functions than management, whereas the management function is carried out by executive officers.

In the Tsarist period, Russian companies were run by an executive body – the management council (*pravlenie*) – whose members were called directors. There was no board of directors. The 1922 RSFSR Civil Code inherited this system of management councils. In contrast, the 1927 Statute on Joint Stock Companies provided for i) a *pravlenie* or a single director, and ii) a board (*sovet*), if the articles of incorporation provide for it. The *pravlenie* were to 'manage all matters and assets of the company' and effect transactions and operations in the name of the company and thus represent the company (Art.87). The board (*sovet*) was set up for 'general direction of affairs and supervision over the activities of the *pravlenie* in accordance with the articles of incorporation' (Art.95).[92] In this sense, the board was closer to the supervisory board, rather than the board of directors.

In the present Law on Joint Stock Companies, the system is complicated. There are the board of directors, and single and collective executive bodies. The board of directors is referred to with 'supervisory board' in brackets. This is confusing, since in Anglo-American countries, while there are boards of directors, there are no supervisory boards, and in the Civil Law countries, the board of directors co-exists with the supervisory board. Czech, Hungarian and Polish company laws have both, although the supervisory board is not always mandatory. In the German *Aktiengesetz*, for instance, it is explicitly provided that the supervisory board is to supervise the management of business.[93] There is no equivalent provision in Russian law.

---

92   *SZ SSSR*, 1927 No.49, item 500.
93   Art.111, para.1, *Aktiengesetz*.

The confusion is compounded by the fact that executive bodies are called directors, or general directors, and in their collective form, management councils or directorates. However, they are not necessarily members of the board of directors. In fact, the term general director seems to come from the socialist period when a single official ran the state enterprise on the basis of 'single responsibility (*edinolichnost'*)'.

(ii) Board of Directors

In Russia, the board of directors determines the general orientation of corporate activities, except for matters reserved for the general shareholders' meeting (Art.64, para.1). The board of directors is not mandatory; in companies with less than 50 shareholders with a vote, the function of the board can be substituted by the general shareholders' meeting (*ibid.*).

Members of the board of directors are appointed by the general shareholders' meeting. Shareholders who holds no less than 2% of voting shares are entitled to propose candidates for membership of the board (as well as the collective executive body and the audit committee). The number of proposed candidates should not exceed the total number of directors (Art.53, para.1).

According to a commentary, the board combines the supervisory function (supervision over the executive body) and the decision-making function on specific problems concerning the activities of the company, e.g. conclusion of major transactions.[94] Thus, the system is considered to be a single-tier system. The most important power of the board of directors in supervising the executive bodies is the appointment and dismissal of the executive bodies.

The board of directors decides on the following matters (Art.65, para.2):

i)   determination of the priority directions of the company's activities;
ii)   convocation of the annual and extraordinary shareholders' meeting;
iii)   approval of the agenda of the general shareholders' meeting;
iv)   determination of the date of the compilation of the list of shareholders who are entitled to take part in the shareholders' meeting;
v)   increase of capital by additional issue of shares in cases where this power has been delegated by the articles of incorporation;
vi)   issuing of bonds and other securities;
vii)   determination of the value of assets, issuing price of shares, and the price of sale of securities in cases provided by the present Law;
viii)   acquisition of issued shares, bonds and other securities in cases provided by the present Law;

---

94   Tikhomirov, *supra*, p.277.

ix)   formation of the executive body of the company and its early termination if the articles of incorporation grant this power to the board;

x)   recommendation as to the remuneration of audit committee members and the auditor;

xi)   recommendation as to the amount of dividends and the method of their payment;

xii) use of the reserve fund and other funds;

xiii) approval of internal documents of the company except those documents which the general shareholders' meeting has the power to approve;

xiv) establishment of branches and representative offices;

xv)   endorsement of major transactions in cases provided by Chapter 11 of the Law;

xvi) endorsement of transactions provided in Chapter 12 of the Law, i.e. transaction with interested parties;

xvii) approval of the registrar and the determination of remuneration.

These matters which fall within the exclusive competence of the board cannot be delegated to the executive body (*ibid.*):

> An open joint stock company Surugutskii Gas Refinery brought an action in the Moscow Commercial Court against a closed joint stock company UKBGI Bank, asking the court to declare void a contract for acquisition of a share in the capital of the latter. The Refinery had acquired a share in the Bank when the Bank was a limited liability company. The Refinery argued that the contract had been signed by its general director without the consent of the board of directors against Article 65 of the Law on Joint Stock Companies [before the 2001 amendment], which provided that the decision on the participation of the company in other organisations etc. was the exclusive competence of the board.
>
> The lower courts acknowledged the claim of the plaintiff. However, upon protest, the Supreme Commercial Court reversed the judgment. The Supreme Commercial Court ruled that the provision in question covered only the 'participation' in another organisation, and did not extend to 'withdrawal'. Since this provision has an exhaustive list of matters which fall within the exclusive competence of the board, it should be interpreted literally, and such an extensive interpretation should not be allowed.[95]

The number of the members of the board for companies with more than one thousand shareholders with a vote, has to be at least seven directors, while if the number of such shareholders is more than ten thousand, there has to be at least 10 directors (Art.66, para.3). The maximum number of directors is to be determined by the articles of incorporation.

---

95   Decision of the Presidium of the Supreme Commercial Court, January 23, 2001, *VVAS* 2001 No.5, pp.36-37.

There is no statutory requirement for the qualification of a director. It is left
to the companies to determine the requirements under the articles of incorporation.
For example, it is possible to provide that directors can only be those shareholders
who have more than 10% of the shares.[96] There are some restrictions under other
laws, such as the Law on the Fundamentals of Government Officials which
prohibits government officials from becoming directors unless so entrusted by
the government.[97]

Irregularities are often seen in the process of appointing board members:

> A group of shareholders initiated an action at a district court in the City of Moscow
> asking the court to declare void a resolution of the general shareholders' meeting of
> a joint stock company SELP. In the shareholders' meeting in 1994, the selection of the
> board members was on the agenda, but none of the candidates obtained the votes
> required. Therefore, it was resolved that a second shareholders' meeting was to be held.
> However, not all shareholders received the notice for the second shareholders' meeting.
> Shareholders who were previously members of the workers' collective and later dismissed
> were not informed of the meeting; the total number of shares held by them exceeded
> 50%.
>
> The executive body of the joint stock company SELP failed to include the candidates
> proposed by the shareholders who were suing the company in the list of candidates for
> the members of the board, despite the fact that there were no flaws in the procedure
> to put forward the candidates. The company claimed that the signatures of the proposal
> had been forged.[98]

Directors may be elected by cumulative voting. In a company with more than
one thousand shareholders with a vote, cumulative voting is mandatory (Art.66,
para.4).

The chairman of the board of directors is elected by the members from among
themselves. The chairman organises the work of the board, convenes the board
and presides over it, and also presides over the general shareholders' meeting
unless otherwise provided by the articles of incorporation (Art.67, paras. 1 and 2).

The meeting of the board is convened by the chairman on his own initiative,
but also upon request of the members of the board of directors, audit committee,
or the auditor, executive body of the company and other persons provided by the
articles of incorporation. The board meeting can be held without an actual meeting.
The quorum can be set by the articles of incorporation, but cannot be less than
50% (Art.68, paras. 1 and 2).

---

96   Shapkina, *supra*, p.188.
97   *SZ* 1995 No.31, item 2990.
98   Mateleva, *supra*, pp.164-165.

(iii)   Executive Bodies

Current activities of the company are directed by a single executive body (director or general director) or a single executive body and a collective executive body (management council (*pravlenie*), directorate(*direktsiia*)). The executive body of the company organises the implementation of the resolutions of the general shareholders' meeting and the board of directors (Article 69, para.2). A single executive body is entitled to act on behalf of the company without power of attorney; more specifically, the executive body is empowered to represent the interests of the company, effect transactions in the name of the company, approve the number of personnel, issue instructions and orders which are binding on all employees (Art.69, para.2).

Executive bodies are appointed and dismissed by the resolution of the general shareholders' meeting, unless this power is given to the board of directors by the articles of incorporation (Art.69, para.3).

Apart from the provision which defines the function of the executive body to be the 'directing of the current activities of the company', there is no explicit provision on the power of the executive bodies. Details of the power of the executive bodies are left to the articles of incorporation.[99] Typical issues which fall within the portfolio of an executive body include the following:

i)   arrangement of an effective operational management of the current business of the company;

ii) arrangement for the conducting of the general shareholders' meeting and the meeting of the board of directors;

iii) preparation and realisation of the company's current business strategy for the purpose of increasing profitability and competitiveness;

iv) preparation and submission to the board of directors of the business plan of the company, financial documents including the balance sheet, the profit and loss report and the proposal for the distribution of the profit and loss;

v)   preparation and submission to the board of directors of draft internal rules and instructions.

If there are both single and collective executive bodies, the articles of incorporation must determine the scope of the power of each body. In such cases, the single executive body, i.e. the director or general director, also combines the function of the chairman of the collective executive body. By the resolution of the general shareholders' meeting, the power of the executive body may be entrusted to a

---

99   Sahpkina, *supra*, p.195.

commercial management organisation or an individual entrepreneur by agreement (Art.69, para.1).

The relationship between the members of the executive body and the company is governed by a contract which is categorised as an employment contract. The contract is signed on behalf of the company by the chairman of the board or a person empowered to do so by the board. The general shareholders' meeting may terminate this contract at any time (Art.69, paras.3 and 4).

Members of the collective executive body may not form a majority of the board of directors. A person who is the single executive body may not simultaneously be the chairman of the board of directors (Art.66, para.2).

> In Gazprom, the articles of incorporation provide that members of the management council (*pravlenie*) can be dismissed by a unanimous vote of the board of directors. However, these people are simultaneously board members, and therefore, a unanimous vote is unlikely to be achieved. This arrangement was contested in the commercial court, which ruled this clause to be against the law. Gazprom reportedly intends to change it to a majority vote, but this will not change the situation, since six management council members occupy the 11 member board of directors.[100]

The actual arrangement of executive bodies differs from company to company. For example, in Gazprom, there is a management council (*pravlenie*) which is a collective executive body, and a chairman, who appears to be the single executive body. In contrast to the management council, the board of directors has outsiders as members, namely because the state still holds a significant portion of its shares. In 1998, the chairman of the board of directors was the Minister of State Property, and the members include the Minister of Fuel and Energy, a professor, the first deputy minister of finance and a local governor. Chairmen of the management council of group companies such as Gazprombank are also members of the board. Of the 25 members of the board of directors at Gazprom, 15 were members of the management council.[101] This was apparently against the Law on Joint Stock Companies which required that members of the collective executive body may not occupy a majority of the member of the board. The Unified Energy System also has a collective executive body in the form of a management council. Members of its board of directors include outsiders such as government and local government officials, while members of the management council do not have a majority on the board.[102] In contrast, Lukoil does not appear to have a management council; instead, it has a single executive body in the person of the president

---

100   *NG*, June 20, 2000.
101   www.gazprom.ru
102   http://ues.elktra.ru

and vice presidents. Its board of directors has outsiders such as the deputy minister for energy, but on the other hand, the president and all vice presidents are simultaneously board members.[103]

(iv)   The Relationship Between the Board and the Executive Body

The Law is almost silent on the relationship between the board of directors and the executive body. A Russian expert raised a question- on whose behalf and against whom does the board perform a supervisory function?[104] In Germany, the supervisory board supervises the board of directors. In Russia, this is not possible, since the board of directors and the supervisory board are one and the same body. Therefore, if the board is to have any supervisory function, it has to be supervising the executive bodies. It was only by the 2001 amendment that a provision to the effect that the executive bodies are subordinate to the board of directors and the general shareholders' meeting was introduced (Art.69, para.1).

In fact, by statute, the board of directors is by no means under an obligation to supervise the activities of the executive bodies in implementing the resolutions of the shareholders' meeting and decisions of the board of directors. Executive bodies, in principle, are controlled by no one, except that they are appointed and dismissed by the board of directors.[105] It is pointed out in Russia that an unsupervised executive body will always sooner or later start ignoring the interests of the company which it manages, more and more subjecting their activities to their own interest which it places above the interests of the company. 'If appropriate measures are not taken, the financial state of the company will start deteriorating'.[106]

The same applies to the relationship between the single and collective executive bodies. One commentator suggests that in practice, the collective executive body has failed to become an independent executive body; it continues to be a body subordinated to the single executive body – the general director.[107]

Under the socialist system, state enterprises were run by the general director under the 'one man management' system, assisted by some officers. There was no effective control over the management. This may still be the case.

---

103   www.lukoil.com
104   Krapivin and Vlasov, *supra*, p.163.
105   *Ibid.*
106   *Ibid.*, p.164.
107   S.Mogilevskii, *supra*, pp.144-145.

6)   Restraints on the Power of the Executive Bodies

As mentioned above, abuse of power by the management of the company at the cost of shareholders is not uncommon in Russia. The Law accommodates two basic means of control over the activities of the management, namely the executive bodies.

(1)   Major Transactions

Approval of the board of directors or the general shareholders' meeting is required in effecting transactions which qualify as 'major transactions (*krupnyie sdelki*)'. Major transactions are defined by the Law as a transaction or several related transactions by the company involving direct or indirect acquisition, or assignment or the possibility of assignment of property whose value is 25% or more of the book value of the assets (Art.78, para.1). Previously, the issuing of ordinary shares or preferential shares which can be converted to ordinary shares over the amount of 25% of the already issued ordinary shares was also regarded as a major trans-action. By the 2001 amendment, this ceased to be a major transaction. On the other hand, there is a general requirement of a three-quarters majority of the general shareholders' meeting for the issuing of additional shares by a closed offer, and the same requirement for the issuing of additional shares by a public offer, provided that the amount of issue exceeds 25% of the already issued shares (Art.39, paras. 3 and 4).

Transactions effected in the course of normal economic activities, such as the sale of property which the company had purchased in the course of business, are excluded, even if the value exceeds 25% of the assets.

The definition of major transactions has been criticised in Russia as having serious shortcomings because of its ambiguous criteria.[108] For example, whether the taking out of loans qualifies as a major transaction was not clear:

> Closed joint stock company, Ost-Invest, brought an action in the Moscow Commercial Court, requesting a loan agreement of January 21, 1998 concluded with a commercial bank, Platina, to be found void.
>
>   The court of first instance ruled that the contract was void on the ground that although the amount of the loan exceeded 50% of the assets of the borrower and there-fore required the approval of the general shareholders' meeting by virtue of Art.79, para.2 of the Law on Joint Stock Companies, the borrower never obtained such an approval. This was upheld by the appellate instance and the cassation instance.

---

108   G.S.Shapkina ed., *supra*, p.219.

Upon protest, the judgment was quashed by the Supreme Commercial Court on the following grounds.

Between the company and the bank, a loan agreement of one million US dollars for 6 months with 24% interest had been concluded. According to Art.77 of the Law on Joint Stock Companies, one of the criteria of a major transaction is the purchase or sales price of the property. However, since a loan agreement does not presuppose a 'price', it cannot be treated in the same way as the purchase or sale of property. Such a transaction does not fall within the purview of the provision on major transactions. Also in accordance with the Joint Decision of the Plenum of the Supreme Court and the Supreme Commercial Court of the Russian Federation No.4/8 of April 2, 1997, these provisions do not apply to transactions which are effected by companies in the process of conducting normal business activities, regardless of the value of property which is acquired or sold. In this case, the loan was used by the company to pay for the products it purchased from a foreign company, i.e. within the scope of normal business activities of the company, and therefore, also from this viewpoint, does not qualify as a major transaction.[109]

On the other hand, there was a contradicting judgment to the effect that a 'contract of *kredit*' may qualify as a major transaction, if the value of the loan and the interest exceeds 25% of the assets on the balance sheet.[110] Provisions on major transactions were also understood to extend to guarantees, if the value of the suretyship exceeded 25% of the assets on the balance sheet.[111] Under the 2001 amendment, the provision has become more specific. Now, it is explicitly provided that *zaem* and *kredit* as well as pledges and suretyships are covered by this provision.

The rule is that major transactions must be approved either by the board of directors or the general shareholders' meeting (Art.79, para.1). Major transactions with a value of between 25% and 50% of the company's assets need to be approved by the board of directors unanimously. If unanimity cannot be reached, the matter can be transferred to the general shareholders' meeting, which may approve the transaction by a simple majority (*ibid.*, para.2). Transactions with a value of more than 50% of assets require a qualified majority of the general shareholders' meeting (three quarters) (*ibid.*, para.3).

Major transactions which were effected without the required approval are void (*ibid.*, para.4).

---

109   Decision of the Presidium of the Supreme Commercial Court, June 15, 1999, *VVAS RF* 1999 No.10, pp.59-60.

110   'Obzor praktiki razresheniia sporov, sviazannykh s zakliucheniem khoziaistvennymi obshchestvami krupnykh sdelok i sdelok, v sovershenii kotorykh imeetsia zainteresovannost', informatsionnoe pis'mo, March 13, 2001, *VVAS RF*, 2001 No.7, p.71.

111   *Ibid.*, p.73.

Whether a transaction is major or not depends on its value. A joint decision of the Plenum of the Supreme Court and the Supreme Commercial Court of the Russian Federation interpreted Article 78 as meaning that the value of the property which is the object of the transaction should be determined by the actual sale or purchase price of the assets as entered in the latest balance sheet, and thus gave some objectivity to the 'market value', but such prices may not always be available.[112] By the 2001 amendment, it is now a statutory requirement that the price of the property which is to be sold should coincide with the book value and that the value of the property to be acquired coincide with the price of its acquisition (Art.78, para.1).

Decisions on effecting major transactions, the subject matter of which is property of a company with a book value between 25% and 50% of the assets of the company, must be approved unanimously by the board of directors, without the director proposing the transaction voting. If a unanimous approval is not obtained, the matter can be transferred by the board to the general shareholders' meeting (Art.79, para.1).

In cases where the object of the transaction has a value of more than 50% of the book value of the company's assets, the decision is to be adopted by the general shareholders' meeting by a three quarter majority of those who are present (*ibid.*, para.2).

> A closed joint stock company, Rosinka Odin, brought an action against an open joint stock company, Russkaia Berezka, in the Moscow City Commercial Court, requesting that part of an additional agreement attached to the contract be declared void. Russkaia Berezka and a third party, Stels Plius, concluded a contract of sale on May 27, 1996, according to which Russkaia Berezka sold Stels Plius packets of shares of various companies at the total amount of 1,121,712,160 roubles (before devaluation). Additional agreement of June 14, 1996 concluded between the above two companies plus Rosinka Odin provided that Rosinka Odin guarantee the performance of the obligation by Stels Plius *vis à vis* Russkaia Berezka by transferring Russkaia Bereska shares of Rosinka Odin as a security. Rosinka Odin argued that although this transaction was a major transaction, necessary procedural requirements were not fulfilled.
>
> The first instance court rejected the claim of the plaintiff. The appellate instance upheld this and so did the court of cassation. The Supreme Commercial Court overruled the judgment of the lower court. The Court found that the relevant clause of the additional agreement was void, since the transaction had been effected without the approval of the board of directors or the shareholders' meeting at Rosinka Odin as required by

---

112 Krapivin and Vlasov, *supra*, p.184.

Article 79 of the Law on Joint Stock Companies although the value of the pledged shares had exceeded the assets of the company.[113]

(2)   *Transactions with interested parties*

In Russia, it is not uncommon for board members and executive officers to abuse their position and pursue their own interests rather than the interests of the company by effecting transactions not at arm's length, but in favourable terms with interested parties:

> Joint stock company Lensnabpechat' brought an action against a limited liability company Interspekt, asking the court to declare void a sales agreement on the production base at Shvalovo. On July 1996, Polikarpov, the general director and the chairman of the board of directors of the plaintiff company and at the same time, acting on a power of attorney issued by the defendant company, signed a sales agreement on this production base. Polikarpov turned out to be simultaneously one of the founders of the defendant company and in fact, held 20% of its capital. A representative of the defendant company, who held 20% of the capital of the defendant company and one of its founders, was at the same time, the deputy general director of the plaintiff company. The Federal Commercial Court of the North-West District found that the transaction was in apparent excess of power by the general director and therefore, void. The argument of the defendant company that the defendant was not aware and could not have been aware of the restrictions on the power of the general director was not accepted by the court.[114]

The Law on Joint Stock Companies first defines the scope of interested parties and then imposes an obligation on the interested parties to disclose information to the company and sets the procedure for the approval of such transactions.

The provision covers the following persons affiliated with the company (Art.81, para.1):

  i)   members of the board;
  ii)   a person who is the single executive body of the company;
  iii) members of the collective executive body;
  iv)   a person or organisation which is entrusted to manage the company;
  v)   shareholders who, together with affiliated persons, hold 20% or more of the voting shares.

---

113 Decision of the Presidium of the Supreme Commercial Court, February 23, 2000, *VVAS RF*, 1999, No.6, pp.42-43.

114 *Arkhiv federal'nogo arbitrazhnogo suda severo-zapadnogo okruga, Kassatsionnoe delo* No.1664/96 (cited in Bushev and Skvortsov, *supra*, pp.157-159).

These persons are regarded to have an interest in a transaction with the company, if such a person, his spouse, parent, child, sister or brother, parent or child by adoption, as well as affiliated person:

i)   is a party, beneficiary, intermediary, or representative in the transaction,

ii) holds 20% or more of the shares in a juridical person which is a party, beneficiary, intermediary, or representative in the transaction, or

iii) occupies a position in the management body of a juridical person which is a party, beneficiary, intermediary, or representative in the transaction, or holds a position in the organisation entrusted to manage the company.

Such transactions are required to be approved in advance by the board of directors or the general shareholders' meeting. In a company with a number of shareholders under 1,000, such transactions are required to be approved by the board of directors by a majority of directors who do not have any interest in the transaction. If the number of non-interested directors is below the quorum, the transaction has to be approved by the general shareholders' meeting (Art.83, para.2). In companies with more than 1,000 shareholders, the transaction is required to be approved by a majority vote of independent directors. If all directors are regarded as having an interest in the transaction, or are not independent directors, the transaction has to be approved by the general shareholders' meeting (*ibid.*, para.3).

In this context, 'independent directors' denotes directors who are not, and have not been for the past one year before the adoption of the decision to approve the transaction:

i)   a single executive body, or a member of the collective executive body, or held a position in the management of the management organisation,

ii)   a person whose spouse, parent, child, brother or sister, parent or child by adoption occupies a position in the above body of the company, management company, or an individual manager entrusted to manage the company, or

iii) an affiliated person of the company.

Approval of the general shareholders' meeting by a majority vote of those shareholders who have no interest in the transaction is required in certain cases, e.g. if the object of the transaction or several interrelated transactions is 2% or more of the assets of the company in the accounts of the last financial period (*ibid.*, para.4). However, those transactions do not need the approval of the general shareholders' meeting, if the terms of the transaction do not substantially differ from the transaction between the company and the person with an interest, effected between the same parties in the course of normal commercial activities of the company before this person was recognised as a person with an interest in the transaction (*ibid.*, para.5).

The persons listed above are under an obligation to provide the board of directors and audit committee as well as the auditor of the company with the following information (Art.82):

i)   on juridical persons in which the person singularly, or jointly with an affiliated person, holds 20% or more shares;

       on juridical persons in which this person holds a position in its management body;

iii)   on the transaction which the person has effected or intends to effect in which this person may be regarded as an interested party.

If such a transaction was effected in violation of the above regulations, the transaction can be found null and void. The person with an interest is liable to the company for the damage resulting from the transaction (Art.84).

A closed joint stock company, Uralskoe Zoloto-Platinovaia Kompania, brought an action against an open joint stock company, Zavod Russkie Samotsvety, and closed joint stock company, Nauchno-Proizvodstvennoe Ob"edinenie ZiP, requesting the court to declare void a contract of exchange concluded between the latter two companies. The plaintiff, who is a shareholder of the defendant Zavod, based the claim on the fact that the contract was concluded by the general director of the Zavod in a conflict of interests, as he owned more than 43% of the voting shares of ZiP at the same time.

At the appellate instance, the court ruled that at the time of registration, the general director of the Uralskoe Zoloto-Platinovaia Kompaniia had 43% of shares of ZiP. This meant that the board of directors' decision was needed for the transaction as it was a transaction between interested parties, but such a resolution had not been adopted.

However, the Supreme Commercial Court referred the case for a new hearing to examine in particular whether or not the general director held the shares at the time of the transaction.[115]

Open joint stock company, Samarskaia Metallurgicheskaia Kompaniia (SAMEKO) ,brought an action against the joint stock company, Inkombank, in the Commercial Court of the City of Moscow, for recognition of a loan agreement as void on the ground that the transaction had been effected with an interested party without following the appropriate procedure.

The agreement was signed by the president of Inkombank on behalf of the Bank and by the general director, V.I.Bogocharov on behalf of the debtor, SAMEKO. At the time of conclusion of the agreement, Bogocharov was at the same time, vice president of Inkombank and a member of the top management of the Bank.

---

115   Decision of the Presidium of the Supreme Commercial Court, May 16, 2000, *VVAS RF,* 2000, No.8, pp.44-45.

The first instance court and the court of the cassation instance acknowledged this transaction as void, since the procedure as required by Art.81 of the Law on Joint Stock Companies had not been followed.

However, upon protest, the Supreme Commercial Court quashed the judgment of the lower court and referred the case for a new hearing, since a contract of assumption of debt had been concluded between Inkombank and another company, Saianskii Aliuminevyi zavod, and therefore, it was questionable whether or not SAMEKO was the appropriate plaintiff.[116]

7)   Audit – Audit committee (*revizionnaia komissia*) and the External Auditor

Supervision of 'financial and economic activities' of the company is entrusted to the audit committee. The term 'financial-economic activities' is not defined in the Law, but the audit committee essentially supervises the accounting of the company and ensures that financial documents are properly prepared for the shareholders' meeting. The committee's responsibility includes checking the correctness of the accounts, particularly the checking of the inventory of assets and debts of the company, and supervision of accounting discipline.[117]

Normally, there are three members of the committee, but in smaller companies it is possible to have one member (*revizor*) only. Members of the audit committee are appointed by the general shareholders' meeting. Shares which belong to the members of the board of directors and other bodies of the company are not given a vote when appointing members of the audit committee. Members of the committee cannot simultaneously be a member of the board or occupy other positions in the company's management (Art.85, para.6).

'Financial-economic supervision' is conducted on the basis of the annual result of the activities of the company as well as on the initiative of the audit committee, a resolution of the general shareholders' meeting or the decision of the board of directors. Shareholders with not less than 10% shares are entitled to request an inspection by the audit committee (*ibid*, paras. 1-3).

Upon request of the audit committee or its members, persons who occupy a position in a management body are obliged to submit documents concerning the financial-business activities of the company. However, there is no sanction against non-compliance, and therefore, the effectiveness of this provision is doubtful. The audit committee is empowered to request the board to convene an extraordinary shareholders' meeting (*ibid*., paras.4 and 5).

---

116 Decision of the Presidium of the Supreme Commercial Court, January 18, 2000, *VVAS RF,* 2000 No.4, pp.45-46.
117 Tikhomirov, *supra*, pp.347-348.

Open joint stock companies are under an obligation to publish their annual report, balance sheet, and the profit and loss report every year (Art.92, para.1). The Law on Banks and Banking Activities imposes a similar obligation on credit organisations.[118] These companies must involve a professional auditor (an external auditor) to check and verify the authenticity of the financial reports on an annual basis. For closed joint stock companies, companies over a certain size in terms of turnover or assets are required to have an external auditor.[119]

The external auditor can be either an individual or a firm, but must be a person or entity who does not have any proprietary relations with the company or its members. Closed type joint stock companies are not generally required to have an external auditor, but upon request of a shareholder with no less than 10% of shares, inspection by an external auditor is required (CivC Art.103, para.5).

The external auditor checks the 'financial-economic activities' of the company on the basis of a contract with the company. The external auditor is appointed by the general shareholders' meeting. The remuneration is determined by the board of directors (Art.86).

The Law on Auditing Activities was enacted in 2001.[120] Auditing is a licensed profession; there is a cabinet decision which sets out the procedure for attestation and the grant of a license. All major accounting firms in the world are operating in Russia.

Upon completion of the auditing of the 'financial-economic activities' of the company, the audit committee and/or an external auditor prepares an opinion which includes:

i)   confirmation of the authenticity of the information contained in the annual report and other financial documents of the company;

ii)   information on the facts of breaches of laws and statutes on accounting and financial reporting in the course of conducting 'financial-economic activities' if there were any.

Accounting standards are provided by the Law on Bookkeeping as well as cabinet decisions and normative acts of the Ministry of Finance.[121] In 1997, the government embarked on a reform of the accounting system for approximation with the

---

118 *SZ RF*, 1996 No.6, item 492.
119 Edict No.408 of the Government, April 25, 1995.
120 *SZ RF*, 2001, No.33, item 3422.
121 *SZ RF*, 1996 No.48, item 5369.

International Accounting Standards. However, the 'evolutionary approach' which has been adopted seems to be taking time.[122]

8)   Liability of Directors and Executive Officers

Members of the board of directors, a single executive body (director, general director), and members of the collective executive body (management council, directorate) are under a general obligation to act in the interest of the company, and to exercise their rights and fulfil their duties in relation to the company conscientiously and reasonably (Art.71, para.1). Directors and others listed above are liable *vis à vis* the company for the damage caused by them to the company by their fault (this includes both acts and omissions). In collective bodies such as the board of directors and the collective executive body, those members who voted against the decision which caused the loss, or did not take part in the vote, are exempted from liability (Art.71, para.2). When determining the basis and scope of liability, normal terms of commercial practice and other circumstances which have relevance to the case must be taken into account (*ibid.*, para.3). If several persons are liable, they bear joint and several liability (*ibid.*, para.4).

Abuse of power by directors and members of the executive body is not rare in Russia.

> A director of a company, Zavod Keramzitovogo Graniia', concluded an agreement of pledge (*zalog*) with the Stroitel'nyi Bank in order to guarantee a debt of a third party who had nothing to do with the company. The agreement was concluded without the consent of the collective executive body or the general shareholders' meeting. The Zavod brought the case to court, asking the agreement to be declared void. However, courts of first instance and the appellate instance rejected the claim. The Supreme Commercial Court quashed the decision and reversed the case to the first instance court on the ground that 'such a transaction could lead to gratuitous assignment of property of the company without the consent of the shareholders'.[123]

The liability of these persons can be pursued either by the company itself, or by shareholders who hold 1% or more of the ordinary shares (Art.71, para.5). In such an action, the single executive body is to act on behalf of the company without power of attorney. If the liability of the single executive body itself is pursued,

---

122 M.Gorsky, 'Accounting Reform in Russia: An Insider's Comments', *BISNIS Bulletin*, 2000 February, p.3.
123 Decision of the Supreme Commercial Court, March 10, 1998 (cited in Tokhomirov, *supra*, p.299, see *VVAS RF*, 1998 No.6).

a power of attorney is issued to another person by the resolution of the general shareholders' meeting, the board of directors, or the collegiate executive body.

Shareholders who hold 1% or more of the shares are entitled to pursue the liability of the directors and others. This 'indirect action' has apparently been modelled on the system of derivative action in the United States. However, this provision merely provides for the general right of shareholders to pursue liability of directors and executive officers but fails to give details. The wording of this provision is ambiguous in the sense that the nature of this action is not clear. It is not explicitly provided that this action is not for the interest of an individual shareholder, but for the interest of the shareholders as a whole or the company and that the damages are payable to the company and not to the plaintiff shareholder. There is no procedural provision either. Even the jurisdiction in such cases, i.e. whether such cases are handled by the commercial courts or ordinary courts, is not certain.

In reality, there has been no reported case of indirect action. Presumably, the time and cost involved as weighed against the gain – even if the plaintiff wins, the compensation will go to the company – discourage the shareholders.

9)   Reorganisation of Companies

The Russian concept of 'reorganisation' covers merger (*sliianie*), absorption (*prisoedinenie*), division (*razdelenie*), spin-off (*vydelenie*) and conversion (Art.15).

Merger is defined as an emergence of a new company, with the transfer of all rights and obligations of one or several existing companies to the new company, with the termination of those existing companies. Companies taking part in the merger are required to conclude an agreement of merger which determines the procedure and conditions of the merger as well as the procedure of converting shares and other securities of these companies. The board of directors of each company proposes the merger and the approval of the merger agreement to the general shareholders' meeting of the company (Art.16, para.2). The resolution has to be adopted by a qualified majority of those present at the meeting. The adoption of the articles of incorporation and the appointment of the board of directors of the newly established company take place at the joint general shareholders' meeting of the companies which are parties to the merger (*ibid.*, para.3).

Absorption denotes a type of reorganisation in which one or several companies are terminated and their rights and obligations are transferred to another company (Art.17, para.1).

In both merger and absorption, provisions of the Law on Competition and the Prevention of Monopolistic Activities are applicable.[124] Thus, if the total amount of assets in the latest balance sheet of those companies involved exceeds 100,000 times the monthly minimum wage, a prior consent of the Federal Anti-Monopoly Office is required. For mergers and absorption with total assets of more than 50,000 times the monthly minimum wage, the Federal Anti-Monopoly Office has to be notified within 15 days of the state registration. Breach of these requirements will result in the court nullifying registration upon the request of the Anti-Monopoly Office.

In division of a company, the company ceases to exist, while the rights and duties of the company are transferred to several newly established companies. The board of directors of the company proposes the division to the general shareholders' meeting and the form, procedure, terms of the division, and other matters concerning the creation of new companies and the method of conversion of shares and securities. The general shareholders' meeting of each newly set up company adopts a resolution on the approval of the articles of incorporation and the appointment of the board of directors. In a division of a company, all the rights and obligations of the company are transferred to the newly established companies in accordance with the divided balance sheet (Art.18).

In a spin-off a company creates one or several new companies and transfers part of its rights and duties, but the company stays in existence (Art.19). The procedure is basically the same as in division.

Conversion (*preobrazovanie*) means transformation of a joint stock company to another type of commercial organisation. The Law provides for conversion either to a limited liability company or production cooperative.

All these reorganisations require a qualified majority vote of the general shareholders' meeting. Those shareholders who voted against reorganisation or were not present at the shareholders' meeting have an appraisal right (Art.75, para.1).

7   LIMITED LIABILITY COMPANIES

1)   Procedure of Establishment

As is the case with joint stock companies, limited liability companies can be set up by a single person (physical as well as juridical). However, a company set

---

124   *VSND RFSFR i VS RSFSR*, 1991 No.16, item 499.

up by a single person cannot be a sole promoter of another company (Art.7, para.2). The number of participants may not exceed 50 (*ibid.*, para.3).

Promoters of the company conclude a shareholders' agreement, prepare the articles of incorporation, and appoint the executive body (Art.11, para.1). Unlike in joint stock companies, the founding agreement (*uchrezhditel'nyi dogovor*) is regarded as a founding document together with the articles of incorporation; its contents are listed in the Law (Art.12, paras. 1 and 2). While in joint stock companies, the agreement of founding the company loses meaning once the company has been established, in limited liability companies, the agreement maintains its validity even after the company has come into being.[125] If both documents do not coincide, the articles of incorporation prevails.

Concerning in-kind contribution, any object which has monetary value can be contributed (Art.15, para.1). According to the Joint Decision of the Supreme Commercial Court and the Supreme Court of the Russian Federation, which is applicable to both joint stock companies and limited liability companies, 'therefore, objects of intellectual property or know-how cannot be contributed'. However, the right to use such property based on a registered licensing agreement can be contributed. Presumably, this is because in licensing agreements, the value of the intellectual property can be ascertained in the form of the royalty.[126]

If there is an in-kind contribution, its value needs to be approved by the promoters. In-kind contribution exceeding 200 times the minimum wage has to be valued by an independent appraiser. In the case of insolvency, promoters and the independent valuer are liable in an additional manner for the excess of the value for three years of the company registration (Art.15, para.2). Articles of incorporation and the approval of the value of in-kind contribution require a unanimous vote of the promoters.

Promoters are jointly and severally liable for the obligations incurred up to the registration of the company. The company is liable for such obligation only when the general meeting of participants subsequently endorses it (Art.11, para.2).

---

125 M.Iu.Tikhomirov ed., *Kommentarii k federal'nomu zakonu ob obshchestvakh s ogranichennoi otvetstvennost'iu*, second edition, Moscow 2001, p.81.

126 Joint Decision of the Supreme Court and the Supreme Commercial Court of the Russian Federation, No.6/ 8, July 1, 1996, item 17, Zhurakovskii and Kalinin, *supra*, p.23.

2)   Articles of Incorporation

In the articles of incorporation of limited liability companies, in addition to the matters required for joint stock companies, the following matters have to be addressed (Art.12):

i)   nominal value of the participatory share of each members;
ii)   information on the procedure and the consequences of the withdrawal of a member from the company;
iii)   information on the procedure of transfer of a participatory share to another person.

3)   The Capital and Participatory Shares

(1)   The Capital

The capital of a limited liability company comprises the nominal value of members' participatory shares. The minimum amount of capital is set at 100 times the minimum wage. Participatory shares of members (participants) are determined by the percentage of or proportion to the capital (Art.14, para.1). The actual value of the participatory shares corresponds to the value of the part of net assets divided in accordance with the size of the participatory share.

The capital can be increased from internal sources, by additional contribution by participants, or, if it is not prohibited by the articles of incorporation, contribution by third parties (Art.17, para.2). For increase of capital by additional contribution of the members, a two-thirds majority of the votes is required. In other words, minority participants may be forced to make an additional contribution. The vote needed can be increased by the articles of incorporation. Participants are required to pay in the contribution within two months of the resolution (Art.19, para.1). The company may increase the capital by soliciting contribution from the members and third parties by a unanimous vote of the members (*ibid.*, para.2). The articles of incorporation must be amended and the amendment must be registered.

The capital can be decreased by the reduction of the nominal value of the participatory share of all participants or by redemption of the participatory shares (Art.19). If, at the end of each financial year after the first, the net assets are less than the capital, the company must reduce the capital (Art.20, para.3). Within 30 days of the adoption of the resolution to reduce the capital, the company must notify creditors in writing of the decrease of capital and also publicise it in the newspaper. Creditors may accelerate the repayment and require the company to repay the debt within 30 days (Art.20, para.4).

It is possible to set the maximum participatory share a single participant may hold, under the articles of incorporation (*ibid.*, para.3).

(2)   Assignment of Participatory Shares

Participants are entitled to sell or otherwise assign all or part of their participatory share to another member without the consent of the company, unless the articles of incorporation have a different provision (Art.21, para.1).

Sale or assignment in other ways of the participatory share to a third party is allowed, unless it is prohibited by the articles of incorporation (*ibid.*, para.2). It is possible to require the consent of all participants for the assignment of a participatory share to a third party under the articles of incorporation.

In case a participant intends to sell the participatory share to a third party, other participants have a right of pre-emption to purchase the participatory share at the price offered to the third party. If the articles of incorporation so provide, the company itself may exercise such a right. Participants who intend to sell the participatory share are under an obligation to notify in writing the remaining members and the company of the price and other terms of sale. If the remaining members and the company fail to exercise the right of pre-emption within 30 days of the receipt of notification, the sale may go ahead. Violation of the right of pre-emption enables other participants and the company to resort to a court procedure for retrieval of the participatory share (*ibid*, para.4).

If the sale of participatory share to a third party is prohibited and other participants refuse to purchase the participatory share, or if the consent of other participants or the company required for the sale is unavailable, the company is under an obligation to purchase the participatory share at the 'actual value' calculated on the basis of the balance sheet of the latest financial period (Art.23, para.2).

(3)   Withdrawal from the Company

Participants may withdraw from the company regardless of the consent of other members. The participatory share held by this member will be transferred to the company. The company must pay the actual value of the participatory share to the withdrawing member within 6 months of the petition to withdraw. The payment can be made in kind, but must be made from the surplus of the net assets over the capital. If no such surplus exists, the capital has to be decreased (Art.26).

Allowing withdrawal from the company with the right to retrieve the investment is probably unique to Russian Law and creates a significant risk to joint venture partners.

(4)   Expulsion of participants

The company may expel a participant under certain circumstances. This power is not unique to Russian law. A similar system exists in German law. It was introduced into Russia in the RSFSR Law on Enterprises and Entrepreneurial Activities of 1990, but was dropped in the Civil Code, and then re-emerged in the 1998 Law on Limited Liability Companies.[127]

A participant who holds 10% or more of the capital may apply to court for expulsion of another member who was in significant breach of his duty, or if, as a result of an act of this member, the company's activity has become impossible or difficult to continue (Art.10). These grounds are considered to be exhaustive, and therefore, it is not possible to add other grounds under the articles of incorporation.[128] In practice, because those grounds are broadly formulated, ultimately, it is left to the discretion of the court to decide whether a member should be expelled or not. A joint decision of the Plenum of the Supreme Commercial Court and the Supreme Court of the Russian Federation has 'slightly expanded' the grounds for expulsion to include 'repeated failure to take part in the general meeting which deprived the company from adopting resolutions which require a unanimous vote.'[129] The participatory share of the expelled member will be transferred to the company and the expelled member will receive the 'actual value' of the participatory share in return (Art.23, para.4).

(5)   Dividends

The company may pay dividends quarterly, semi-annually, or annually (Art.28). Dividends cannot be paid on the same grounds as with joint stock companies, but in addition, if the company has not paid the 'actual value' of the participatory share to a participant in cases of expulsion or withdrawal, or refusal to give consent on sale of participatory shares, dividends cannot be paid (Art.29).

---

127 O.Petnikova, 'Zashchita prav uchastnikov obshchestva s ogranichennoi otvetstvennost'iu', *PiE*, 2000 No.11, pp.15-16.

128 Tikomirov ed., *Kommentarii k federal'nomu zakonu ob obshchestvakh s ogranichennoi otvetstven-nost'iu...*, *supra*, p.73.

129 Joint Decision of the Supreme Court and the Supreme Commercial Court of the Russian Federation No.14, December 9,1999, item 17, Zhurakovskii and Kalinin, *supra*, p.73.

4)   Issuing of Bonds and Securities

Limited liability companies are allowed to issue bonds and other securities. This is in contrast to most other jurisdictions where limited liability companies may not issue bonds. Russian law, however, imposes some restrictions. Firstly, bonds cannot be issued in excess of the amount of the capital. Secondly, bonds have to be secured. Thirdly, bonds can be issued only in the third financial year of the existence of the company after the accounts for the first two years have been approved (Art.31).

5)   Rights and Duties of Participants

Participants of limited liability companies have the following statutory rights (Art.8):

    i)   the right to participate in the management of the company, including the right to take part in the general meeting of the participants, to elect and be elected to the executive body, and to propose items to be included in the agenda of the general meeting of the members etc;
    ii)   the right to have access to information;
    iii)   the right to share the profit;
    iv)   the right to sell or otherwise assign the participatory share to other participants;
    v)   the right to withdraw from the company at any time without the consent of other participants;
    vi)   the right, in the case of the liquidation of the company, to share the remaining assets.

i) also includes the right to contest the resolutions and decisions of the management bodies of the company in court in cases where they were against the law or other legislative acts, articles of incorporation, or infringed the rights and legal interests of the participants (Art.43,para.1). As is the case with the corresponding system in the Law on Joint Stock Companies, the court has the discretion to keep the resolution in effect, if the vote of the person who is contesting the resolution would not have affected the outcome, or the violation was not substantial and did not cause any harm to this person (*ibid.*, para.2). It is worth noting that unlike the Law on Joint Stock Companies, it is not only the resolution of the general meeting, but also the decisions of the board of directors, and the single and collective executive bodies that are explicitly covered (*ibid.,* para.3).

6)   Management Bodies

(1)   General Meeting of Participants

The highest body of the company is the participants' general meeting. Participants
have the right to participate and vote. The voting right is granted in proportion
to the participatory share which each of them holds. However, under the articles
of incorporation, it is possible to adopt a different means of distribution of votes,
but only by a unanimous vote of participants (Art.39, para.1). The following
matters fall within the exclusive competence of the general meeting (Art.33,
para.2):

i)	determination of the basic direction of the company;
ii)	amendment of the articles of incorporation and the founders' agreement;
iii)	formation and early termination of terms of the executive body;
iv)	appointment and early termination of terms of the audit committee;
v)	approval of the annual report and balance sheet;
vi)	adoption of the resolution regarding the distribution of profit;
vii)	approval of internal rules and regulations;
viii)	appointment of auditor and determination of the remuneration;
ix)	approval of the issuing of bonds and other securities;
x)	adoption of the resolution on reorganisation and liquidation of the company;
xi)	appointment of the liquidation committee.

Extraordinary participants' meetings can be convened by the executive body on
its own initiative or upon request of the board of directors, the audit committee,
or the auditor. A participant who has more than a one-tenth of participatory share
is entitled to request the company to convene an extraordinary meeting (Art.35,
para.2). The executive body must decide whether or not to convene a general
meeting within five days of receiving the request. The request can be refused only
on limited grounds such as in cases where the proposed agenda does not fall within
the competence of the general participants' meeting. If the general participants'
meeting is to be convened, it has to be convened within five days of receiving
the request. If the executive body does not make any decision or refuses to convene a meeting, then the body or person who made the request, may convene the
meeting (*ibid.*, paras. 2-4).

    In preparation of the general participants' meeting, any participant may propose
items to be included in the agenda. Participants may take part in the meeting via
a representative. The meeting is opened by the single executive body or the
chairman of the collective executive body, who conducts the election of the

chairman of the meeting (Art.37). It should be added that the participants' meeting can be held without an actual meeting (Art.38).

Amendment to the articles of incorporation requires a two-thirds majority. Changes to the founders' agreement and the resolution for reorganisation and liquidation must be adopted by a unanimous vote (Art.37, para.8).

As a rule, these matters cannot be transferred to the competence of the board of directors, but as an exception, the formation and early termination of terms of the executive body may be left to the board of directors.

(2) The Board of Directors

The establishment of the board of directors (supervisory board) is not mandatory. The general participants' meeting may set up the board of directors which is granted the power to:

i) form the executive body and terminate its terms early;
ii) approve major transactions;
iii) approve transactions with interested parties;
iv) prepare, convene and conduct the general members' meeting and the board of directors (Art.32, para.2).

(3) Executive Bodies

Direction of the current activities of the company is entrusted to a single executive body (general director, president), or a single executive body and a collective executive body (management council, directorate) jointly (Arts.40 and 41). What is different from the Law on Joint Stock Companies is that there is an explicit provision that the executive body is subordinate to the general members' meeting (Art.32, para.4).

7) Restraints on the Power of the Executive Bodies

(1) Major Transactions

Similar to joint stock companies, there are regulations on major transactions applicable to limited liability companies. The decision to effect major transactions, i.e. transactions exceeding 25% of the value of the company's assets, lies with the general participants' meeting (Art.46, paras. 1 and 3). If there is a board of directors, major transactions whose value is over 25% but less than 50% can be authorised by the board, if the articles of association so provide (*ibid.*,4). Major transactions effected without required consents are void (*ibid.*, 5):

> A participant brought an action against a limited liability company asking the court to declare void a contract of sale effected by the company. The company sold equipment and an inventory whose value exceeded 50% of the value of the assets without the resolution of the general participants' meeting. The claim was accepted by the court on the ground of Article 46 of the Law on Limited Liability Companies.[130]

However, it should be noted that, unlike in joint stock companies, the above requirements can be totally removed by the articles of incorporation (*ibid.*,para.6).

(2)   Transactions with Interested Parties

Members of the board, the single executive body, members of the collective executive body as well as participants who hold 20% or more of the capital alone or in conjunction with affiliated persons, are not allowed to effect transactions with interested parties without the consent of the general meeting of participants (Art.45, para.1). The general meeting may give consent to the transaction by a majority vote without the interested participants voting (*ibid.*, para.3). If there is a board of directors, this power to give consent can be entrusted to the board, except in cases where the value of transaction exceeds 2% of the assets of the company determined on the basis of the last financial year (*ibid.*, para.7).

Transactions are regarded as those with interested parties in cases where the above persons, spouses, parents, children, sisters and brothers as well as their affiliated persons are (*ibid*, para.2):

i)   party to the transaction with the company or acting in the interest of a third party against the company.

ii)   holding 20% or more of the participatory share of a juridical person which is a party to the transaction with the company or which acts in the interest of a third party against the company, or

iii)   holding a position in the management body of a juridical person which is a party to the transaction with the company or which acts in the interest of a third party against the company.

---

130 'Obzor praktiki razresheniia sporov, sviazannykh s zakliucheniem khoziaistvennymi obshchestvami krupnykh sdelok i sdelok, v sovershenii kotorykh imeetsia zainteresovannost', informatsionnoe pis'mo, March 13, 2001, *VVAS RF*, 2001 No.7, p.79.

Members of the board, the single executive body, members of the collective executive body as well as the participants mentioned above are under an obligation to disclose the information listed in the Law to the general participants' meeting (*ibid.*, para.2).

Those transactions effected in violation of this provision are null and void (*ibid*, para.5).

8)   Liability of the Directors and Executive Officers

The above persons are under an obligation to act in the interests of the company in a conscientious and reasonable manner. They are liable to the company for damage caused to the company by their fault. Those who voted against the act in question or did not take part in the vote are exempted from liability (Art.44, paras. 1 and 2).

As is the case with joint stock companies, breaches of duties by the directors and others are not uncommon:

> The general director of company Liudmila, which was a successor to a limited liability company (TOO), forged a document needed to provide a non-residential building which belonged to the company as collateral and personally received a loan from the Saratov Bank – part of the Sverbank. Eventually, the general director defaulted and the building became the property of the Bank. The court ruled that the Bank was unaware and could not have been aware that there was no resolution of the general meeting concerning the loan by offering the building as a collateral and that the general director had no power to effect the transaction. In such cases, the consequences must be borne by the juridical person, in whose name the director had acted in bad faith.[131]

Indirect (derivative) action is available to participants, but as is the case with the Law on Joint Stock Companies, no details are given (*ibid.*, para.5).

9)   Audit

The company may, under the articles of incorporation, set up an audit committee or have an internal auditor (*revizor*). In a company with 15 or more participants, this is mandatory. Members of the audit committee may not be a member of the board of directors, a collective executive body, or a single executive body (Art.32,

---

131   Decision of the Presidium of the Supreme Commercial Court, February 11, 1997, *VVAS RF*, 1997 No.5, pp.102-103.

para.6). The audit committee is appointed by the general participants' meeting for checking the 'financial-economic activities' of the company (Art.47, paras.1 and 2).

In order to check and authenticate the accuracy of the annual report and the balance sheet, as well as to check the current state of business, the company may involve a professional auditor unrelated to the company. By request of any participant, the audit can be conducted by a professional auditor as above, at the expense of this participant (Art.48).

The requirement of publicity on their activities is less stringent in limited liability companies than in joint stock companies. Limited liability companies are under no obligation to publish their annual report. Only when they are making a public offer of bonds and other securities are they required to publish the annual report, balance sheet and other information (Art.49).

5

INSOLVENCY LAW

1 HISTORICAL BACKGROUND

The history of insolvency legislation in Russia goes back to the 1800 Statute on Bankruptcy (*Ustav o bankrotakh*). The enactment of a new law was discussed extensively in the Tsarist period and even a draft law based upon the German model was published, but it was not adopted as it was seen as an 'imitation of Western statutes'.

In the planned economy, the sole owner of enterprises was the state. Despite the façade of the enterprises being separate entities from the state and operating on their own balance sheet, loss-making enterprises were supported by the state, which was actually redistributing profits made by other enterprises. There was little need to have the assets of the debtor-enterprise distributed among the creditors who were also state enterprises, or rehabilitating the enterprise on the latter's initiative. These enterprises did not have sufficient assets of their own which could be disposed of in the first place. Thus, there was no system to deal with insolvent enterprises under the socialist system.

In the process of transition to the market economy, the necessity of such a system as a prerequisite to the transition was acutely felt. In 1992, the Law on the Insolvency (Bankruptcy) of Enterprises was enacted. As was the case with other laws enacted in this early period, this Law lacked consistency and internal logic. As one Russian commentator put it, it was 'like a car which was difficult to start, and once it starts, inadequately responds to the attempts to manipulate it and moves in all directions'.[1] Therefore, a new Law was prepared and was enacted as the Law on Insolvency in 1998.[2]

In the three-year process of preparing the new Law, the 'best laws of the contemporary world', the US Bankruptcy Code, the UK Insolvency Act, the German

---

1   V.V.Stepanov, *Nesosoiatel'nost' v Rossii, Frantsii, Anglii, Germanii*, Moscow 1999, p.139.
2   *SZ RF*, 1998 No.2, item 222.

Insolvenzordnung and the French Law were extensively studied. The end result was that, from a Russian perspective, 'in terms of the conceptual parameter, the new Russian Law can be placed at the same level as the US, German, English and French law which regulate insolvency'.[3] It is based upon the idea that in an optimal system of insolvency law, liquidation should not have preference to reorganisation (rehabilitation) or *visa versa*, i.e. a balance should be struck between the interest of creditors and debtors.[4]

Shortly after the Law took effect, a 'simplified procedure' of insolvency was introduced by a government decision (Decision No.476) in the light of the looming financial crisis. This decision introduced the debt-equity swap through auction. However, the new system was criticised for creating a watershed for abuses and insider dealing. Under this system, it was pointed out that managers of the debtor-organisation, in collusion with speculators with financial resources would have a major role and may well compromise the auction.[5] There were instances where irregularities were suspected.[6]

This procedure was eventually abolished, and currently, the Law on Insolvency and the Law on the Insolvency of Credit Organisations are the two basic laws in this area.

Whether the insolvency procedure has been utilised in Russia in an adequate manner is often questioned. It is pointed out that the initiation of the procedure in fact became an inexpensive alternative to hostile takeover, provided that there is a potential alliance between the administrator, judges and the officials of the Federal Agency on Financial Restoration.[7] This proved to be true in the Sidanco case (see below).

2   THE 1998 LAW ON INSOLVENCY

In Russia, the term *bankrotstvo* denotes the entire procedure dealing with in-solvency, while the term *konkurs* denotes the procedure for the sale of the debtor's assets and the distribution of the proceeds among the creditors. In the Tsarist period, the term *konkurs* was commonly used. The current Russian Law is entitled *zakon o bankrotstve*. It accommodates both the procedure aimed at rehabilitation

3   Stepanov., *supra*, pp.161-162.
4   *Ibid.*, p.169.
5   *Ibid.*, pp.163-164.
6   A.Radygin, 'Sovstvennost' i integratsionnye protsessy v korporativnom sektore', *VE*, 2001 May, pp.31-32.
7   *Ibid.*, p.33.

of the debtor as well as the procedure for liquidation. In the following, *bankrots-tsvo* will be translated as insolvency to cover the entire procedure accommodated in the 1998 Law on Insolvency, while bankruptcy will be used in a narrower sense to cover the *koknkurs* procedure, i.e. the liquidation procedure.

The Law on Insolvency has adopted a 'one stop' system in which once the application for the recognition of insolvency has been accepted and the court recognises the debtor as insolvent, depending on circumstances, different measures and proceedings can be applied.

These are:

i)   observation;
ii)   external administration;
iii)   bankruptcy proceeding;
iv)   amicable settlement.

The commercial court has exclusive jurisdiction in bankruptcy cases, regardless of whether the debtor is a juridical person or an individual (Art.28, para.1). The court of the location of the debtor has jurisdiction (Art.29, para.1).

The Law is applicable to insolvency of juridical persons as well as individuals. Concerning juridical persons, as a rule, commercial organisations as well as non-commercial organisations such as consumer cooperatives and funds are covered, but state enterprises are excluded (Art.1, para.2). There is a separate Law on the Insolvency of Credit Organisations which sets out special rules applicable to credit organisations [see Chapter 12 Banking Law].

Insolvency is defined as the inability of the debtor to pay monetary debt in full and/or to perform obligations for mandatory payment (taxes, levies, and other payments)(Art.2). For juridical persons, this is indicated by the fact that the debtor failed to satisfy a monetary claim or perform an obligation for mandatory payment for more than three months after the due date (Art.3, para.2). There is also a requirement that the debt should exceed 500 times the minimum wage (Art.5).

This arrangement is simpler than the 1992 Law which required that the debt owed be higher than the value of the debtor's assets or 'the structure of the balance sheet was not satisfactory'. This requirement was difficult to apply in practice. Besides, it led to a situation where directors of enterprises, by manipulating the assets and debts, 'managed to dispose of the debtor's assets for a substantial period without being penalised'.[8]

---

8   V.V.Vitrianskii, *Lektsii po problemam regulirovaniia bankrotstva*, Moscow 1996, p.6.

On the other hand, there are cases under the current arrangement where small creditors initiate the insolvency proceedings despite the opposition of large creditors:

> In 1999, an insolvency proceeding was initiated against Sidanco, the then fifth largest oil company, by an unknown company. The amount of claim this company held was actually 0,1% of the total debt of the company. Proceedings were initiated against Sidanco's production subsidiaries too. In relation to one of the subsidiaries, the creditor who filed for recognition of insolvency had been offered payment, but reportedly, the court ignored it and went ahead with the proceeding.[9]

It is pointed out that a paradoxical situation is observed where enterprises which have sufficient assets are dragged into the insolvency procedure because there was an opportunity for competitors taking control of them, while hopeless enterprises escaped the procedure because no one wanted to take control of such enterprises. It is proposed to require the initiator of the procedure to prove that there is no other way of recovering the debt than insolvency procedure.[10]

3   THE PROCEDURE

1)   Initiation of the Proceedings

Creditors as well as debtors are entitled to initiate the proceedings aimed at having the debtor recognised as insolvent. The debtor is entitled to apply for an insolvency recognition as if there are circumstances which clearly demonstrate that the debtor will not be in a state to perform the obligation (Art.7, para.2). The head of the debtor-organisation is under an obligation to apply in cases where satisfaction of the claim(s) results in the debtor's impossibility to fully satisfy the other creditors' claim.

In addition, procurators and the Ministry of Tax and Levies are empowered to initiate proceedings. A large portion of bankruptcy cases are initiated by the tax agency (the Ministry of Taxes and Levies). In 2000, 43,7% of the cases were initiated by the tax agency, while 20% were initiated by creditors. Obviously, the tax agency uses the bankruptcy procedure as an effective device for collecting unpaid taxes.[11]

---

9   *East European Energy*, 1999 September issue, pp.11-13.
10   Radygin, *supra*, pp.32-33..
11   Supreme Commercial Court, 'Rassmotrenie del o bankrotstve v 2000 godu', [www.akdi.ru].

In the absence of any objection by the creditor, the debtor may declare itself insolvent and liquidate itself (Art.24).

Reflecting the economic climate after 1998, in 2000, the commercial court accepted more than 19,000 applications for bankruptcy proceedings; this was 74% more than 1999. Proceedings were initiated with 15,000 companies and organisations.[12]

2)   Observation

Once the application for the recognition of the debtor as insolvent has been accepted by the court, the observation procedure starts (Art.56; in March 2001, the Constitutional Court found this provision unconstitutional to the extent that it does not give an opportunity to the debtor to contest the decision).[13]

The primary purpose of this procedure is to investigate the financial state of the debtor and to enable creditors to decide whether to opt for rehabilitation or liquidation.

A temporary administrator is appointed by the court, but the incumbent management is not removed. However, the incumbent management is required to obtain the consent of the administrator for the disposal of immovable assets, or other property which exceeds 10% of the assets in the balance sheet in value, to take out loans, or to provide guarantees. The management body is also prohibited from effecting reorganisation, creating juridical persons or participating in another juridical person, paying out dividends, and issuing bonds. The court may remove the head of the debtor organisation if measures to preserve the assets are not taken, he or she obstructs the work of the temporary administrator, or otherwise acts against the law (Art.58, paras.1-4).

It is often the case that the creditor who files the application for the initiation of the procedure exercises considerable influence over the choice of the temporary administrator, and as a consequence, gains control over the entire procedure.[14]

The temporary administrator must analyse the financial state of the debtor and also establish the creditors and the amount of their respective claims (Art.61, para.1). In order to take part in the first creditors' meeting, creditors are to present their claims to the debtor within one months of the notice of the court's acceptance

---

12   *VVAS* 2001 No.5, p.11.

13   Decision of the Constitutional Court, March 12, 2001 [Inforis].

14   A.S.Alexandrovich, 'Bankruptcy Law, and Economic Medicine: How Russia's New Bankruptcy Legislation Facilitated Recovery From the Nationwide Financial Crisis of August 17, 1998', *Cornell International Law Journal*, vol.34, 2001, p.114.

of the application for the recognition of insolvency (Art.63, para.1). This stage is crucial to creditors, since if their claim is not acknowledged at this stage, they will not be able to take part in the creditors' meeting and would fail to influence the procedure:

> In a case involving Sidanco's and another subsidiary, Kondpetroleum, the temporary administrator refused to acknowledge the existence of a claim by Sidanco, and the court upheld this decision. Sidanco argued that this was an abuse of power by the administrator who was close to Sidanco's competitor, but the court rejected this argument.

At the first creditors' meeting, creditors are to discuss whether to i) apply to court for the introduction of external administration, or ii) apply for the recognition of insolvency and the initiation of the bankruptcy procedure, in other words, take measures to rehabilitate the company or liquidate it and distribute the proceeds of the sale of assets (Art.65, para.1). If the meeting resolves to introduce external administration, the length of external administration and the candidate for the external administrator must be decided at the same time (Art.66).

It is the court which makes the final decision. Based upon the resolution of the creditors' meeting, the court decides whether to recognise the debtor as insolvent, initiate the bankruptcy procedure, or endorse an amicable settlement (Art.67, para.1).

3)   External Administration

External administration is a procedure for composition which is designed to restore the solvency of the debtor by creditors agreeing on various concessions, including waiver of part of the claim.

Upon the introduction of external administration, the head of the debtor-organisation is removed from the position and the management body's power is terminated; the external administrator takes over. At the same time a moratorium on the payment of monetary debt is introduced. Seizure of the debtor's assets is not allowed other than within the framework of this procedure (Art.69). Execution of judgments for proprietary claims is suspended, except for claims on unpaid wages, compensation for damage to the life or health of people and moral damages (Art.70, para.2). Performance of obligations can be rejected under certain circumstances within three months of the introduction of external administration (Art.77).

External administrators are recommended by creditors, but are appointed by the court. The court is not bound by the recommendation, at least not in an explicit manner. The administrator is appointed from the list of registered administrators kept by the Federal Agency on Financial Restoration. He is required to be a registered entrepreneur with a specialist knowledge and not connected to either the debtor or the creditor (Art.14). In many cases, the temporary administrator is appointed as the external administrator. This gives rise to cases where the creditor who initiated the procedure manages to control the entire procedure through an administrator who is close to this person.

The external administrator must prepare an inventory of the assets of the debtor. Creditors are entitled to present their claims to the external administrator during the course of the external administration. The administrator examines the claims and registers them based upon the result of this examination. Creditors may file an objection with the court as to the decision of the administrator (Art.75, paras.1-3).

Certain transactions can be found null and void by the court upon application of the external administrator:

i) transactions of the debtor with interested parties, the performance of which harms or may harm the interests of creditors;

ii) transactions of the debtor with a creditor or others concluded or performed after the application for the recognition of insolvency was filed, or within 6 months before the application was filed, provided that such transactions result in a preferential fulfilment of a claim of a creditor to the others;

iii) similar transactions to those above which are related to the paying out of a portion of the assets to the members of the debtor-organisation in relation to this person's withdrawal from the organisation.

In the last two instances, not only the administrator, but the creditors are entitled to apply to court in order to have the transaction voided (Art.78).

The external administrator prepares a plan of external administration within one month of his appointment and submits it to the creditors' meeting. This plan must contain a proposed measure for the restoration of the solvency of the debtor and its timing (Art.82). These measures include (Art.85):

i)   changing the profile of production;
ii) closing of loss-making production;
iii) sale of part of the debtor-organisation;
iv) assignment of claims of the debtor;
v)   sale of subsidiaries (business) of the debtor by auction.

The creditors' meeting may endorse the plan, or resolve to apply to court for recognition of the debtor as insolvent and to initiate the bankruptcy procedure. They may also opt for amicable settlement. The plan is regarded to have been endorsed by the creditors' meeting, if it is supported by half of the votes present at the meeting (Art.83, paras.3 and 4). It is not clear from this provision whether the court has the right to reject the plan or not. On the other hand, in order to apply to court for the initiation of the bankruptcy procedure, a majority of all votes of the creditors is needed (Art.14, para.1).

As a rule, the length of external administration is 12 months; it can be extended for 6 months (Art.68, para.4). However, the court may extend this period, provided that there is sufficient ground to assume that the extension would result in the restoration of solvency of the debtor (Art.84).

Every year, around 1,100-1,200 companies come under external administration. In 2000, external administration was introduced in 1,069 companies. In 907 cases, the company was recognised as bankrupt and the bankruptcy procedure started. 296 cases ended with amicable settlement between the creditors and debtors. Only in 50 cases, the debtor became solvent.[15] Therefore, the effectiveness of external administration is often questioned.[16]

The primary problem with external administration is the quality of external administrators. According to the report of the commercial court, no corpus of qualified administrators has been formed. 'In fact, the incompetent and un-professional external administrators and the absence of an effective means of controlling them often results in the liquidation of companies'. Some administrators who are qualified totally lack experience. On the other hand, many administrators handle the procedure of 8-10 large companies simultaneously.[17] External administrators are in practice, free from control and the result is the 'theft of basic assets of the enterprises, violation of the rules of auction for the sale of assets etc'.[18]

What is more, the neutrality of the administrators of the interested parties is questionable:

In a case involving Chernogorneft, which was the largest production subsidiary of Sidanco, a competitor of Sidanco had been collecting claims *vis à vis* this subsidiary. The competitor floated a massive amount of bonds to finance this operation. Eventually, this competitor came to hold a substantial claim to the subsidiary directly and indirectly.

At the beginning of the procedure, EBRD, US Export-Import Bank and other creditors were not allowed to vote for the candidates for the post of external administrator, but eventually, a new creditors' committee chaired by EBRD was formed and worked for the restoration of the company. However, the competitor applied to court for the removal

---

15   Supreme Commercial Court, 'Rabota arbitrazhnykh sudov Rossiiskoi Federatsii v 2000 godu', [www.arbitr.ru].
16   *VVAS* 2001 No.5, pp.11-12.
17   'Rabota...', *supra*.
18   *Ibid.*

of the external administrator. The commercial court, on appeal, accepted this and replaced the administrator who was said to be close to the competitor. The Supreme Commercial Court quashed this decision, but soon afterwards, reinstated the same administrator.

In the creditors' meeting which followed, since the amount of registered claims of the EBRD was reduced by the court and the claim of the US Exim Bank had been repaid shortly before, the competitor's side had a majority, and another administrator close to the competitor was appointed. In the end, the creditors' meeting later resolved that Chernogorneft be sold by auction. Despite objections from Sidanco and foreign creditors, the auction went ahead, and a company related to the competitor successfully acquired Chernogorneft at a low price. Similar questionable incidents took place in relation to other subsidiaries and Sidanco itself.

In the year 2000, a compromise was reached, but was not fully implemented. Finally, in July 2001, a deal was announced to the effect that a holding which owns the competitor will acquire a 44% stake in Sidanco, and the same competitor returns Chernogorneft to Sidanco. The competitor's group will come to hold 84% of Sidanco, while a foreign investor – BP-Amoco – will maintain 10% as was the case before the incident.[19]

4)   Bankruptcy

If the court finally recognises the debtor to be insolvent, a decision to this effect is made, and the bankruptcy procedure begins. With the initiation of the bankruptcy procedure, all monetary claims become due. As a rule, transactions involving the disposal of the property of the debtor are not allowed. The seizure of the debtor's assets and other restrictions on them are terminated and new measures are not allowed. The head of the debtor-organisation is removed from management (Art.98, para.1).

With the recognition of the debtor as insolvent, the court appoints the bankruptcy administrator(s) (Art.99). All powers of management of the debtor-organisation, including the power to dispose of the debtor's assets, shift to the bankruptcy administrator upon the appointment (Art.101, para.1). The bankruptcy administrator's functions include the following (*ibid.*, para.3):

i)   management of the debtor's assets, preparation of the inventory and valuation of the assets;

ii)   analysis of the debtor's financial state;

iii)   presentation of claims *vis à vis* third parties who are in debt to the debtor;

iv)   giving notice of impending dismissal to the employees;

---

19   *Project Finance International*, June 16, 1999, p.47, October 6, 1999, p.52; *The Moscow Times*, November 24, 26, 1999, August 3, 2001; *Kommersant* , March 2, May 16, 2000.

v)   refusal of performance of the obligation of the debtor;

vi)   search for and retrieval of the debtor's property in possession of third parties.

The bankruptcy estate comprises all properties of the debtor existing at the time of the initiation of the bankruptcy procedure and properties found in the course of the procedure. Properties which are excluded from circulation, e.g. items of cultural or historical significance, proprietary rights which are related to the person of the debtor, including licences for carrying out specific types of activities etc. are excluded from the estate (Art.103, paras. 1 and 2).

Secured properties are not excluded from the bankruptcy estate. This was not the case in the 1992 Law. This is said to be because the Civil Code, which was enacted after the 1992 Law, has a provision to this effect (Art.64, para.1), and the Law on Insolvency could not provide otherwise. A more substantial reason is that the security rights are regarded as rights *in personam*, and not real rights in Russia.

The bankruptcy administrator, after preparing the inventory and having the assets valued, sells these properties by public auction, unless the creditors' meeting or creditors' committee determines otherwise. The administrator may personally organise the auction, or entrust it to a specialised organisation for auction (Art.112, paras. 1 and 3).

After paying the cost, the order of satisfaction from the estate is as follows (Art.106):

first rank   claims of individuals based upon the liability of the debtor for causing damage to life and health

second rank   payment of retirement money and wages, and royalty for author's rights (copyright)

third rank   secured claims

fourth rank   tax obligations and payments to the extra-budget funds (pensions and social insurance)

fifth rank   other claims

Payment of claims based upon tort liability which comes first is effected in the form of capitalising the payment.

In 2000, 15,143 bankruptcy proceedings were imitated, while 7,775 proceedings were completed.[20]

---

20   'Rassmotrenie…', *supra.*

5)   Amicable Settlement

An amicable settlement can be made between the debtor and the creditors. This is possible only after the claims of the first and second rank are satisfied. The settlement has to be endorsed by the court (Art.123, paras. 1 and 2).

6

GENERAL RULES OF THE LAW OF OBLIGATIONS

1 GENERAL

Book Three of the Civil Code is divided into two sections: general rules of the law of obligations and general rules of contract law. Individual types of obligation are provided in Book Four, which is in Part Two of the Code enacted one year after Part One. Book Four not only contains obligations arising from various types of contracts, but also obligations arising out of tort and unjust enrichment. This structure is in line with the tradition of Russian civil law under the influence of the European system. The draft Civil Code of 1905 was also arranged in this way.

2 PERFORMANCE OF OBLIGATION

1) Manner of Performance

The general rule is that an obligation should be performed in accordance with the terms of obligation and the requirement of the law and other legal acts, and in their absence, in accordance with the business practice (*obychai delovogo oborota*) or other normally applicable requirements (Art.309).

Business practice means 'accumulated and widely applied rules of conduct in a particular area of entrepreneurial activity' (Art.5). Business practice against the law is not applicable. Some other laws, such as the Law on International Commercial Arbitration, use the term *torgovyi obychai* (commercial custom). There are three requirements for business practice to be applied; it has to be accumulated, i.e. continuous and sufficiently defined in its content, has to be widely applied, and not against the law.[1]

---

[1] O.N.Sadikov ed., *Komentarii k grazhdanskomu kodeksu Rossiiskoi Federatsi, Chasti Pervoi*, enlarged edition, Moscow 1999, p.17.

2)   Time of Performance

If the obligation presupposes a fixed date or period of performance, it has to be performed on that day or within the period. If no date or period is determined, the obligation must be performed within a reasonable period after the obligation emerged. With an obligation which was not performed within a reasonable period, or obligation by presentation, the debtor must perform the obligation within 7 days of the creditor requiring the performance, unless otherwise provided by law and other legal acts, business practice or emanates from the content of the obligation (Art.314). Performance of obligation ahead of the agreed time is allowed in principle. However, in obligations involving entrepreneurial activities, performance ahead of time is allowed only when it is provided by law, legal acts, business practice or emanates from the content of the obligation (Art.315).

3)   Place of Performance

If the place of performance of obligation is not provided by law and other legal acts, or contract, or is not apparent from business practice or the content of the obligation, the place of performance is determined by the following rules:

    i)   obligation to transfer land, building, installation and other immovables – the place of the location of the property;

    ii)   obligation to transfer goods and other property which presupposes transportation – place of the location of the first carrier for the delivery to the creditor;

    iii)   other obligation of entrepreneurs to transfer goods and other property – place of production or storage if these places were known to the creditor at the time of the emergence of obligation;

    iv)   monetary obligation – place (location) of the creditor at the time of the emergence of the obligation;

    v)   all other obligations – place (location) of the debtor.

4)   Currency of Performance

Monetary obligations must be denominated in roubles. They can also be determined as a rouble equivalent of foreign currency or units of payment. In such cases, the exchange rate is determined by the official rate at the time of payment (Art.317, paras. 1 and 2). The basic law which regulates currency transactions is the Law on Foreign Currency Regulation and Control of 1992.

5)   Performance by Deposit

Depositing money or securities is deemed to be performance of obligation (Art.327). Debtors are entitled to place money or securities in deposit with the notary public or, in cases provided by law, with the court if the obligation is impossible to perform for the following reasons:

i)   absence of the creditor or the person empowered by the creditor to accept performance at the place of performance of obligation;

ii)   absence of legal capacity of the creditor and the absence of a legal representative;

iii)   apparent difficulty in determining who the creditor is, especially when there is a dispute in this regards between the creditor and a third party;

iv)   failure on the part of the creditor to accept performance or other delay on his part.

The procedure for depositing money and securities is provided by the Basic Law on Notary Public.[2]

6)   Counter-Performance

When the performance of an obligation presupposes performance of an obligation by the opposite party *vis à vis* the other party, if the opposite party does not offer performance or there are circumstances which demonstrate that the obligation will not be performed within the agreed period, the other party is entitled to suspend the performance of his obligation, or refuse performance and demand compensation (Art.328, paras. 1 and 2).

3   OBLIGATION WITH MULTIPLE PARTIES

As a rule, if there are several debtors and/or creditors, each creditor has the right to demand performance and each debtor has a duty to perform obligation in the same proportion as the others (Art.321).

The Code also provides for joint and several obligations and claims. In joint and several obligation (obligation with multiple debtors), the creditor is entitled to demand from all debtors simultaneously, or separately, performance in full or in part. Each debtor continues to be liable until the obligation is performed in

---

2   *VSND RF i VS RF*, 1993 No.10, item 357.

full (Art.323). A debtor is not entitled to set up an objection to the creditor based upon the relationship between his co-debtors and the creditor to which he is not a party (Art.324). For example, even if one of the debtors has a counter claim against the creditor, other debtors are not entitled to rely on this counter claim.

Obligation related to entrepreneurial activities with several debtors or creditors are joint and several, unless law and other legal acts, or terms of obligation provides otherwise (Art.322).

4   CHANGE OF THE PARTIES

1)   Assignment of Claims

The right (claim) which belongs to the creditor can be assigned by a juristic act or shift to another person by law (Art.382, para.1). As an exception, claims which are inseparable from the personality of the creditor cannot be assigned. These include the right to alimony and the right for compensation of damage on life or health of an individual (Art.383). Also assignment is not allowed if it is against the law and other legal acts, or contract (Art.388). Thus, it is possible to restrict the right to assign the claim by a contract.

For assignment of claims, the consent of the debtor is not needed, unless otherwise provided by law or contract. If the debtor was not notified in writing of the assignment of the claim, the new creditor bears the risk of disadvantageous consequences; performance of obligation to the original creditor is regarded as an appropriate performance in such cases (Art.382, para.3). A consent of the debtor is needed, however, if the identity of the creditor has an essential meaning to the debtor (Art.388, para.2).

The rights of the original creditor are transferred to the new creditor in the same scope and with conditions which existed at the time of the assignment. What is particularly important is that the rights which secure the performance of the obligation, e.g. pledge, as well as other rights related to the obligation, such as the right to unpaid interest, shift to the new creditor (Art.384). Whether the agreement concerning the place of dispute settlement would be transferred together with the claim was disputed at the former Foreign Trade Arbitration Commission in Moscow in 1984. The Commission concluded that the agreement was independent from the main contract and could not be transferred.[3] Whether this con-

---

3   Sadikov ed., *Komentarii k grazhdanskomu kodeksu Rossiiskoi Federatsii, Chasti Pervoi*, first edition, Moscow 1996, p.379.

clusion can be maintained under this provision in the Civil Code was at issue in the following case:

> By an agreement concluded in 1996, a Belgian company assigned to a US company a claim against a Russian joint stock company for repayment of a loan. The US company, which opened an office in Russia, brought an action against the Russian company for the enforcement of the claim in the Russian commercial court. The original loan agreement had an arbitration clause, referring the dispute to the Stockholm Arbitration Institute. The US company, in bringing the case to a Russian court, was of the view that the arbitration clause was independent of the loan agreement, had a procedural nature, and therefore, had not been transferred together with the claim to the assignee of the claim.
>
> The Russian commercial court ruled that the right to bring the case to court was one of the component parts of the claim and should be recognised to have been assigned to the new creditor together with the claim by virtue of Article 384 of the Civil Code.[4]

The debtor is entitled to refuse performance until the new creditor presents evidence that the claim has been transferred to this person. The assignor of the claim is under obligation to provide documents which certify the claim and relevant information to the new creditor (Art.385). The debtor may set up the objection he had against the original creditor also against the new creditor up to the moment of notice of assignment (Art.386).

The assignor of the claim is liable to the assignee for the invalidity of the claim which has been assigned, but is not liable for the non-performance of the claim unless the assignor guaranteed performance by the debtor to the assignee (Art.390).

2)   Assumption of Debt

Transfer of debt by the debtor is allowed only with the consent of the creditor (Art.391). The new debtor is entitled to set up objections against the claim based upon the relation between the creditor and the original debtor (Art.392).

---

4   'Obzor sudebno-arbitrazhnoi praktiki razresheniia sporov po delam s uchastiem inostrannykh lits', Informatsionnoe pis'mo, Supreme Commercial Court, February 16, 1998 No.29, item.15, in V.Zhura-kovskii and V.Kalinin, *Kommentarii i primenenie zakonodatel'stva arbitrazhnymi sudami Rossisskoi Federatsii*, Moscow 2000, pp.212-213.

5   TERMINATION OF OBLIGATION

1)   General

Obligations are terminated on the following grounds (arts.407-419):

  i)   performance;
  ii)   substitute performance (*otstupnoe*);
  iii)   set-off;
  iv)   merger of the status of creditor and debtor;
  v)   novation;
  vi)   discharge of debt;
  vii)   impossibility of performance;
  viii) act of government;
  ix)   death of a physical person or liquidation of a juridical person.

2)   Substitute Performance

Performance of obligation can be substituted by another kind of action by agreement of the parties (Art.409). Substitute performance has been practised for many
years, but the present Civil Code has, for the first time since 1922, accommodated
a provision on it.[5] The Code refers to transfer of property as a substitute performance for payment of money, but it can be in other forms, such as provision of
service.

   Substitute performance is widely practised in Russia due to the 'ineffectiveness
of pledge as a means of securing performance'.[6] A contract of substitute performance by transferring property (collateral) from the debtor to the creditor is
concluded simultaneously with the basic loan contract. This is a contract with
condition precedent and comes into effect by the debtor defaulting in the basic
loan contract. The basic loan contract is terminated by substitute performance.
The court practice seems to acknowledge this as 'substitute performance of obligations secured by pledge'. In principle, all agreements of pledge which provide
for the transfer of the collateral to the creditor in case of default are null and void,

---

5   O.Iu.Shilokhvost, *Otstupnoe v grazhdanskom prave*, Moscow 1999, pp. 60-132.
6   *Ibid.*, pp.213-216.

but as an exception, if the agreement qualifies as substitute performance or novation, it is valid.[7]

3)   Set-off

Set-off is possible between countering claims of the same nature which are due, have no fixed time of performance, or become due on presentation. It is effected by an act of one of the parties (Art.410). The requirement of the 'same nature' means that the object of the claim should be of the same kind, e.g. money. Set-off is not allowed when the counter claim is extinct by prescription, is a claim on compensation for damage caused on health or life of an individual, is a claim on alimony, or life annuity (Art.411).

If a claim has been assigned, the debtor is entitled to set-off his counter-claim against the original creditor also against the new creditor. This is possible when this counter claim against the original creditor existed before the debtor was notified of the assignment and the claim was due, the time of performance was not determined, or was to become due on presentation (Art.412).

4)   Novation

Obligation can be terminated by novation, i.e. agreement of the parties to replace the original obligation by another obligation with different object or manner of performance. The basic difference of novation with substitute performance is that in novation, a new obligation emerges. Novation is not allowed with obligations on compensation of damage caused on health or life of an individual, or payment of alimony (Art.414, paras. 1 and 2). It should be noted that novation terminates 'supplementary obligations' related to the original obligation unless otherwise provided by the agreement between the parties. 'Supplementary obligations' in this context includes means of securing the performance of obligation, e.g. agreement of pledge or guarantee (except for bank guarantee).[8]

---

7   Joint Decision of the Supreme Court and the Supreme Commercial Court, 'O nekotorykh voprosov, sviazannykh s primeneniiem chasti pervoi Grazhdankogo kodeksa RF', July 1, 1996, No.6/8, item 46, in Zhurakovskii and Kalinin, *supra*, p.42.

8   Sadikov ed., *Kommentarii…* first edition, *supra*, pp.403-404.

5)   Impossibility of Performance

Impossibility of performance also terminates obligations, i.e. an obligation is terminated if performance became impossible due to circumstances in which neither party is responsible. Naturally, impossibility of performance is excluded in monetary obligations. If impossibility of performance was caused by an intentional or negligent act of the creditor, the creditor is not entitled to demand return of the performed part of the obligation (Art.416). On the other hand, if impossibility of performance was caused by fault on the part of the debtor, the obligation is not terminated, but is changed; the debtor is liable for non-performance of obligation.[9]

6   LIABILITY FOR THE BREACH OF OBLIGATIONS

Debtors are liable for compensation caused to the creditor by non-performance or inadequate performance of obligation (Art.393, para.1). As a rule, this is a liability based upon fault (intent or negligence). The present Code has introduced a definition of fault for the first time. Thus, a person is found to have not been at fault, if this person has taken all measures for the adequate performance of the obligation with the standard of care and foreseeability which are required of this person in accordance with the nature of the obligation and terms of business (Art.401, para.1).[10] The absence of fault has to be proved by the person who is in breach of obligation (*ibid.*, para.2).

In most jurisdictions, the absence of fault should be no defence in monetary obligations. However, in Russia, there have been cases where fault was required in pursuing the liability for the delay of performance in monetary obligations of government institutions:

> A government institution was sued for the delay in payment for the service provided by a joint stock company. The Supreme Commercial Court denied the argument of the defendant that the penalties were unreasonable, but found that the delay of payment was due to the delay in the allocation of funds to the government institution from the federal budget and that this could mean that the institution was not at fault.[11]

---

9   *Ibid.*, p.405.

10   M.I.Braginskii ed., *Nauchno-prakticheskii kommentarii k chasti pervoi grazhdanskogo kodeksa Rossiiskoi Federatsii,* second edition, Moscow 1999, p.521.

11   D.V.Murzin ed., *Grazhdanskii kodeks RF s postateinymi materialami iz praktiki VAS RF*, Moscow 1999, pp.402-403. See also S.V.Sarbash, *Arbitrazhnaia praktika po grazhdanskim delam*, Moscow 2000, pp.379-384..

For those involved in entrepreneurial activities, the Code is stricter. As a rule, a person who failed to perform obligation or performed obligation in an inadequate manner while performing entrepreneurial activities is liable for compensation, unless it is proved that adequate performance was impossible due to *force majeure*, i.e. circumstances which are extraordinary and impossible to prevent under the given conditions (*ibid.*, para.2). *Force majeure* include natural disasters like earthquake, flood, severe change of temperature, as well as 'military activities', epidemics, and large scale strikes as well as acts of government. Acts of government includes declaration of quarantine, prohibition of transport, and international trade sanctions.[12] The Code explicitly provides that breach of obligation by a third party in relation to the debtor, absence of the goods in the market, or absence of money with the debtor are not *force majeure* (*ibid.*, para.3);

> A limited liability company – a bakery – 'Magazin No.60' brought an action against an electricity company for compensation of damage of 134,486,500 roubles. The damage was caused by the interruption of the electricity supply to the company, due to an accident involving the transmission cable. The defendant argued that the interruption was caused by the technical violation of the use of electricity by the plaintiff. The defendant also pointed out that the amount of the claimed compensation was excessive. The Supreme Commercial Court ruled that the accident happened outside the scope of responsibility of the plaintiff. The Court did not find any evidence which proved the fault of the plaintiff or the existence of grounds for exempting the liability of the electricity supplier.[13]

> A foreign trading company with a representative office in Russia brought an action against a Russian foreign trade organisation for payment of the price for the sugar supplied to this Russian organisation. The defendant claimed that the money was transferred to a foreign bank in accordance with the term of the contract with the trading company, but was stolen from the bank, and argued that it could not be held liable for the fault of a third party. The commercial court, by referring to the Vienna Convention on the International Sale of Goods, ruled that the defendant had failed to prove that the act of a third party in this case was a 'hindrance out of control'.[14]

If non-performance or inadequate performance of the obligation was caused by a fault of both parties, the court must accordingly reduce the amount of liability of the debtor. The court is entitled to do the same if the creditor by intention or

---

12 Sadikov ed., *Komentarii…*enlarged edition, *supra*, p.654.

13 Decision of the Presidium of the Supreme Commercial Court, November 4, 1997, *VVAS RF*, 1998 No.2, pp.32-34.

14 'Obzor sudebno-arbitrazhnoi praktiki razresheniia sporov po delam s uchastiem inostrannykh lits', *supra*, pp.201-202.

negligence contributed to the increase of damage caused by non-performance or inadequate performance or failed to take reasonable measures by the debtor for the reduction of damage (Art.404).

An act of employees of the debtor in performance of an obligation is regarded as an act of the debtor. The debtor is liable for the act of employees for non-performance or inadequate performance (Art.402). If the debtor entrusted the performance of an obligation to a third party, the debtor is liable for non-performance or inadequate performance by this person unless the law provides that the third party is liable (Art.403).

The debtor is liable for the damage caused by non-performance or inadequate performance of an obligation (Art.393, para.1). The basic provision on compensation is located in the General Part of the Code. The principle of full compensation is adopted (Art.15, para.1). Damages cover both real damage and lost income. Thus, the cost which the person had incurred and will incur to restore his rights and loss and damage on the property as well as the lost income which the person would have received under normal conditions of civil transaction had his rights not been infringed, are compensated (*ibid.*, para.2). Although The Code provides for compensation of moral damage in the General Part (Art.15), this is understood not to apply in the breach of contractual obligations.

Full compensation means that as a result of compensation, the assets of the creditor should be the same as it would have been, had the obligation been performed in an adequate manner. In some jurisdictions which adopt this principle, the scope of damage which is to be compensated is limited by the concept of 'adequate compensation'. The same idea seems to apply in Russia – the compensation has to be 'adequate'. 'The creditor should not receive anything more than necessary to have his rights restored'.[15] One commentator suggests that a creditor who claims lost income beyond reasonable scope may be found to be abusing the rights (Art.10).[16]

The Civil Code does not have detailed provisions on compensation. The only such provision concerns the price. As a rule, when determining the amount of compensation, price of goods and services in question on the day of performance by the debtor at the place where the obligation was to be performed is to be taken into account; if the obligation was not voluntarily performed, the price on the date of action to bring the case to court should be taken into account (Art.393, para.3). In cases of inflation, if the creditor proves that he had taken all measures to prevent the damage or reducing the damage, the price which is a result of inflation

---

15   Braginskii ed., *supra*, p.490.
16   *Ibid.*, p.491.

may have to be taken into account, since the damage at the time of the court action is to be compensated.[17]

The right to full compensation for the breach of performance can be limited by law or contract. Sometimes, the amount of compensation is limited to penalties, to the value of goods or service, or to the real damage and not the expected income, i.e. the loss sustained but not the income foregone. In some cases, a ceiling is set for the amount of compensation. However, limitation on the amount of compensation by standard form contracts or contracts in which the creditor is a physical person acting as a consumer, is void, if the amount of compensation for such instances or such kinds of violations is determined by law, or the contract had been concluded before the incident occurred (Art.400, para.2).

In order to claim compensation, the plaintiff must prove 1) the breach of obligation by the defendant, 2) existence of a causal link between the non-performance or inadequate performance and the damage, and 3) the scope of damage caused by the breach on the part of the defendant.

Contracts often provide for penalties (*neustoika* -sometimes called *peni* or *shtraf*) for non-performance or inadequate performance. Penalties usually take the form of monetary payment. The relationship between penalties and compensation for damage varies. The general rule is that compensation covers the damage which is not covered by penalties (Art.394, para.1). However, there are variations. In some cases, penalties are all that the creditor is to receive (liquidated damages), such as in the transport industry. In other cases, penalties are charged in addition to compensation of damage. There are also instances where alternatively, penalties or compensation is available (*ibid*.).

Penalties can be reduced by discretion of the court if apparently disproportional to the result of the breach (Art.333). This power of the court is said to be widely utilised due to the 'extremely low standard of contract' which often provides for 5-10% penalties a day![18]

For non-performance of monetary obligations, including use of other person's money as a result of its unlawful retention, refusal to return the money, and other delay in payment or unjustified receipt or saving of other person's money, interest must be paid on the amount of the money. The rate of interest is determined by the bank interest rate applicable at the place of residence of the creditor on the day of performance (Art.395, para.1). If the damage incurred by the creditor by an unlawful use of money by another person is more than the interest payable, the creditor may claim the difference as well (*ibid*., para.2).

---

17 D.V.Murzin, *supra*, pp.31-32. Also *VVAS RF*, 1993 No.11, p.185.
18 Braginskii ed., *supra*, p.498.

7

MEANS OF SECURING CLAIMS

1   General

The Russian Civil Code has a separate chapter on the securing of performance of obligations. The starting provision in this chapter provides as follows:

> Performance of an obligation can be secured by a penalty (*neustoika*), a pledge, the withholding of the object, a suretyship, a bank guarantee, earnest money, and other means provided by law or contract (Art.329, para.1).

Penalties, pledges, withholding of the object, suretyship, and bank guarantees are covered in subchapters in this part. Withholding of the subject and bank guarantees are novelties of the Code, while other means existed in the socialist code.

The list of the means of securing performance of obligation is by no means exhaustive. The above-mentioned provision refers to 'other means provided by law or contract'. The Code itself has another provision which provides that when it is agreed in the contract that the title to the product is to be retained by the seller until payment or fulfilment of other conditions, the seller is under an obligation not to alienate or otherwise dispose of the product (Art.491). This provision also allows the parties to agree on other means of securing obligations under a contract. This may be relevant in determining the validity of atypical security rights (see below).

Furthermore, the Law on Banking and Banking Activities provides that the repayment of credit can be secured by a pledge on movables and immovables, including state and other securities, bank guarantees and other means provided by federal law or contracts (Art.33).[1]

---

[1]   *VSND RF i VS RF*, 1992 No.9, item 391.

2   Real Security Rights (Pledge)

1)   The Concept

The Russian term *zalog* is usually translated into English as 'pledge'. The Civil
Code provides that by virtue of *zalog*, the creditor has a right to have the claim
satisfied from the assets of the debtor in priority to other creditors in case of the
debtor's default. Thus, in this context, *zalog* means security rights in general. The
Code divides *zalog* into two categories; pledges with or without transfer of the
collateral to the creditor. *Zalog* over immovables is hypothec (*ipoteka*), while
pledges on other properties do not seem to have a specific name under the Code.
The 1992 Law on Pledge (*zalog*) called it *zaklad*. The 1998 Law on Hypothec
reconfirmed that *zalog* on immovables was hypothec. This arrangement was the
reverse in the Tsarist law. There was no specific term for the *zalog* on immovables,
while *zalog* on movables was called *zaklad*.[2]

Other methods of securing the performance of obligations are not called *zalog*.
The Code provides that an obligation can be secured by other means provided
by law or agreed by the parties. Thus, retention of title, which is covered in the
part dealing with contract of sale, is not *zalog* per se. Atypical security rights do
not seem to be regarded as *zalog* either.

A pledge is regarded as a right *in personam* rather than a real right under the
Code. Provisions on pledges are part of the law of obligations and not the law
of property. This is different from German, French and English law, but it is
similar to the Dutch Civil Code on which the Russians had modelled the Code.
Those who took part in the preparation of the Code also pointed out that this is
a Russian tradition from before the Revolution.

Indeed, the *Svod zakonov* had provisions on security rights in the part dealing
with contracts. Volume X (Civil Law) of the *Svod zakonov* was composed of four
books. It started with the rights and duties of the family, followed by the procedure
of obtaining and consolidating property rights in general. This part basically
covered property rights. It was followed by the procedure of obtaining and consolidating property rights in specifics. This latter part contained provisions on, *inter
alia*, the obtaining of property by gift, sale, and inheritance. Book Four contained
provisions on contracts. There was a chapter here which was devoted to the means
of securing the performance of obligations. This included suretyship, pledges, and
penalties for delay.[3] A 'pledge' was defined as a right to receive payment from

---

2   D.I.Meier, *Russkoe grazhdanskoe pravo*, St.Petersburg 1902, pp. 434-435.
3   *Ibid.*, pp.43-48.

the proceeds of sale of the collateral in case of default.[4] Thus, a pledge was not regarded as a right over the collateral, but rather, a right to demand that the debtor sell the collateral and to have the claim satisfied from the proceeds. Presumably, this was why it was not made part of property law, but part of the law of obligations. On the other hand, some lawyers in the Tsarist period maintained that *zalog* was a real right. According to Verblovskii, 'an essential feature of the right to pledge is its nature as a real right (*veshchnoe pravo, dingliches Recht*)'.[5]

The present Code seems to have followed the model of *Svod zakonov*. However, some problematic effects are deducted from the nature of a pledge as a right *in personam*. An example is the Law on Insolvency. Under the current Law of Insolvency, secured claims are not excluded from the bankruptcy estate as they used to be under the previous law. This is explained as being a result of the fact that a pledge is a right *in personam*; only objects of real rights are qualified for exclusion from the bankruptcy estate.

2)   The Statutes

At present, there are two statutes other than the Civil Code which provide for pledges. In 1998, a new Law on Hypothec was enacted. This Law has clarified some matters which were left ambiguous by other laws. In addition, the Law on Pledge of 1992 is still valid, insofar as it does not contradict the Civil Code and the 1998 Law.

There are some other laws which are relevant and supplement the system of security. First, there is the Law on Registration of Immovables and Related Transactions which was enacted in 1997. Although the system of registration is still in the process of development, it is hoped that this Law will bring order into the present chaotic registration system where local authorities set up their own rules. Second, there is the Law on Civil Enforcement Procedure of 1997. Third, a new Law on Insolvency was enacted in 1998 to replace the 1992 Law.

There are laws which are yet to be enacted or to be modernised. First of all, the Code of Civil Procedure, which has a section on the sale of assets, is yet to be amended in line with other laws. This Code was enacted in 1964 and has been amended since the collapse of socialism, but still requires some change in order to introduce a proper system of the realisation of assets of the debtor. Furthermore, according to the Civil Code, a new law which deals with security on the "goods in circulation", e.g. inventories, is to be enacted, but has not materialised so far.

---

4   *Ibid.*, p.432.
5   F.A.Brokgaus et al eds., *Entsiklopedicheskii slovar' brokhaus*, St.Petersburg, vol. 23, p. 189.

3)   Objects of Pledge

The Code provides that any property can be the object of a pledge, including proprietary rights (claims), but excludes property which is withdrawn from circulation and claims which are inseparably linked with the personality of the creditor (Art.336, para.1). A commentary to the Code suggests that the basic requirement to be an object of pledge lies in its nature as a commodity.[6] In fact, the Code, in the General Part, refers to the capability of circulation (*oborotsposobnost'*) of the objects of civil law rights (Art.129). Objects of rights under the Code are freely disposable and can be transferred to another party unless it is withdrawn from circulation or the circulation is restricted. What specifically the term 'withdrawn from circulation' means is not necessarily clear. A commentary on the Civil Code refers to natural resources on the continental shelf and in exclusive economic zones, and cites forests as well as assets related to national defence as examples. Gold or silver which is not processed into ornaments cannot be traded freely either.[7] On the other hand, in stark contrast to the socialist system, while subsoil resources belong to the state, once they are exploited, they can belong to private entities and can be pledged.

The 1992 Pledge Law was slightly different in that it provided that any property which is disposable could be an object of a pledge. It was more specific on the pledge of rights. It was provided that the right to possess and use a property including leases as well as other rights, and claims emanating from obligations and other proprietary rights qualified as objects of a pledge.

The 1998 Law on Hypothec lists the following objects of hypothec (At.5, para.1):

i)   pieces of land;
ii)   enterprises, as well as buildings, installations and other immovables used for entrepreneurial purposes;
iii)   residential houses, flats and parts of them which comprise one or several separate rooms;
iv)   *dacha*, garden houses, garage and other structures of a consumption nature;
v)   aircraft, ships and satellites.

Whether land can be pledged (hypothecated) was not clear until the 1998 Law was enacted. A provision of the Civil Code which sets out the content of ownership of land lists the right to pledge the property as one of the attributes of owner-

---

6   M.I.Braginskii and V.V.Vitrianski, *Dogovornoe pravo*, Moscow 1997, p.414.
7   O.N.Sadikov ed., *Kommentarii k grazhdanskomu kodekusu Rossiiskoi Federatsii, chasti pervoi*, enlarged edition, Moscow 1999, pp.584-585.

ship (Art.260, para.1). However, this provision was yet to take effect, pending the adoption of the new Land Code (the new Land Code was finally adopted in October 2001). Even without this provision, as long as the 'circulation' of the given piece of land is not prohibited, it was thought that land could be hypothecated. The 1998 Law made this clear. On the other hand, this Law also has a provision which sets out exceptions. Thus, land which belongs to the state or municipality and agricultural land cannot be hypothecated (Art.63, para.1).

A practical problem is that there is no proper market which determines the value of the land.

'Goods in circulation' can also be the object of a pledge. The goods remain in the possession of the titleholder, but the 'composition and the identity' of the goods may change, provided that the total value does not fall below the agreed amount. Goods which are disposed of by the pledger cease to be the object of the pledge, while goods which newly come into the possession of the pledger become an object of the pledge.

Details on this type of pledge are not given either in the Code or the 1992 Law. The former creates some confusion by referring to *tverdyi zalog*, i.e. firm pledge. A new Law is expected to be enacted on this matter.

Rights are pledgeable. However, the Code does not have specific provisions on the pledge on rights. The only reference to rights as objects of a pledge is a provision which requires that rights embodied in securities be transferred to the pledgee or deposited with a notary public unless otherwise agreed in the contract (Art. 338, para.4). Therefore, at this moment, the 1992 Law on Pledge is applicable here. Furthermore, the 1998 Law on Hypothec accommodates a provision on hypothecs on leases (*arenda*) of immovables. This provision provides that rules applicable to the hypothec of immovables are applicable with modification to the lease (Art.5, para.5). This is unusual, since a hypothec is supposed to be placed on immovables, and not on rights to immovables. It should be noted that as a rule, a lease cannot be hypothecated without the consent of the owner. Furthermore, in the case of default by the debtor, the creditor is not entitled to take over the lease; the lease has to be realised, i.e. sold by auction![8]

Securities can be pledged. In fact, the pledge of securities is widely utilised and is one of the few means through which juridical persons and individuals can receive a loan from a bank. Furthermore, it is, in many instances, the only collateral the creditor accepts. When the Central Bank extends loans to banks, treasury bonds are the only security accepted.[9]

---

8   V.Smirnov and Z.Lukina, *Kommentarii k federal'nomu zakonu ob ipoteke*, Moscow 1999, pp.30-31.
9   A.A.Makovskaia, *Zalog denezhnykh sredstv i tsennykh bumag*, Moscow 1999, pp.25-26.

Whether money in an account can be the object of a pledge is a matter of conention. The problem is whether the money in the account can be seized by a secured lender in preference to others in the case of default by the debtor:

> Sverbank initiated an action against Pakamar Bank claiming that the contract of pledge concluded between them was void. The pledged object was the 'money in the corresponding account'. The Supreme Commercial Court found this contract to be null and void by virtue of Article 168, since money in a corresponding account was not transferable, while the Civil Code presupposes that the collateral should be transferable.[10]

The Supreme Commercial Court summarised this case as demonstrating that 'the object of a pledge cannot be specified as money in the bank account'.[11] However, this decision is being criticised by academics. Perhaps the pledge should have been arranged as a pledge on the claim of the debtor to the money in the bank account.[12]

Using foreign currency as the object of a pledge is said to entail no problem.[13]

The available type of pledge depends on whether the object of the pledge is an immovable or not. A hypothec is available only for immovables. On the other hand, transactions involving immovables including contracts of hypothec are subject to registration. The 1997 Law on the Registration of Immovables and Related Transactions is applicable here. This Law covers the above-mentioned real properties except for aircraft, ships and satellites. It is, however, applicable to them for the time being until respective federal laws are enacted

The Code lists land, subsoil reserves, demarcated water objects, and other property which is firmly attached to the land, i.e. cannot be removed without unreasonable harm to its purpose of use, as immovables. These include forests, perennial plants, buildings and installations. Also aircraft, ships, and satellites are regarded as Immovables. Under a separate provision, an enterprise as a whole is made an immovable (Art.130, para.1).

---

10 Decision of the Presidium of the Supreme Commercial Court, July 2, 1996, *VVAS RF* 1996 No. 10, p.68.

11 'Obzor praktiki razresheniia sporov, sviazannykh s primeneniem arbitrazhnymi sudami norm grazhdanskogo kodeksa Rossiiskoi Federatsii o zaloge', informatioannoe pis'mo VAS RF, January 15, 1998, item 3, in V.Zhuranovskii and V.Kalinin, *Kommentarii i primenenie zakonodatel'stva arbitrazhnymi sudami Rossiiskoi Federatsii*, Moscow 2000, p.109.

12 Sadikov ed., *supra*, p.585.

13 Braginskii and Vitrianski, *supra*, p.416.

4)   Form of Contracts and Registration

The Code requires that a contract of pledge must be in written form. A pledge of immovables (hypothec) as well as any pledge which secures a claim subject to notarisation, must be notarised in addition (Art.339, para.2).

In a contract of pledge, the object of the pledge, its value, the nature, and the amount and time of performance of the secured obligation must be specified (*ibid.*, para.1):

> A bank brought an action against a joint stock company for the repayment of a debt and at the same time, the seizure of two automobiles which had been pledged. In the contract, the object of the pledge was specified as 'automobiles and other means of transport which belong to the debtor'. During the hearing, it was found that the debtor had several automobiles in its possession. The court found this contract not to have been concluded, since the object of the pledge was insufficiently identified. In addition to the type of the property ('automobile'), individual characters of the object which allow the object to be distinguished from similar objects must be specified.[14]

The Law on Hypothec provides for essential elements to be specified in the contract (Art. 9).

Security rights over a property presuppose an appropriate system of publicity, particularly when the collateral remains in the possession of the debtor. The Code distinguishes two types of pledge; pledges with and without the transfer of the collateral to the creditor. Pledges on immovables (hypothec) and on 'goods in circulation' belong to the latter. The Code provides that a hypothec must be registered; otherwise, the contract is void (Art.339, para.3).

The system of registration of immovables was almost absent in Russia until recently. For land, there was a limited register which included some information as to the right of the entity which was in possession of the land under socialism. However, this registration was basically for the purpose of accounting (*uchet*) and had no meaning of publicity. In fact, access to these registers was limited. The same applied to registration of other properties like automobiles.

Until 1997, it was the task of the committees on land resources and land reallocation attached to the local government to register rights on land. However, since it was not clear whether a hypothec was a right which could be registered with the committee, there were cases where the committee simply refused to register such rights. After all, it was only in the early 1990s that the committee started to develop a register on the rights over land. In one case, a commercial

---

14   *Supra*, 'Obzor...', item 2.

bank applied for the registration of a hypothec over a piece of land, which was refused by the committee. The bank appealed to the commercial court, which eventually ordered the committee to register the hypothec.

In this respect, the enactment of the Law on the Registration of Immovables and Related Transactions in 1997 was a major step forward. Under this Law, a unified state register on immovables and related transactions is to be developed. Rights on immovables covered by this Law include ownership rights, as well as 'encumbrances' such as servitude, leases, hypothecs and trust rights. Instead of the land committee, it is the Ministry of Justice and its local agencies which are to have jurisdiction over registration.

Registration of immovables should be distinguished from registration of other properties which are registered by different agencies; e.g. aircraft are registered at the Ministry of Civil Aviation, automobiles are registered by the Ministry of Internal Affairs, and construction machinery by the State Technological Inspectorate. The registration procedure for these properties has improved in the past several years. Now, not only ownership, but also pledges can be registered. This also applies to share registers.

What is different is that for these properties, registration is not a prerequisite to the rights taking effect. In one case, a creditor tried to foreclose a car which had been pledged. The debtor argued that since the pledge had not been registered, it had no effect. The commercial court of first instance accepted this argument. However, on appeal, the court ruled that registration was not a prerequisite for a pledge on cars.[15] In contrast, registration is a prerequisite for a hypothec, i.e. pledge on immovables, to take effect.

For a hypothec, registration is the only means by which the rightholder can prove the existence of the right. The validity of registration can only be contested by court procedure.

A bank in Moscow initiated an action against a closed joint stock company at the Commercial Court of Moscow Province asking the court to order the defendant company to register the contract of pledge of September 30, 1997. As a third party, the Registration Chamber of the Province was brought into the procedure.

A loan agreement between the bank and the defendant was concluded on August 1, 1997, and in order to secure this loan, the defendant was to transfer the assets including movables and immovables located in the town of Pushkin to the bank by the contract of pledge dated September 30, 1997. The contract was notarised and accounted for by the Bureau of Inventory of the District. However, according to the Civil Code (Art.117) and the law of Moscow Province, property rights and transactions involving them were

---

15   *Ibid.*, item 1.

required to be registered by the Registration Chamber of Moscow Province. The defendant failed to do this, so the bank initiated the action.

The first instance court acknowledged the claim and ordered the Registration Chamber to register the contract on May 25, 1998. The contract was eventually registered on September 21, 1998.

Upon protest, the Supreme Commercial Court reviewed the case. The problem was that according to the Civil Code (Art.433, para.3), contracts which are subject to registration are deemed to be concluded by registration. Therefore, the contract in question was concluded not on September 30, 1997, but on September 21, 1998. However, the Register of the Registration Chamber of Moscow Province indicated that as late as December 1, 1997, the title to the pledged assets was held not by the plaintiff, but by two other closed joint stock companies on the basis of a certificate issued by the Registration Chamber. There was no entry as to the encumbrance on the property.

The Supreme Commercial Court ruled that the first instance court, when ordering the contract to be registered, failed to ascertain whether the property actually belonged to the defendant or not, and therefore, the case should be reversed to the original instance.[16]

It is important to note that the Law on Registration of Immovables and Related Transactions expressly declares that the register is open to the public. In the past, it was difficult for the interested party to have access to the register. Under the new Law, the agency which manages the register is under an obligation to provide information on the registered Immovables. The Law on Hypothec has a similar provision.

5)   Multiple Pledges

It is possible to create security for different claims on the same property. In such cases, the creditor who has security with priority receives payment from the proceeds of the sale of the collateral ahead of the others, and the creditor with security of an inferior rank receives payment only after that. The 1992 Law provided that creating security on the same property which has already been made an object of security was possible, but only when there is no agreement against it. The pledger was obliged to notify all the subsequent pledgees of the existing pledges. For non-compliance with this requirement, the pledger was to be held liable. The Civil Code has a similar arrangement (Art.342), but whether this has any practical meaning is questionable.

---

16   Decision of the Presidium of the Supreme Commercial Court, May 30, 2000, *VVAS RF* 2000 No.8, 29-30.

Subsequent creditors are protected only if there is a proper system of registration which the person who intends to create security can refer to for information on prior security:

> A Japanese company EIP initiated an action against a limited liability tourist company and a regional bank in the Khabarovsk Regional Commercial Court asking the court to acknowledge the contract of pledge of immovables concluded between the defendants on September 13, 1996 to be valid.
>
> As a result of a tri-partite contract, concluded between 1993 and 1995, EIP was under an obligation to provide a loan to the company 'Greenline Express' for constructing a hotel in Khabarovsk. The tour company, as the owner of the hotel, was to provide EIP with the ownership and use of the hotel in the case of default by Greenline Express. On May 1,1996 and February 18, 1997, the tour company assumed the debt of Greenline Express and concluded a contract with EIP to the effect that the company would transfer the title to the hotel in the case of default *vis à vis* EIP.
>
> However, at the same time, the tour company concluded a loan agreement with a bank on September 4, and a contract of pledge on the hotel with the bank on September 13, 1996. EIP sued the tour company and the bank to have this agreement recognised as void. The grounds for this action was 1) non indication in the contract of pledge of the ownership of the property, and 2) failure on the part of the tour company to disclose the obligation to EIP.
>
> Both the appellate instance and the cassation instance rejected the claim, on the ground that these were not legitimate reasons for denying the validity of the pledge. On the other hand, according to the Supreme Commercial Court, lower courts recognised the right of pledge of EIP on the hotel without sufficient grounds and found the pledge by the bank to be inferior to the pledge by EIP. This was not upheld by the Court Russian Law, which is applicable in this case, sets certain requirements as to the content of the pledge agreement, and also requires government registration. The contract is deemed to be concluded by registration. The Court reversed the case to examine whether these requirements were met by EIP.[17]

The 1998 Law on Hypothec has some provisions on subsequent hypothecs. The creation of a subsequent hypothec is allowed only when it is not prohibited by prior hypothec agreements. If, despite the prohibition, a subsequent hypothec is created, the court may declare subsequent hypothecs void. This applies regardless of whether the subsequent pledgee was aware of the prior hypothec or not (Art.43, para.3). Most significantly, the law provides that subsequent hypothecs can be registered and that the priority of hypothec is determined by the order of registration (*ibid.*, para.1).

---

[17] Decision of the Presidium of the Supreme Commercial Court, December 14,1999, *VVAS RF* 2000 No.5, 34-35.

However, for other properties such as motorcars, or construction machinery, there is no protection as in the case with a hypothec, since registration is not a prerequisite of the effect of a pledge.

If a subsequent hypothecary creditor applies for enforcement, then, prior creditors may also apply, regardless of whether the claim is due or not.

6) Transfer of Collaterals

The Civil Code provides that the pledger may assign the collateral, offer it for lease, for gratuitous use, and by other means dispose of it, as long as it is not against the law or contract, or does not emanate from the nature of the pledge, only with the consent of the pledgee. Agreements which restrict this right of the pledger are void (Art.346, para.2). There is a different arrangement regarding an encumbrance on the collateral in the Law on Hypothec.

In cases where the title to the collateral is transferred to a third party, the pledge remains with the property. The person who obtained the title replaces the pledger and becomes liable for the debt (Art. 353, para.1).

Incidentally, the fact that the pledge follows the collateral seems to demonstrate the fact that the pledge is in fact a real right, rather than right *in personam*.

While the Civil Code is silent on the effect of disposal of the collateral without the consent of the pledgee, the Law on Hypothec has a provision on this matter. Thus, if the collateral was assigned without the consent of the pledgee, the pledgee has a choice of:

i)   voiding the transaction between the pledger and the third party, or
ii) accelerating the performance of the claim and seizing the collateral regardless of to whom the collateral belongs.

If the third party who obtained the collateral had known, or should have known that the assignment was effected without the consent of the pledger, the third party is liable to the pledgee jointly with the pledger for the non-performance of the obligation, but within the value of the collateral (Art. 39).

While the Civil Code allows the pledger to offer the collateral for the lease, or non-gratuitous use of a third party in principle only with the consent of the pledgee, the Law on Hypothec differs from the Code in this respect. Under this Law, unless otherwise provided by a federal law or contract, the pledger may lease the collateral, offer it for temporary use with compensation and create servitude without the consent of the pledgee. The period of such encumbrance should not exceed the period of the claim secured by the pledge (Art.40, para.1). These encumbrances can be created in excess of the period of the claim only with the consent of the pledgee. In the case of the enforcement of a pledge, those encumbrances created after the conclusion of the pledge agreement without the consent of the pledgee can be discharged by a court judgement (Art. 40, paras. 1 and 2).

Thus, the Law on Hypothecs has attempted to adjust the interests of the pledgee and the users of the property by slightly deviating from the Civil Code.

The Law on Hypothec explicitly makes it an obligation of the pledger to disclose the existence of all the encumbrances on the collateral. These include pledges, leases, life-long use, and servitude. Non-compliance with this requirement gives a right to the pledgee to accelerate the claim or to modify the terms of the agreement (Art.12). This is in contrast to the Civil Code in which this obligation extends only to pledges of priority rank and does not cover leases or servitude.

The Law on the Registration of Immovables and Related Transactions requires that in addition to the real rights, hypothecs, trusts, and leases be registered (Art.4, para.1). Registration is the only means of proving the existence of such rights. If one looks into the register, even without disclosure by the pledger, the existence of immovables rights and other rights in effect should be evident. Thus, theoretically, those who enter into a transaction on immovables are protected from unknown encumbrances on the property.

7)   Transfer of the Right of the Pledgee

The right of the pledgee can be assigned to a third party in the manner provided for in the Civil Code for the assignment of rights. The assignment is valid only when the claim which is secured by the pledge is assigned to the same person (Arts. 355, 382-390). The same rule is set out in the Law on Hypothecs. Under this Law, the assignment of the rights of pledge is presumed to accompany the assignment of the claim (Art. 47).

The Law on Hypothec has introduced a novelty – the hypothecary certificate (*zakladnaia*). This is a type of nominal security which embodies the claim secured by the hypothec as well as the hypothecary right over the collateral. It is issued by the agency which handles registration of hypothecs upon request of the first pledgee. The rights embodied in the certificate are assigned by way of endorsement on the certificate. It is also possible to pledge the certificate (Arts. 13-18).

8)   Enforcement of Real Security Rights

This is the most controversial area in the Russian law on pledges. Even the latest law, the Law on Hypothec, is not without inconsistencies in this respect. In fact, according to one commentator, this is the part which contains serious contradictions.[18]

What is striking is that a real security right is not always enforceable when the debtor has defaulted.

The Code provides for a moratorium for the pledger. Thus, upon the request of the pledger, the court may postpone the public sale of the collateral for up to one year (Art.350, para.2). According to a commentary, this applies in cases where, for example, the pledger had pledged his only property, such as an apartment flat. The pledger is to be given a chance to repay the debt before his flat is foreclosed.[19] Naturally, this is a great disadvantage to creditors.

Furthermore, the Law on Hypothec provides that in obligations which require periodic payments, the collateral can be seized only in cases where there was a systematic breach of terms in repayment by the debtor, i.e. where the repayment was not made in compliance with the date of repayment three times in 12 months unless otherwise provided in the contract (Art. 50, para.2).

Russian law distinguishes between seizure (*obrashchenie vzyskaniia*) of the collateral and its realisation (sale – *realizatsiia*). The 1992 Law on Pledge provided for a judicial procedure in principle. Thus, in order to seize the collateral, unless the law provided otherwise, a judgement of the court, commercial court or arbitration tribunal was needed. However, it was possible to seize the property on the basis of a notarised enforcement agreement in a non-contentious manner. Realisation of the collateral was to be effected in accordance with the Code of Civil Procedure, unless the 1992 Law provided otherwise, or the parties had agreed to a different arrangement (Art.28, para.1).

The present Code of Civil Procedure was enacted in 1964 and was substantially amended in 1995, but it is insufficient. A new Code is being prepared.

Concerning realisation of the collateral, the present Code of Civil Procedure has a brief chapter on auctions, which is apparently not enough. A new Law on Civil Enforcement was enacted in 1997 to supplement it, but there are still problems. A Russian lawyer pointed out that when the Law on Civil Enforcement

---

18   B.D.Zavidov, *Kommentarii k Federal'nomu Zakonu Rossiiskoi Federatsii ob Ipoteke*, Moscow 1999, p. 73.
19   Braginskii and Vitrianskii, *supra*, p. 431.

Procedure was enacted, sufficient attention was not paid to provisions on the conducting of public auctions.[20]

The Civil Code, in contrast to the 1992 Pledge Law, restricts the use of the notarised enforcement agreement. The Civil Code distinguishes between immovables and movables. In the case of movables which have already been transferred to the pledgee, unless the law provides otherwise, the parties may agree not to use court proceedings for seizure. This is only natural, since there is no point in returning it to the pledger only for it to be seized. Concerning immovables, the Civil Code provides that satisfaction of the claim without recourse to the court is allowed on the basis of a notarised contract, only if the contract was concluded after the default (Art.349, para.1). Furthermore, the Code proceeds to provide that such agreements can be invalidated by the court upon the petition of an interested party, whose right was affected by such a contract. Interested parties in this context means, according to the commentary, secured lenders of a prior rank, or the owner of the collateral. An example is when the price of the collateral was incorrectly determined.[21]

According to the resolution of the Plenum of the Supreme Court and the Supreme Commercial Court of July 1, 1996, a clause in the contract of pledge which provides for the right of the creditor to take possession of the collateral immediately and directly is void.[22] A book on this subject suggests that such a clause used to be common.[23]

This antipathy against enforcement without recourse to the court is evident in the 1997 Law on Civil Enforcement Procedure. Previously, under the Code of Civil Procedure, along with court judgements and arbitral awards, notarised agreements of enforcement were listed as one of the grounds for enforcement. However, the 1997 Law on Civil Enforcement considerably limited the use of the notarised agreement, only allowing it to be used in alimony cases. In fact, this approach had already been clear in the 1992 Provisional Statute on Pledge, which was prepared by the Institute of Private Law in Moscow. Later, this Institute played a major role in preparing the Civil Code.

The preference of court procedure, or more precisely, the ban on arrangements by notarisation, is clearly based upon a social policy consideration. Proponents of this approach maintain that with notarised agreements, at the time the document is formulated, the existence and validity of the secured claim as well as the

---

20   Zavidov, *supra*, p.79.
21   Braginskii and Vitrianskii, *supra*, pp. 429-430; Sadikov ed., *supra*, p.598.
22   Joint Decision of the Plenum of the Supreme Court and the Supreme Commercial Court, 'O nekotorykh voprosakh, sviazannykh s vvedeniem v deistvie chasti pervoi grazhdanskogo kodeksa RF', July 1, 1996, item 46, in Zhuranovskii and Kalinin, *supra*, p.42.
23   A.A.Vishnevskii, *Zalogovoe pravo*, Moscow 1995, p. 87.

possibility of recovering the claim by other means are not ascertained, and therefore, it entails a risk for the debtors. Particularly at a time when the consumer credit industry is flourishing and citizens are pledging their flats which are their sole property, it is thought to be 'unethical' to let creditors foreclose the property without recourse to court.[24]

A further problem for the creditor is that the realisation of the collateral has to go through a public sale (*publichnyi torg*). The Civil Code provides that the realisation of the pledged property is to be effected by public sale as provided in the Code of Civil Procedure, unless other procedure is provided by law (Art.350, para.1).

There is some controversy as to whether the 'other procedure' means procedure of sale other than by public sale, or procedure other than that provided by the Code of Civil Procedure. In other words, is it possible to avoid public sale if there is a law to that effect, or does it simply mean that the Code of Civil Procedure does not have to be applied at all? For example, is it possible to realise property through a sale on a commission basis?[25] Some Russian lawyers maintain that the 1992 Law should be applicable here. Thus, in interpreting the above-mentioned provision of the Code, 'other procedure provided by law includes the procedure provided by the 1992 Law'. The 1992 Law allows the parties to agree to an alternative means of realising the pledged property. Therefore, the parties are free to avoid mandatory public sale by agreement.[26]

However, a commentary to the Civil Code denies the possibility of resorting to means other than public sale. 'The possibility of sale on a commission basis is excluded'.[27]

The Civil Code provides that a public sale can take two forms; auction and tender bid (Art.447, para.4). The distinction between them is that in an auction, the highest bidder in price wins, while in a tender, 'the most suitable person to solve the task' or 'who made the best offer' wins.[28] In other words, the price is not decisive in a tender bid. Presumably, as can be seen by the fact that the tender bid is utilised in the privatisation process for the sale of state enterprises, the tender bid may be intended to be used in the realisation of collaterals such as enterprises.

---

24 Braginskii and Vitrianskii, *supra*, p. 428.
25 Vishnevskii, *supra*, pp. 90-91.
26 O.I.Sviridenko, 'Pravovoe regulirovanie zaloga v bankovskom kreditovanii, VVAS, 1998 No. 8, p. 76.
27 O.N.Braginskii ed., *Komentarii k chasti pervoi Grazhdanskogo Kodeksa Rossiiskoi Federatsii dlia predprinimaatelei*, first edition, Moscow 1996, p. 303.
28 Sadikov ed., *supra*, p.722; B.A.Zavidov, *Analiza zaloga v grazhdanskom prave*. Moscow 1999, p.73.

The 1998 Law on Hypothec seems to adopt yet another approach. This Law provides for the seizure of the collateral in the same manner as the Civil Code. The property – in the case of hypothec, it is an immovable – is to be seized by court procedure, except in cases where the parties agreed to the enforcement by a notarised document after the default. As for the realisation of the seized property, the Law provides that in principle, it should be realised by a public sale (Art.56, para.1). The procedure for a public sale is to be determined by procedural law, unless there are provisions in the Law on Hypothec.

Then, what is the 'procedural law' in this context? The Code of Civil Procedure has a part on the enforcement of judgements and the realisation of property. There was a provision in the part dealing with the realisation of the property of individuals which allowed a sale on a commission basis through a state or cooperative trading house. Property of the state and that of state enterprises were treated in a different way (Art. 398). Now that private enterprises play a major part in the economy, this differentiation of private entities and state enterprises is not appropriate. The Law on Civil Enforcement Procedure has replaced the relevant part of the Code of Civil Procedure, although it is not satisfactory, particularly on realisation of collaterals.

This Law on Civil Enforcement Procedure provides that movable property is to be sold by a specialised shop on commission or another contractual basis, whereas for immovables, sale has to be conducted by a specialised organisation with a licence to deal with immovables in accordance with the procedure set out by federal law (Art.54, paras. 1 and 2). Such federal law is yet to be enacted.

What is confusing is that the Law on Hypothec, while maintaining the principle of mandatory public sale, provides that the court may, with the consent of both parties, allow the realisation of the property by auction (*ibid.*, para.2). The Law seems to juxtapose public sale and auction.

Public sale, according to the Law on Hypothec, is organised and handled by the agency to which the procedural law has entrusted the enforcement of judgements, unless otherwise provided by federal law. The Law on the Bailiffs' Office was enacted in 1997. There is no doubt that the office of bailiffs is to handle public sales.

The procedure starts with an announcement of public sale, at least one month before the sale. The starting price is declared at this stage. Those who intend to take part are obliged to place a deposit of up to 5% of the value of the property at sale. At the sale, only those who take part in the sale and those who are entitled to use the property or have a real right on the property may be present. The bidder who bid the highest price is the winner. This person must pay the price within five days of the sale. Within five days of the payment, the successful bidder concludes a sales contract with the organiser (Art.57).

The procedure described above fits the description of public auction in other countries. However, the Law on Hypothec has a separate provision on auction in addition to public sale. It provides that as an organiser of the auction, a specialised organisation is selected with the consent of the pledger. This organisation is in a contractual relationship with the pledgee and acts in the name of the pledgee. It is not clear from the wording of this provision who selects the organisation. The successful bidder enters into a sales contract with the organiser of the auction. The auction is, as a rule, conducted in public (Art. 59, para.1).

Comparing public sale and auction under the Law on Hypothec, it is evident to Western lawyers that they would both be considered an auction in other jurisdictions. It is only that the organiser is different; in public sale, it is the bailiff's office, while in auction, it is specialised organisations for auction. On the other hand, there is no reference to a tender bid in the Law on Hypothec.

Thus, the Law on Hypothec, which is the latest law in this field, has maintained the principle of mandatory public sale of the pledged property, but expanded the concept to include auctions by specialised organisations – auction houses. To be fair, reportedly, at the time of the preparation of the Civil Code, the necessity of commercial organisations being involved in auctions was already acknowledged.[29]

On the other hand the Law on Civil Enforcement Procedure provides that the seized property is to be realised by specialised licensed organisations in accordance with the procedure provided by legislation. It does not refer to the bailiff's office. This is an example of the inconsistency in related legislation which one often encounters in Russia.

The reason why public sale was made mandatory in the Civil Code is presumably because in this way, instances such as pledgees taking advantage of commissioned sale and acquiring the property at an unfairly low price, can be avoided. There has to be an element of competition in order to keep the sales price higher. The arrangement seems to be primarily based upon social policy considerations, i.e. the protection of the pledger. As one commentator pointed out, 'under no circumstances can the pledgee automatically become the owner of the pledged property'.[30] Another commentator stated that 'this rule protects the interest of the weaker party, since it ensures that the collateral is sold at market price'.[31]

However, this requirement of mandatory court involvement and public sale is inevitably time consuming and costly, and is therefore being criticised in Russia

---

29 Braginskii ed., *supra*, p.303.
30 *Ibid.*, p.304.
31 Sadikov ed., *supra*, p.601.

as 'a sufficiently inconvenient arrangement which apparently does not meet the needs of contemporary times'.[32]

Apart from the time and cost, another problem with the mandatory public sale is that it is not suitable to pledges on claims. The 1992 Law on Pledge devoted a chapter to pledges on 'rights'. It provided that object of a pledge could be the right to possess and use property including the right to lease, and other rights (claims) emanating from obligations, as well as other proprietary rights (Art.54). This means that claims can be pledged in the same manner as proprietary rights, such as intellectual property rights.

If public sale or auction is mandatory, problems arise with the realisation of a pledge on rights. There is no problem in realising them by public sale or auction, if the given right is embodied in securities, for example, if company shares were pledged. However, if it is a simple money claim, such a claim is normally unsuitable for auction, although this may be possible if there is a developed factoring market for certain categories of claims.

Let us assume that A has a claim against B. B, in turn, has a claim against C. B pledges his claim against C as a security for his debt to A. According to the present Russian Law, A cannot realise the claim other than by public sale or auction. It is unrealistic to think of a 'market' for such claims unless debtor C is a major company. A possible solution is to let A exercise the right of B *vis à vis* C, i.e. let A replace B as a creditor within the scope of A's claim by court order.

In fact, the 1992 Law has such an arrangement with a limited scope. The pledgee is entitled to apply to court to have the pledged right transferred to himself in cases of non-fulfilment of some obligations such as the duty not to assign the right to a third party (Art.57). However, this does not include the default of the pledger on the secured obligation. Therefore, under the current law, even a claim against an individual has to be sold at auction or public sale, which does not seem to be rational.

The case cited earlier regarding the pledge of 'the money in the bank account' demonstrates the inadequateness of this arrangement. The Supreme Commercial Court ruled that the provisions of the Civil Code require that the claim be satisfied out of the proceeds of the sale of the pledged property, and therefore, the possibility of realisation was one of the fundamental traits of the object of pledge. From the nature of 'non-cash money', in the view of the Supreme Commercial Court, money in a bank account cannot be realised and therefore, cannot be pledged. However, in this case, the object of pledge could have been construed as the claim

---

32   Sviridenko, *supra*, p. 74.

of the company (lender) against the account holding bank and not the 'money in the account' *per se*. It is a normal practice elsewhere in the world to pledge such a claim for finance.

The requirement of a mandatory public sale is justified by the fact that it ensures that the collateral will be realised at a fair price. However, the pledgee substituting the pledger in a claim by court procedure will not harm the pledger, since the pledgee substitutes the pledger only to the extent of his claim against the pledger, and the amount of this claim is already fixed. There is no more possibility of unfairness to the pledger here than in a public sale.

9)   Real Security Rights and Bankruptcy Procedure

As Russian commentators agree, the nature of a pledge lies in the right to have a claim satisfied out of the proceeds from the pledged property in priority to other creditors. However, this is not necessarily the case under Russian Law.

The first Law on Insolvency in the Russian Federation was enacted in 1992. This Law excluded secured property from the bankruptcy estate. The 1992 Law was replaced by a new Law on Insolvency in 1998.[33] In contrast to the 1992 Law, the 1998 Law does not exclude the pledged property from the bankruptcy estate.

Secured claims do have priority to unsecured claims, but are inferior to two other categories of claims. One is the claim for compensation arising from damage caused to the life or health of people, and the other is the claim for wages and retirement payments. These claims, particularly the first category, can be substantial if there was e.g. environmental damage caused by the pledger.

The justification for not excluding secured claims from the bankruptcy estate is primarily that a pledge is a not a real right, but a right *in personam*. It is also pointed out that the provision of the Civil Code on the liquidation of juridical persons, has such an arrangement (Art.64).

What is more, the Civil Code provides in a chapter on bank accounts that in cases where the amount in the bank account is not sufficient to satisfy all the claims, tort claims are of the first rank, followed by wages and retirement payments, and then, by tax and other mandatory payments. Money claims come after tax payments, and moreover, there is no distinction here between secured and unsecured claims (Art.855).

In any case, this does not seem to be consistent with the nature of pledges.

---

33   *SZ RF*, 1998 1998 No.2, item 222.

3   ATYPICAL SECURITY RIGHTS

As mentioned above, the procedure for the enforcement of a pledge is rigid and does not meet the requirements of creditors who prefer quick, inexpensive and less complicated enforcement. The procedure for enforcement itself is not clear in some cases.

As one commentator pointed out, 'because of restrictions imposed by the laws, a pledge does not give creditors in most cases confidence of speedy and full satisfaction of the claim through seizure of the pledged property'.[34] Another commentator found 'essential shortcomings of the pledge system' in that:

> ...the system, in a majority of cases, does not give creditors confidence in full and prompt satisfaction of the claim, since court procedure, which requires cost and time, is mandatory for enforcement

This author proceeded to point out that because of these shortcomings, in order to avoid risk, banks should conclude an agreement to have the title to the property combined with an agreement of reverse sale.[35]

In some jurisdictions where speedy, uncostly, and uncomplicated enforcement of security rights is not always available, eventually, alternative methods of security have developed. This is also the case with Russia.

In practice, varieties of transactions are being used as alternative means of securing obligations. Parties often resort to novation, or substitute performance (*otstupnoe*). They agree to terminate the contract and conclude another agreement, which, in effect, is an agreement to transfer the title of the pledged property to the pledgee. However, novation is accompanied by a risk of litigation by interested parties such as other creditors, since, as the original transaction has been terminated and replaced by a new agreement, whatever priority they had is gone.[36] This is particularly true when the debtor was declared bankrupt. It is most likely that the effect of such an agreement would be denied by the administrator, or even the procurator.

---

34 G.Adamovich, 'O nekotorykh sposobakh obespecheniia kreditnykh obiazatel'stv, *KhiP*, 1996 No. 9, p. 41.
35 M.Chirkova, 'Otsenka zaloga kak sposoba obespecheniia vozvratnosti kredita', *VVAS RF*, 1998 No. 8, p. 38.
36 K.Sklovskii, 'Zalog, arest imushchestva, isk kak sposoby obespecheniia prav kreditora', *RIu*, 1997 No. 2, p. 26.

Substitute performance became an issue in the following case:

An open joint stock company, the Company for the Assistance of Regional Development, brought an action at the Commercial Court of Primorskii Region against the Russian Tikhookeanskii Bank, claiming compensation of 1,595,417,775 roubles for the damage caused by an unlawful act by the Bank in taking away and disposing of the property of the company. The plaintiff also claimed that the contract of sale (substitute performance) of July 7, 1995 was void.

The court of first instance acknowledged the claim. At the appellate and cassation instances, the judgment was upheld.

The Supreme Commercial Court quashed the judgment and referred the case to a new hearing on the following grounds. The plaintiff was a debtor of the bank by the loan agreement of October 14, 1994. The plaintiff defaulted, and the Bank received two notarised documents on which basis, a bailiff seized the property as a substitute performance. The property was valued by an expert to be worth 857,765 thousand roubles. By the enforcement judgment of the Lenin District Court of Vladivostok of July 7, 1995, the property was transferred to the Bank as repayment of the debt. On the same day, enforcing the judgment of the court, the Bank sold the property to a third party at the price of 857,759,445 roubles. However, this was before the judgment had taken effect and therefore, the Bank had acted unlawfully in selling the property. On the other hand, the Court noted that the lower courts failed to take into account that as a result of the sale, the debt of the plaintiff was reduced by 857,765 thousand roubles, and therefore, it was wrong to claim this amount as damages.

The Court referred the case to a new hearing in order to examine the lawfulness of the contact of substitute performance and other arrangements which served as a basis of the plaintiff's claim.[37]

One way of securing a claim is by selling the property to the creditor at the outset. This is called a 'REPO' – sale and repurchase operation. The creditor purchases a property from the debtor with an obligation to resell it to the debtor. The payment for the first sale is equivalent to the amount of debt, while the resale price, which is agreed in advance, is repayment of the debt, and therefore, interest is added. In case the debtor (the seller) failed to tender payment for resale, the second agreement is simply rescinded and the first buyer (the creditor) will retain the title. Thus, theoretically, there are two different contracts of sale, but they are usually combined into a single agreement.

A variation of this arrangement is a preliminary agreement of a revert sale with a condition subsequent of the debtor's repayment. If the debtor defaults, the condition is not fulfilled, and therefore, agreement of sale does not come into

---

37 Decision of the Presidium of the Supreme Commercial Court, March 31, 1998, *VVAS RF*, 1998 No.6, pp.51-52.

effect. Another variation is the use of contracts for management of property by entrustment.

However, there may be some problems concerning these arrangements, since these alternative means are designed to circumvent the cumbersome requirements of a statutory pledge.

The Civil Code provides that sham transactions, i.e. transactions which conceal another transaction, are void. In such cases, provisions for the transaction which the parties genuinely desired (the concealed transaction) are to be applied (Art. 170). There is a likelihood that an unfaithful pledger may claim that such an arrangement is sham and therefore, void. If the above-mentioned alternative transactions are found to be sham, then provisions on statutory pledges, instead of sale, will be applicable and various restrictions which the parties intended to avoid will have to be applied.

There is also a problem concerning publicity. If the title over immovables shifts to the creditor, even provisionally, this has to be registered. Then, technically, the creditor is free to dispose of the property to a third party. There may be a dispute between the debtor seeking to retrieve the property once he has repaid the debt, and the third party who acted on the belief that the registered owner was the genuine holder of the right.

The Commercial Court used to be fairly cautious in dealing with the problem of the validity of atypical security rights, but in the following case, the court found the sale to be a sham:

An 'industrial investment company' Evroresursy sued a bank Diamant, demanding that shares held by the Bank be returned to the Company. The parties concluded a contract of sale for 97,774 units of shares of another company for five million roubles on March 4, 1996. The contract was duly performed. However, they also concluded a contract under which the Bank was under an obligation to sell back the same amount of shares of the same company after May 6, 1996 at seven million roubles. However, this contract was rescinded by the Bank, because the Company failed to pay the price for the shares. In fact, there was a loan agreement concluded between the same parties concluded on March 14 of the same year.

The Supreme Commercial Court found that these three contracts were interrelated and inseparable, and that the contract of sale of shares was intended to conceal the contract of pledge of shares. The Court declared the sale contract to be void as a sham contract and applied the provision of a pledge to this transaction. Since the Bank had no grounds to hold the shares, the court ordered the Bank to return the shares to the

Company. In exchange, the Company was ordered to return five million roubles to the Bank.[38]

An open joint stock company initiated an action against the Moscow Interregional Commercial Bank, asking the court to acknowledge a loan agreement and an agreement of pledge as void. The Bank had extended a loan of 100 billion roubles (before denomination) at 25% annual interest. In the accompanying contract of pledge, the company transferred to the Bank its own bills of exchange of the amount of 125 billion roubles. The court, with the perspective of applying Art.170 (sham transactions), reversed the case to the lower court for further examination of the intention of the parties.[39]

Thus, at least, this type of atypical security right failed to be endorsed by the court. However, Article 329 of the Civil Code which is a general provision on the means of securing the enforcement of obligations, lists suretyship, bank guarantees, pledges, and in addition, other means provided by law or contract. The Law on Banks and Banking Activities has a similar provision. The Civil Code guarantees freedom of contract. There seems to be room for atypical security rights. In the light of these open-ended provisions on the list of the means of securing obligations, it may be possible to argue that contracts involving atypical security rights are contracts which are not specifically referred to in the Civil Code, but perfectly legitimate under the principle of the freedom of contract. The requirement of court procedure and public sale can be construed as being applicable only to statutory pledges.

4   SURETYSHIP AND BANK GUARANTEE

Under Russian Law, suretyship has been one of the traditional means of securing the performance of an obligation. However, under socialism, the use of suretyship was very much limited. The 1964 Civil Code provided for suretyship and guarantee. The latter was in fact a variation of suretyship, the basic difference being the latter having the superior body of the state enterprise as a guarantor. Even this institution was limited in scope. Guarantee was finally abolished by the 1991 USSR Fundamental Principles of Civil Legislation as something unique to the planned economy.[40]

---

38   Decision of the Presidium of the Supreme Commercial Court, October 6, 1998, *VVAS RF,* 1999 No. 1, pp.59-60.
39   Decision of the Presidium of the Supreme Commercial Court, January 23, 2001 [Inforis].
40   S.N.Bratus and O.N.Sadikov eds., *Kommentarii k grazhdanskomu kodeksu RSFSR,* Moscow 1982, p.257. Braginskii ed., *supra,* pp.448-449.

In suretyship, the surety and the debtor are jointly and severally liable to the creditor in the case of non performance or inappropriate performance of an obligation by the debtor, unless the law or contract provides for the liability of the surety as supplementary (Art.363, para.1). In contrast to the 1964 Code, the present Code allows suretyship which guarantees an obligation which is to emerge in the future (*ibid.*, para.2). Sureties that jointly secured a claim are jointly and severally liable to the creditor (*ibid.*, para.3).

A contract of suretyship requires written form. Terms of suretyship can be agreed in a separate contract, or in the contract of the obligation which is secured by suretyship. The Supreme Commercial Court held valid a suretyship in which the undertaking of the surety was entered in writing in the contract of loan.[41] In any case, the acceptance of a surety by the creditor is required.[42] In banking practice in Russia, the surety sends a letter to the bank-creditor guaranteeing the repayment of the debt by the debtor. This practice is said to be valid under the current Code, since the subsequent act of the bank-creditor in extending the loan signifies the acceptance of suretyship by the creditor.[43]

The surety is entitled to a defence *vis à vis* the creditor which the primary debtor can raise. The surety does not lose this right even if the debtor waived the defence or acknowledged the claim (Art.364).

The right of the creditor is transferred to the surety once the latter performs the obligation. Upon performance by the surety, the creditor must provide the surety with documents certifying the claim and transfer the claim secured by suretyship to the surety (Art.365, paras.1 and 2).

Suretyship is terminated if:

i)   the obligation secured by suretyship is terminated;
ii)   there was a change to the secured obligation which resulted in the increase of liability on the part of the surety or other unfavourable consequences without the consent of the surety;
iii)   the secured obligation is assigned to a third party in the absence of the surety giving consent to the creditor to provide a guarantee for the new debtor;
iv)   the creditor refused to accept adequate performance offered by the debtor or surety;
v)   the term of suretyship expires; if there is no such term, it expires if the creditor, within a year from the time the secured obligation became due, failed to initiate an action against the debtor (Art.367).

---

41   Braginskii ed., *ibid.*, p.452.
42   Sadikov ed., *supra*, p.615.
43   Braginskii ed., *supra*, p.452.

A creditor brought an action against a surety, after failing to have his claim satisfied by the debtor. The surety and the debtor bore joint and several liability *vis à vis* the creditor. It was agreed between the creditor and the debtor (borrower) that the creditor could unilaterally change the rate of interest. In accordance with this agreement, the creditor had informed the debtor and the surety of the increase in the rate of interest.

The court, however, dismissed the claim of the creditor on the basis of Article 367. The argument of the creditor that the surety consented to the change by concluding the suretyship contract containing such terms was rejected by the court. The court ruled that an express consent of the surety to accept liability in accordance with the changed secured obligation was lacking.[44]

There is no requirement as to the qualification of the surety in the Civil Code. However, in cases where entities related to the state are involved, care should be taken. The court found a suretyship contract void on the ground that the state unitary enterprise which acted as a surety exceeded its power in becoming a surety for an obligation of a debtor, with whom the enterprise had no production relations. Furthermore, state treasury enterprises or institutions may not be a surety, since it may result in the liability of the owner – the state – without its knowledge. By law, the state bears supplementary liability for the debt of those entities.[45]

Bank guarantees did exist in a limited scope under socialist law as part of suretyship, but the present Civil Code accommodated it in a separate chapter. In a bank guarantee, the bank or other credit institution, upon request of another person (principal), assumes an obligation *vis à vis* the creditor of the principal (beneficiary) and pays the guaranteed amount upon presentation of the claim by the beneficiary (Art.368). In exchange of the bank guarantee, the principal pays remuneration to the guarantor – the bank. Incidentally, even if a bank guarantee was given without remuneration, it does not affect the relationship between the guarantor and the beneficiary; the guarantor is not entitled to refuse performance *vis à vis* the beneficiary.[46]

The obligation assumed by the guarantor, in relation to the beneficiary, does not depend on the basic obligation which is secured by the guarantee (Art.370). A bank guarantee is, as a rule, irrevocable (Art.371).

The guarantor may refuse payment if the demand or documents attached to it does not coincide with the terms of the guarantee, or the period of the guarantee had expired (Art.376, para.1).

---

44   'Obzor praktiki razresheniia sporov, sviazannykh s primeneniem arbitrazhnymi sudami norm grazhdanskogo kodeksa Rossiiskoi Federatsii o poruchitel'stve', informatioannoe pis'mo VAS RF, January 20, 1998, item 6, *VVAS RF*, 1998 No.3, p.92.

45   Sadikov ed., *supra*, p.614.

46   *VVAS RF*, 1997 No.6,p.82.

5   OTHER MEANS OF SECURING PERFORMANCE OF OBLIGATION

1)   Penalty

A penalty (forfeiture or fine) is an amount of money set by law or contract which
the debtor is under an obligation to pay in cases of non-performance or inappropriate performance of an obligation, but in particular, in cases of delay of performance (Art.330, para.1). What is important is that the creditor does not have to prove
damage. This is an obligation based upon fault, and therefore, if the debtor is not
liable for non-performance, inappropriate performance or delay, he does not have
to pay the penalty (*ibid.*, para.2).

It should be noted that agreement on a penalty has to be in writing. Non-
compliance will result in its invalidity (Art.331).

A peculiarity of Russian Law on penalties is that the agreed amount of a
penalty can be reduced by the court, if the amount is 'apparently disproportionate
to the consequence of the breach of the obligation'(Art.333). This provision was
applied in a case where the obligor was to receive one billion roubles for the
breach of a contract worth 30 million roubles, and also in a case where a penalty
was set 1.5 times higher than the value of the contract, and the amount of penalty
was reduced by the court.[47]

Furthermore, in cases of delay, a penalty is not to be imposed in addition to
interest for delay. According to the commercial court, 'two different means of
liability cannot be applied to one and the same breach'.[48]

2)   Withholding of the Object

Withholding of an object means that the creditor, who is in possession of an object
which is to be transferred to the debtor, may retain it in cases where the debtor
has failed to perform an obligation, to reimburse the cost related to the object,
or to pay other damages on time. If both parties are entrepreneurs, then the
requirement of a relationship between the obligation and the object is dropped
(Art.359).

This is not merely a right of retention; the creditor has the right to have his
claim satisfied from the proceeds of the sale of the object which has been withheld
(Art.360).

---

47   Sadikov ed., *supra*, p.580.
48   Decision of the Presidium of the Supreme Commercial Court, May 26, 1998, *VVAS RF* 1998 No.8,
      pp.34-35.

3)   Earnest Money

Earnest money is defined as the money paid to the opposite party from the amount which is due to this party to prove the conclusion of the contract and to secure its performance (Art.380,para.1). The agreement for payment of earnest money has to be in writing (*ibid.*, para.2).
The effect of earnest money is:

i)   if the obligation was terminated by the agreement of the parties or by impossibility of performance before the performance has started, the earnest money is returned;

ii)   If the obligation was not performed by the fault of the party which paid the earnest money, the money stays with the opposite party;

iii)   if the obligation was not performed by the fault of the opposite party, this party is under an obligation to return twice the amount of the earnest money.

In addition, the party which is responsible for the non-performance is liable for compensation minus the amount of earnest money (Art.381).

8

GENERAL RULES OF CONTRACT LAW

1   GENERAL

A contract is defined as an agreement of two or more persons on the establishment, change or termination of civil law rights and obligations. It is a juristic act. As is the case with the German BGB and the Dutch Civil Code, provisions relevant to contracts can be found in several different places in the Code. First of all, rules on juristic acts (*sdelka* -transactions) which are contained in Book One of the Code are applicable. These include the public order provision and abuse of rights provision. Secondly, the provisions in Book Three, general rules of obligation, such as provisions on performance and termination of obligations, are applicable unless the part on contracts has different provisions (Art.420). Thirdly, rules accommodated in Book Three, general rules of contracts, such as those on offer and acceptance, and rescission, are also applied. Finally, provisions on individual contracts can be found in the Book Four.[1] Within the Civil Code, the rule that a special norm has priority to a general norm applies.

2   FREEDOM OF CONTRACT

A significant novelty in the Civil Code is that the principle of the freedom of contract has been enshrined there. Article 421 provides as follows:

> Individuals and juridical persons are free to conclude a contract. Compulsion to conclude a contract is not allowed except in cases where it is provided by the present Code or law, or by a voluntarily assumed obligation.

---

1   M.I.Braginskii and V.V.Vitrianskii, *Dogovornoe pravo*, Moscow 1997, pp.16-17.

Parties may conclude a contract which is provided or not provided by law or other legal acts.

Terms of the contract are determined by the discretion of the parties except in cases where the content of the terms are determined by law or legal acts.

Freedom of contract in the Russian Civil Code, as in other jurisdictions, encompasses i) freedom of concluding a contract, ii) freedom of selecting the opposite party, and iii) freedom of determining the terms of the contract.

In the socialist period, there was no such freedom. Contracts between enterprises (they were called plan-contracts) were subordinated to the state economic plan. Under the dominance of the state economic plan, enterprises had no choice but to conclude contracts with a particular party as the plan dictated. The parties were not free to negotiate the terms of the contracts, nor even the price. In fact, there was a procedure at the then State Arbitration Commission (*gosarbitrazh*) to compel the parties to conclude a contract.

Naturally, freedom of contract has its limits under the present Civil Code, as is the case in other industrialised countries. In Russia, there are the following exceptions to the freedom of contract:

First, the Code has a concept of 'public contracts'. This is a new concept which was introduced by the Law on the Protection of the Rights of Consumers of 1992.[2] 'Public contracts' are those concluded by commercial organisations and which establish the duty of the organisation to sell goods, provide services or work, which, the organisation, by nature of its activities, must perform for everybody who turns to it for such goods, work or service. Examples of these activities include the retail trade, public transportation, communication, energy, medical services and hotels (Art.426, para.1). The uniqueness of public contracts is that i) commercial organisations are not entitled to refuse the sale of goods or the provision of work or services other than in instances provided by law (*ibid.*, para.3), ii) the price of goods, work, or services and the terms of contract should be the same for all, unless the law allows preferential terms to be applied to a specific category of consumers (*ibid.*, para.2), and iii) in case of refusal on the part of the commercial organisation to conclude a contract, the organisation may be forced by law to conclude a contract. Beside these 'public contracts', in government supply contracts, selected Russian companies are under an obligation to conclude a contract with the government and supply goods or provide services.[3]

---

2   Originally enacted in 1992, substantially amended by *SZ RF* 1996 No.3, item 140.
3   Sadikov, *Kommentarii...,* k *Grazhdanskomu Kodeksu Rossisskoi Federatsii, chasti pervoi,* enlarged edition, p.674. *SZ RF* 1996 No.1, item 6.

Second, there are standard form contracts in which the freedom of contract is substantially limited. Standard form contracts are those contracts whose terms are determined by one of the parties in a standard form and can be accepted by the opposite party only as an 'adhesion' to the entire contract (Art.428, para.1). The Civil Code provides some protection to consumers from standard form contracts. The opposite party in a standard form contract may demand rescission or alteration of the contract if the contract deprives this party of the rights normally provided in this type of contract, excludes or limits the liability of the other party for the breach of an obligation, or includes other disadvantageous terms which this party, based upon his reasonably understood interest, would not have accepted had he been given a chance (Art.428, paras. 1 and 2). This applies even when the contract is not against the law or legal acts. It is not quite clear how effective this right would be. On the other hand, since this is for the protection of individuals (consumers), this is not applicable if the contract involved entrepreneurial activities by the opposite party and this party had known or should have known under what terms the contract was concluded (*ibid.*, para.3).

Third, naturally, contracts must conform with mandatory provisions of the law and legal acts valid at the time of the conclusion of the contract (Art.422, para.1). A similar provision concerning juridical acts exists in the General Part (Art.168). However, this provision in the contract law part is slightly different in that it refers to the law and legal acts valid *at the time of the conclusion* of the contract. If a law which was adopted after the conclusion of the contract has a mandatory provision different from the law existing at the time of the conclusion of the contract, terms of the contract retain the effect insofar as the new law does not provide otherwise (Art.422, para.2). A similar 'grandfathering clause' concerning tax and other mandatory payments exists in the amended Foreign Investment Law in relation to major projects (Art.9).

3   CONCLUSION OF CONTRACTS

A contract takes effect and becomes binding on the parties from the time of its conclusion (Art.425, para.1). A contract is deemed to have been concluded if an agreement with all the essential terms of the contract has been reached in the required form between the parties. Essential terms in this context are the terms on the object (subject matter) of the contract, terms which are determined as essential by law or legal acts, terms necessary for the given type of a contract, as well as other terms, to which agreement is required by one of the parties (*ibid.*). A contract is concluded by the offer of one party and the acceptance of the offer by the other (*ibid.*, para.2).

An offer is a presentation to one or several specific persons which is sufficiently definite and reflects the intention of the offeror to regard a contract to be concluded upon acceptance by the opposite party. The offer must contain the essential terms of the contract (Art.435, para.1). The offer binds the offeror from the time it was received by the offeree (*ibid.*, para.2). An offer which has been received by the offeree cannot be withdrawn by the offeror for the period established in the offer for its acceptance, unless otherwise reserved in the offer, or unless the withdrawal emanates from the nature of the offer or the circumstance in which the offer has been made (Art.436).

Acceptance is a response by the offeree to the offer. The acceptance has to be in its entirety and without reservation. As a rule, silence is not an acceptance. Acts on the part of the offeree which implement the terms of the contract, such as accepting the goods, providing services etc., within the period of acceptance is regarded as acceptance unless otherwise provided by law, a legal act or the offer itself. Acceptance can be withdrawn until it has reached the offeror (Art.438). If the period of acceptance is fixed in the offer, the contract is concluded when the offeror receives the acceptance from the offeree within this period (Art.440). If a period of acceptance is not fixed in a written form, the contract is concluded if the offeror received the acceptance within the period established by law or a legal act, and if such a period does not exist, within the period normally needed for the acceptance (Art.441, para.1). If the offer has been made orally without indicating the period for acceptance, the contract is considered to be concluded if the offeree immediately expresses its acceptance (*ibid.*, para.2).

4   INTERPRETATION OF CONTRACTS

Following the 1990 Fundamental Principles of Civil Legislation of the USSR, the Civil Code has a provision on the interpretation of contracts. The Code provides that first, the literal meaning of the words and expressions in the contract should be considered. If this fails, the meaning of the term should be established from other terms and conditions of the contract and the meaning of the contract as a whole (Art.431). Thus, the expressed intention of the parties is crucial:[4]

> A contract of lease provided that the rent was to be indexed to the rise in the tariff for electricity. Whether this meant that the rise in the tariff was linked merely to the part of the rent covering the electricity, or the rent as a whole was unclear. The commercial court found the latter to be the case, since this clause was accommodated in the part

---

4   Braginskii and Vitrianskii, *supra*, pp.216-217.

of the contract entitled 'the amount of rent and the procedure of payment' and because the 'words and expressions contained in this part gave a basis for the conclusion that this part provided for the mechanism of the increase of rent, and not merely the increase of the electricity payment'.[5]

If this method is not sufficient to ascertain the content of the contract, then, the actual common intention of parties should be clarified by taking into consideration the purpose of the contract. In such cases, all appropriate circumstances, including the negotiations which preceded the conclusion of the contract, and communications as well as the practice established between the parties, custom of trade and subsequent conduct of the parties are to be taken into account (*ibid.*):

> In a contract of joint participation in the construction of an apartment block, the owner of was under an obligation to transfer 10 flats of a total of 919 square metres, but in reality, 10 flats of only total 685 square metres were transferred. The shareholders brought an action to have the remaining space transferred. The claim was dismissed, since the building did not have 10 flats whose total size reached 919 square metres. The court found that the contract merely obliged the owner to transfer 10 flats of a different size.[6]

5   REVISION AND RESCISSION OF CONTRACTS

As a rule, revision and rescission of a contract is possible by agreement of the parties, unless law or the contract provides otherwise. The Code provides that a contract can be revised by the judgment of the court upon application of one of the parties only when there was a substantial breach of contract by the opposite party and in other occasions as provided by the Civil Code, law or the contract. 'Substantial breach' means a breach 'which causes the other party to suffer a loss which significantly reduces what this party may legitimately expect by concluding a contract' (Art.450, para.2). Another provision of the Civil Code prohibits the unilateral refusal of performance or the unilateral change of obligations (Art.310). It is important to note that other than in cases where a law or a contract entitles a party to a unilateral change or rescission, the revision or rescission of a contract has to be effected via a court judgment.

---

5   Decision of the Presidium of the Supreme Commercial Court, February 18,1997, *VVAS RF*, 1997 No.6, p.45.
6   Decision of the Presidium of the Supreme Commercial Court, June 17,1997, *VVAS RF*, 1997, No.9, p.36.

On this matter, the Supreme Commercial Court has published a 'Review of the Court Practice of Settling Disputes involving Conclusion, Revision, and Rescission of Contracts'.[7] Thus, for example, the failure of the buyer to pay for a real property as provided in the contract of sale is a substantial breach of a contract. Similarly, a failure to pay for a privatised object is a ground for a unilateral rescission of the contract of privatisation. Failure on the part of the contractor to complete the construction work within the agreed time limit and exceeding the projected cost were found to be grounds for rescission of the contract. On the other hand, in a case where the lessee failed to pay the rent many times, to make repairs, and even subleased the property without the consent of the lessor, the defendant submitted evidence that the breach had been rectified within a reasonable period. The court dismissed the claim of the lessor to rescind the contract.

If a creditor fails to accept the performance of an obligation without justifiable reason, this serves as a ground for rejecting rescission by the opposite party:

> A joint stock company brought an action against a limited liability company in order to rescind the contract of sale of a non-residential property for the failure of the defendant to pay the price. The court dismissed the claim, since it was ascertained that the plaintiff/seller had failed to accept the payment by the buyer and the buyer had deposited the amount. By virtue of Article 327, para.1 of the Civil Code, if an obligation cannot be performed due to the failure on the part of the creditor to accept performance, the amount in question can be deposited with a public notary.[8]

The Civil Code has a special provision on the revision and rescission of contracts on the ground of change of circumstances (Art.451, para.1):

> A significant change of circumstances on which one of the parties relied at the time of the conclusion of the contract is a ground for the revision or rescission of the contract, unless otherwise determined by the contract or unless this emanates from the nature of the contract.

> A change of circumstances is significant if the circumstances changed to the extent that if the parties were reasonably able to foresee it, they would not have concluded the contract or they would have concluded the contract under substantially different terms.

There are four basic requirements for the application of this provision:

---

7   Informatsionnoe pis'mo VAS RF, May 5, 1997, in Zhurakovskii and Kalinin, *supra*, pp.142-148; D.V.Murzin ed., *Grazhdanskii kodeks RF s postateinymi materialami iz praktiki VAS RF,* Moscow 1999, pp.464-471.

8   Murzin, *supra*, p.469.

i)   at the time of the conclusion of the contract, the parties relied on the fact that no such change of circumstances would occur;

ii)   the change of circumstances was the result of a phenomenon which, after it had happened, was insurmountable by the interested party with the care and alertness which are required of this party by the nature of the contract or the terms of business;

iii) the performance of the contract without revision of its terms harms the relationship of the proprietary interest of the parties and results in a loss on the part of the interested party to such an extent that this party would be deprived of what he had legitimately expected on concluding the contract;

iv)   it cannot be derived from commercial custom or the substance of the contract that the risk should be borne by the interested party.

This provision is a novelty which was introduced for the first time by the present Civil Code. Since the concept of change of circumstances is not common in the Anglo-American jurisdiction, when this was introduced, some foreign lawyers were apprehensive, since it was suspected to be an attempt to reduce the binding effect of contracts. However, this concept is familiar to lawyers in the Civil Law countries. In fact, the Swiss Civil Code has long had this concept, and so has the Dutch Civil Code which served as a model for the Russian Civil Code. A Russian expert points out that this has been recognised as 'one of the most important principles of contemporary contract law', which is demonstrated by the fact that it is incorporated in the 'Principles of International Commercial Contracts' prepared by UNIDROIT.[9]

The effect of the change of circumstances is that the parties are able to renegotiate the contract in order to bring it in line with the changed circumstances or to rescind the contract. If they fail to reach an agreement, the contract can be rescinded. If one of the parties brings the case to the court for rescission of the contract, in principle, the court must allow the rescission of the contract.[10] On the other hand, the contract can be revised by the court in exceptional circumstances where rescission of the contract is against the interests of society or where it results in a loss to the parties that significantly exceeds the cost necessary for performing the contract under changed circumstances (Art.452, para.4).

The commercial court has been cautious in acknowledging that the change of circumstances has occurred. In one case, the court denied the application of this provision to a lease agreement, concerning the determination of the amount

---

9   A.S.Komarov, 'Izmenenie obstoiatel'stv i dogovornoe otnoshenie', in A.L.Makovskii ed., *Grazhdan-skii kodeks Rossii*, Moscow 1998, pp.337-348.

10   *Ibid.*, p.350.

of rent.[11] In another case, the court denied that the bankruptcy of the creditor was a change of circumstances.

> The bankruptcy administrator of joint Stock company, Tserta Bank, brought an action against a limited liability company Firma BAK in order to have the credit agreement of February 9, 1998 to be rescinded and the amount of the loan, 300,000 roubles, and the interest, 33,750 roubles, to be seized from the defendant. In this case, the Bank was to provide a loan over five years with 5% interest to Firma BAK. The first instance court acknowledged the claim and the appellate instance as well as the cassation instance court upheld the judgment. Upon the protest of the deputy president of the Supreme Commercial Court, the Supreme Commercial Court reversed the judgment. Tserta Bank was declared bankrupt after the conclusion of the loan agreement. The Bank applied for rescission of the loan agreement to the court on the ground that the bankruptcy of the Bank was a substantial change of circumstances.
>
> However, in the view of the Supreme Commercial Court, the contract can be rescinded only when the four requirements set out in Article 451 are met. Bankruptcy of the creditor which occurred as a result of a risky credit policy is not regarded as a substantial change of circumstances and does not qualify as a change of circumstances resulting from a cause which the interested party, in this case, the Bank, could not have overcome with due care. Therefore, Article 451 is not applicable in this case.[12]

In a third case, the Supreme Commercial Court rejected the claim of the party for the revision of a construction contract due to the increase in the price of materials. The Court ruled that in order to revise the terms of the contract, all four requirements of Article 451, para.2 should be met, and in addition, pointed out that revision of the contract was possible, in accordance with para.4, only in exceptional cases where rescission of the contract is against the interests of society or where it results in a loss to the parties that significantly exceeds the cost necessary for performing the contract under changed circumstances.[13]

In order to claim revision or rescission of a contract, the interested party must first propose such a revision or rescission to the opposite party. Only when the interested party receives a refusal to revise or rescind the contract from the opposite party, or fails to receive a reply within the period determined by law or a contract, or in the absence of such a period, within 30 days, can he apply to court for revision or rescission (Art.452).

Revision or rescission of a contract takes effect from the time of the agreement by the parties to this effect, or, in cases where the revision or rescission is made

---

11   Decision of the Presidium of the Supreme Commercial Court, January 12, 1999 [Garant].
12   Decision of the Presidium of the Supreme Commercial Court, June 15, 1999 [Garant].
13   Decision of the Presidium of the Supreme Commercial Court, October 6, 1998, *VVS RF*, 1999 No.1, p.61.

by court procedure, from the time the judgment enters force. As a rule, the parties are not entitled to demand the return of that which has been transferred to the opposite party as performance of obligations up to the time of the revision or rescission of the contract (Art.453, para.4). However, if a substantial breach of contract by one of the parties served as a ground for revision or rescission of a contract, the opposite party is entitled to claim damages for revision or rescission of the contract (para.5).

9

INDIVIDUAL CONTRACTS

1   GENERAL

Part Two of the Civil Code covers individual contracts, together with tort and unjust enrichment. There are altogether 28 types of contracts provided in the Code ranging from sale, exchange to public tender and even wagering. These include contracts which are normally concluded between individuals as well as also commercial contracts which have entrepreneurs involved. In fact many of the commercial contracts, (i.e. contracts in which at least one of the parties is an entrepreneur) such as factoring, financial leases, franchising and entrustment of the management of assets have been newly incorporated in the Code. The problem is that the provisions on some of these newly incorporated types of contracts such as financial leases are not necessarily well thought through.

This list of contracts is not exclusive. Based upon the principle of freedom of contract, parties are free to conclude contracts which are not directly provided by law (*Innominatkontrakt*) unless the contracts are against the law. The Code also provides that parties may conclude contracts which encompass different types of contracts as provided by law and other legal acts (mixed contracts). Provisions on the types of contracts which compose the elements of the contract in question are applied to such contracts unless otherwise agreed by the parties or unless they emanate from the nature of the contract (Art.421, para.3).

Many provisions of the part on contracts are of an optional nature, i.e. it is possible to provide otherwise by agreement of the parties.

2   CONTRACTS OF SALE

1)   Types of Contract of Sale

A contract of sale is defined as a contract in which the seller is obliged to transfer the ownership of a thing (goods) to the buyer, while the buyer is under an obligation to accept it and pay the price (Art.454, para.1).

Contract of sale part of the Civil Code starts with the general part which sets out rules which are applicable to all kinds of contracts of sale. This is followed by specific types of contracts such as i) retail contracts, ii) supply contracts, iii) government procurement, iv) supply of agriculture products (*kontraktatsiia*), v) energy supply contracts, vi) sale of immovables, and vii) sale of enterprises.

A retail contract is a contract in which the seller, who is an entrepreneur in retail sales, sells goods for personal, family, domestic, and other uses not related to entrepreneurial activities. It is a 'public' contract, i.e. the seller is not allowed to refuse to enter into a contract if someone makes an offer. Supply contracts are those under which the supplier/entrepreneur supplies goods to another person for entrepreneurial activities and other purposes not related to personal, family, or domestic use.

Government procurement covers both contracts with the federal government and with the constituent entities of the Russian Federation. Government procurement is effected in two forms: a state contract for the needs of the state, and a state supply contract (Art.525, para.1). The former is compulsory on the opposite party, i.e. the opposite party is not entitled to refuse the supply, unless it is granted on the basis of tender. Compulsory conclusion of a contract is allowed only when provided by law, and on a compensation basis (Art.526, Art.527, para.2). State supply contracts are ordinary government procurement contracts and provisions of the supply contract are applicable.

2)   General Rules

(1)   Object of Sale

The object of sale can be anything which is regarded as an object of civil law rights in the Code, except for those excluded from circulation or whose circulation is restricted (Art.129, para.1). It should be noted that land and other natural resources can also be an object of sale to the extent it is allowed by the law on land and other natural resources (*ibid.*, para,3)[see Chapter 10 Property and Land Law].

A contract of sale can be concluded regarding goods which are in the possession of the seller at the time of the conclusion of the contract as well as goods which are to be acquired by the seller in the future (Art.455, para.2).

(2)   Performance and Acceptance

The obligation on the part of the seller is regarded to be performed at the time of either (i) delivery of the goods to the buyer or to the person designated by the buyer, if the seller is under an obligation to deliver the goods under the contract, or (ii) providing of the goods for the disposal of the buyer, if the goods, under the contract, are to be transferred to the buyer or a person designated by the buyer at the location of the goods. In the latter case, goods are provided for disposal when the goods are ready at the time and place determined by the contract and the buyer is notified of the readiness of the goods in accordance with the terms of the contract (Art.458, para.1).

If the seller fails to transfer the goods to the buyer, the buyer is entitled to refuse performance of the contract on his part. If the seller refuses to transfer an individually specified thing, the buyer may claim damages (arts.463 and 398).

The buyer is under an obligation to accept the goods except in cases where he is entitled to a replacement or to refuse performance. The buyer also has a duty to cooperate with the seller: he is obliged to perform acts which, in the light of normally presented requirements, are necessary for ensuring the transfer and acceptance of the goods, unless otherwise provided by law or other legal acts (Art.484, paras. 1 and 2).

(3)   Transfer of Risk

As a rule, the risk for accidental loss or damage of goods is transferred to the buyer when, by law or contract, the seller is regarded to have performed his obligation to transfer the goods to the buyer. The risk during transportation is transferred to the buyer from the moment of conclusion of the contract of sale, unless the contract provides otherwise or there is a different commercial custom (Art.459, para.2).

(4)   Third Parties

The seller is under an obligation to transfer the goods to the buyer without any encumbrance by rights of a third party, unless the buyer agreed otherwise. A breach of this obligation will result in the right of the buyer to demand a reduction in price or rescission of the contract, if it is not proved that the buyer had known or should have known of the existence of the third party's right in the goods. The same applies when there is a claim on the goods which the seller was aware of, and this claim is subsequently found by an established procedure to have grounds (Art.460).

If the object of sale was taken away from the buyer by a third party on a ground which had existed before the performance of the contract, the seller is liable for the damage unless the seller proves that the buyer had known or should have known the existence of such a ground. An agreement to exempt or limit the liability of the seller in such cases is void (Art.461).

Exemption of the liability of the seller if he proves that the buyer should have known the existence of the third party's right is rather questionable in that it gives too much protection to the seller who was aware of the existence of such a right.

If a third party initiates litigation *vis à vis* the buyer for taking away of the object of sale on a ground which had emerged before the performance of the contract, the buyer must cause the seller to take part in the proceedings and the seller is under an obligation to take part on the side of the buyer. If the seller was not invited, the seller is exempted from liability, if he successfully proves that had he participated, he could have prevented the third party from taking away of the property (Art.462).

(5)   Quality of Goods

The seller has a duty to transfer to the buyer the goods whose quality corresponds to the requirements set out in the contract. If there are no requirements in the contract, the seller is under an obligation to provide goods which are prepared for the purpose for which goods of the kind are normally used for. If the buyer had informed the seller of the specific purpose for use of the goods, the seller must provide goods for that particular purpose (Art.469, paras. 1 and 2). If, there is a mandatory requirement as to the quality of the goods, the seller, who is engaged in entrepreneurial activities, is under an obligation to provide the goods which correspond to such mandatory requirements (*ibid.*, para.4).

The buyer who received goods with inappropriate quality may, by his choice, require the seller to effect the following (Art.475, para.1):

i)   a commensurate reduction of the price;
ii)   the free removal of defects within a reasonable period;
iii)   the reimbursement of the cost for the removal of the defect incurred by the buyer.

If there was a substantial breach of the requirement of quality, defined by the Code as an irreparable defect, a defect which cannot be removed without disproportional cost or time, or repeatedly appearing defects, the buyer may choose from the following alternatives (*ibid.*, para.2):

i)   refuse the performance of the contract of sale and require the reimbursement of the money paid for the goods

ii)   require the replacement of the defective goods with those which meet the quality requirements

In retail sale, the buyer is entitled to require the replacement even if there is no substantial breach regarding the quality of goods (Art.503, para.1).

As a rule, the seller is liable for the defect of the goods if the buyer has successfully proved that the defect of the goods or the cause of the defect had emerged before the transfer of the goods to the buyer. Only when the seller has guaranteed the quality of the goods, the burden of proof shifts to the seller; the seller must prove that the defect of the goods or the cause of the defect emerged after the transfer of the goods to the buyer as a result of the breach of the rules of use or storage by the buyer, an act of a third party, or by *force majeure* (Art.476).

The procedure of inspecting the quality of the goods is established by law and other legal acts, mandatory requirements of the state standards, or the contract. In the absence of such a procedure, the inspection is carried out in accordance with commercial custom or other normally applicable requirements to the given goods (Art.474, paras.1 and 2):

> Limited liability company 'Firma SDM-Service' brought an action at the Commercial Court of Krasnodarsk Region against the joint stock company Agrokompleks claiming compensation for the supply of substandard bricks.
>
> The first instance court dismissed the claim on the ground that the plaintiff had failed to prove that the bricks were substandard. This was upheld by the appellate instance. Upon protest, the Supreme Commercial Court quashed the original judgment.
>
> In this case, the inspection of the brickwork on the 7th floor on May 13, 1996 revealed that the bricks were cracking and collapsing. The bricks were sent to the laboratory for technical examination. The plaintiff had submitted the report of this test as well as a report prepared with the participation of a director of a construction material plant. The director had agreed that the bricks were substandard.
>
> The reason why the first instance court dismissed the claim was because the plaintiff had failed to follow the procedure set by an instruction of the former USSR *gosarbitrazh* on the acceptance of products.
>
> The Supreme Commercial Court found this to be unjustifiable, since the contract between the parties of March 5, 1996 was governed by Part Two of the Civil Code and the above instruction was not applicable any more. According to Article 513, para.2 of the Code, the buyer is under an obligation to inspect the quantity and quality of the

accepted goods in accordance with the procedure set by law and other legal acts, the contract or commercial usage. The contract was silent on this matter.

The Court also noted that the lower court failed to examine the result of a random test referred to in the report. The Court concluded that the plaintiff's claim should be satisfied.[1]

As a rule, the buyer must inform the seller of the breach of the terms of the contract regarding quantity, quality, packaging etc. within the period determined by law, and other legal acts or the contract. If such a period is not determined, the claim has to be presented within a reasonable period by taking into account the nature and purpose of the goods (Art.483, para.1). There is a separate provision for discovering defects. If there was no guarantee period or period of use specified, the defect should be found within a reasonable period, but less than 2 years of the transfer of goods to the buyer unless law or the contract provides for a longer period. If a period of guarantee or usage is established, the claim has to be presented within this period (Art.477).

For sale of goods to consumers, there is a special law – the Law on the Protection of Consumers of 1996.[2] Consumers in this Law means individuals who order, acquire or use the goods exclusively for personal needs not related to the gaining of profits. Consumers are guaranteed the right to information on the manufacturer and the seller of the goods as well as the goods themselves (Arts.8-12). Manufacturers and sellers are liable for inappropriate information. There are detailed provisions on the consequence of sale of goods with inadequate quality (Art.18).

3)   Sale of Immovables

The definition of immovables is given in the General Part of the Civil Code (Art.130). The sale of immovable requires a written form – a single document signed by the parties (Art.550). Previously, some transactions on immovables, e.g. sale of accommodation, required notarisation, but with the introduction of the system of state registration, this became unnecessary, except for transactions on hypothecs.

An important requirement of the sale of immovables is that in the contract, information which allows the demarcation of the immovable which is to be

---

1   Decision of the Presidium of the Supreme Commercial Court, December 23, 1997, *VVAS RF*, 1998 No.5, pp.46-47.
2   *SZ RF*, 1996 No.3, item 140 (originally enacted in 1992).

transferred must be specified. This is an 'essential term' of the contract as provided in the general part of the contract law (Art.432). If there is no such information, the parties to the contract are deemed to have failed to agree on the terms, and therefore, the contract is void (Art.554). This may be rather difficult in a sale of land where, in many areas, with the insufficient development of the Land Register, the demarcation of the land is not clear.

Transfer of immovables by the seller and acceptance by the buyer are effected by a 'transfer document' or other document signed by both parties. The seller's duty to transfer the object is considered to be fulfilled by the handing over of the object to the buyer and the signing of the transfer document (Art.556, para.1).

Transfer of title of immovables is subject to state registration. The contract itself takes effect between the parties at the time of conclusion. The significance of state registration is that only after the registration, may the buyer become a titleholder in relation to a third party. In cases where one of the parties fails to register the transaction, the court, upon the petition of the other party, may render a decision to register the transaction. The party who failed to register without justifiable grounds is liable for damages to the other party.

True to the tradition of Russian law, the Civil Code provides that if a building, installation, or other immovable is sold, the right over the piece of land which the immovable occupies and which is needed for its use is transferred to the buyer together with the title to such an immovable (Art.552, para.1). The right over the land which the buyer obtains depends on the right which the seller had held. If the seller had a title -ownership right over the land, then the buyer may acquire either an ownership right, a right of lease, or another right over the land as pro- vided by the contract of sale (*ibid.*, para.2). If the seller did not have the title over the land, nevertheless, he is entitled to sell the building, installation etc., without the consent of the owner of the land, provided that it is not against the terms of use of the land determined by law or contract. In such cases, the buyer obtains the right to use the land on the same terms as the seller (*ibid.*, para.3).

Conversely, if a piece of land on which a building, installation, or other immovable of the seller is located is sold, the seller retains his right to use the land which is occupied by the building etc., and the land which is needed for its use. The terms of use are to be determined by the contract of sale. In the absence of contractual provisions, the seller retains the right of servitude over the land (Art.553).

Since most of the immovables – land, buildings, and enterprises – used to be state -owned, the title of the current seller emanates from state or municipal property. However, the process of the transfer of title to the private sector was at the best, murky. Therefore, the title of the seller is often contested in court:

A deputy procurator of the Perm Province brought an action in the Commercial Court of the Perm Province 'for the interest of the state' to declare void the decision of the city government of the Solikamsk on the sale of a non-residential building and the contract of sale between a municipal enterprise of the retail trade, Sosenka, and an open joint stock company Sosenka. The claim was based on the ground that property which belonged to the municipality had been transferred to the company in breach of the privatisation law.

The retail enterprise Sosenka was set up by the city committee for the administration of municipal assets in 1992. The premise of the shop was used on the basis of a lease agreement between the enterprise and the committee which was renewed every year. In 1998, the premise was transferred for the right of economic management of the enterprise by the decision of the city government, and permission for the sale to the then newly established joint stock company Sosenka was granted on the condition that the latter fully assume the debt of the enterprise.

The first instance court and the appellate instance dismissed the claim of the procurator on the ground that the sale of the premise was effected in accordance with articles 215, 295 and other provisions of the Civil Code. However, the Supreme Commercial Court pointed out that the lower courts failed to take into account that enterprises are prohibited from alienating assets directly needed for production purposes which belong to its economic management. Such a transfer is void on the basis of Art.168, regardless of the existence of the owner's (the city government's) consent. The case was referred to a new hearing.[3]

Thus, the buyer can never be certain whether the seller's title to the immovable is free from any pretension.

4)   Sale of Enterprises

There are separate provisions for the sale of enterprises in addition to the provisions on the sale of immovables, although, according to the Civil Code, enterprises are immovables. If the object of sale is a state or municipal property, the Law on Privatisation also applies.

By a contract of sale, an enterprise as a whole – a 'proprietary complex' – is transferred to the buyer. This includes the trade name, trademark, service mark and other means of identification. The contract has to be in writing, and is subject to registration. Not only the title, but the contract itself has to be registered. Therefore, the contract only takes effect upon registration (Art.560, para.3).

---

3   Decision of the Presidium of the Supreme Commercial Court, October 19, 1999, *VVAS RF*, 2000 No.1, pp.43-45.

Before the signing of the contract, an act of inventory, a balance sheet, an opinion of an independent auditor on the composition and the value of the enterprise, and a list of all the debts with an indication of the name of the creditors, nature, amount and the time of payment, must be prepared and inspected by the parties (Art.561).

There are protections for creditors. Creditors must be notified of the sale in writing by one of the parties before the transfer of the enterprise to the seller. Creditors who did not give consent to the transfer of debt to either the seller or the buyer are entitled to require, within three months of receipt of the notice, the termination of the claim or accelerated payment and compensation of loss by the seller. Creditors may also require the contract of sale to be recognised as void in its entirety or in part. The creditor may initiate litigation within a year from the time he became aware of the transfer, or should have become aware of the transfer. After the transaction, the seller and the buyer bear joint and several liability for the debt for which the creditor's consent was not obtained (Art.562).

An enterprise is deemed to have been transferred to the buyer from the date of the signature of the transfer act by both parties. From this moment, the risk of accidental loss or damage shifts to the buyer (Art.563).

The consequence of the transfer of enterprise with defects, including the quality of the assets, is determined by the provisions on the seller's liability in the general part of the contract of sale. Particularly important is that the buyer is entitled to the reduction of price if a debt which was not indicated in the contract of sale or the transfer act was transferred to the buyer, unless the seller proves that the buyer was aware of such a debt at the time of the conclusion of the contract and the transfer of the enterprise (Art. 565, para.3). The buyer is entitled to rescind the contract or to require a revision of the contract, if the enterprise is not fit for the purpose indicated in the contract due to a defect to for which the seller is liable, provided that such a defect has not been removed in accordance with the terms, procedure, and time as set by law and other legal acts or contract, or removal of the defect is impossible (*ibid.*, para.5).

3   CONTRACTS OF LEASE

1)   The Concept and Types of Lease

There are two Russian terms for lease: *arenda* and *naem*. The term *arenda,* according to a Tsarist Russian source, originates from the Latin *reditta*. It denotes a lease of immovables, i.e. a contract by which a person provides immovable property to another for a fixed period for a rent.[4] The concept of *imushchestvennyi naem* also existed at that time, but there was a clear distinction between *arenda* and *naem*. The object of *arenda* was of a 'productive nature', while *naem* was for objects of an 'instrumental character'.[5]

Thus, *arenda* was historically used in relation to the lease of a means of production. There was no wonder the term *arenda* did not appear in the civil codes of the socialist period when means of production were monopolised by the state. Instead, the term '*imushchestvennyi naem*' was used for a limited scope of properties. Leases of land and enterprises existed in the NEP period, but disappeared in the late 1920s. Under socialism, not only the object of '*imushchestvennyi naem*' was limited, but its length was also limited to a maximum term of 10 years.[6]

A significant change was introduced by the Fundamental Principles of the Law on Lease of the USSR in 1989. It was not only that the term *arenda* was officially restored. This Law defined a lease as a contract of possession and use (not disposal) of land and other natural resources, enterprises and other proprietary complexes as well as all other properties needed by the lessee for economic and other activities. These objects which were hitherto unavailable for lease could now be leased by entities such as state enterprises and local governments. Juridical persons and individuals including foreign ones were allowed to be lessees. While this Law remained in force only until 1992, it marked a radical turn to the market economy in that it enabled individuals and private entities to establish a business on the basis of leased assets. In fact, by leasing state enterprises and eventually purchasing them, which was allowed by this Law 'spontaneous privatisation' of state enterprises in the form of management and/or employees' buy-out rapidly spread. In this sense, together with the Law on Cooperatives, it contributed to the acceleration of transition to the market economy.

The current Civil Code has a chapter on leases (*arenda*) and another chapter on leases (*naem*) of residential premises. The chapter on leases (*arenda*) is further divided into different types of lease. After the general part applicable to all kinds of lease (*arenda*), there are provisions on hire (*prokat*), the lease of means of transportation, the lease of buildings and installations, the lease of enterprises, and finance lease (*lizing*). Hire denotes a contract in which the lessor leases movables as a permanent entrepreneurial activity (Art.626, para.1). A finance lease is defined as a contract in which the lessor is under an obligation to acquire a property designated by the lessee from the seller and provide it to the lessee for

---

4   F.A.Brokgaus et al eds., *Entsiklopediicheskii slovar'*, vol.II, St.Petersburg, 1890, pp.54-55.
5   Brokgaus, *supra*, vol.XX, p.450.
6   Art.277, 1964 Civil Code of RSFSR.

possession and use for entrepreneurial purposes of a fixed period in exchange for payment (Art.665).

2)   General Rules

The object of leases can include all durable property, from land and other 'natural objects', enterprises and proprietary complexes, buildings, installations, equipment, means of transportation and other things which do not lose their natural attributes through their use. It is possible to determine types of property whose lease is prohibited or restricted by law (Art.607, para.1), but present, there is no such law. Information which enables the object of a lease to be identified has to be indicated in the contract; otherwise, the contract is regarded not to have been agreed and concluded (*ibid.,* para.3).

A contract of a lease for more than a year, or in cases where at least one of the parties is a juridical person, regardless of the term, must be concluded in writing. A contract of the lease of an immovable is subject to state registration (Art.609, paras. 1 and 2).

The length of the lease is determined by the contract. If there is no such term, the lease is regarded to be for an indeterminate period. This means that either party may terminate the lease with one month's notice (in the case of immovables, three month's notice).

As a rule, it is the owner of the property who may be a lessor. In addition, those who are empowered to do so by law or by the owner may lease the property under their control. Thus, unitary enterprises may lease state property only with the consent of the owner, since they do not have a title to the assets entrusted to them.

The lessor is liable for a defect of the property provided to the lessee which inhibits its use wholly or partly, even if he was not aware of such a defect at the time of the conclusion of the contract. The lessor is not liable if the defect could have been discovered by the lessee at the time of inspection or check at the time of the conclusion of the contract or transfer of the property (Art.612, paras. 1 and 2).

Providing the property for lease is not a ground for termination or modification of the right of a third party in this property, e.g. servitude or a pledge. When concluding a contract of lease, the lessor is under an obligation to disclose to the lessee all the rights of the third party on the object of the lease. The failure of the lessor to fulfil this duty results in the right of the lessee to demand reduction of rent, or rescission of the contract and payment of damages (Art.613).

The lessee may, with the consent of the lessor, sublet the property, assign the rights and duties of the lessee to another person, provide the leased property for the gratuitous use of another person, pledge the right of lease, and to contribute it to the capital of a company. In these cases, except for the assignment of the rights and duties of the lessee to another person, the lessee remains liable to the lessor (Art.615, para.2).

Rescission of the lease is effected only via court procedure. Upon the action of the lessor, the contract can be rescinded by the court if the lessee (Art.619):

i)   uses the property with a substantial breach of the terms of the contract or the purpose of the property, or repeatedly breached the terms;
ii)   substantially worsened the property;
iii) failed to pay the rent in time more than twice, or;
iv)   in cases where capital repair is the responsibility of the lessee, failed to carry out such a repair.

The lessee may take an action in court to rescind the contract in the following instances (Art.620):

i)   the lessor failed to provide the property for the use of the lessee, or created obstacles for its use in accordance with the terms of the contract or the purpose of the property;
ii)   the property has a defect which inhibits its use and this defect was not known to the lessee before, and could not have been detected by the lessee on inspection;
iii) the lessor failed to carry out a capital repair which he is under an obligation to carry out, or;
iv)   the property, due to a cause not attributable to the lessee, has turned out to be unsuitable for use.

The lessee who has appropriately performed his obligation, has a right of pre-emption ahead of others to conclude a contract for a new period, if the terms offered by the others are the same as the lessee's, unless otherwise provided by law or contract. The lessee must inform the lessor of the intention to renew the contract within a reasonable period in advance. If the lessor refused to conclude a contract with the lessee, but within one year of the expiry of the contract, concluded a contract of lease with another person, the previous lessee has the following choices (Art.621, para.1):

i)   bring an action to court requiring the rights and duties of the lessee in the new contract to be transferred to him and claim compensation for not renewing the contract, or;
ii)   only claim compensation for not renewing the contract.

If the lessee continues using the property after the expiry of the term and the lessor does not object, the contract is deemed to have been renewed on the same terms for an undetermined period (*ibid.*, para.2).

The Code provides for the right of the lessee to purchase the object of the lease. Thus, by law or contract, it is possible to provide that the title to the leased property is to be transferred to the lessee on the expiry of the lease, or that even before the expiry, the lessee may purchase the property by paying the full purchase price as determined by the contract (Art.624, para.1). This right of the lessee to purchase the leased property was first introduced by the above-mentioned Fundamental Principles on Leases of 1989. In the case of a lease of a state enterprise, the lessee was entitled to purchase the enterprise by deferred payment and convert it to a joint stock company or other forms of business entities. In the formal privatisation process which started in 1992, commercial companies which the workers' collectives set up were allowed by law to have the offices, buildings, structures leased to them on a long term basis and were given a preferential right eventually to purchase them.[7]

3)   Lease of Buildings and Installations

The lease of buildings and installations has to be effected in a written form; breach of this requirement makes the contract void. Contracts of lease of buildings and installations with a term of one year or more are subject to state registration and are regarded as concluded at the time of registration (Art.651).

Under the lease of a building or installation, the right to use the land which it occupies and which is needed for its use is transferred to the lessee. If the lessor is the owner of the land, the lessee obtains the right to lease or other rights as provided by the contract (Art.652, paras.1 and 2). Even if the lessor is not the owner of the land, the lessor may still lease the building or installation standing on it without the consent of the owner of the land, providing that the lease of the property is not against the conditions of use of the land as provided by the law or contract (*ibid.*, para.3).

If the land on which the building or installation is located changes hands, the lessee of the building or installation maintains the right to use the land which it occupies and which is needed for the use of the building or installation on the same terms which existed until the sale of the land (Art.653).

---

7   See S. Johnson and H. Kroll, 'Managerial Strategy for Spontaneous Privatization', *Soviet Economy*, 1991, p. 281 ff.

4)   Lease of Enterprises

Contracts of lease of enterprises must be concluded in a written form and are subject to state registration. They are considered to be concluded from the time of the registration. A breach of form makes the contract void (Art.658).

In the lease of an enterprise, creditors of the enterprise are given the same right as in the case of the sale of an enterprise. Creditors must be notified of the lease of the enterprise in writing. Creditors who did not give a written consent to the lease are entitled, within three months of the notice, to require termination of the debt or accelerated repayment of the debt with compensation for loss. Creditors who failed to be notified are entitled to the same claim within one year of the day when he became aware, or should have become aware of the lease. After providing the enterprise for lease, lessor and lessee are jointly and severally liable for the debt which was transferred to the lessee without the consent of the creditor (Art.657).

4   CONTRACTS OF COMMISSION, AGENCY, AND MANDATE

1)   The Concepts

In a commission contract (*kommissiia*), one party (commission agent) undertakes an obligation to effect one or several 'transactions (*sdelka*)' entrusted by another party (commission principal) for remuneration in his own name, but at the expense of the commission principal (Art.990, para.1). In a transaction with a third party, the commission agent obtains rights and assumes duties even if the name of the commission principal was indicated in the transaction or the principal directly dealt with the third party (*ibid.*, para.2).

In a contract of mandate (*poruchenie*), one party is under an obligation to effect a certain legal act (*iuridicheskie deistviia*) in the name of, and at the expense of, the other party (Art.971, para.1). Remuneration is not an essential component of a mandate, although remuneration can be provided by law, other legal acts or contract.

An agency contract (*agentirovanie*) is defined as a contract in which one party (agent) undertakes an obligation to effect a juristic act or other acts entrusted by the other party (principal) for remuneration in his own name, but at the expense of the principal, or in the name of the principal and at the expense of the principal (Art.1005, para.1).

In Russian Law, an agent may either act in his own name or in the name of the principal. If the agent has acted in his own name *vis à vis* a third party but at the expense of the principal, the agent obtains rights and assumes duties even if the principal was referred to in the transaction or the principal had directly performed the obligation in relation to the third party. In this 'commission type model', the agent is under an obligation to transfer the rights and duties to the principal. When the agent acted in the name of the principal, the principal obtains rights and assumes duties directly (Art.1005, para.1).[8]

There seems to be a significant overlap between these three types of contracts. In fact, if a person is to effect a juristic act in the name of another person, it can be either by mandate or agency. If a juristic act is to be effected in the name of the person himself, it can be either by commission or agency. Acts performed by the commission agent, agent, and the person with a mandate are juristic acts (including 'transactions'), but in the case of agents, they can effect non-juristic – factual acts as well. Provisions on mandate and commission contracts are applicable to agency contracts insofar as they are not against the provisions of agency contracts, depending on whether the agent has acted in the name of the principal or in his name (Art.1011).

This confusing state of legislation has a historical background. Commission contracts and contracts of mandate had been accommodated in the socialist civil codes, while agency contracts, which came from Anglo-American Law, is new to Russian Law. The agency contract was added as a new category of contract with the transition to the market economy in order to cope with situations e.g. where an agent not only undertakes the task of selling products, but also to advertise and market the products. This is a combination of juristic acts (sale) and factual acts (advertisement) which cannot be fully covered by either mandate or commission contracts, so a new type of contract in the form of agency had to be introduced.[9]

It should be added that in the General Part of the Civil Code, there is a provision on 'commercial representation' (*kommercheskoe predstavitel'stvo*). A commercial representative is a person who constantly and independently represents an entrepreneur in the name of this entrepreneur in concluding contracts in the area of business activities (Art.184). Although this resembles an agency, reference is made to commercial representation in the chapter on contracts of mandate (Art.973, para.3).

---

8   O.N.Sadikov ed., *Kommentarii k grazhdanskomu kodeksu Rosiiskoi Federatsi, chasti vtoroi*, enlarged edition, Moscow 1999, p.592.

9   M.I.Braginskii ed., *Kommentarii chasti vtoroi Grazhdanskogo Kodklsa Rossiiskoi Federatsii dlia predprinimatelei*, first edition, Moscow 1996, p.p.306-307.

2)   Commission Contracts

In a commission contract, the commission principal retains the title to those properties which he has transferred to the commission agent or those which the commission agent has acquired at the expense of the commissioner (Art.996, para.1).

The commission principal has a duty to remunerate the commission agent. The commission principal must also reimburse the cost incurred by the commission agent for performing his duty, except for the storage (Art.1001). If the commission contract was not performed due to a cause which is attributable to the commission principal, the commission agent retains the right to remuneration (Art.991).

The commission agent is under an obligation to perform his duty in the manner which would be the most advantageous for the commission principal, bound by the latter's instruction; if there is no instruction, he must perform his duty in accordance with commercial custom or normally applicable requirements. If the commission agent effected a transaction in better terms than those instructed by the commission principal, the additional profit is to be divided between the parties, unless the parties had agreed otherwise (Art.992).

The commission agent is liable for the loss, shortage, and damage of the property of the commission principal in his possession (Art.998, para.1).

Commission contracts can be terminated on the following grounds (Art.1002):

i)   refusal on the part of the commission principal to perform the contract;
ii)   refusal on the part of the commission agent to perform the contract in cases provided by law or contract;
iii)   death, declaration of incapacity, limited capacity, or disappearance of the commission agent;
iv)   recognition of an individual entrepreneur as insolvent (bankrupt).

The commission principal may, at any time, revoke the commission. In such cases, the commission agent is entitled to compensation (Art.1003, para.1).

The commission agent is not entitled to refuse performance of the commission contract unilaterally unless otherwise provided by the contract, except in cases where the contract was concluded for an indefinite period. In the latter case, the commission agent may refuse performance with 30 days' notice (Art.1004, para.1).

3)   Agency Contracts

In agency contracts, if the principal grants to the agent a general power to act in the name of the principal, the principal may not refer to an absence of power on the part of the agent *vis à vis* a third party, unless he proves that the third party had known or should have known of the restriction of power on the agent (Art.1005, para.2).

In the contract, it is possible to provide for an obligation of the principal not to conclude a similar contract with another agent who is active in the same territory determined by the contract, or to refrain from conducting activities by himself analogous to those which are the object of the agency contract. By the same token, the agent may be placed under an obligation not to conclude an analogous agency contract with another principal in the territory which in all or part, overlaps with the territory covered by the agency contract (Art.1007, paras. 1 and 2).

On the other hand, terms of an agency contract by which the agent is allowed to sell products, execute works, or provide services only for a specific category of buyers, or only to those who are located or resident in the territory, are void (Art.1007, para.3). This is explained to be because by these terms, some people will be excluded in advance from being potential consumers (buyers, customers).[10]

In the process of the performance of an agency contract, the agent is under an obligation to submit a report to the principal as provided by the contract. If there is no such clause in the contract, the agent has a duty to report to the principal in the course of performance or at the end of the performance of the contract. If the principal has an objection to the report, he has to inform the agent within three days of the receipt of the report; otherwise, he is considered to have accepted the report (Art.1008).

Unless otherwise provided by the contract, the agent is entitled to contract a subagent for the purpose of performing the agency contract, but has to remain responsible *vis à vis* the principal for the act of the subagent (Art.1009, para.1).

Agency contracts are terminated on the following grounds:

i)   refusal of performance by either party of a contract concluded without a fixed period of validity;
ii)   death, declaration of incapacity, limited capacity, and disappearance of the agent;
iii)   recognition of an individual entrepreneur as insolvent (bankrupt).

4)   Contracts of Mandate

The person under mandate must perform his duties in accordance with the instructions of the principal. The instructions must be 'lawful, enforceable, and specific'. The person under mandate may deviate from the instruction if it is necessary for

---

10   *Ibid.*, p.309.

the interests of the principal and there was no time to inquire with the principal or the person under mandate had failed to receive a reply to the inquiry. The person under mandate must inform the principal of such a deviation without delay, once the communication has become possible (Art.973, paras 1 and 2).

A person under mandate acting as a 'commercial representative', i.e. a person who perpetually and independently represents an entrepreneur in concluding contracts in the area of entrepreneurial activities (Art.184, para.1), may be granted a right to deviate from the instructions without advance consultation with the principal (Art.973, para.3).

4   CONTRACTS RELATED TO BANKING

1)   Contracts of Loan and Credit

The current Civil Code has a chapter on contracts of loan and credit. This is subdivided into contracts of loan, credit, and 'products and commercial credit'.

In the RSFSR Civil Code of 1964, provisions on loan and credit contracts were accommodated in separate chapters and were scarce. In contracts of loan, with the absence of commercial banks, the creditors were invariably state banks. There was only one provision on extending loans to 'organisations' including state enterprises which provided that the loans to various entities were granted in accordance with the economic plan by state banks in accordance with the procedure established by legislation. Loans between enterprises were allowed only in cases provided by legislation.[11]

The Civil Code distinguishes between loan (*zaem*) and credit (*kredit*). The RSFSR Civil Code of 1923 and 1964 both only provided for *zaem*. Credit was first referred to in the USSR Fundamental Principles of Civil Legislation of 1990, but not as a separate type of a contract. *Zaem* and *kredit* were regarded as one and the same contract (Art.113). In contrast, under the current Civil Code, *zaem* and *kredit* are provided as different types of a contract.

In *zaem*, the lender transfers money or other things determined by their generic nature to the ownership of the borrower, and the borrower is obliged to return the same amount of money or things of the same generic nature to the lender within the agreed period. A contract of *zaem* is a *contrat réel*, i.e. it is deemed to be concluded at the time of the transfer of money or other things (Art.807, para.1). A contract of *zaem* concluded between juridical persons must take a

---

11   Art.392, Civil Code of the RFSFR of 1964.

written form; the same applies to contracts between individuals of the amount of 10 times or more of the minimum wage (Art.808). The lender is entitled to receive interest out of the money or other things transferred to the borrower (Art.809).

Although interest is not a constituent element of a contract of loan, unless otherwise provided by law or contract, the lender is entitled to interest as provided by the contract. If the terms regarding the amount of interest are not provided in the contract in which the lender is a juridical person, the rate of interest is determined by the bank refinancing rate at the place of the lender on the day of repayment by the borrower. Unless otherwise agreed between the parties, the interest is payable every month until repayment (Art.809, paras. 1 and 2). There is no restriction on the level of interest charged in *zaem* and *kredit* contracts.

Variations of *zaem* are promissory notes (*veksel'*), ordinary bonds (*obligatsiia*) and government bonds. If the borrower issued a promissory note which certifies an unconditional assumption of debt by the issuer (simple promissory note) or by another person indicated on the note as a payer (bill of exchange), the relationship between the parties is regulated by the Law on Promissory Notes and Bills of Exchange. If there is a contradiction between the Civil Code and this law, provision of the latter prevails (Art.815). Until 1997, the Statute on Bills of Exchange and Promissory Notes, which was attached to the decision of the Supreme Soviet of the RSFSR in 1991 was applicable. In fact, this was a 'reconfirmation' of the 1938 Law which was enacted following the ratification of the 1930 Geneva Convention by the USSR in 1937. Although after the 'reform of the credit system' in the early 1930s, there was no need for bills of exchange or promissory notes within the country, they were thought to be necessary for foreign trade, and therefore, the USSR ratified the Geneva Convention. Basic rules of the Convention have been incorporated in the Statute.

The Law on Promissory Notes and Bills of Exchange was enacted in 1997, It has taken into account the 1988 UN Convention on International Bills of Exchange and International Promissory Notes which was signed, but not ratified by the former USSR.[12]

The Civil Code also provides that a contract of *zaem* can be concluded by the issuing and offering of bonds. Bonds are securities which certify the right of the possessor to receive its nominal value or its proprietary equivalent plus interest from the issuer (Art.816). In a contract of state *zaem*, the borrower is the Russian Federation, and the lenders are individuals or juridical persons. A contract of state *zaem* is concluded by acquisition of state bonds and other securities by the lenders.

---

12   *SZ RF* 1997, No.11, item 1238.

It should be noted that the terms of state bonds may not be altered (Art.817, paras. 1, 3 and 4).

In contrast with *zaem*, in contracts of *kredit*, lenders (creditors) are banks or other credit organisations. It is not a *contrat réel*; signing of a contract is sufficient. The creditor is obliged to offer the agreed amount under agreed terms to the debtor, and the debtor is under an obligation to repay the money and the interest (Art.819, para.1). *Kredit* contracts must be concluded in a written form. As a rule, provisions on *zaem* are applicable to *kredit* contracts.

The Civil Code provides that creditors are entitled to refuse the granting of credit provided by a contract wholly or partly, if there are circumstances which demonstrate that the money will not be returned on time (Art.821, para.1).

The borrower is naturally under an obligation to return the borrowed sum to the lender. If the period of return is not determined or the sum is to be returned on demand by the lender, the borrowed sum should be returned to the lender within 30 days of the demand by the lender. While a loan without interest can be returned before maturity, a loan which bears interest can be returned prematurely only by agreement of the parties (Art.810, paras. 1 and 2).

If the borrower fails to return the loan (*zaem* and *kredit*) in time, the borrower must pay interest for delay as provided in the general part of the Law of Obligations of the Civil Code, i.e. at the bank discount rate on the day the performance was due (Art.395).

If the borrower fails to provide security as provided by the contract, and also in cases where the means of security was lost or worsened due to a cause not attributable to the lender, the lender is entitled to require the premature return of the loan and the payment of interest (Art.813).

2)   Commercial Credit Contracts

Contracts in which one party transfers money or generic goods to the ownership of the other party, can be regarded as credit contracts. Those include advance payments, deferred payments, and payments in installations. As a rule, provisions on *zaem* and credit are applicable to these arrangements (Art.823).

3)   Bank Deposit (*bankovskii deposit*) Contracts

In contracts of bank deposit, the bank accepts the money paid in by the depositor or for the benefit of the depositor and is under an obligation to return the amount with interest as provided by the contract (Art.834, para.1). The deposit account serves only the depositary purpose, i.e. the account cannot be used for settlement etc. Juridical persons may not transfer the deposited money to another person's account (*ibid.*, para.3).

A bank deposit can take the form of payment on demand, or fixed term (Art.837, para.1).

Interest is paid on the deposit. The interest rate is to be determined by the contract, but in the absence of an explicit provision, the rate is determined by the bank refinancing rate at the place of business of the creditor/juridical person (Art.838, para.1).

4)   Bank Account (*bankovskii schet*) Contracts

In bank account contracts, the bank is under an obligation to accept and credit the money to the account opened by the client, and execute the instructions of the client on transfer of the money, payment and other operations (Art.845, para.1). Regarding payment, the distinction between bank account contracts and contracts of entrustment of payment (see below) becomes blurred. The bank is entitled to use the money in the account, provided that it guarantees free disposal of the money in the account by the client (*ibid.*, para.2). It is possible to open a credit account from which a payment can be made regardless of the absence of money in the account (Art. 850, para.1).

A contract of bank account is a public contract, i.e. the bank is obliged to conclude a contract when requested by the client to do so in an appropriate manner. The bank is liable for an ungrounded refusal to open an account (Art.846, para.2).

The problem is the withdrawal of money from the account. There is no question that the client is entitled to withdraw money by instructing the bank. However, the Code also provides for withdrawal of money *without* the instruction of the client. Grounds for such withdrawal are court judgments, and 'instances provided by laws or contracts between the bank and the client' (Art.854, para.2). At present, the Ministry of Tax and Levies is empowered to withdraw unpaid tax and penalties from the account of juridical persons without recourse to judicial procedure. The same applies to unpaid customs duties, pensions, social security contributions and medical insurance payments by employers.[13]

---

13   Sadikov ed., *supra*, p.424.

5)   Payment Contracts

This is a new section introduced by the present Civil Code. Previously, there was
only one provision concerning payment in the 1964 Civil Code. Payment was
regulated by subordinate legal acts, primarily by normative acts of the Central
Bank. With the enactment of the new Civil Code, payment is regulated by banking
regulations only when so provided by the Code and other laws (namely the Law
on Banks and Banking Activities) and only to the extent that they do not contradict
the provisions of the Code.[14]

Payments in Russia are not entirely free from restrictions. The Civil Code
provides that payments where at least one party is an individual who is not
engaged in entrepreneurial activities can be effected by cash without restriction.
However, payment between juridical persons, and between juridical persons and
individuals involving the performance of entrepreneurial activities are to be effected
in a non-cash form. As a rule, payment in a non-cash form is effected through
banks and other credit organisations where an account is opened (Art.861).

The Civil Code lists various methods of payment by taking into account
international rules and practices. The list is not exhaustive:

    i)   payment by order;
    ii)   payment by letter of credit;
    iii)   incasso payment;
    iv)   payment by cheque.

Provisions on letters of credit in the Civil Code were prepared with the ICC Rules
taken into consideration.

As for cheques, the Geneva Convention on Cheques of 1932 was ratified by
the USSR. There was a Statute on Cheques which was revived in 1993 which
followed the lines of the Geneva Convention. However, this Statute was repealed
by the enactment of the Civil Code. The current Civil Code has made efforts to
toe the line with the 1932 Geneva Convention on the Unification of Cheques.[15]

6)   Contracts of the Management of Entrusted Property

Auxiliary businesses of credit organisations as listed in the Law on Banks and
Banking Activities include '*trast* operations', i.e. attract and invest assets and

---

14   *Ibid.*, p.443..
15   *Ibid.*, p.474.

manage securities as entrusted by customers'. In the property law part of the Civil Code, there is a provision which refers to the management of entrusted property (*doveritel'noe upravlenie*), but does not use the term *trast* (Art.209). The special part of contract law contains a chapter on the same matter, but does not use the term *trast* either (Chapter 53).

In the management of entrusted property, a party transfers property to another person for a fixed period, and the latter manages the property for the interest of the former or a person designated by the former (Art.1012, para.1). Important differences between this arrangement and the trust under the Anglo-American system are that the title to the property does not shift to the entrusted party (*ibid.*, para.2), and that it is not necessarily a tri-partite arrangement between the parties and the beneficiary.[16]

Contract on the management of entrusted property is used in mutual funds and pension funds as well as in the process of privatisation.[17]

5   Some other Contracts

1)   Contracts of 'Commercial Concession'

In a contract of commercial concession, a party (holder of the right) is obliged to provide the other party (concessionaire) for a fixed period, or without determination of the period, with the right to use the complex of exclusive rights which belong to the rightholder, including the right to the name of the company and/or commercial identification, the right to protected commercial information, trade marks and service marks (Art.1027, para.1). Parties to this contract are commercial organisations and individuals registered as entrepreneurs (*ibid.*, para.3).

Commercial concession contracts are subject to registration. Registration is effected by the agency which registers juridical persons and individual entrepreneurs (Art.1028, para.2). Contracts whose object is protected by patent need to be registered by the Patent Agency as well (*ibid.*).

This type of contract should not be confused with the concession contracts in the area of the natural resources law or the construction and operation of infrastructure. In fact, the term 'franchising' is often used to denote this type of contract in Russia.

---

16   E.Reid, 'The Law of Trust in Russia', *Review of Central and Eastern European Law*, 1998 No.1, pp.50-51.

17   *Ibid.*, pp.52-55.

2)   Joint Venture Contracts

Joint venture contracts are denoted as 'contracts of simple partnership (*prostoe tovarishchestvo*)' in the Civil Code. In this kind of a contract, two or more parties are under an obligation to invest in a joint scheme and join forces with the goal of making profits or achieving other goals without forming a juridical person (Art.1041, para.1).

As is the case with other typical contracts provided by the Civil Code, most of the provisions are of an optional nature and as such, can be modified by contracts.

The contribution is presumed to be equal among the parties, but the parties may agree otherwise (Art.1042, para.2). The property which the joint venture obtained or produced belong to the co-ownership with shares of the participants, unless otherwise agreed by the parties (Art.1043, para.1). It should be noted that creditors of the participants are entitled to require the split of the share of the debtor-participant from the common property of the joint venture (Art.1049). Participants are liable for the debt of the joint venture jointly and severally, if the joint venture is involved in entrepreneurial activities (Art.1047, para.2).

The contract of joint venture is terminated on grounds including the following (Art.1050; para.1):

i)   bankruptcy of the participant;
ii)   rescission of the contract with a fixed period by the participant;
iii) withdrawal of the participant from a contract without a fixed period;
iv)   splitting of a share of the participant by a creditor.

However, these do not apply, if the contract provides that the contract would continue to be valid among the remaining participants (*ibid.*).

Another important ground of the termination of a joint venture contract is change of circumstances. In addition to the general provision on the change of circumstances in the general part of the contract law (Art.450, para.2), there is a special provision in the Chapter on Joint Venture Contracts to this effect. Thus, in a contract of joint venture with a fixed period, or a fixed purpose as a condition pending, participants are entitled to rescind the contract between themselves or with the remaining participants with a justifiable ground and on the condition that the real damage caused to the remaining participants is compensated (Art.1052). No definition of the 'justifiable ground' is given. According to a commentary, 'the effect of the contract can be preserved by the agreement of the remaining parties', as is the case with the provision on the termination of the contract.[18]

---

18   Sadikov ed., *supra*, p.645.

10

LAW ON PROPERTY AND LAND

1   Ownership Right and other Real Rights

The concept of real rights (*veshchnoe pravo*) was known in Tsarist Russia. The draft Civil Code of the Tsarist period had Book Two devoted to real rights. However, in the socialist period, this concept totally disappeared, since the scope of property to which individuals were entitled to claim came to be severely restricted. Particularly noteworthy was the fact that land and other 'means of production' ceased to be private property and were subject to administrative law, and not civil law. Therefore, the civil law concept of real rights had little use. It was revived only by the 1990 Law on Ownership and the Fundamental Principles of Civil Legislation of the USSR.

Part one, Book Two of the Civil Code is entitled 'Ownership Rights and other Real Rights'. It comprises 8 chapters, but Chapter 17 which covered the rights over land did not come into effect at the same time as the rest of the Code. This Chapter was to take effect only when the new Land Code was adopted and came into effect. It finally took effect when the long-awaited Land Code was adopted and came into effect in November 2001.

Real rights, in contrast to rights *in personam*, are absolute rights, i.e. they can be set up against an unlimited scope of people, while rights *in personam* can be claimed only *vis à vis* the opposite party. Thus, a real right maintains effect even with the transfer of the title of the property. For example, even if the title to a piece of land shifts from the state to the municipality, the right of permanent (indefinite) use of land remains intact, since it is a real right (Art.216, para.3). In contrast, traditionally, it was understood that a right *in personam* e.g. a lease, could not be set up against the change of ownership over the leased property; the lease lost effect through the sale of property by the lessor. However, this distinction has become blurred; the lease of immovables has come to be protected in a way similar to real rights.[1]

A real right being an absolute right, the holder of the right retains the right even when he looses loses the possession of the property. The owner of a property has the right to require the return of the property from the unlawful possessor of the property (Art.301). This action of *vindikatsiia* (lat. *vindicare*) is commonly utilised:

> On the basis of a capital construction contract, a joint stock company sent a crane and five bulldozers to a *kombinat*. After the completion of the construction work, the company could not retrieve the machinery since the *kombinat* retained it. In fact, the crane was there, but the bulldozers had disappeared. The company sued the *kombinat* and demanded the return of the machinery on the basis of Article 301. The Supreme Commercial Court ruled that the object of this action could only be the property in the possession of the defendant. The *kombinat* was ordered to return the crane, but since the bulldozers were no longer in its possession, the claim was dismissed on this part. It was suggested that the plaintiff sue for compensation.[2]

An owner is entitled to claim for the elimination of an infringement upon his right to ownership. He may require the removal of any kind of infringement on the possession, use and disposal of the property, even if the infringement does not involve deprivation of possession (Art.304):[3]

> In a dispute concerning an office building, the plaintiff, a company with limited liability which owned the building, brought an action against a joint stock company which leased an adjacent building. This company closed the only access to the premise of the plaintiff. Based on Article 304, the commercial court ordered the defendant to cease the obstruction of the use of the office premises by the plaintiff.[4]

This right is also extended to possessors of properties who are not owners, e.g. state and municipal unitary enterprises which have the right to economic management or operational administration (Art. 305).

Real rights are created by law only; a new type of right cannot be created by individuals by e.g. contracts.

---

1   See BGB Art.571.
2   'Obzor praktiki razresheniia sporov, sviazannykh s zashchitoi prav sovstvennosti i drugikh veshch-nykh prav', *VAS RF* in D.V.Murzin eds., *Grazhdanskii kodeks RF s postateinymi materialami iz praktiki VAS RF*, Moscow 1999, p.295.
3   A.N.Guev eds., *Postateinyi kommentarii k chasti pervoi grazhdanskogo kodeksa Rossiskoi Federatsii*, second edition, Moscow 1999, p.375.
4   Murzin eds., *supra*, p.300.

2   THE RIGHT OF OWNERSHIP

1)   The Content of the Right of Ownership

The right to ownership is the most fundamental real right. In relation to other real rights, the right to ownership is the basic right, while other real rights are 'restrictive rights' on ownership.[5] Ownership has been defined in Russia during the Tsarist period as the right to possess, use and dispose of an object. The same applied in the socialist period, the only difference being that these rights were limited in one way or another.

Under socialism, there were various restrictions on property rights (e.g. there was a limit to the number and size of the accommodation one could own). There was in fact no concept of 'private ownership', but only 'individual ownership'. In contrast, the present Constitution declares that the right of private ownership is protected by law (Art.35, para.1). Every person is entitled to have property under his ownership, and possess, use, and dispose of it by himself or jointly with others (*ibid.*, para.2). This is understood to include foreign nationals. Furthermore, individuals and their associations may also privately own land (Art.36, para.1). However, this part does not extend to foreign nationals.

The present Civil Code provides that owners of property are attributed the right of possession, use, and disposal of that property (Art.209, para.1). Disposal in this context means to decide the legal fate of the property and includes sale, gift, lease, and pledge.[6] The Civil Code declares that the owner may, at his discretion, transfer the title of his property to another person, transfer the right to possess, use and dispose of the property while remaining an owner, pledge or encumber it, or dispose of it in other ways, insofar as it is not against the law or legal acts, and does not infringe rights and the lawfully protected interests of others (*ibid.*, para.2).

On the other hand, the owner bears the risk of the loss and destruction of the property (Art.211). The owner's property may be taken to satisfy his obligation (Art.24).

The right of ownership can be limited by law, but as is the case with civil law rights in general, it can be limited by federal law only, and to the extent necessary for the defence of the constitutional system, moral, health, rights and the legally protected interests of other persons as well as for the defence and national security of the state (Art.1, para.2).

---

5   O.N.Sadikov ed., *Kommentarii k grazhdanskomu kodeksu Rossiiskoi Federatsii, chasti pervoi,* enlarged edition, Moscow 1999, p.416.

6   *Ibid.*

2)   Owners

The Constitution acknowledges private, state, municipal and other forms of ownership and provides that they are protected in an equal manner (Art.8). This provision is reproduced in the Civil Code (Art.212, para.1). This is in contrast with the socialist period, when the 'primacy of state ownership' was the rule and the state monopolised the ownership of 'means of production', including land and other natural resources and state enterprises.

Property may be owned by individuals and juridical persons as well as the Russian Federation, constituent entities of the Russian Federation, and municipalities (*Ibid.*, para.2).

(1)   Ownership by Individuals and Juridical Persons

Property which belongs to individuals or any juridical person, except for unitary enterprises, state and municipal institutions (*uchrezhdenie*), is private property. Individuals and juridical persons may own any property except for those properties which, by law, they are not allowed to own. Thus, they can own various immovable properties including enterprises as proprietary complexes, flats and houses (Art.213, para.1). The Constitution also guarantees private ownership of land and natural resources (Art.9, para.2, Art.36, para.1). However, despite the constitutional guarantee, private ownership over land has not fully developed. Private ownership of other natural resources is significantly restricted by various laws such as the Forestry Code and the Sub-soil Law.

The quantity and the value of the property which is owned by physical persons or juridical persons are not restricted except for restrictions established by law for the purpose of protecting the constitutional system, moral, health, rights and the legally protected interests of others, the defence of the state and national security (Art.213, para. 2). A commentary suggests that there can be restrictions on the size of a piece of land which individuals and juridical persons may own.[7]

(2)   State and Municipal Ownership

The Civil Code provides for state and municipal ownership as separate types of ownership. Some lawyers use the concept of public ownership to cover both state

---

7   *Ibid.*, p.422.

and municipal ownership; the common denominator is the public-law characteristics of the state and the municipality.[8]

Under socialism, the state monopolised the ownership of means of production. All land, natural resources, and state enterprises were owned by a single entity, the Soviet State. The current system is different in that i) state ownership not only means ownership by the federal state, but also by constituent entities of the Russian Federation (state ownership), ii) municipalities (local self-governments) have also come to own properties (municipal ownership), and iii) privatisation of the property owned by the state has taken place. It should be noted that while the Constitution uses the term 'local self-government'(e.g.Art.131), the Civil Code uses the term 'municipalities (*munitsipal'noe obrazovanie*)' (e.g. Art.215).

Objects of state ownership are those properties owned by the Russian Federation (federal property) and constituent entities of the Russian Federation (property of constituent subjects) (Art.214, para.1). Thus, 'state' in this context includes both the Federation and the constituent entities. Unitary enterprises (state or municipal enterprises) do not own the properties, e.g. land or factories, buildings etc. which are entrusted to them, but merely have a right of economic management or operational administration; their assets are owned by the state or municipality. The same applies to institutions (*uchrezhdenie*) (Art.214, para.4). Assets of the state which are not entrusted to unitary enterprises and establishments comprise the state treasury (*kazna*) and the treasury of the constituent entities of the Russian Federation (*ibid.*, para.4).

One of the problems with state ownership is the demarcation of ownership over assets between the Russian Federation and constituent entities. The issue emerged immediately after the collapse of the USSR, but so far, has not been solved.[9] The procedure for the allocation of assets between the Russian Federation and constituent entities was supposed to be regulated by law, but no such law existed, and therefore, the 1991 decision of the RSFSR Supreme Soviet, which transferred a significant part of the state property including state enterprises to constituent entities and municipalities, was in force until 2001.[10] The federal legislature finally managed in 1999 to enact a law which sets out the basic principles of demarcating ownership, and in 2001, the Law on Demarcation of State Ownership on Land was enacted.[11]

---

8   Braginskii ed., *Nauchno-prakticheskii komenntarii k chasti pervoi Grazhdanskogo kodeksa Rossiiskoi Federatsi*, second edition, Moscow 1999, p.338.
9   G.E.Bystrov, 'Zemel'naia reforma v Rossii: pravovaia teoriia i praktika', *GiP*, 2000 No.4, pp.52-53.
10 *VSND RF i VS RF,* 1992 No.3, item 89.
11 *SZ RF,* 2001, No.30.

Properties which are under the right of ownership of the city, village settlement, and other municipalities are municipal property. Agencies of municipalities exercise the ownership rights (Civil Code Art.215). As is the case with state property, assets of municipalities comprise assets consolidated with municipal enterprises and institutions, as well as assets which directly belong to the treasury.

This concept of municipal ownership did not exist under socialism; local entities did not have their own title over any assets. The process of devolution which started after the collapse of the USSR found its reflection in the management of property. By virtue of the above-mentioned decision of the RSFSR Supreme Soviet of 1991, a large part of state assets including land, enterprises, accommodations, office buildings and other buildings were transferred to the municipality.

In theory, those properties which are under state or municipal ownership are to be registered as such in the Register. However, until such a register is completed, the document which certifies the ownership is the list of public properties prepared in accordance with a statute adopted in 1992 upon a presidential order.[12]

Attachment of the land and other natural resources under state or municipal ownership is allowed only when provided by law (Art.126, para.1).

State and municipal property can be transferred by its owner to the ownership of physical or juridical persons by way of privatisation (Art.217). Privatisation is not limited to state enterprises, but to other kinds of assets such as land, accommodations, buildings, and other properties. There is a separate Law on Privatisation.[13] Provisions of the Civil Code on the manner of acquisition and termination of ownership are applied only insofar as the Law on Privatisation does not provide otherwise (Art.217).

3)   Acquisition and Termination of the Right of Ownership

The right of ownership over things (property) can be acquired on various grounds. The rules are as follows (Art.218):

i)   the right of ownership over a thing newly created by a person belongs to this person;

ii)   the right of ownership over fruits, products, and income received as a result of the use of property is acquired in accordance with the rules set out in the General Part of the Civil Code;

---

12   *Ibid.*, p.339.
13   *SZ RF*, 1997 No.30, item 3595.

iii)   the right of ownership over a property which already has an owner may be
       acquired by another person on the basis of a contract of sale, exchange, gift and
       other juristic acts for assigning it;

iv)   in the case of the death of a physical person who is the owner of a property, the
       property is transferred to another person by inheritance, by statute, or will;

v)   in the case of the reorganisation of a juridical person which is an owner of a
       property, the property is transferred to the ownership of the juridical person which
       is a successor to the reorganised juridical person;

vi)   a person may acquire the right of ownership over a property which has no owner,
       a property whose owner is not known, or a property whose owner waived the
       right to ownership or lost the right of ownership on grounds provided by law
       (arts.225-228);

vii)   the right of ownership can be acquired by acquisitive prescription.

In acquisitive prescription, a person (physical or juridical) acquires ownership
of an immovable property if this person, in good faith, openly and without interruption possessed the property in question as his own property for 15 years. For
properties other than immovables, this period is 5 years (Art.234, para.1).

A person who acquired for value a property from a person who does not have
the right to assign it may nevertheless acquire the right of ownership if he acted
in good faith, i.e. the purchaser was not aware and could not have known that
this person had no right to assign it (a purchaser in good faith). This applies to
cash and securities as well. Exceptions are where the owner had lost the property,
the property had been stolen or otherwise alienated against the will of the owner
from the owner himself or from the person to whom the owner had given possession of the property (Art.302, para.1):

The State Property Fund brought an action *vis à vis* a joint stock company and a limited
liability company, asking the court to declare void the contract of sale of 1,500 shares
by the limited liability company to the joint stock company and apply the consequences
of void transactions. The State Property Fund had sold shares of a company created
on the basis of a privatised state enterprise to the limited liability company, but later,
this transaction was recognised by court as void, since the shares should have been
distributed through a closed offer. The limited liability company was ordered by the
court to return the shares to the Fund, but by the time the judgment was rendered, the
company had sold part of the shares to the joint stock company.

The Fund argued that the sales contract between the companies was void, since
the seller – the limited liability company – did not have the title to these shares and
could not have effectively sold the shares. The lower court rejected this argument, and
the Supreme Commercial Court upheld this on the ground that a claim of the owner
(or an agency entrusted by the owner) to retrieve property in possession of a person

who acquired it by contract as a third party should be examined under Article 302. This provision is applicable to securities, including shares.[14]

Normally, in other jurisdictions, this action is available only for movables, and is not applicable to immovables which can be registered. However, in Russia, there is no statutory restriction to this effect:

> An individual entrepreneurial entity brought an action against a company with limited liability for the return of the building of a shop. The plaintiff argued that the disputed property had been sold by the plaintiff to a joint stock company (the buyer) under duress. The defendant company which purchased the property from the buyer (the third party) claimed protection under Article 302. The contract of sale between the plaintiff and the buyer had been found null and void by the commercial court on the ground that there had been a threat of force on the plaintiff by the buyer. However, during the period of the possession of the building, the buyer pledged the building for various loan agreements with the bank. Since the buyer defaulted, the building was sold at an auction organised by the district court and the defendant in this case successfully bid for the building. The Supreme Commercial Court dismissed the claim on the ground that the defendant had purchased the property through an auction legitimately organised by a court bailiff and that the owner had no right under Article 302.[15]

On the other hand, the fact that the property was registered would probably lead to the conclusion that the person who obtained the property should have been aware that the seller was not the legitimate owner.

The right of ownership can be terminated on the following grounds (Art.235, para.2):

i)   assignment of the property to another person;
ii)   waiver of the right of ownership by the owner;
iii) the loss or destruction of the property;
iv)   other instances provided by law.

Compulsory acquisition of property is allowed in cases of seizure based upon obligations (Art.237), requisition (Art.242), and confiscation (Art.243). The Code explicitly provides that nationalisation may be effected on the basis of law with compensation for the value of the property and any other damage caused (Art,235,

---

14 'Obzor praktiki razresheniia sporov po sdelkam, sviazannym s razmeshcheniem i obrashcheniem aktsii', informatsionnoe pis'mo VAS RF, April 21,998, *VVAS RF* 1998 No.6, item.7, in Zhurakovskii and Kalinin, *Kommentarii i primenenie zakonodatel'stva arbitrazhnymi sudami Rossiiskoi Federatsii*, Moscow 2000, p.235.
15 Murzin eds., *supra*, p.298-299.

para.2). Nationalisation means transfer of the property to the Russian Federation or its constituent entities; transfer to municipal ownership is not allowed.[16] It should be added that the Foreign Investment Law of 1999 guarantees that nationalisation or requisition of the assets of foreign investors will not be effected unless based upon a federal law or an international treaty (Art.8, para.1). At the moment, there is no law which enables nationalisation.

4)   Co-ownership

Property which is owned by two or more persons is under co-ownership (*obshchaia sobstvennost'*). Co-ownership is divided into two categories: share ownership – a form of common ownership with the share of each co-owner determined (*dolebaia sobstvennost'*) and joint ownership – without such shares (*sovmestnaia cosbtvennost'*) (Art.244, paras. 1 and 2). Co-ownership is presumed to be share ownership unless the law provides that the property in question be under joint ownership (*ibid.*, para.3). Examples of joint ownership include matrimonial property and the property of a farming household (*fermer'skoe khoziaistvo*).[17]

The property under share ownership is disposed of by the unanimous consent of co-owners. Co-owners are entitled to sell, give away as a gift or by will, pledge or otherwise dispose of the share. If the share is to be sold to a person other than a co-owner, other co-owners have a right of pre-emption to purchase the share at the price and other conditions at which it has been offered to the other. For this purpose, the co-owner who intends to sell the share to an outsider is under an obligation to inform the co-owners of the intention to sell and the price and other conditions of sale (arts.246 and 250).

In share ownership, the property can be divided by the agreement of the co-owners. A co-owner may demand the split of his share from the common ownership. If no agreement is reached among the co-owners on the manners and terms of the division, the co-owner who demanded the division of his share may apply to court for the withdrawal of his share in kind. If this is not possible without unreasonable damage to the property, the co-owner who intends to withdraw is entitled to reimbursement in cash (Art.252, paras. 1-3).

In joint ownership, the co-owners jointly possess and use the property. For the disposal of the property, unanimous consent is needed (Art.253, paras.1 and 2). Division of the property or the withdrawal of a co-owner is possible. In such cases, the share of each co-owner has to be determined; the shares are to be equal,

---

16   Guev eds., *supra*, pp.404-405.
17   Sadikov ed., *supra*, p.475.

unless otherwise provided by law or agreed by the co-owners (Art.254, paras.1 and 2).

It should be noted that creditors of the co-owner in both share ownership or joint ownership may request the division of the shares in cases where other assets of the co-owner is insufficient to cover the debt. If, in such cases, division of the property is impossible without damaging it, the creditor may require the debtor to sell the share to the remaining co-owners (Art.255).

3   The Right of Economic Management and Operational Administration

The right of economic management (*pravo khoziaistvennogo vedeniia*) is a right of unitary enterprises to possess, use, and dispose of the assets and properties in accordance with the terms and purposes set by the owner. The owner is either the state (the Russian Federation and its constituent entities) or municipalities. The entity is not entitled to dispose of immovables entrusted to it by sale, placement as a security, or contribution to the capital of a commercial company without the consent of the owner (Art. 295, para.2).

The right of operational administration (*pravo operativnogo upravleniia*) is exercised by some unitary enterprises and institutions, including government agencies. It is stricter than the right of economic management in that not only immovables, but properties in general cannot be disposed of without the consent of the owner. The state, on the other hand, is entitled to take away 'excessive' properties, or properties which are not used in accordance with the purpose of the enterprise or institution (Art.296). Unitary enterprises which are based on this right over the assets are called treasury enterprises (*kazennye predpriiatiia*).

In fact, the concept of the right of operational management was conceived in the 1940s by A.V.Benediktov for explaining the rights of state enterprises under the system of state monopoly over means of production. After the collapse of socialism, the state has been distancing itself from being directly involved in production and commercial activities. The right of economic administration was introduced later as a 'transitional form from state monopoly to private entrepreneurship.[18] The number of enterprises with the right of operational management is in decrease.

---

18   V.P.Pavlov, 'Pravo khoziaistvennogo vedeniia', in A.Ia. Sukharev ed., *Rossiiskaia iuridicheskaia entsiklopediia*, Moscow 1999, pp.2251-2252.

4   REGISTRATION OF THE RIGHT OF OWNERSHIP AND OTHER REAL RIGHTS

The right of ownership and other real rights on immovables, encumbrance on these rights, as well as the creation, transfer, and termination of these rights are all subject to state registration (Art.131,para.1). Although they are not real rights, leases and trustee rights of management by entrustment are also subject to registration. Registration is not merely for authentication of these rights; it is a prerequisite of those rights having effect. The registration of transactions involving immovables is different; these transactions take effect on the conclusion of a contract, not on registration.

There was no unified system of land registration under socialism. Since land and other immovables were not in circulation, there was no real need for registration. There was a system of land survey and accounting (*uchet*), but this was merely a record keeping system for the state. The means and the agency of recording differed, depending on the type of land and the region.

The move for land registration began in 1993 with a presidential decree. Registration was to be handled by the land commission and its local entities – local committees on land resources and redistribution. Since 1994, in some regions, land registration was introduced, but it was only in 1997, when the new Law on the Registration of Immovables and related Transactions was enacted, that a uniform system of registration was introduced throughout the country.[19] According to this Law, the Ministry of Justice is to administer the Unified State Register on these rights. It should be added that some kinds of immovable property are subject to another form of registration by other agencies. As late as 2001, the Ministry of Justice reported that the development of local registries has been completed; there are 1,400 local registries and their outlets with 2,000 registry officials.[20]

The register is not always accurate:

The administration of a district issued a certificate of consolidation of land of 6.12 hectares for an indefinite term of use to a joint-stock company, instead of the original certificate for 5 hectares. As a result, 1.12 hectare of land was taken away from the user of the adjacent land. No measures of acquisition or redistribution as provided in the 1990 Land Code were taken. In fact, there had been a dispute on this 1.12 hectare. The commercial court found the decision of the district administration to be null and void.[21]

---

19   *SZ RF*, 1997 No.30, item 3594.
20   'Novost' Ministerstva Iustitsii RF', www.scli.ru/news
21   V.Kostiuk, 'Pravovye problemy regulirovaniia zemel'nykh otnoshenii i sudebnaia praktika v usloviiakh formirovaniia zemel'nogo zakonodatel'stva' *KhiP*, 2000, No.3, p.31.

In cases where the entry in the register and the factual state of affairs conflict, in some jurisdictions, the entry in the register prevails. However, this is not the case in Russia. This is understandable in a country where the register has just begun to develop. On the other hand, the registry is responsible for the accuracy and authenticity of the information contained in the register and is liable to errors by fault.

The objects of registration are 'immovables and relevant transactions'. Thus, the Law distinguishes between the immovables and the transactions involving immovables. Rights on immovables which are subject to registration are:

i)   right of ownership;
ii)   right of economic management;
iii)   right of operational administration;
iv)   life-long, inheritable right of possession;
v)   indefinite right of use;
vi)   hypothec;
vii)   servitude.

The following transactions involving immovables are subject to registration:

i)   contracts of sale of residences and flats;
ii)   contracts of gift involving immovables;
iii)   lease contracts of immovables exceeding one year (if the party is a juridical person, regardless of the length, it must be registered);
iv)   contracts of management of immovables by entrustment.

According to a commentary, these two kinds of registration do not overlap.[22] For example, a contract of sale of a piece of land does not require registration, but the transfer of the title as a result of the contract requires registration. The intention of the legislature may have been to enable the lease of immovables (not a real right) to be able to be registered. However, it is not clear why registration of the contract and the resulting title both have to be registered in transactions involving residences and flats, while only the registration of the title is sufficient in land transactions. The commentary explains that when the situation is complex and state supervision is needed not only for the transfer of rights, but also for the juristic acts themselves, registration is needed for both.[23]

---

22 P.V.Krashninnikova ed., *Postateinyi kommentarii k federal'nomu zakonu o gosudarstvennoi registratsii prav na nedvizhennoe imushchestvo i sdelok s nim*, Moscow 2000, pp.42-43.
23 *Ibid.*

As a general rule, the acquisition of the right of ownership by means of contract takes effect, by transfer of the object, unless otherwise provided by law or contract. However, if state registration is required for the transaction, the right to ownership is acquired only by registration, unless the law provides otherwise (Art.223, para.2). Another provision in the contract law part provides that the performance (*ispolnenie*) of a contract of sale of immovables by the parties before the state registration of the transfer of title does not serve as a basis for changes in relation to a third party (Art.551, para.2). Thus, the buyer of an immovable has no power to act as the owner of this property before registration. A contract transferring the property to another person by the buyer before registration of his title is considered to be void:

> A joint stock company sold a building to an individual entrepreneur. The buyer did not pay the price to the seller nor register the building in his name. Then, this entrepreneur sold the building to a third party, and disappeared with the money which he received from the third party. The joint stock company brought an action asking for the contract between the individual entrepreneur and the third party to be declared void. The court found that since the individual private company did not acquire the ownership right due to the failure to register (Art.223, para.2), he had no power to dispose of the property, and therefore, the sale between the individual entrepreneur and the third party was void. The court also took into account that the third party had failed to check the title of the entrepreneur to the building, particularly in the Register, and therefore, acted 'on his pain and risk'.[24]

Thus, when purchasing immovables, the buyer is expected to check the register and ensure that the seller really has got the title.[25]

On the other hand, it is not clear from the Civil Code what would happen if the seller sold the immovable after the sale to the buyer, but before registration, to a third party. In such cases, the second buyer had relied on the register which showed that the seller was still the title holder. A commentary suggests that the seller loses the right to dispose of the property once the contract has been performed.[26] The position of the seller is often justified by the above-mentioned Article 551, para.2 of the Code which can be interpreted as stating that the seller retains the title until registration and is entitled to dispose of the property. However, this interpretation is criticised as allowing abuse of rights by one of the

24 'Obzor praktiki razresheniia sporov, boznikaiiushchikh po dogovoram kupli-prodazhi nedvizhnosti', informatsionnoe pis'mo VAS RF, November 13, 1997, *VVAS RF*, 1998 No.1, p.82.

25 S.F.Savkin, 'Sudebno-arbitrazhnaia praktika po sporom, sviazannym s zashchitoi prava sobstvennosti i drugikh beshchnykh prav', *VVAS RF*, 1998 No.10, pp.67-68.

26 Sadikov ed., *supra*, p.139.

parties to the transaction.[27] The Supreme Court ruled in a similar situation as follows:

> Golovenko brought an action against the company 'Russkaia Nedvizhimost' and Fomen-ko, asking the court to recognise his ownership of a flat, registration of the contract of sale of this flat, and also to recognise the auction in which the flat had been sold to Fomenko as void. Golovenko and the company concluded a contract of sale of the flat in April 1995 and the price was duly paid by the buyer – Golovenko. According to the contract, a written contract was to be handed to Golovenko, but the company failed to do so, and therefore, Golovenko was unable to register the transaction. In July 1995, the flat was seized and sold at a public auction in which Fomenko was the successful bidder. Fomenko brought an action against Golovenko and claimed that the original sales contract between the company and Golovenko was void and that Golovenko should be evicted, because the contract had never been registered. The Supreme Court dismissed the claim of Fomenko and ruled that Golovenko failed to register the contract and the title against his will, and therefore, Golovenko's claim should be satisfied.[28]

After the performance of the contract, if a party fails to cooperate in the registration, the other party may initiate an action against this party. The court, in such cases, examines the existence of a valid contract between the parties and the fact of the transfer of the property, and may render a judgment on state registration of the property. The party which failed, without justifiable reason, to cooperate may be obliged to pay damages for the delay in registration (Art.165, para.3).

It is not clear how the court is to effect registration. The 'information letter' of the Supreme Commercial Court suggests that the judgment of the court serves as the basis for the obligation of the registering agency to register the transaction.[29] In a case where a bank brought an action against a company for its failure to register the contract of pledge (pledge of a complex of movable and immovables) the lower court did not involve the registration chamber as a party, but merely invited it as a third party joining in the side of the defendant. This was found to be wrong by the Supreme Commercial Court, which suggests that in such cases, the agency of registration should be brought in as a defendant as well.[30]

The Register of Immovables is open to the public. The agency which administers the register is under an obligation to provide any person with information

---

27   Savkin, *supra*, pp.67-68.
28   G.Mishchenko, 'Federal'nyi zakon "o gosudarstvennoi registratsii prav na nedvizhimoe imushchestvo i sdelok s nim" i grazhdansko zakonodatel'stvo', *KhiP* 1999 No.10, pp.39-40.
29   'Obzor praktika rasreshenii sporov, vosnikaiushikh po dogovoram kupli-prodazhi nedvizhnosti', informatsionnoe pis'mo, *VVAS RF*, 1998 No.1, p.81.
30   Decision of the Presidium of the VAS, May 30, 2000, *VVAS RF*, 2000 No.8, pp.29-30.

on the fact of registration and the rights which have been registered (Art.131, para.4).

5   LAND LAW

1)   The Abolition of the State Ownership of Land

The modern history of land ownership in Russia goes back to the mid-19th century. By the Emancipation in 1861, peasants were allocated agricultural land in return for the payment of redemption. The title to the land was given not to individual peasants, but to village communes. It was only after 1906 that through a reform initiated by P.A.Stolypin, the prime minister, individual ownership of land by peasants emerged. However, the reform failed in 1914, and the village communes remained the predominant owners of land until the October Revolution.

     One of the first decrees which the Bolshevik government issued after the October Revolution was the renowned Decree on Land. Private ownership of land was abolished altogether without any compensation; land was placed under the control of the local land committees together with the buildings, implements, livestock and everything pertaining thereto. It was prohibited to sell, buy, pledge, or otherwise dispose of land. The right to use land was acknowledged to all citizens, but the use of paid labour was not allowed.[31] This was confirmed by another decree of February 1918. While these decrees were primarily aimed at rural land, yet another decree issued on August 1918 totally abolished the private ownership of land by individuals as well as enterprises in the urban area.[32] In fact, the peasants interpreted these decrees as authorising the seizure and redistribution of large estates. The bulk of the agricultural land in European Russia was actually taken over by the peasants and used in a traditional manner. An observer pointed out that the Bolsheviks did not achieve socialisation, but instead, individualisation of land.[33]

     In the 1922 Civil Code, rights over land were excluded, and instead, came to be regulated by the Land Code, which was part of administrative law.[34] The Land Code, which was enacted in the same year, was rather different from the decrees which had been issued after the October Revolution. Although it repeated the phrases of the preceding decrees on the abolition of private ownership of land,

---

31   *SU RSFSR* 1917 No.10, item 150.
32   *SU RSFSR* 1918 No.62, item 674.
33   V.Gsovski, *Soviet Civil Law*, vol.1, Ann Arbor 1948, pp.693-694.
34   *SU RSFSR* 1922 No.68, item 901.

subsoil, water and forests and replacement by state ownership, the village commune and the individual household were entitled to select any type of land tenure, including individual enclosure similar to that introduced by the Stolypin reform. Individual peasants and their communes were granted the right of 'immediate toil tenure of land without time limit'.[35] It is no wonder that the Land Code was dubbed the *Magna Carta* of landowners. It was inevitable that the Land Code went into oblivion in the late 1920s when these individual peasants were labelled *kulaks* ('rich' peasants) and 'liquidated as a class'. Land, together with all sorts of natural resources, came to be solely owned by the state.

After the collapse of socialism, this system radically changed. A substantial part of the land has been 'de-étatised' since then. The process started primarily with agricultural land. Already towards the end of socialism, in February 1990, members of collective and state farms were given the right to the land which belonged to those farms, if they desired to set up a farmer's business by the Fundamental Principles of Land Legislation.[36] Such a transfer of land to private ownership was effected in a gratuitous manner. The RSFSR Law on Land Reform of December 1990, declared that land and other natural resources were the 'property of the people' and that the state monopoly of land was to be abolished. Various forms of ownership over land, including private ownership, were acknowledged. In the process of reform, land was to be distributed to individuals enterprises, institutions, associations and companies. Regarding distribution to individuals, land was to be transferred to their ownership for individual gardening as well as farming and other agriculture related purposes. No payment was required for the land up to a certain limit. On the other hand, unlike in the Central and Eastern European countries, land was not to be returned to those who were the owners before the Revolution.[37] This was followed by a similar provision in the Land Code of 1991. In 1992, the scope of private ownership was extended in that the subject of ownership came to include all juridical persons, and the available land extended to non-agricultural land.

Since the early 1990s, collective and state farms were reorganised into agricultural enterprises based upon private ownership, and private farmer's households were created. There are currently around 270,200 farmer's households to which 6.2% of agricultural land belongs. 63% of agricultural land is under the co-ownership (share and joint ownership) of members of the agricultural commercial organisations.[38] 108 million hectares of agricultural land was eventually trans-

---

35   Gsovski, *supra*, pp.698-703.
36   I.A.Ikonitskaia, *Zemel'noe pravo Rossiiskoi Federatsii*, Moscow 1999, pp.21-26.
37   *VVS RSFSR* 1990 No.26, item 327.
38   Bystrov, *supra*, p.47.

ferred to farmers and 12 million rural inhabitants became landowners and were issued a 'certificate of the right of ownership'.[39]

In the urban areas, the 1991 Land Code provided that urban land would be made available for individual ownership for a limited range of purposes such as gardening. The 1998 edict of the government decreed that land is either sold or leased in the urban area by the state or municipal government by auction in which 'any person may take part'.[40] However, in reality, the lease is still the predominant form of releasing land from state ownership. There is strong scepticism towards the fully-fledged private ownership of land. A commentator stated as follows:

> Rules of city and town planning are mandatory for companies, state agencies as well as individuals. Local administrative agencies are empowered to give instructions to the subjects of rights over the land in order to ensure the compatibility of economical development and the optimal use of the natural environment. However, if private ownership of land is to be introduced, it would be difficult for administrative agencies to interfere with the use of land, even when it is necessary. In the urban area, there is a necessity for limiting private ownership of land and making the lease the basic form of land use.[41]

In reality, in major cities such as Moscow, following the above idea, the lease is the basic form of land use.

On the other hand, the circulation of land is severely limited. The amendment to the 1978 Constitution in 1991, while acknowledging private ownership of land, introduced a 10 year moratorium on the sale of land. This moratorium was gradually lifted, first in relation to subsidiary farming plots and *dacha* businesses, gardening, and individual housing construction. A presidential decree of 1993 allowed individuals and juridical persons who are owners of land to transfer land by inheritance, gift, lease, exchange, and investment in companies, including those with foreign investment. The 1993 Constitution granted the owners the right to freely possess, use, and dispose of land insofar as they do not cause any damage to the environment or infringe the rights and interests of other persons (Art.36). The Civil Code repeats this and allows circulation within the limit established by law, but is vague on the actual scope of permissible circulation (Art.209, para.3).

---

39 Ikonitskaia, *supra*, p.67.
40 *VVAS RF*, 1998 No.3, pp.15-21.
41 S.A.Bogoliubov, *Zemliia i pravo*, Moscow 1998, pp.100-101.

Land for subsidiary farming, *dachas,* and possibly housing in the rural areas can be sold. There is also 'no restriction on the sale of agricultural land'. The new Land Code of 2001 does not seem to set excessive restrictions on the circulation of land either. But in reality, as far as agricultural land and land for housing as well as land for entrepreneurial use are concerned, circulation of land is very much limited.

2)   Legal Framework of the Land Law

Despite the above developments towards de-étatisation of land, a systematic legal basis for these developments had been absent until 2001, when the new Land Code was finally adopted and took effect. The 1991 Land Code was amended in 1993 after the adoption of the Constitution and a majority of the provisions were deleted. Since then, several drafts of the Land Code had been submitted to the Duma, but failed to become law. The primary points of disagreement were reported to be the permissible scope of private ownership and of the circulation of land. There was more or less a common understanding that the re-emergence of large scale land ownership should be prevented. Some people were apprehensive of the possible growth of speculative transactions which may lead to an accumulation of land in the hands of a small number of people, once free circulation of land is allowed. On the other hand, there was a view that unless free circulation of land is allowed, private ownership is incomplete.

While the new Land Code was not in place, primary sources of regulations concerning land were presidential decrees, edicts of the government, orders and instructions of the State Committee for the Management of State Property as well as the laws of the constituent entities of the Russian Federation. The Constitution provides that the conditions and procedure of the use of land are determined on the basis of federal law (Art.36, para.3). However, various constituent entities of the Russian Federation have adopted laws which seemingly contradict the provision of the Federal Constitution. For example, the constitution and Land Law of Dagestan deny private ownership of land. The Constitution of the Sakha Republic does not recognise private ownership of agricultural land.[42] There is no clear demarcation between the land which belongs to the Russian Federation, constituent entities, and municipalities. Some entities have enacted their own constitution and laws and claim ownership over land and natural resources in the Republic. For

---

42   Kostiuk, *supra,* p.30.

example, the Land Code of Kareliia does not recognise federal ownership over land.

There were confusions everywhere. The number of disputes involving land has been increasing; in 1999, the commercial court handled 2,507 cases of disputes involving the use of land; the number has more than doubled since 1996.[43] A Russian specialist characterises the state of land law by its 'insufficiency, lack of system, contradiction, ambiguity, and instability'.[44] In the absence of comprehensive and clear legislation, the market for land has reportedly become subject to corrupt and ambiguous deals.[45] There was even a view that the new Land Code was delayed by some people who do not want it, since with the absence of the Code they can operate without being penalised.[46] According to another Russian specialist, the present system of disposal, possession and use of land in fact restricts access to land resources, does not allow redistribution of land and transfer of land to entities who can effectively manage it. The system of guaranteeing the right to land is lacking.[47] The absence of the market made secured financing by land impossible.

The new Land Code was adopted in October 2001 and took effect on the day of its publication. Accordingly, Chapter 17 of the Civil Code also took effect. The taking of effect of the new Land Code and Chapter 17 certainly is certainly a major step forward, but there remains an enormous task of aligning existing legislation, namely the laws of the constituent entities, with them.

3)   The New Land Code

The new Land Code of 2001 provides that proprietary relationship concerning the possession, use, and disposal of land as well as transactions with land is to be regulated by civil legislation, unless otherwise provided by the land, forestry, water, subsoil legislation, environmental, and other special federal laws (Art.3). This is a reconfirmation of the fact that land relations are basically civil law relationships, not administrative law relationships.

The Code recognises state and municipal ownership of land as well as ownership of land by individuals and juridical persons. Individuals and juridical persons enjoy 'equal access' to the acquisition of land. In principle, land under state and

---

43   'Sudebno-arbitrazhnaia statistika', *VVAS RF* 2000, No.3, p.8.
44   Bystrov, *supra,* p.49.
45   *Ibid.*, p.51.
46   *Ibid.*
47   Kostiuk, *supra*, p.29.

municipal ownership can be offered to individuals and juridical persons for their ownership (Art.15, para.2).

Whether foreign nationals can own land was hitherto not clear. In 1992, as part of the privatisation of state and municipal enterprises, those who became owners of a privatised enterprise including foreign nationals and juridical persons were allowed to acquire the land of these enterprises as well.[48] However, this part of the decree concerning the right of foreign nationals was deleted in 1997. The 1993 Constitution does not specifically refer to the right of foreign nationals to own land. The Foreign Investment Law of 1999 merely provides that acquisition of land, natural resources, buildings, installations and other immovables is to be effected in accordance with the law of the Russian Federation and constituent entities (Art.15).

The draft Land Code did not give foreign individuals and juridical persons the right to ownership of land; they were merely entitled to a lease.[49] The new Land Code does not explicitly prohibit land ownership by foreign nationals, nor does it explicitly declare such a right of foreign nationals. It merely provides that the right of foreign individuals and juridical persons to own land is to be determined by the Land Code and federal laws (Art.5, para.2). However, the Land Code itself is silent on this matter, except that foreign individuals and juridical persons are prohibited from owning land in the border areas (Art.15, para.3). The only other federal law which refers to the right of foreign nationals on land is the above-mentioned Foreign Investment Law. Therefore, it is not clear whether land ownership by foreign nationals is allowed in areas other than the border areas as the Land Code seems to suggest, or, whether only a lease is available as the Foreign Investment Law provides. It should be noted that the Land Code has a provision that rules on land accommodated in other federal laws must comply with the provisions of the Land Code (Art.2, para.1).

Owners of land are under an obligation to use the land in accordance with the purpose of the land, e.g. if it is purported to be for housing, it should not be used for industrial purposes, the owner must not cause damage to the environment and the soil, he must pay in a timely manner the payment for land, and observe planning, construction, ecological, sanitary, fire and other regulations (Art.42).

The ownership of land is terminated by assignment of land to another person by the owner, waiver of the right of ownership by the owner, and compulsory withdrawal of land by the procedure established by civil legislation (Art.44). Land

---

48   *VVS i SN RSFSR*, 1992 No.25, item 1427.
49   Ikonitskaia, *supra*, p.70.

can be withdrawn in a compulsory manner from the owner for the needs of the state or municipality in exceptional cases as follows (Art.49):

i)   implementation of international obligations of the Russian Federation;

ii)   allocation of objects of state or municipal significance, if there is no alternative site;

iii)   other cases provided by federal law or law of constituent entities.

Compulsory withdrawal of land for the need of the state or municipality can be made only with advance compensation equal to the value of the land, and on the basis of court judgment (Art.55, para.2). If the owner so wishes, alternative land of an equal value is provided (Art.63, para.1). Chapter 17 of the Civil Code has similar provisions on those matters.

While the permissibility of free circulation of land was a much debated issue before the enactment of the new Code, there is no declaration of free circulation of land in the new Code. Instead, there is a provision on restrictions on the circulation of land. As a rule, land which is excluded from circulation cannot be an object of private ownership, or an object of transactions provided by the Civil Code. There is a list of such land which is excluded from circulation, which includes natural reserves and national parks as well as land occupied by military and nuclear energy installations. The list is not particularly extensive or unreasonable. Land is to be circulated in accordance with the Civil Code and the Land Code. However, concerning agricultural land, a separate federal law is expected to be enacted (Land Code Art.27).

There is a specific provision on the sale of land. First of all, only the land which is accounted for in the land survey can be an object of sale. The seller is under an obligation to provide information on all encumbrances on the land to the buyer (Art.37, para.1). The following terms of sale are void (*ibid.*, para.2):

i)   sale with the seller's repurchase option;

ii)   sale with terms restricting the creation of hypothec, lease, and the effecting of other transactions;

iii)   sale with terms limiting the liability of the seller when a third party asserts his right over the land.

was a common instrument for securing claims, but has now been made void by the Land Code.

4)   Rights on Land other than Ownership

Chapter 17 of the Civil Code, which has now come into effect with the Land Code, accommodates provisions on the right of ownership and other real rights over land. The Civil Code lists the following rights on land in addition to the right to ownership:

i)   the right of life-long, inheritable possession;
ii)   the right of permanent (indefinite) use of land;
iii)   servitude
iv)   lease
v)   gratuitous use

The right of life-long, inheritable possession is a right very similar to ownership which emerged towards the end of socialism, when 'it was still terrifying to talk publicly about private ownership of land'.[50] This is a right to possess and use land, and is inheritable. The power to dispose of land is very much limited. In the past, this right has been granted in the rural areas by local administrative agencies.[51] Although it was a concept of the transitional period and was abolished in the early 1990s, it was restored in the Civil Code (Art.265). The new Land Code still retains this, but only insofar as the person has obtained this right before the new Land Code took effect (Art.21, para.1).

The right of permanent (indefinite) use of land, according to the Land Code, is the right to possess and use land which is under state or municipal ownership. This is a gratuitous right; no rent is payable. This right is not available to individuals; it is only for government and municipal institutions, federal treasury (*kazennyi*) enterprises, and state and municipal representative bodies (Art.20, para.1). The new Land Code also provides for free use of land, but this is for a fixed period (Art.24).

Servitude is a right of limited use of land by neighbours. Servitude may be established for passing through the land, the passage of livestock, laying of cables etc. Servitude retains its effect even when the title to the land is transferred. Servitude can be created by contract, or by law. The new Land Code leaves 'private servitude', i.e. servitude created by agreement, to the Civil Code and provides only for 'public servitude' (Art.23, para.1). Public servitude can be created by federal law and normative acts and the law and normative acts of the constituent entities (*ibid.*, para.2). These include servitude for crossing a piece

50   Bogoliubov, *supra*, p.300.
51   Ikonitskaia, *supra*, p.85.

of land, for the use of land to repair cables and transportation infrastructure, for drainage etc. (*ibid.*, para.3).

The lease of land is provided for by the Civil Code as a typical contract in the part on the Law of Obligation.

11

TORT (OBLIGATIONS ARISING FROM THE CAUSING OF HARM) AND UNJUST ENRICHMENT

1   GENERAL RULES

Obligations arising from the causing of harm (*deliktnoe obiazatel'stvo* – tort) is covered in Part Two of the Civil Code as obligations arising from non-contractual grounds. This arrangement, which is in line with the Pandekten system, was adopted by the draft Civil Code in the late Tsarist period and has been inherited by the 1922 and 1964 RSFSR civil codes. Tort law under socialism was, in principle, no different from tort law in the West. Instead of the 'grand scheme of state compensation from public funds' as envisaged by some Marxists, the system still continued to be that of private law tort.[1]

The structure of the part on tort in the current Civil Code is strikingly similar to that in the previous civil codes. First, there is a general provision on tort liability based upon fault, combined with a provision on a non-fault principle for 'sources of increased danger'. Second, various forms of government tort liability are covered in the Civil Code. Third, in addition to the general rules on tort, there are additional provisions on the liability of minors, parents, employers, persons without capacity to act etc. Fourth, liability for causing damage to the health or the life of a person is covered in a separate subsection.

The general provision on tort provides as follows (Art.1064):

1. Damage caused to the person or property of a physical person and also damage caused to the property of a juridical person are subject to full compensation by the person who caused the damage.

The obligation to compensate can be imposed by law on a person who is not the person who caused the damage.

An obligation may be imposed on the person who caused the damage to pay compensation to the victim at a level above that of the actual damage by law or contract.

---

1   W.Gray, 'Soviet Tort Law: New Principles Annotated', in W.Lafave ed., *Law in the Soviet Society*, Urbana 1965, p.181.

2. The person who caused the damage can be exempted from liability if he proves that the damage was not caused by his fault (*vina*). By law, it is possible to provide for compensation despite the absence of fault on the part of the person who caused the damage.

3. Compensation of damage may be denied, if the damage was caused by the request or with the consent of the victim, and the act is not against the ethical principles of society.

    Damage caused by a lawful act is subject to compensation in cases provided by law.

Thus, the general rule is that the tortfeasor is liable for full compensation of the damage based upon the principle of fault. The burden of proof of fault lies with the tortfeasor.

For liability to emerge, there has to be (i) an occurrence of damage, (ii) unlawfulness of the act of the tortfeasor, (iii) causal links between (i) and (ii), and (iv) fault on the part of the tortfeasor.[2] (ii) is not explicitly provided by law, but is 'presupposed'.[3] Damage caused by necessary defence does not have to be compensated, insofar as it was within the permissible scope of actions undertaken in necessary defence (Art.1066). In cases of extreme necessity, the act of the person who caused the damage is understood to be lawful under Russian Law, but nevertheless, this person is liable for damages (Art.1067).

Damage is understood as a material harm in the form of a decrease in the value of the property of the victim and/or a worsening of non-material welfare (life, health etc.). The General Part of the Civil Code has a provision which defines the concept of loss (*ubytok*) (Art.15, para.2):

Loss is understood as the cost, which the person whose right has been infringed, spent or has to spend in order to recover his rights, loss or damage to his property (real damage) and also loss of future income which this person would have received in normal conditions of civil transactions had this right not been infringed (loss of future income).

    If the person who infringed a right has received an income as a result of the infringement, the person who had his rights infringed may require compensation, in addition to the compensation for other losses, for the loss of future income of an amount not less than this income.

---

2   O.N.Sadikov ed., *Kommentarii k grazhdanskomu kodeksu Rossiiskoi Federatsii, chasti vtoroi*, enlarged edition, Moscow 1999, p.666.

3   *Ibid.*, p.666.

This provision is accommodated in the general part presumably to cover both tort compensation and compensation arising from non-performance or inappropriate performance of obligations.

Thus, loss includes real damage plus the loss of future income. It should be added that there is a provision in the part on contracts of supply which sets out rules for the calculation of loss in cases of rescission of a contract of supply (Art.524).

Another provision in the general part which is relevant in this respect is the provision on the compensation for moral damage (Art.151). This provision is part of a chapter on 'non-material welfare and their protection'. Compensation for moral damage is indeed a novelty in the post-socialist period. It was introduced by the 1990 Fundamental Principles of Civil Legislation of the USSR and inherited by the current Civil Code (see below).

The above general provision is based upon fault on the part of the tortfeasor. This includes both intentional acts and negligent acts. An intentional act is defined in a commentary as an unlawful act which the tortfeasor not only has foreseen, but has also desired, or at least, he has allowed the harmful result to happen. Negligence is defined as the 'lack of caution, foreseeability, care etc., required under the given circumstances'.[4]

In contrast, there is a provision which provides for non-fault liability as follows (Art.1079):

> Juridical and physical persons whose activities are related to increased danger to the surroundings (use of means of transportation, mechanisms, high-voltage electrical energy, atomic energy, explosive substances, strongly-acting poisons etc.; carrying out of construction works and other activities connected to such works) are under an obligation to compensate for damage caused by the sources of increased danger, unless it is proved that the damage has occurred as the result of an insurmountable force or an intentional act of the victim.

The effect of this provision is that the juridical persons and physical persons whose activities involve increased danger to the surroundings are liable, unless they prove that the damage has occurred as the result of an insurmountable force or an intentional act of the victim. Insurmountable force is understood as 'extraordinary and unpreventable circumstances under the given conditions' (Art.401, para.3).

This is an exception to the general rule of tort liability based upon fault. Although this is an exception, this provision has been fairly extensively applied since the time of socialism. A similar provision had existed in the socialist civil

---

4   *Ibid.*, p.667.

codes; the listed activities included those of industrial enterprises and installations, transport organisations, and car possessors. Damage caused by traffic accidents was covered by this provision, not by the general tort provision. Thus, in cases of traffic accidents, the tortfeasor bears non-fault liability.

The current Code merely lists examples of activities associated with an increased danger to the surroundings. The object is regarded as a source of increased danger if it represents the 'large scale of its destructive power which cannot be controlled in the light of the given state of safety technology'. There have been cases where the provision was applied to the keeping of animals in a zoo and a circus, as well as the dumping of toxic waste above the permissible level in the environment.[5] The resolution of the Plenum of the Supreme Court of the Russian Federation of 1994, which was published before the enactment of the Civil Code, but is still applicable, suggests that such activities are those whose implementation creates an increased probability of the occurrence of damage caused by the impossibility of people fully controlling them, as well as activities involving the use, transportation, and storage of objects, substances etc. of a production and commercial nature which have the same characteristics as above.[6]

The person (juridical or physical) who is in possession of the sources of increased danger on the basis of ownership, right of economic management, right of operational administration, lease, *trast* etc. is liable for damages in such cases. This person is exempted from liability, if he proves that the source of increased danger left his possession by an unlawful act (*ibid.*, para.2). It is important to note that persons who are employed by the possessor of these sources are not liable; it is the 'possessor' in the above sense, who is liable. Thus, in a car accident, it is not the chauffer, but the 'possessor' of the car, who is held liable.

Those who jointly caused damage are liable jointly and severally for damages (Art.1080). In cases where the damage was caused by joint acts involving increased danger to a third party, the possessors of the source of increased danger are jointly and severally liable (Art.1079, para.3):

> Spouses G initiated an action against joint stock company Sergievskavtotrans and an individual L for the compensation of for the loss and moral damage caused by the death of their son A who died in a collision of two cars, one owned by this company and driven by Iu, and another car driven by L. L and the passenger of the latter car, A, died in the accident.

---

5   S.N.Bratus and O.N.Sadikov eds., *Kommentarii k grazhdanskomu kodekusu RSFSR*, Moscow 1982, p.533.
6   *BVS RF* 1994 No.7, p.6.

The collision was caused when a pedestrian suddenly came running, against traffic rules, in front of the car driven by Iu, and in order to avoid hitting the pedestrian, the car steered into the opposite lane in which the other car was driving.

The first instance court, the district court, acknowledged the claim in full. In the second instance, the court reduced the moral damages by 80% as well as the damages for the material loss. The case eventually reached the Supreme Court by protest. The Court rejected the protest and upheld the original judgment.

The Supreme Court ruled that this was a case where the provision of the Civil Code involving sources of increased danger (Art.1079) was applicable. In this case, Iu was found to have had no technical possibility of avoiding hitting the pedestrian by applying the emergency brake. The pedestrian was later pursued in court for criminal responsibility, but was discharged by an amnesty. The Supreme Court acknowledged that Iu as well as L had not acted unlawfully, and they were never pursued for administrative or criminal responsibility, but nevertheless, the company who employed Iu, and the driver L were found to be liable for the death of A. The Court ruled that the occurrence of the collision is in itself a ground for the liability of possessors of the sources of increased danger. The counter argument that the diversion of the other car into his lane should be regarded as an 'insurmountable force' was not accepted by the Court.[7]

In addition, Article 1096 of the Civil Code (product liability) and the Law on Atomic Energy and the Merchant Shipping Code provide for non-fault liability.[8]

Fault on the part of the victim is also taken into account when determining the level of compensation. The rule is that if the victim was grossly negligent in a manner which contributed to the occurrence or increase of damage, the amount of compensation is to be reduced accordingly. If the victim was grossly negligent and the liability of the tortfeasor was on a non-fault basis, the amount of compensation may be reduced or the compensation may be denied altogether. On the other hand, in cases of the death of the breadwinner, the fault of the victim is not counted (Art.1083, para.2).

A unique feature of Soviet/Russian Law is that the court is entitled to reduce the amount of compensation by considering the financial state of the individual, unless the act was intentional (Art.1083, para.3).

Injunctions are available under the current Civil Code. The Code provides that the danger of causing damage in the future is a ground for an action to prohibit activities which create such a danger (Art.1065, para.1). In addition, if the damage which has already occurred was a result of the utilisation of enterprises, installations, or production activities which continue to cause damage and threaten further damage, the court may oblige the defendant to suspend or ter-

---

7   *BVS RF* 2001, No.5, pp.1-2.
8   *SZ RF* 1995 No.48, item 4552; 1999 No.

minate such activities. However, the court may dismiss the claim for suspension or termination, if it considers this to be against social interests (*ibid.*, para.2).

2   SPECIAL RULES

There are some provisions which cover specific rules of tort liability.

i)   Liability for damage caused by a minor below 14 years of age

In such cases, the parents are liable, unless they prove that the damage was caused not by their fault (Art.1073).

ii)   Liability for damage caused by a minor between 14 and 18 years of age

As a rule, these minors are liable for damage caused by them under the general rules of tort, but if they do not have income or assets, the parents are liable, unless they prove that the damage was caused not by their fault (Art.1074).

iii)   Liability for damage caused by a person who was declared incapable to act

The guardian or the organisation which is under an obligation to supervise this person is liable, unless they prove that the damage was caused not by their fault (Art.1076).

iv)   Liability for damage caused by a person declared partly incapable to act (limited capability)

This denotes those who have alcoholic or narcotic dependency. They are liable for the damage caused (Art.1077).

v)   Liability for the damage caused by a person who is not capable of under-
        standing the meaning of his act

This covers the acts of those people who are perfectly capable to act, but have
temporarily lost the capability to understand the meaning of their acts, or are unable
to be guided by such an understanding by e.g. a serious mental disease, a deceived
state, or loss of consciousness. In such cases, the court may, by taking into account
the financial state of the victim and the tortfeasor and other circumstances, make
the tortfeasor fully or partly liable (Art.1078).

vi)   Liability of a juridical person or a physical person for the damage caused
        by an employee in the course of discharging his employment duties

The employer is liable in such cases. In this context, the term 'employees' does
not only mean those people employed on the basis of an employment contract
governed by labour law, but also those who work under a civil law contract,
provided that the person acts or is supposed to act on instruction and is under
the control of the employer for the safe conduct of work. Furthermore, commercial
organisations and production cooperatives are held liable for the activities of their
members in implementing entrepreneurial, production and other activities of the
commercial organisations and production cooperatives (Art.1068). For this liability
to emerge, basic prerequisites of tort must exist in relation to the employee, i.e.
the employee has to be at fault, his act has to be unlawful, and the the causal links
should exist.[9] In court procedure, the employer is the defendant, and the actual
tortfeasor – the employee is a third party participant.[10]

3   LIABILITY FOR CAUSING DAMAGE TO THE LIFE OR HEALTH OF AN
        INDIVIDUAL

The Code has a separate chapter on compensation for damage caused to the life
or health of an individual.
        The rule is that for causing disability or another harm to the health of a person,
the loss of wages (income) which he had or could have definitely had, the cost
which became necessary as a result of the harm including medical care, supplementary diet, medicine, artificial limbs, treatment in sanatoriums, acquisition of

---

9   Sadikov ed., *supra*, p.671.
10   *Ibid.*

special means of transportation, training for another profession etc., is recoverable, provided that they are needed and cannot be obtained without payment (Art.1085, para.1). In determining the lost income, pensions and other payments the person is entitled to receive are not deducted (*ibid.*, para.2). This is a marked difference from the socialist civil codes which deducted pensions and other payments and made the amount of damages to be meagre.

In cases of a death of the bread-winner, the following persons are entitled to damages (Art.1088, para.1):

    i)   dependants who are not capable of working;

    ii)   children of the deceased who were born after his death;

    iii)   either parent or spouse or other members of the family who did not work and were dependent on the deceased such as children, grandchildren, brothers and sisters below 14 years of age, or those above 14, but who need care for health reasons;

    iv)   a person who was dependent on the deceased and who lost his working capability within five years of his death.

A person who has the right to claim damages for the death of the bread-winner is entitled to the portion of the wages (income) of the deceased which this person had been receiving or had the right to receive for his subsistence (Art.1089, para.1). The period of compensation for damage depends on the category of these people. For example, minors are paid damages up to the age of 14, while invalids are paid during the period of invalidity (*ibid.*, para.2).

As a rule, compensation for damage to the life or health is paid as a monthly payment. The court may order a lump sum payment if there is a reasonable ground to do so, but this cannot exceed three years' payment (Art.1092, para.1). If the working capability of the victim subsequently decreased, the victim may require an increase of the monthly payment, while in the opposite case, the tortfeasor may require a decrease of the payment (Art.1090). Furthermore, if the price of subsistence increases, the payment must be indexed with the prices. The increase of the minimum wage also affects the payment (Art.1091).

4   MORAL DAMAGE

One of the novelties in the post-socialist period is the introduction of compensation for moral damage. The Fundamental Principles of the Civil Legislation of the USSR of 1990 introduced this system for the first time in the history of Russian Law. There were discussions on this matter in the early 20th century and the draft Civil

Code in the Tsarist period accommodated a provision on compensation for moral damage, but the Code was never enacted.[11]

Under the socialist system, compensation for moral damage was denied, since it might result in an unfair 'windfall profit' for the victim. Compensation was limited to real damage. However, there were proposals to introduce this system, particularly after some Eastern European countries introduced it.

The current Civil Code has a provision on moral damage in the General Part, since it is intended to cover not only tort, but contractual liabilities as well (Art.151). The resolution of the Plenum of the Supreme Court of the Russian Federation of 1995 defines moral damage as follows:

> moral or physical suffering caused by an act (or omission) which harms an immaterial benefit which belongs to an individual by birth or by law (life, health, personal integrity, business reputation, privacy, personal and family secrets etc.), or infringes his personal non-proprietary rights (right to use the name, copyright and other rights in accordance with the laws protecting the rights on the results of intellectual activities) or which infringes the proprietary rights of individuals.[12]

This includes 'psychological experience related to the death of the next of kin, the impossibility of continuing active social life, and the loss of work.

As a corollary, it is only individuals, not juridical persons, who are entitled to claim compensation for moral damage. 'Since juridical persons cannot feel physical or moral pain, it is impossible to cause them moral damage'.[13]

The Civil Code provides that moral damage is subject to compensation in monetary terms. However, there are no precise criteria as to the determination of the amount of compensation.[14] The Code provides that the court should take into account the level of the fault of the person who caused the harm (if fault is required) and other contributing factors. The court must also consider the moral and physical suffering of the victim (Art.151). There is a requirement of reasonableness and fairness as well (Art.1101, para.1).

The rule is that moral damage to non-proprietary rights is subject to compensation without restriction, while moral damage to proprietary rights is subject to compensation only in cases that are provided by law (Art.1099, para.2).

In principle, fault is a prerequisite of compensation for moral damage. However, in the following cases, fault is not required (Art.1100):

---

11   R.A.Beliatskii, *Vozmeshchenie moral'nogo vreda*, St.Petersburg, 1913, p.52.
12   *BVS RF*, 1995 No.3, p.9.
13   Decision of the Supreme Commercial Court, December 1, 1998, *VVAS RF* 1999 No.2.
14   B.D.Zavidov and O.B.Gusev, *Grazhdansko-pravovaia otvetstvennost'*, Moscow 2000, pp.485-486.

i)   damage caused to the life or health of an individual by sources of increased
     danger:

ii) damage caused to an individual as a result of unlawful conviction, arrest, detention
     etc.;

iii) damage caused by the dissemination of information which harmed honour, dignity,
     or business reputation

For example:

> E, who was driving a car, collided with another car driven by K. E was convicted of
> a breach of traffic rules and of causing bodily harm to K and was also ordered to pay
> 3 million roubles (before denomination) as compensation for moral damage by the district
> court. However, the presidium of the provincial court quashed this judgment on the
> ground that the district court failed to take into account the actual financial state of E,
> who was a pensioner, married and with two children (minors). The amount was eventual-
> ly reduced to 500 thousand roubles.[15]

Concerning defamation, under the socialist civil codes, publication of rebuttal was
the only remedy. The 1990 Fundamental Principles of Civil Legislation introduced
compensation of moral damage for defamation. The present Code inherited this
provision:

> A senior doctor of a hospital, Shorokhov, brought an action against the editor of the
> newspaper 'Tribun' and the senior assistant procurator of the City of Syktyvkar for
> compensation for moral damage caused by the publication of an article in the newspaper.
> Y was the author of the article which, according to the plaintiff, was untrue and harmed
> his honour and dignity.
>   The City Court ruled in favour of the plaintiff and ordered the newspaper to pay
> five million roubles and Y to pay one million roubles. The judgment was upheld by
> higher courts. The protest brought to the Presidium of the Supreme Court of the Russian
> Federation was also dismissed.
>   The newspaper published an article which claimed that the re-registration of a small
> enterprise Sana into a joint stock company was effected for the purpose of separating
> Shorokhov from other founders, and that the commercial activity of this enterprise was
> aimed at reselling bandages at a high price to the hospital where Shorokhov worked.
> The City Court had earlier ruled in favour of Shorokhov and ordered the newspaper
> to publish a rebuttal by Shorokhov in another procedure. The Supreme Court ruled that
> under such circumstances, the City Court had acted lawfully in finding that due to the
> publication of an article which was untrue and which harmed the honour and dignity
> of the plaintiff, moral damage, which requires compensation by the editor of the news-
> paper and the author, had occurred. The City Court was right in determining the amount

---

15   *BVS RF*, 1995 No.4, p.15.

of compensation for the moral damage by taking into account the nature and the content of the publication, the level of dissemination of the information which harmed his honour and dignity as well as his reputation, and other contributing factors.[16]

5 PRODUCT LIABILITY

There are some provisions on product liability in the chapter on tort. Thus, damage caused to the life, health or property of individuals, or the property of juridical persons as a result of design, formula, or other defects of goods, work, or services as well as a result of inaccurate or insufficient information on goods, work, or services is to be compensated by the seller, the manufacturer of the goods, or the person who performed the work or provided the service, regardless of whether this person was at fault or not, and whether there was this person was in a contractual relation with the victim or not (Art.1095).

There are not so many judgments on product liability. The following is a rare case where the victim claimed compensation for extended damage:

> The plaintiff brought an action against the manufacturer of a television which caused a fire in his flat. The plaintiff claimed compensation for material damage of 4,167,568 roubles for the ruined flat and furniture, and for moral damage of 2,500,000 roubles. The court took into account that the suffering of the victim had been compounded by the delay in responding to the claim, and also that the plaintiff, who was an aged person, had been deprived of the opportunity of enjoying watching television. The court acknowledged compensation for moral damage of 1,000,000 roubles.[17]

The victim may choose whether to sue the seller, the manufacturer, or others. Sellers, manufacturers, or providers of work or services are exempted from liability if they prove that the damage occurred as a result of an insurmountable force, or as a result of a breach on the part of the consumer of the rules of use or storage of the goods or the results of the works or services (Art.1098). The burden of proof lies with the seller, manufacturer, or the provider of work or service.

The Law on the Protection of the Rights of Consumers of 1996 has more detailed provisions on this matter.[18] However, if there is an overlap, the provisions of the Code has priority.

---

16 Decision of the Presidium of the Supreme Court, July 10, 1996, in *Spory o zashchite chesti, dostoinstva i delovoi reputatsii; sbornik dokumentov*, Moscow 2000, pp.24-27.
17 Cited in *Kompensatsiia za moral'nyi vred*, Moscow 1998, p.69.
18 *SZ RF* 1996 No.3, item 140.

6   GOVERNMENT TORT LIABILITY

It has been a tradition since socialist times to cover government tort liability in the Civil Code.

It is a constitutional right of the people to claim damages against unlawful acts of the government or government officials. The Civil Code provides as follows (Art.1069):

> damage caused to individuals or juridical persons as a result of unlawful acts (or omissions), including the enactment of acts against the law or other legal acts, by a state agency, agencies of local self-government or their officials is subject to compensation.

The 1999 Foreign Investment Law also has a provision on the liability of state agencies (Art.5, para.2). They are to be liable in accordance with the Civil Code.

Not only are acts or omissions of these agencies or officials covered in this provision, but also the enactment of unlawful normative or non-normative acts. 'Officials' in this context means only those key personnel who perform the function of a representative of power or 'organisational-dispositionary, administrative-economic' power, i.e. prerogative power.[19] The act should have been effected in the course of duty. Otherwise, the liability is covered by general tort rules.

The above provision does not explicitly require fault on the part of the government or municipal agencies or officials. However, the Supreme Commercial Court is of the view that when applying this provision, general requirements of tort including the existence of fault should be met:[20]

> An individual entrepreneur P brought an action against the Federal Financial Administration of the Puskov Province for the damage caused by the unlawful confiscation and the destruction of goods. The judgment of the district court which had served as a basis of the confiscation was quashed by a higher court. The Court ruled that the act of destroying confiscated goods was unlawful. It also acknowleged that the liability as provided in Article 1069 presupposes the existence of components of tort required by the general provision of tort (Art. 1064).[21]

The Law on the Protection of Natural Environment of 1997 also provides for compensation for environmental damage:

---

19   Sadikov ed., *supra*, p.673.
20   Decision of the Presidium of the Supreme Commercial Court, December 8, 1998 in A.N.Dolzjenko et al eds., *Sudebnaia praktika po grazhdaskim delam*, Moscow 2001, pp.911-913.
21   Judgment of the Federal Commercial Court of the North-Western Region, April 10,2000, *ibid.*, pp.922-924.

The State Far-Eastern Marine Environmental Protection Agency brought an action against the Pacific Fleet for compensation of 37,531,482,500 roubles (before denomination) for polluting the environment by arbitrarily dumping waste in the sea. The first instance court acknowledged the claim for compensation of up to 12,749,482,500 roubles. The court of the appellate instance upheld this. The Supreme Commercial Court, however, reversed the judgment on the ground that compensation of damage in such cases should be calculated on the basis of the actual cost of restoring the polluted state of environment.[22]

7   UNJUST ENRICHMENT

A person who, without a ground established by law, other legal acts or juristic acts, obtained or kept property at the expense of another person must return this property to the latter (Art.1102, also see exceptions in Art.1109). A person who assigned his right to another person on the ground of a non-existing or invalid obligation is entitled to have the *status quo ante* restored (Art.1106).

As a rule, property which represents unjust enrichment has to be returned in kind (Art.1104). If this is impossible, the actual value of the property at the time of the acquisition shall be returned, together with the damage resulting from the subsequent change of its value, if the person failed to return the property without delay when he became aware of the fact of unjust enrichment (Art.1105, para.1). Furthermore, all income which this person has received or would have received from the property, if this person was aware, or should have been aware of the fact of unjust enrichment should be returned with the property (Art.1107, para.1):

A small enterprise Meditsina-Tekhnologiia-Servis brought an action against the city administration of Shlissel'burg at the Commercial Court of the City of St.Petersburg and Leningrad Province claiming 1,571,983 roubles as unjust enrichment in relation to the defendant occupying a building of 860 square metres which the plaintiff owned. The first, appellate and cassation instances all rejected the claim of the plaintiff. However, the Supreme Commercial Court, upon protest, acknowledged the claim. In this case, the owner of the disputed property was established as the plaintiff in another proceeding. However, the defendant continued to occupy the building, and failed to maintain it properly. The Supreme Commercial Court found this to be an unjust enrichment and reversed the case to the first instance court.[23]

---

22   Decision of the Presidium of the Supreme Commercial Court. February 18, 2000, *ibid.*, pp.915-916.
23   Decision of the Presidium of the Supreme Commercial Court, April 4, 2000, *ibid.*, pp.948-949.

12

BANKING LAW

1 HISTORICAL BACKGROUND

The origin of the modern banking system in Russia goes back to the financial reform of 1859. The State Bank of Russia was founded in 1860, followed by some private credit institutions. At the beginning of the 20th century, the Russian banking system comprised the State Bank, the State Savings Bank and some other government banks plus various social and private credit institutions. This included around 50 commercial banks which were formed as joint stock companies and in addition, 300 city credit societies and banks.[1]

Immediately after the October Revolution, these banking institutions were nationalised by the Decree on Nationalisation of Banks. Banking business was declared to be under a state monopoly. Activities of foreign banks were prohibited by 1918.

At the beginning of the New Economic Policy in 1921, the State Bank of the RSFSR was founded which was later transformed into the USSR State Bank. Some specialised state banks such as the Foreign Trade Bank and the Agricultural Bank were set up around this time. During the period of the New Economic Policy, the state monopoly of banking was forgotten temporarily and some private credit organisations in the form of mutual credit societies were allowed to be set up.[2] However, these institutions were phased out by the end of the 1930s.

The socialist system of banking could be characterised as a mono-bank system in contrast with a two-tier banking system of state banks and commercial banks. The State Bank, being the issuer of money, together with a selected number of specialised banks, was the sole credit institution. At the end of socialism, in addition to the State Bank, there were the All-Union Bank for Financing Capital

---

1 O.Kuschpeta, *The Banking and Credit System of the USSR*, Leiden 1978, pp.17-21.
2 G.A.Tosunian et al., *Bankovskoe pravo Rossiiskoi Federatsii, obshchaia chast'*, Moscow 1999, pp.272-303.

Investment (*Stroibank*), the Foreign Trade Bank, and the Workers' Savings Bank. Under socialism, the State Bank acted as a cashier or a settlement house for the government. All State enterprises and organisations had an account with a local branch of the State Bank and were under an obligation to pay all the money into this account and effect payments through the bank. This enabled financial resources to be pooled in the State Bank and be reallocated. After all, this system was designed for the state to closely monitor state enterprises for the ultimate goal of fulfilling the state economic plan. On the other hand, individuals could use only cash for payments and maintain saving accounts only.[3]

2   THE EMERGENCE AND DEVELOPMENT OF COMMERCIAL BANKS

The system started to change in 1987, when the last economic reform under socialism was attempted. In the proposed new system, the State Bank was to be transformed into a genuine central bank, leaving other functions to newly created specialised state banks such as the Industrial Construction Bank (*Promtsroibank*) and the Agricultural Development Bank (*Agrostroibank*). In addition, the Foreign Trade Bank and the Savings Bank were reorganised and were given more independence from the State Bank.[4]

In 1988, the Law on Cooperatives was enacted. This Law was a watershed for private entrepreneurship which had previously been banned by law. According to a Russian specialist, 'for the first time since the New Economic Policy (in the 1920s), individual freedom in the area of labour activities was significantly expanded'.[5] The Law allowed associations (unions) of cooperatives to set up cooperative banks. Cooperative banks were not only a clearing house, but were expected to ensure the development of cooperatives by financing their activities from resources which primarily comprised deposits from cooperatives as well as other organisations (including ministries) and individuals.

In reality, the banks which mushroomed after 1988 were mainly 'wildcat' banks formed by state enterprises and local governments. They primarily accepted deposits from members and borrowed on the cheap interbank credit market to finance their own enterprises. Those banks applied for credits at subsidised rates from the State Bank and used this money to extend loans to the state enterprises.

---

3   M.Lavigne, *The Economic of Transition*, 2nd edition, New York 1999, pp.13-14.
4   J.E.Johnson, 'The Russian Banking System: Institutional Responses to the Market Transition', *Europe-Asia Studies*, 1994 No.6, pp.977-978..
5   Tosunian, *supra*, p.324.

Approximately four-fifths of all Russian commercial banks were set up by one or more state enterprises.[6]

In the light of the increased autonomy of state enterprises by the economic reform in the 1980s, namely the expansion of their right to retain part of the profits, and the newly introduced freedom of entrepreneurial activities for individuals, non-government banks rapidly developed in Russia on the basis of this Law. In 1998 and 1999, 150 commercial banks and cooperative banks were founded out of the money accumulated in particular branches of industry.[7] By the end of 1990, the number of 'commercial banks' exceeded one thousand.[8] In this way, a two-tier system of banking, i.e. a system with a Central Bank and independent commercial banks, emerged in Russia in the late 1980s.

The question was where the initial capital for these 'commercial banks' came from. 'Ministries, state committees, large state enterprises, government organs, state financial institutions, the Communist Party affiliates' – these were the entities which were already doing business on their own account. For example, Toko Bank, which went bankrupt in 1998, but until then, was the 6th largest commercial bank, was created by *Gossnab*, the state supply and distribution system. Oneksim Bank was created by large foreign trade organisations. Many of them operated as 'pocket banks' of the state enterprises which created them. Also there is no doubt that the capital accumulated in the 'second economy' under socialism poured into these banks.[9] As one observer put it rightly, 'Russian banks were deformed from the beginning'.[10] These banks helped their clients convert their state –owned assets into cash, circumvent foreign exchange regulations and transfer profits to offshore accounts.[11]

The reform of state banks belatedly followed. In 1990, the Law on the USSR State Bank and the Law on Banks were enacted. With the collapse of the Soviet Union, the Central Bank of the Russian Federation (Bank of Russia) was founded in 1990 on the basis of the RSFSR Bank, part of the USSR State Bank. On December 20, 1991, the USSR State Bank was formally abolished and its assets and debts within the territory of the RSFSR were transferred to the Bank of Russia. At the RSFSR level, in December 2, 1990, the Law on Banks and Banking Activities was enacted. This Law is still in force with subsequent amendments.[12]

---

6   Johnson, supra, p.979.
7   N.D.Eliashibili, *Bankovskoe pravo*, Moscow 1999, p.6.
8   Tosunian, *supra*, pp.323-329.
9   T.Gustafson, *Capitalism Russian Style*, Cambridge 1999, p.81.
10 *Ibid., supra*, p.83.
11 *Ibid., supra*, p.83.
12 *SZ RF,* 1996, No.6, item 492.

In the first half of the 1990s, 'commercial banks' continued to prosper. From 1993 to 1996, the number of registered credit organisations increased from 1,700 to 2,600.[13] In the period of high inflation, these credit organisations became accustomed to a fast-and-loose style closer to loan-sharking, currency speculation, and arbitrage than conventional banking.[14] Ensuring access to soft credit for the state enterprises which founded them was the banks' major task. For instance, in 1993, *Promstroibank*'s 30 largest shareholders were all clients.[15] Their managers were more concerned with the interests of the enterprises which controlled them, rather than with the soundness of their banks.[16] On the other hand, banks did not pay interest for around 70% of the total liabilities. This included budgetary organisations' accounts, which, since 1993, the state had allowed commercial banks to handle.[17] In a word, 'Russian banks did remarkably little to attract funds, subsisting largely on the basis of resources made available to them at little or no cost, and did relatively little lending except to the state'.[18]

In 1998, Russia fell into a serious financial crisis which led to the government's default on domestic debts and subsequent devaluation of the rouble. Various causes of the financial crisis have been pointed out. These include the general deterioration of the economy, the growing government deficit, the increase in foreign debt, the collapse of the financial market in South-East Asia etc.[19]

The Russian banking system had been in a critical state as early as autumn 1997. In May 1998, Toko Bank, which was one of the larger banks, got into difficulties and eventually had its licence withdrawn. Measures implemented by the government to counter the financial crisis in August 1998 turned out to be the final blow to the banking industry. Top ranking banks such as the Imperial Bank, and the SBS Agro Bank defaulted in August. By then, there were 511 loss making banks; in August alone, 140 credit organisations collapsed. There was a 'run on the bank'.[20]

The government default and devaluation of roubles, however, merely triggered the failure of the banks. Actually, the systemic crisis of the banking system had been prepared by 'economic-, social- and political-legal developments of the

---

13 'Vankovskii krizis: tuman rasseibaetsia?', *Voprosy ekonomiki*, 1999 No.5, p.5.
14 Gustafson, *supra*, p.87.
15 W.Tomspon, 'Old Habits Die Hard: Fiscal Imperatives, State Regulation and the Role of Russia's Banks', *Europe-Asia Studies*, 1997 No.7, p.1170.
16 Tompson, *supra*, p.1171.
17 *Ibid.*, p.1165.
18 *Ibid.*, p.1176.
19 In general, see T.Malleret et al., 'What Loaded and Triggered the Russian Crisis', *Post-Soviet Affairs*, 1999 No.2, p. 107ff. Tosuniain, *supra*, pp.330-338.
20 'Russia's Banking Crisis', *Russian Economic Trends*, 1998 No.3, p.39.

country' since 1991.[21] A survey of 18 banks (15 of which are among the 30 largest banks) conducted by the Bank Review Unit of the World Bank in autumn 1998 suggests that the massive failure of the banks was primarily the result of mismanagement of funds by bank managers. Connected lending and excessive risk taking in the forex market were the most destructive factors. The main sources of banks' capital deficit were bad loans (45%), followed by forex and transaction losses (37%). The failure of the government to redeem treasury bonds accounted for less than 18%. The survey also revealed that 14 of the 18 banks had negative capital in September – October 1998, and all of Russia's top five banks were among them.[22]

In 1999, the Chairman of the Central Bank stated as follows:

> The roots of such a serious crisis definitely go much deeper. The causes of the crisis are: insufficiently qualified management of banking risks, particularly foreign currency risk and credit risk, undercapitalisation of many banks, extreme increase of operations in the financial market, including pure speculations instead of more labour-consuming and often less profitable operations with the real sectors of the economy. We should also be reminded that the low level of financial discipline of many borrowers substantially increased the credit risk of the banks.[23]

In early 1999, the Central Bank reported that a quarter of the existing banks were not sustainable, and 149 of them were 'apparently bankrupt'.[24] The government was rather slow in responding to the situation. Individual banks were rescued by the Central Bank by cash injection and 'repo' loans in a highly opaque manner. It was only in July 1999, almost one year after the crisis, that the Central Bank found the courage to withdraw licences from some of the bigger violators of banking regulations and credit rights.[25] The Central Bank came under significant political pressure in the process. In the case involving the Imperial Bank, which held Gazprom and Lukoil accounts, but had made headlines for theft and asset stripping, the Bank had its licence revoked in August 1998. In June 1999, however, the licence was reinstated as a result of the appeal of the Minister of Fuel and Energy and major creditors to the Central Bank.[26]

---

21 Tosunian, *supra*, p.330.
22 'Banking Sector', *Russian Economic Trends*, 1999 No.2, p.85.
23 V.V.Gerashchenko, 'Akutual'nye problemy bankovskoi sistemy v 1999 godu', www.cbr.ru.
24 S.Aleksashenko et.al, 'Bankovskii Krizis: tuman rasseivaetsia?', *VE* 1999 No.5, p.31.
25 'Banking sector', *Russian Economic Trends*, 1999.2, p.87.
26 A.S.Alexandrovich, Bankruptcy Law, An Economic Medicine: How Russia's New Bankruptcy Legislation Facilitated Recovery From the Nationwide Financial Crisis of August 17,1998', *Cornell International Law Journal*, 2001, vol.34, pp.110-112.

The number of withdrawals of licences had been strikingly high in Russia even before the crisis, reflecting the dubious nature of some of the banks. In 1997 and 1998, licences were withdrawn from 334 and 229 banks respectively.[27] On the other hand, after 1998, the number of withdrawals has surprisingly dropped.[28] There were many banks whose licence had been withdrawn, but the bank itself was yet to be liquidated.

In February 1999, the long-awaited Law on the Insolvency of Credit Organisations was enacted. A new agency – Agency for Restructuring of Credit Organisations (ARKO) – was founded in March.[29] The Law on the Restructuring of Credit Organisations, which sets out the procedure for restructuring credit organisations by ARKO, was enacted in July 1999.[30] However, Bank owners and managers had been given plenty of time to strip assets from the banks by transferring them into 'bridge banks'.[31] This happened, for example, with Bank MENATEP, which was the fifth largest bank in Russia. By the time the Law on the Insolvency of Credit Organisations was adopted, the Bank was reduced to a mere shell whose assets had been transferred to an independent 'sister bank' which continues to operate. Some of the assets had been hidden abroad.[32]

As late as early 2001, it is reported that the Russian banking system has not really recovered from the crisis. By January 2001, aggregate capital was restored only to 60% of the pre-crisis level.[33] Lack of transparency in financial reporting and the absence of reliable information about the condition of banks, particularly about their loan portfolios, are among the serious obstacles to recovery.[34]

3   SOURCES OF BANKING LAW

Apart from some provisions of the Federal Constitution, e.g. Article 75 on the emission of currency and defending of its stability by the Central Bank, banks and other credit organisations are primarily regulated by laws and subordinate legal acts.

---

27   K.T.Tifomirov, *Postateinyi kommentarii k Federal'nomu zakonu "O nesostoiatel'nosti' kreditnykh organizatsii"*, Moscow 2001, p.IX.
28   'Banking sector', *Russian Economic Trends*, 1999.2, p.92.
29   *SZ* 1999, No.9, item 1097.
30   *SZ* 1999 No.28, item 3477.
31   K.Eggenberger, 'Bank Restructuring: Developments in 1999', *Russian Economic Trends*, 1999 No.4, p.27.
32   Alexandrovich, *supra*, p.108.
33   'Banking Sector', *Russian Economic Trends*, 2001, March p.63.
34   *Ibid.*, pp.62-63.

On the regulatory side, two federal laws are relevant. One is the Law on the Central Bank (Bank of Russia) and the other is the Law on Banks and Banking Activities (both originally enacted in 1992). The latter provides that banking activities in Russia are regulated by the Constitution, federal laws and normative acts of the Central Bank (Art.2). However, this list is incomplete in that decrees of the President and edicts of the government which do regulate banking activities in reality, were 'omitted by mistake' in the legislative process.[35]

There are also the Law on Insolvency of Credit Organisations and the Law on the Restructuring of Credit Organisations which were enacted in the aftermath of the 1998 banking crisis.[36]

On the transaction side, the Civil Code is the major source of law. The Code covers the following transactions:

i)   bank guarantee;
ii)   loan;
iii)   credit;
iv)   factoring;
v)   bank deposit;
vi)   bank account;
vii)   payments;
viii)   bank storage.

Subordinate acts include normative acts of the Central Bank as well as the former USSR State Bank. Normative acts of the Central Bank take the form of rules (*ukazanie*), statutes (*polozheniia*), instructions (*instruktsiia*), as well as letters and telegrams. Instructions can be fairly comprehensive, such as the Instruction No.49 on the Procedure for Registration of Credit Organisations and Licensing of Banking Activities of September 27, 1996. Letters of the Central Bank often cover important matters such as the Letter No.14 on the Conditions of Opening Banks with Foreign Participation of April 8, 1993. These acts may not contradict federal laws and do not have retrospective effect.

Decrees of the President are subordinate to the Constitution or the federal laws. However, the President is empowered to take emergency measures in order to defend the sovereignty and independence of the nation, and defend its integrity (Constitution Art.80, para.2). This power does not require a legal basis.

Edicts of the government 'ensure implementation of the single financial, credit and monetary policy' (Constitution, Art.114). Those edicts are enacted on the basis

---

35   V.A.Belov, *Bankovskoe pravo Rossii; teoriia, zakonodatel'stvo, praktika*, Moscow 2000, p.21.
36   *SZ* 1999 No.9, item 1097.

of, and for the implementation of, the Constitution, federal laws and presidential decrees (Art.115).

The Constitution also provides that 'the universally accepted principles and norms of international law and international treaties of the Russian Federation' are an integral part of the legal system of the Russian Federation (Art.15, para.4). What specifically constitutes 'universally accepted principles and norms of international law' in the area of banking law is not clear in court practice, and academic views vary. The Geneva Convention of Unified Rules on Cheques, Unified Rules on promissory Notes and Bills of Exchange, the UNIDROIT Convention on International Factoring, and the UNIDROIT Convention on Finance Lease, *inter alia*, are understood to incorporate these principles and rules.[37]

In addition, commercial custom serves as a source of law insofar as it is not against mandatory statutes or binding contracts (Civil Code, Art.5, para.2). Commercial custom is referred to in the Civil Code in the part covering banking transactions (e.g. Art.836 and 848). International commercial custom applied in banking practice includes ICC Uniform Rules on Incasso Transactions, Rules for Demand Guarantees, Contract Guarantees, as well as the Uniform Customs and Practice on Documentary Credits.

4   THE CENTRAL BANK (BANK OF RUSSIA)

Under the Law on the Central Bank, the Bank has a dual nature; on the one hand, it is a state agency which administers the monetary-credit policy and is the 'bank of banks', while on the other hand, it is empowered to effect civil law transactions with Russian and foreign credit organisations as well as the Russian State (the government of Russia). The Central Bank is a juridical person. According to the Law on the Central Bank, the Bank has a power to extend loan up to one year by taking securities and other assets as a collateral, to buy and sell promissory notes and bills of exchange, government bonds and obligations, to issue guarantees and provide suretyship, and to effect other commercial transactions provided by law.[38]

The Bank performs the following functions:

i)   preparation and implementation of the monetary-credit policy of the state in conjunction with the government;

ii)   emission of the currency and organisation of its circulation;

---

37   Tosunian, *supra*, p.132.
38   Eriashibili, *supra*, pp.14-16.

iii) acting as a creditor of the last resort for credit organisations by organising the system of refinancing;

iv) establishment of rules for payment in Russia;

v) establishment of rules for banking operations, bookkeeping and auditing for the banking system;

vi) registration of credit organisations and granting licenses;

vii) supervision of credit organisations;

viii) registration of emission of securities by credit organisations;

ix) regulation of foreign currencies;

x) determination of the procedure for payments with foreign states;

xi) control of foreign currency transactions;

xii) organisation of the balance of payment for the Russian Federation.

In its regulatory and supervisory capacity, the Central Bank

i) sets the numerical targets in order to ensure the prudence of credit organisations,

ii) opens of correspondent accounts, keeping of minimum mandatory reserve for credit organisations,

iii) finances credit organisations,

iv) ensures the liquidity of the banking system by buying and selling government securities,

v) establishes the rules for banking operations, and

vi) supervises the observance of banking laws and the normative acts of the Central Bank and inspects the activities of credit organisations.

5   CREDIT ORGANISATIONS

The Law on Banks and Banking Activities was originally enacted in 1990, but underwent major amendments in 1996. Until 1996, the core concept of this Law was 'banks'. Banks were defined as commercial juridical persons founded in any organisational-legal form, which, on the basis of the licence issued by the Central Bank, are entitled to solicit deposits, extend loans, perform payment, and conduct other banking operations and other transactions which are not against the law or against the purposes provided in the articles of incorporation.[39] This approach was supplemented by 1996 amendments which introduced the concept of credit organisations.

Credit organisations are defined as juridical persons which, for profit, based upon the licence granted by the Central Bank, are entitled to conduct banking

---

39 Tosuniian, *supra*, p.192.

operations listed in the Law (Art.1). Credit organisations are divided into banks and non-banks.

The Law lists the following banking operations (Art.5):

i)   taking of deposits from juridical and physical persons;

ii)   managing of the money deposited in the bank's name and account on the condition of return, profit basis, and limited term;

iii) opening and managing of accounts of juridical and physical persons;

iv)   arranging payments upon instruction by customers;

v)   incasso transactions, bills of exchange transactions, payment and settlement by documents;

vi)   purchase and sale of foreign currencies in cash and non-cash form;

vii) solicitation for deposit and investment of precious metals;

viii) issuing of bank guarantees.

There is a list of auxiliary businesses including finance lease and consulting service. On the other hand, credit organisations are prohibited from being engaged in production, trading and insurance business (for insurance, there is the Law on Insurance).

Banks are credit organisations which have an exclusive right to perform all of the first four banking operations. Non-banks are also credit organisations, but are entitled to perform specific banking operations provided by the Law (Art.1). It should be noted that in Russia, there is no segregation of banking and securities business. Based upon the general banking licence, banks may issue, purchase, sell, register, and possess in deposit various kinds of securities. Banks may also manage property entrusted by juridical and physical persons.

As of May 31, 2001, there are 2,100 registered credit organisations of which 1,322 are operating. The difference between the number of registered institutions and operating ones are those which had the licence withdrawn and/or liquidated. The number of operating credit organisations is much lower than the figure in 1998 when it was 1,697. There are only 41 are non-bank institutions.

Of these credit organisations, 130 had foreign participation, including 23 fully foreign-owned entities.[40]

---

40   Goskomstat, *Rossiia v tsifrakh 2000*, Moscow 2000, pp.291-292; See also www.cbr.ru/eng/statistics

Table 5 Registration of Credit Organisations as of October 1, 2001

Registered Credit Organisations in Total	2,059
Registered Banks	2,018
Credit Organisations with License withdrawn	738
Credit Organisations which were liquidated	954
Operating Credit Organisations with a General Licence	1,322
Banks with a general Licence	1,281
Credit Organisations with Foreign Participation	130
100% Foreign Capital	23
Over 50% Foreign Capital	12

Registered Capital (million roubles) 242,564
(Central Bank of Russia; www.cbr.ru/statistics)

The size of banks varies. There are around 100 banks with a capital of over 300 million roubles, but more than half of the banks have less than a 20 million rouble capital.[41] There are 295 entities with a capital of 40 billion roubles or more.

Table 6 Size of the Registered Capital as of October 1, 2001

Amount of Capital (million roubles) Number of Credit Organisations

Up to 3	13	(10,1%)
3 to 10	236	(17,9%)
10-30	318	(24,1%)
30-60	253	(19,1%)
60-150	164	(12,4%)
150-300	93	(7,0%)
300 and over	124	(9,4%)

---

41   *Rossiia v tsifrakh 2000, supra*, p.292.

Credit organisations can be founded as 'commercial organisations on any form of ownership'. This means that credit organisations can be either joint stock companies, limited liability companies or companies with supplementary liability. Credit organisations must have the word 'bank' or 'non-bank organisation' as well as the organisational form of the company attached to their name. They are required to take the form of a joint stock company.

6   LICENCE FOR BANKING TRANSACTIONS

Credit organisations are subject to registration with the Central Bank. Credit organisations receive the right to perform banking transactions on the basis of a licence granted by the Central Bank.

Registration and the issuing of licences can be refused on the following grounds (Art.16):

i)   candidates for the head of the executive body and/or the chief accounting officer do not meet the required qualifications, such as the completion of high legal or economic education and experience as a head of a department of a credit institution for 2 years, and the absence of bankruptcy within two years or previous criminal conviction;

ii)   unsatisfactory financial state of the founders or their non-performance of tax payment and other mandatory payments to the state;

iii)   non-compliance of the submitted documents with the requirements of the law.

Licence can be withdrawn on the following grounds (Art.20):

i)   establishment of the fact that information on which the licence was based turned out to be untrue;

ii)   delay of starting banking operation for more than a year from the issuing of licence;

iii)   establishment of the inaccuracy of accounting;

iv)   performance of banking operations which are not included in the licence;

v)   non-compliance with federal laws regulating banking activities and normative acts of the Central Bank, if disciplinary measures were applied more than once within a year;

vi)   unsatisfactory financial state of the credit institution, non-performance of obligation *vis à vis* depositors and creditors which serve as a ground for filing for bankruptcy.

7   SUPERVISION OVER CREDIT ORGANISATIONS

The Central Bank is the regulatory and supervisory agency over credit organisations. The Bank exercises permanent supervision over the observance of banking legislation and normative acts of the Central Bank, namely the mandatory numerical requirements established by the Bank (Law on the Central Bank, Art.55,).

Between 1992-1995, the Central Bank gradually created a system of supervision and inspection over credit organisations. However, supervision by the Bank can hardly be regarded as effective as has been demonstrated by the 1998 banking crisis.

The Law on the Central Bank provides for the mandatory reserve which is to be deposited by credit organisations with the Central Bank. There is also a requirement for the minimum capital, which is currently set at 24,420,000 roubles by the Central Bank.

Although Russia is not a member of the Basel Committee, it has been represented in preparing prudential rules by the Committee. In principle, these rules are accommodated in Russian banking legislation. Instruction of the Central Bank sets out the numerical requirements on the following aspects:[42]

i)   capital adequacy ratio;
ii)   liquidity ratio;
iii)   limit of exposure to a single borrower;
iv)   maximum credit risk;
v)   maximum exposure to a single creditor;
vi)   maximum amount of credit/guarantees to insiders and shareholders;
vii)   maximum amount of bill of exchange debt;
viii)   maximum use of capital to purchase shares of other companies.

These requirements had already been in place before the 1998 crisis. However, it turned out that many banks, including a majority of the top 15 banks, had actually failed to meet these requirements. This is presumably due to the lack of transparency in the banks' accounting and lax supervision by the Central Bank. The report of the Central Bank on the inspection of banks in the first half of 1998 (i.e. the period leading to the banking crisis) revealed various violations and non-fulfilments of the prudential requirements. 'In many credit organisations, the capital was artificially inflated by an inaccurate reflection of the financial activities on the balance sheet'. 'In almost all credit organisations, the true financial state of

---

42   *Instruktsiia* of the Central Bank, No.567-U of May 27, 1999.

the borrower was not evaluated'. Arranging of security for lending was also reportedly inappropriate.[43]

The failure of the Central Bank in supervising credit organisations was duly acknowledged by the Bank in the 'Basic Directions of Unified State Monetary-Credit Policies for 2001'. The Bank declared that:

> Measures to improve the requirements for the licensing of credit organisations should be taken. Special care should be taken in analysing the financial state of the founders of the institution and examining the possible influence of interrelationship between the founders. The Bank intends to analyse more carefully the structure of the real owners of credit organisations and the capability of the institutions to implement prudential regulations after the reorganisation procedure, and assess more strictly the quality of bank management......The Bank intends to strengthen supervision so that the real state of affairs of credit organisations is reflected on the accounts and reports... Efforts should be continued to oust those banks from the market which do not have the capability to survive and whose existence in the market negatively affects the confidence of creditors and investors. Efforts to liquidate banks whose licence has been withdrawn should be strengthened.[44]

The Central Bank is empowered to inspect credit organisations and issue binding orders. In cases where credit organisations acted in breach of laws or normative acts, the Bank may demand these institutions to rectify the violation, impose fines up to 0,1% of the minimum capital, or restrict a specific activity of the institution for up to 6 months.

If the credit organisation in question fails to comply with the order of the Bank to remove violations, and also in cases where the violation or the operation by the institution created a real threat to the interest of the depositors, the Bank is empowered to:

i)   impose fines up to 1% of the paid-in capital (but less than 1% of the minimum capital);

ii)   demand the credit institution to implement measures for financial rehabilitation, including restructuring of the assets, and/or replacement of the management;

iii) change the mandatory numerical requirements for the institution for the period of up to 6 months;

iv)   prohibit the credit institution from performing banking operations included in the licence for up to 1 year or prohibit opening of a branch for the same period;

---

43   *Informatsionnoe soobshchenie* of the Central Bank, August 20, 1998.
44   The Central Bank, *Osnovnye napravleniia edinoi gosudarstvennoi denezhno-kreditnoi politili na 2001 god.*, 2001.

v)   initiate temporary administration for up to 18 months;

vi)   withdraw licence.

(Art.75, the Law on the Central Bank)

8   BANK CONFIDENTIALITY

The Law on Banks and Banking Activities protects confidentiality of banking information (*bankovskaia taina*). However, as exceptions, banks and other credit organisations are obliged to provide information on the banking operations and account details of juridical persons and individuals engaged in entrepreneurial activities to the following institutions (Art. 26):

i)   ordinary courts;

ii)   commercial courts;

iii)   Accounting Office of the Russian Federation;

iv)   Ministry of Tax and Levies and the tax police;

v)   investigating agencies with the approval of the procurator on an ongoing case.

9   RESTRUCTURING AND LIQUIDATION OF CREDIT ORGANISATIONS

In the aftermath of the banking crisis of 1998, the Law on the Insolvency of Credit Organisations was enacted in February 1999 as a special law to the Law on Insolvency.[45]

The Law provides for 1) measures for the prevention of bankruptcy of credit organisations, and 2) special rules (in relation to the general insolvency procedure) on rehabilitation and liquidation procedure for credit organisations.

Measures for the prevention of bankruptcy are (Art.3):

(a)   financial rehabilitation;

(b)   interim administration;

(c)   reorganisation.

Those measures for the prevention of bankruptcy are to be applied if the credit organisation

---

45   *SZ* 1999 No.9, item 1097.

i)   failed to satisfy a monetary claim of a client more than once in the past 6 months, and/or failed to make mandatory payments for up to three days, due to absence or insufficiency of funds in the corresponding account,

ii)   failed to satisfy a monetary claim of a client and failed to make mandatory payments for more than three days, due to absence or insufficiency of funds in the corresponding account,

iii) allowed absolute decrease of its capital by 20% as compared to the highest amount in the last 12 months and at the same time, failed to satisfy one of the numerical requirements of the Central Bank,

iv)   failed to fulfil the capital adequacy requirement, or

v)   failed to fulfil the liquidity requirement for more than 10% in the past 10 months

(Art.4).

Preventive measures are applicable only when 'defects of the activities of the credit organisations do not directly threaten the interest of creditors and depositors'.[46]

If the grounds for preventive measures emerge, the management of the credit organisation is under an obligation (under the threat of criminal penalty) to take measures (a) and/or (c). The Central Bank is empowered to demand the credit organisation in question to take those measures if any of the above grounds emerge, and also to initiate interim administration (Art.3, para.2).

(a)   Financial rehabilitation

Financial rehabilitation can take the following forms (arts. 7 and 8):

i)   granting of financial assistance to the credit organisation by the founders and other persons;

ii)   changing of the structure of assets and debts;

iii) changing of the organisational structure.

The changing of the structure of assets and debts includes improvement of loan portfolio, curtailing of costs and expenses of management, and sale of assets (Art.9). The changing of organisational structure includes shedding personnel and abolition of subdivisions and branches (Art.10).

(b)   Interim Administration

Interim administration is a procedure initiated by the Central Bank which is introduced when credit organisations:

---

46   Trofimov, *supra*, p.11.

i)   failed to satisfy a monetary claim of a client and failed to make mandatory payments for more than seven days, due to absence or insufficiency of funds in the corresponding account,

ii)   allowed absolute decrease of its capital by 30% as compared to the highest amount in the last 12 months and at the same time, failed to satisfy one of the numerical requirements of the Central Bank,

iii)   failed to fulfil the capital adequacy requirement,

iv)   failed to fulfil the liquidity requirement for more than 20% in the past month,

v)   failed to comply with the order of the Central Bank to replace the management, or to take measures of financial rehabilitation or reorganisation within the established period, or

vi)   there is a ground for withdrawal of the licence in accordance with the Law on Banks and Banking Activities (Art.17).

During the period the body of interim administration is in operation, the incumbent management's power can be restricted or suspended (Art.16). In cases where the power of the incumbent management is restricted, the interim administrator takes part in working out the measures for financial rehabilitation and supervises its implementation (Art. 21). If the power of the incumbent management is suspended, the administrator replaces the management and basically performs the function of the interim administrator under the general Law on Insolvency (Art.22).

(c)   Reorganisation

The Central Bank may demand credit organisations to reorganise themselves. Reorganisation takes the form of mergers (Art.32).

The other law in this area is the Law on the Restructuring of Credit Organisations also enacted in 1999. In fact, the Agency for the Restructuring of Credit Organisations (ARKO) was founded earlier in 1999, but its power was defined later by this Law. ARKO is a non-profit organisation – a 'state corporation' – financed by the state (Art.28).

The Law defines 'restructuring' as 'complex measures adopted by credit organisations for overcoming their financial instability and restoring capability of payment or measures for implementing the procedure for liquidation of credit organisations' (Art.2, para.1). For the purpose of implementing these measures, ARKO was created. Credit organisations can be transferred to the management of ARKO if the shortfall of the capital adequacy is less than 2%, but failed to satisfy a monetary claim of a client and/or failed to make mandatory payments for more than 7 days, due to absence or insufficiency of funds in the corresponding account (Art.3).

The Law provides for the investigation of credit organisations and their restructuring. Investigation is conducted by ARKO in order to determine the possibility of taking the given credit organisation under its management after receiving a proposal from the Central Bank (arts,6 and 7). Once ARKO accepts the proposal, it may adopt the decision to decrease the capital of the credit organisations to the level to meet the capital adequacy requirement or increase the capital (Art.10).

ARKO has the power to:

i)   take measures for financial rehabilitation of credit organisations;

ii)   increase and decrease the capital of credit organisations;

iii)   take decisions of the reorganisation of credit organisations;

iv)   sell or otherwise dispose of the shares of credit organisations which belong to ARKO;

v)   initiate an action in court for recognising transactions effected by credit organisations within the last three years as void;

vi)   extend loans, place deposits, provide security, and other financial assistance to credit organisations;

vii) implement other measures to restore the financial status of credit organisations;

viii implement procedure for liquidation of credit organisations.

(Art.14, para.1)

However, it is reported that ARKO lacks the necessary resources to complete its task, and the power struggle with the Central Bank continually impairs ARKO's work.[47]

---

47   Alexandrovich, *supra*, p.104.

13

NATURAL RESOURCES LAW

1   PRODUCTION SHARING SYSTEM V. LICENSING SYSTEM

The current Russian system for the exploration and production of natural resources takes the form of either production sharing or licensing.

The production sharing system was first introduced in Indonesia in the 1960s. Since then, it has spread to over 65 countries in the world.[1] The Russian Federation was the first among the CIS countries to enact the Production Sharing Law in 1995. Other than Russia, the Ukraine has a Production Sharing Law.

The traditional system for the exploration and production of natural resources in Russia was the licensing system. Companies were granted a licence by the government for such purposes. The basic law in this respect was the Subsoil (*nedra*) Code of the RSFSR enacted in 1976. After the collapse of socialism, a new Law on Subsoil was enacted in 1992; this Law is still in force with amendments following the enactment of the Constitution and the Law on Production Sharing in 1995.[2] The licensing system is the primary form of the exploration and development of subsoil for Russian companies, while production sharing is mostly used for projects with major foreign participation.

It was the Sakhalin 1 and 2 Oil Projects which first introduced the scheme of production sharing. These projects preceded the adoption of the Law on Production Sharing, but are 'grandfathered' by the respective contracts and the Law on Production Sharing.

The Law on Production Sharing defines production sharing as follows (Art.2, para.1):

---

1   Y.Shchukin, 'Update on PSA Legislation: A Russian Perspective', *BISNIS Bulletin*, April 2001, p.5.
2   *VSND RSFSR i VS RF*, 1992, No.16, item 834; *SZ* 1995 No.10, item 823.

Production sharing is an agreement by which the Russian Federation provides the investor on a non-gratuitous basis and for a fixed period, with an exclusive right to explore and develop natural resources in the block indicated in the agreement, and the right to carry out the work related to it at the investor's expense and risk.

This arrangement is different from the traditional scheme based upon licensing in the following ways.

Firstly, a production sharing agreement is a civil law contract between the host country and the investor(s). The present Civil Code explicitly provides for the possibility of the state entering into a contract with a private entity. The Russian Federation, constituent entities of the Russian Federation, and local self governments (municipalities) are entitled to be a party to civil law contracts (Art.124, para.1). These entities are liable under their obligation for the assets they own (Art.126, para.1).

This is in contrast with the licensing system in which the host country appears as a sovereign state vested with prerogative power.

A relationship governed by civil law is preferred by investors to a public law relationship, because in the former, the host country and the investor are on an equal footing and bilaterally bound by an agreement, whereas in the latter, there is no guarantee that the host country will not unilaterally change the arrangement, e.g. withdraw the licence. The withdrawal of a licence may be subject to court appeal, but investors have doubts about the neutrality of the national court. It is thought that in the production sharing regime, the position of the investor would be firmer than in the licensing regime.

Secondly, parties to the production sharing agreement can negotiate and agree to share the output of the project. Instead of paying various taxes and duties, except for profit tax, the investor is to simply share the products with the host government in a predetermined ratio. In this way, taxes and other payments are 'replaced by a share in the product'.[3] This effectively shields the investor from frequent changes to tax laws. Considering the number of taxes and mandatory payments at different levels and the frequent changes brought to them in Russia, this was thought to be a great advantage.

In fact, in the earlier oil projects in Russia with foreign participation based upon the licensing system, foreign investors suffered disadvantages from changes in taxes and duties as well as the instability of exemptions initially granted to them.

---

3   S.Sosna, *Kommentarii k federal'nomu zakonu o soglasheniiakh o razdele produktsii*, Moscow 1997, p.10.

Thus, the attraction of the production sharing system is that it provides the investor with a relatively stable regime in a complex and rapidly changing legal and political environment.[4]

At present, the enactment of the Law on Concession is being contemplated. In a concession contract, the state, unlike in production sharing, acts as a subject of prerogative power and grants private entities rights to perform certain activities reserved to the state such as the right to exploit natural resources for a fixed period. It is governed by administrative law, not by private law.[5] Concession was referred to in the 1991 Foreign Investment Law of the RSFSR as one of the possible forms of foreign investment. There was an abortive attempt to enact a concession law in the early 1990s. The effort has now been renewed. If enacted, the system of concession may gradually replace the present licensing system.[6]

2   ADOPTION OF THE PRODUCTION SHARING LAW AND ITS AMENDMENTS

The Production Sharing Law was enacted in 1995 after a fierce and prolonged struggle in the *Duma*. Opponents of the Law argued that the system would result in a loss of revenue to the state, based upon a misunderstanding that investors were to be granted tax exemptions and privileges. They supported the licensing regime based upon the Subsoil Law. The draft Production Sharing Law was heavily revised following proposals from the opponents, some of them being made at the last moment. The Law which was eventually adopted was a product of political compromise, and as such, was confusing and contradictory. What was more, the Law lacked consistency with the existing laws such as the Subsoil Law. Opponents of the Law endeavoured to maintain the licensing system based on the Subsoil Law. It was not surprising that a major amendment had to be contemplated shortly after its adoption.

The problem was not limited to the above. The production sharing system represents an autonomous regime. This means that it involves special rules in relation to the general rules accommodated in related laws such as the Subsoil Law, the Law on the Continental Shelf, the Law on Exclusive Economic Zones, the Water Code as well as various tax laws.

---

4   D.Slade and E.Chung, Production Sharing Legislation in the Russian Federation: A Current Assessment', *OGLTR*, 1998 issue 4, p.123.

5   I.A.Drozdov, *Dogovory na peredachu v pol'zovanie prirodnykh resursov*, Moscow 2001, pp.98-102.

6   J.Zvorykina, 'Building an Efficient Concession System for Russia', *Capital Perspective*, November-December 2001, pp.33-35.

Draft laws for the amendments to the Production Sharing Law and related laws had been submitted to the Duma in 1996, but they remained there for three years. In the meantime, several blocks were designated by law for production sharing. The delay in amending the imperfect Production Sharing Law and in removing contradictions with related laws affected existing investors heavily, and discouraged prospective investors; some companies withdrew from the planned projects. It is worth noting that the currently operating production sharing projects were all signed before the adoption of the 1995 Law.

The proposed amendment to the Production Sharing Law and related laws continued to be discussed in Parliament for two years. Finally, in 1998, a compromise was reached against the backdrop of the financial crisis in Russia which demonstrated the need for foreign investment in the oil and gas sector, and in early 1999, a major amendment to the Production Sharing Law was adopted. Shortly afterwards, the long-awaited amendments to the related laws were enacted. This was a significant step in the direction of making the system workable.

However, this was certainly not the end of the story. These amendments were not without political compromise. As can be seen below, there were indeed some positive changes such as increasing the autonomy of the production sharing regime. On the other hand, onerous requirements to foreign investors such as the local contents requirement were introduced.

Another problem is the delay in the adoption of normative acts which enables production sharing to become operational. Such delay is hampering the progress of production sharing projects. The list of enabling normative acts includes:

i)   regulations on the procedure for preparing, signing, implementing and monitoring the implementation of production sharing agreements;
ii)   rules on the commercial discovery declaration;
iii) rules on formation and the use of the liquidation fund;
iv)   rules on cost recovery;
v)   ordinance of the Ministry of Tax and Duties on the presentation of documents establishing the right of the investors to be exempted from VAT;
vii) rules on customs control.

3   AUTONOMY OF THE PRODUCTION SHARING SYSTEM

One of the biggest advantages of the production sharing system is that it constitutes a more or less independent and autonomous regime which is free from arbitrary interference by the host government. However, in Russia, this is still not fully achieved. The dualism of the production sharing and the licensing systems continues to exist, and therefore, investors in production sharing projects are still required to obtain licence from the government.

The Production Sharing Law is based upon the idea of the autonomy of the production sharing agreement, i.e. that production sharing projects should be solely regulated by the Production Sharing Law. However, the Law before the 1999 amendment referred to the Subsoil Law as follows (Art.3, para.2):

> Terms of the use of subsoil, provided by the production sharing agreement shall not contradict the requirements of the Subsoil Law.

The problem is that the Production Sharing Law requires the investor in a production sharing scheme to obtain a licence as provided by the Subsoil Law. This is not consistent with the nature of production sharing, since production sharing is supposed to be based upon a contract (a production sharing agreement) and not on a licence. The Production Sharing Law provides that the use of subsoil under a production sharing system is based upon a contract (Art.4, para.1). However, it also provides that a licence which 'certifies' the right to use subsoil is to be granted by the government within 30 days of the signing of the contract (*ibid.*, para.2). According to the Subsoil Law, the licence is a document which certifies the right to use subsoil. Therefore, technically, there is no difference in the nature of the licence in the Production Sharing Law and the Subsoil law. This requirement of a licence in a production sharing project is regarded as a major inconsistency.[7]

Investors would like to avoid having the licence revoked unilaterally by the government. In this respect, the Production Sharing Law before the 1999 amendment had provided that the licence to use subsoil was to be terminated on the grounds provided by the Production Sharing Law *and* the Subsoil Law. The Subsoil Law at that time had a fairly broad list of grounds for termination.

A related problem is the assignment of the licence. The Production Sharing Law allows the assignment of the rights and duties of the investor to a third party, subject to the consent of the state. The requirement of the consent of the host government is not uncommon. The problem was that the Law required the licence to be rewritten (Art.16, paras. 1 and 2). There was apprehension that this provision might justify the interference of the Subsoil Law with production sharing agreements.

The 1999 amendment to the Production Sharing Law marked a major step towards the strengthening of the autonomy of the production sharing regime.

First, the general provision cited above was amended as follows:

---

7   Sosna, *supra*, p. 47.

Terms of the use of subsoil established by the agreement shall coincide with Russian Legislation.

At least, specific reference to the Subsoil Law was deleted. Furthermore, the part on the termination of the licence was replaced by a new paragraph:

'The right to use subsoil blocks can be restricted, suspended, or terminated in accordance with the terms of the agreement concluded in accordance with Russian legislation.'

The Subsoil Law was also amended in this respect. It now provides that special rules on the use of subsoil on the basis of production sharing are to be established by the Law on Production Sharing (Subsoil Law, Art.1). The right to use subsoil in accordance with a production sharing agreement can be terminated, suspended or restricted on the terms and in the manner provided by the agreement (Art.20, para.3). These amendments represent an important step towards the strengthening of the autonomy of the production sharing regime.

On the other hand, there was no explicit amendment to the Production Sharing Law concerning the assignment of a licence, but the Subsoil Law was amended and a new paragraph was added (Art.17-1, para.3):

An assignment of the right to use the block to entities involved in entrepreneurial activities on the basis of production sharing and the rewriting of the licence for the use of the block shall be carried out in accordance with the Production Sharing Law.

4   PRODUCTION SHARING LAW

1)   Parties to the Production Sharing Agreement

The parties to the production sharing agreement are the Russian Federation on the one hand and investors on the other. The Russian Federation is represented by the Federal Government and the executive bodies of the constituent entities in whose territory the block is located. Investors can be Russian and foreign individuals and juridical persons, as well as a consortium of juridical persons, which, in itself does not have juridical personality (Art.3, para.1). In the latter case, provisions of the Civil Code on simple partnership are applicable. The Production Sharing Law provides that in such cases, the participants are jointly and severally liable *vis à vis* the State (*ibid.*, para.2).

The 1999 amendment introduced a new requirement in relation to the composition of the consortium.

The requirement that both the central and the local government should represent the host government – the 'dual key' system – emanates from the Constitution which provides that the Federation and the constituent entities jointly decide on the issues of possession, use and disposal of subsoil. The Sakhalin 1 and 2 agreements were signed by the President and the Governor of Sakhalin Province. In practice, the relationship between the Russian government and the government of the constituent entities is often complicated. This may cause problems for investors, and in order to simplify the matter, a body called the authorised state body is set up on the Russian side for each project.

For the coordination of activities related to production sharing, a government committee for coordinating the activities of the federal executive bodies and the constituent entities was set up in 1997. This committee comprises the representatives of the Ministry of Energy, the Ministry of Natural Resources, the Ministry of Tax and Duties, the Ministry of Foreign Economic Relations and Trade, and the Customs Committee. The tasks of this committee include the review of the list of blocks offered for production sharing and the examination of the actual projects before they are submitted to the government and also the coordination of the activities of the central and local governments and investors in implementing production sharing agreements.[8]

2)   Blocks Available for Production Sharing

The list of blocks which are offered for production sharing, as a rule, must be established by law. Only small blocks can be made available on the basis of the decision of the government. Thus far, there are around 25 blocks available for production sharing.

The grounds for including a block in the list include the following (Art.2, para.4):

i)   absence of financial and technological resources for a new large field of minerals, from the utilisation of which the level of exploitation of minerals in the Russian Federation as a whole necessary for the social and economic security of the nation, and also for the construction of production infrastructure, particularly in the continental shelf in the remote and deprived regions, is ensured;

ii)   necessity of introducing high cost technology for the exploitation of difficult-to-develop minerals which exist in the complex mineral-geological conditions and which are as yet left undeveloped;

---

8   Edict of the Government of September 2, 1997 [Inforis].

iii)   necessity for the region to have its own fuel-energy resources, the creation of
        new jobs, or the ensuring of optimal social-economical conditions for under-
        developed regions where the employment level is low;
iv)   existence of the obligation on the part of the Russian Federation for conducting
        negotiations on the terms of the agreement and the existence of the outcome of
        the tender or auction for the offering of a block of minerals for use by production
        sharing.

An important change in the direction of limiting production sharing was introduced
by the 1999 amendment. There is now a 'cap' on the total amount of reserves
to be offered for production sharing. The current law provides that the reserves
offered for production sharing shall not exceed 30% of the reserves of minerals
prospected and accounted for by the state (Art.2, para.3).

This 30% figure has been criticised as arbitrary. When the amendments were
discussed, a 10% limit for strategic resources and 20% limit for other resources
had been proposed; there was no economic rationale for such figures. Besides,
the denominator – the total reserve accounted for by the government, is not
available to the public. The register of reserves itself is based upon the Subsoil
Law. For every type of mineral in each field, a register which contains information
of the size of the reserve, its quality, the extent of development etc., is prepared.
At the time of the amendment, it was pointed out that with around 25 blocks to
be offered, the 30% limit would be almost exhausted. In the discussion for further
amendments to the Law, there is a proposal to increase this percentage to 40%
or to exclude the existing projects from it.[9]

3)   Procedure for the Conclusion of a Production Sharing Agreement

In principle, a production sharing agreement is concluded on the basis of tender
or auction. Exceptions to this requirement include the following (Art.6, para.2):

i)   the interest of defence or security of the state requires the agreement to be con-
        cluded with a specific investor;
ii)   the announced tender or auction failed because there was only one bidder;
iii)   the investor is a user of subsoil before the exploration and development of useful
        minerals under other terms based upon Russian law.

---

9   M.Subbotin, 'Aktual'nye problemy sovershenstvovaniia zakonodatel'stva o soglasheniiakh o razdele
     produktsii', paper submitted to the conference 'Oil, Gas and Law' on November 14-15, Moscow.

The last exception means that if an investor has a licence under the Subsoil law and has been involved in the exploration and development of subsoil in the block, this investor is entitled to negotiate a production sharing agreement without tender or auction. In such cases, the agreement can be concluded with this particular investor, or other juridical persons or a consortium of juridical persons established with the participation of this investor. Such juridical persons and their consortium are to be determined by the edict of the Russian government.

The procedure for preparing a production sharing agreement is not regulated in detail at the moment. Terms of the use of subsoil and the draft agreement for each object of subsoil use are prepared by a government committee with the consent of the executive body of the appropriate constituent entity.

The agreement is signed by the central and the local government, but in projects which involve blocks which are on the continental shelf and/or in the exclusive economic zone, the government of the Russian Federation signs the agreement with the consent of the executive body of the relevant constituent entity.

It is important to note that agreements involving a block of subsoil on the continental shelf and/or in the exclusive economic zone as well as agreements concluded without tender or auction must be confirmed by federal law, i.e. have to be approved by the parliament (Art.6, para.1). This is because of the desire of the parliament to keep control of the projects destined for production sharing.

Despite some positive developments since 1999, the procedure for realising production sharing projects or any natural resources project is poorly regulated and is excessively complicated. Various permissions are required before concluding the production sharing agreement. For example, if the project involves the use of the continental shelf, separate permissions are required for building artificial islands, installations and facilities (Law on the Continental Shelf, arts.16-20). For the use of public land, which is almost inevitable, the Land Code provides for a procedure to obtain permission and have the land allocated. Streamlining of the procedure for obtaining various permissions is now being planned.

4)   Terms of the Production Sharing Agreements – Obligations of the Investor

By the 1999 amendment to the Production Sharing Law, some onerous requirements on the investor have been introduced (Art.7, para.2).

First, for participation in the project as subcontractors, suppliers, and transporters, Russian juridical persons are to be given preferential rights. This provision had already been in the Law before the 1999 amendment, but there, the preferential right was limited to instances where 'other terms were the same'. This meant that Russian companies were to be preferred only when the terms offered by them were the same as those offered by foreign companies. This part of the provision was dropped by the 1999 amendment. Now, even when Russian companies offer less advantageous terms, they will be preferred to foreign companies.

Second, a minimum of 80% of the workers in the project must be Russian nationals. The recruitment of foreign workers and specialists is allowed only at an early stage of the project by agreement, or in cases where there are no workers and specialists who are Russian nationals.

Third, there is a local content requirement; 70% of the total value of the orders for equipment and materials for geological exploration, production and preliminary refinement of useful minerals must go to Russian juridical persons or foreign juridical persons engaged in entrepreneurial activities in Russia and registered as taxpayers.

Fourth, when carrying out a project in the territory where ethnic minorities lead their traditional life and conduct economic activities, measures provided by Federal Law for the protection of their lifestyle must be taken by investors, and furthermore, compensation must be paid.

Investors are also under an obligation to:

i)   implement measures for the prevention of any harmful influence on the environment and eliminate the outcome of such an influence;

ii)   take out insurance for the compensation payable for the potential damage to the environment;

iii) liquidate all installations, structures and other assets after completion of the work based upon the agreement and clean up the environment.

5)   Cost Recovery, Production Sharing and Taxes

The produced natural resources are shared between the state and the investors. Normally, in production sharing agreements, the products are divided into several portions. The first portion is allocated to the host country as a 'royalty production'. This varies between 10 to 15%. The second portion is the cost recovery production, which the investor is entitled to. This part is designed to cover the cost incurred by the investor. The third portion is the profit production which is to be shared by the parties.[10]

---

10   B.Taverne, 'Production Sharing Agreements in Principle and in Practice', M.R,David ed., *Upstream Oil and Gas Agreements*, London 1996, p.81.

The Russian Production Sharing Law has a provision on profit production and compensation (cost) production. There is no royalty production; royalty is payable separately at the time of the conclusion of the contract.

The Law provides that profit production is shared between the state and the investor in accordance with the production sharing agreement (Art.8). The agreement accommodates the terms and procedure for determining, *inter alia*, the total amount of production and its value, the cost production portion, and the sharing of profit production. It is also possible to agree on different methods of production sharing – e.g., direct sharing which was introduced to the Law by the 2001 amendment (Art.8, para.2).

The investor has the title to the cost production and his part of the profit production. It is important to note that mineral resources which have been transferred to the investor can be used as collateral.

As mentioned earlier, in a production sharing scheme, the payment of taxes and other mandatory payments is replaced by the sharing of the production, i.e. profit production. In this regards, the Russian Production Sharing Law provides that with the exception of profit tax and unified social tax, the investor is exempted from taxes and duties for the period of the agreement.

The 2001 amendment to the Production Sharing Law introduced another method of production sharing – direct sharing. In this scheme, the investor is exempted from all taxes and duties except the unified social tax and regional and local taxes and duties provided by the Tax Code. The main difference with the ordinary method is that the investor is exempt from profit tax (Art.13, para.1).

Value added tax is payable in the ordinary production sharing, since it is technically difficult to exempt the investor from value added tax on the purchase of each and every purchase of goods and services, but it is to be reimbursed. There was a confusing provision in the Production Sharing Law on reimbursement and investors in the existing production sharing projects had difficulties in having the value added tax reimbursed. This was replaced by a new paragraph which simply leaves the matter to the Tax Code (Art.13, para.3).

Investors are still subject to the following payments:

i)   bonuses at the time of the conclusion of the agreement and/or the achievement of a certain result;
ii)   rentals (annual payment for the prospecting and exploration work);
iii)   royalties, determined as a percentage of the amount of production or to the value of the production;
iv)   payment for the use of land and other natural resources.

In addition, excise is payable on the sale of the production. Furthermore, if the project involves the use of the continental shelf, payment for the use of the continental shelf is required (Law on the Continental Shelf, Art.40).

In July 2001, Chapter 26 of the Tax Code Part Two, which covers the 'tax on the exploitation of mineral resources' was enacted. A special regime for production sharing is acknowledged in this Chapter (Art.346).

6)   The Right to Export the Production and Access to the Pipeline

The share of the production to which the investor is entitled can be exported in accordance with the terms and manner determined by the production sharing agreement without being subject to quotas (Art.9, para.2). In the past, there were restrictions on the export of 'strategic materials' which included oil and gas. This provision seemingly benefits investors, but it should be noted that this is subject to the Law on the State Regulation of Foreign Economic Activities which allows the introduction of export quotas under certain circumstances.

This Law, which was enacted in 1997, empowers the government to impose restrictions on the export and import of goods.[11] It allows the government to introduce quota restrictions on export and import on the grounds of national security and the protection of the domestic market (Art. 15). Export and import can also be prohibited or restricted on grounds including the necessity of preventing exhaustion of irreplaceable resources (Art. 19). However, whether this Law is compatible with the WTO regime, if Russia is to join, is questionable.

The Production Sharing Law guarantees the access of the investor to the oil and gas pipeline on a contractual basis. Under the current system in Russia, trunk oil pipelines are owned and managed by a single company – Joint Stock Company Transneft. Transneft manages, services and develops the trunk pipeline system. The company is charged with ensuring the transport of crude oil in appropriate volumes and by routes specified in the transportation (export) schedule prepared by the Government Inter-Ministerial Committee. The schedule is based upon annual transport contracts which producing companies negotiate with Transneft. The contracts specify the amount and quality of crude oil to be transported, the starting and final points of shipping, routes, and the terms and schedule of payment. Quarterly and monthly allotments are calculated using the oil companies' certificates of their own annual production.

The same applies to gas pipelines, which are owned by Gazprom.

---

11   *RG*, July 12, 1997.

In reality, access to the oil pipelines was not always easy for foreign operators due to the pressure on Transneft by Russian oil companies. The system of allocating the pipeline capacity is not transparent, due to the bias towards the government-backed programmes and all sorts of side deals.

Incidentally, Transneft is a company which is regarded as a 'natural monopoly' and therefore, although the Production Sharing Law provides for a 'contractual basis', the tariff for the transportation will have to be set by the government. There has been a proposal to enact a law on the use of trunk pipelines, but this has not been realised.

Responding to the pressure by oil producing companies to improve export route access, Transneft adopted 'The Concept for Future Development of Trunk Pipelines in Russia' in 1999.[12]

7)   Stability of the Production Sharing Agreement – Grandfather clause

One of the important reasons for investors preferring production sharing to conventional licensing schemes lies in its relative stability achieved by eliminating the possible changes in law and unilateral action by the host government.

The Production Sharing Law provides that:

> Terms of the agreement maintain their effect for the entire period of the validity of the agreement. Changes to the agreement are allowed only by the consent of both parties except by the request of one of the parties in cases of significant changes of circumstances in accordance with the Civil Code (Art.17, para.1).

Furthermore, the Law has a 'grandfather clause' which provides as follows (Art.17, para.2):

> If, within the period of the validity of the production sharing agreement, a norm which worsens the commercial outcome of the activities within the framework of production sharing is established by the legislation of the Russian Federation, its constituent entities or legal acts of the local self-governments, the agreement shall be revised as though the commercial outcome which the investor could have received had the legislation of the Russian Federation, its constituent entities or legal acts of the local self-governments valid at the time of the conclusion of the agreement had been applicable. Manners of introducing such changes shall be determined by the agreement.

---

12   N.Mikhailov, 'Russia's Pipeline System and Oil and Gas Transportation Projects', *Bisnis internet*, August 2000 [www.bisnis.doc.gov].

It should be noted that this provision is not applicable if the changes involve requirements for the safety of work, the protection of subsoil, the environment and the health of the inhabitants.

Afterwards, a similar provision was introduced in the Foreign Investment Law by the amendment of 1999. The amended Law defers for seven years the application of subsequent laws which would:

i)   change taxes, customs duties, or extra-budgetary contributions;
ii)   increase the total tax burden of a foreign investment project;
iii)   introduce a more restrictive investment regime.

However, this provision is applicable only to 'priority investment projects', i.e. projects over 100 million roubles included in the list prepared by the government.

8)   Dispute Resolution

The Production Sharing Law provides that disputes between the State and the investor concerning the implementation, termination and validity of the production sharing agreement shall be resolved by the ordinary court, the commercial court and arbitration institutions (*treteiskii sud*). The latter includes foreign commercial arbitration institutions (Art.22). Some production sharing agreements provide for arbitration in Stockholm.

5   SUBSOIL LAW

While production sharing will probably be the primary form of large natural resources projects with foreign participation, there may still be other projects based upon the licensing system. The Subsoil Law will remain the basic law for such projects. Furthermore, this Law contains some provisions which are relevant to all kinds of use of subsoil.

The Production Sharing Law provides that relations which are not regulated by the Law, including relations emerging from the use of land and other natural resources, shall be governed by the Subsoil Law and other legal acts of the Russian Federation. On the other hand, relations which emerge from prospecting, exploration and the development of mineral resources, the sharing of productions, as well as transportation, refinement, storage, use, sale and other means of disposal, are to be regulated by the production sharing agreement (Production Sharing Law, Art.2, para.2).

In this respect, at least the provisions of the Subsoil Law which provide for the 'rational use and protection of subsoil' as obligations of the subsoil user seem to be applicable to production sharing projects.

The Subsoil Law has a provision on the ownership of the subsoil. Subsoil in the territory of the Russian Federation and useful natural resources, energy resources etc. are state properties. Problems of possession, use and disposal of subsoil fall within the joint jurisdiction of the Russian Federation and the constituent entities. Blocks of subsoil may not be sold, donated, inherited, invested, pledged, or disposed of in any other manner. On the other hand, the right to use subsoil can be assigned or transferred to another party insofar as federal laws allow their circulation. In contrast with unextracted resources, resources which have been extracted may remain under the ownership of the state, constituent entities, and the municipality as well as to private entities (Subsoil Law, Art.1-2).

The subsoil Law provides for the payment for the use of subsoil resources. In addition, there is a payment for the reproduction of a mineral basis (Art.39). Chapter 26 of the Tax Code still retains this payment, but a special regime for production sharing is available.

The Subsoil Law also provides for grounds for early termination of the licence which include:

i)   breach on the part of the licencee of essential terms of the licence;
ii)   repeated violations of rules by the licencee for the use of subsoil;
iii)   occurrence of an emergency situation such as an epidemic and military action;
iv)   failure on the part of the licencee to commence the use of subsoil on a pre-agreed scale;
v)   liquidation of the licencee.

(Art.20)

Termination of the production sharing agreements is governed by the Production Sharing Law, and not the Subsoil Law.

It should be added that the provision on dispute settlement involving the use of subsoil previously did not acknowledge commercial arbitration. By a subsequent amendment, commercial arbitration was added as an alternative (Art.50).

6   NATURAL RESOURCES PROJECTS AND THE ENVIRONMENT

One of the basic requirements towards the users (licensees) of natural resources is the protection of environment. The Subsoil Law lists the 'prevention of pollution of the subsoil, particularly by storing oil and gas and other toxic substances underground, or abandoning harmful substances and waste of production as well as waste water' as an obligation of the licensee (Art.23, para.1, (8)). Prevention of harmful effects on the environment and the removal of the result of such effects are also obligations of the investor under the Production Sharing Law (Art.7, para.2).

In one of the production sharing projects, the disposal of waste from drilling was found by environmental assessment as harmful on a protected species of fish. There was also a lawsuit by an environmental group when the government allowed the project to go ahead. In the end, investors were required to spend a significant amount to dispose of these wastes without affecting the environment.

The basic law on environmental protection is the Law on the Protection of Natural Environment of 1991. In addition, laws such as the Land Code, the Water Code, the Forestry Code, the Law on the Continental Shelf, and the Law on the Protection of Atmosphere provide for environmental protection.[13]

The actual environmental standards (*predel'no dodopustimye kolichestvo*) are set by normative acts enacted by the Ministry of Natural Resources (which absorbed the former State Committee of Ecology) in consultation with relevant agencies.

The Law on the Protection of the Natural Environment has a set of provisions which deals with the basic requirements as to the siting, planning, construction, reconstruction, commencing of exploitation and exploitation of enterprises, installations and other objects (arts. 40-44).

For the construction and reconstruction of these objects, an environmental review (*ekologicheskaia ekspertiza*; environmental impact assessment) is required.[14] The Law on the Protection of the Natural Environment provides that in siting, a technical and economic justification of the project, design, construction, reconstruction, introduction into operation of enterprises and installations in the area of industry, agriculture, transport, energy, water and communal industry, or when building electric and telephone lines and pipelines, building canals and other objects which directly or indirectly affect the environment, the requirement for the environmental safety as well as for the protection of the health of inhabitants should be met and measures for the protection of nature, rational utilization and reproduction of natural resources and rehabilitation of the natural environment should be taken (Art.40, para.1). For this purpose, financing and working of all projects and programmes require a positive conclusion of the environmental review (Art.36, para.2).

---

13   See *Ekologicheskoe pravo: sbornik normativnykh aktov*, Moscow 1998.
14   S.Bogoliubov, *Ekologicheskoe pravo*, Moscow 1999, pp.176-185.

Environmental review is regulated by the Law on Environmental Review of 1995.[15] Environmental review at the federal level covers 'technical and economic basis and design of construction, reconstruction, expansion, technical refurbishment, conservation and liquidation of objects of economic activities, regardless of administrative subordination or the form of ownership which encompass more than two constituent entities'. Construction of objects with foreign investment which exceeds 500,000 US dollars as well as production sharing projects are also subject to review at the federal level (Art.11).

State environmental review at the federal level is conducted by an expert committee comprising independent experts appointed for each particular case by the Ministry of Natural Resources. The environmental review is not immune from outside pressure:

> In the environmental review of the project for a high speed train link between Moscow and St.Petersburg, there was allegedly psychological pressure from those specialists who prepared the technical and economic basis (TEO) of the project and the head of the train company on members of the expert committee. The conclusion of the committee was appealed to the Federal Procuracy which made some recommendations to the Ministry.[16]

In order to apply for the review, the entrepreneur is required to have obtained a positive conclusion or consent from supervisory agencies at various levels. These include permissions from various central and local administrative agencies. The number of such permissions and licences can be large. Furthermore, the site has to be determined and allocated by the local government, based upon the Land Code. The government is currently working on the simplification of the procedure for obtaining these permissions and licences.

There is a general presumption that any planned economic activity is potentially dangerous to the environment (Art.3). The focus of the review is the 'technical and economic basis (TEO)' of the project which is commissioned by the entrepreneur and submitted to the expert committee.

The time needed for the review depends upon the complexity of the case, but may not exceed 6 months (Art.14). The cost of the review is borne by the entrepreneur (Art.28, para.1).

Individuals as well as organizations may conduct their own 'social' environmental review as contrasted with the state environmental review before or simultaneously with the state environmental review. The conclusion is submitted to the Ministry of Natural Resources, and once granted legal effect by the latter, it

---

15 *SZ RF* 1995 No.48, item 4556.
16 M.M.Brinchuk, *Ekologicheskoe pravo*, Moscow 1998, p.329.

is forwarded to relevant parties (Art.25). The cost is borne by the individual or the organization (Art.29).

There is a separate set of rules applicable to environmental impact assessment for construction of objects in projects with foreign participation required by the decision of the Ministry of Construction.[17]

Conclusions of these commissions are published in the official gazette.

In the review of the draft agreement for the development of Komsomol'sk oil field on a production sharing basis, the expert committee examined the possible impact of the project on the environment. It was pointed out that the production and transportation of hydrocarbon fall within the category of high environmental risks with the probability of accidents. The project failed to take into account Russian legislation in the area of environmental protection. The contract lacks a clause which provides for the obligations of the investors to take measures for the prevention of harmful effect on the environment and the removal of such an effect. After examining the technical and economic justification of the project, the expert committee found the operator to be unsuitable. In conclusion, the basic goal and concepts of the project were positively appraised by the committee, but a revision of the draft agreement was recommended.[18]

For the breach of environmental law, disciplinary, criminal and civil liability is applicable. Persons who are engaged in activities involving increased danger to the environment have an aggravated burden to prove that they had not acted by intention or negligence.

---

17   Decision of the Ministry of Construction, February 16, 1995
18   Order of State Commission on Ecology, No.24, January 28,1997. [Inforis].

14

TAXATION

1   HISTORICAL BACKGROUND

The system of taxation in Russia was abolished after the October Revolution, but was restored in the 1920s in the period of the New Economic policy. After the completion of the 'socialist industrialisation' in the 1930s, corporate tax was gradually replaced by 'income from the socialist economy'. With the overall '*étatisation*' of the economy, 'direct administrative methods' were used for siphoning off the profits of state enterprises and redistributing them through the budget. On the other hand, indirect tax in the form of circulation tax (*nalog s oborota*) occupied a significant part of the income of the state. It was only towards the end of socialism when individuals were officially allowed to be involved in entrepreneurial activities as individual entrepreneurs or members of a cooperative that direct tax on individuals was introduced in a large scale.[1]

At the end of 1991, Russia embarked on the path of fiscal reform. New taxes were introduced in succession. These included the tax on the profit of enterprises and organisations, value added tax, and individual income tax. In the same year, a brief Law on the Fundamental Principles of the Taxation System was enacted.[2]

The tax system in Russia has been notorious for its failings which include:

i)   an excessively large number of federal and local taxes;
ii)   frequent changes in the law and its interpretation;
iii)   broad taxable basis and narrow scope of deductible expenses;
iv)   vague and contradictory provisions of tax laws;
v)   poor and often unfair enforcement.

---

[1]   D.G.Chernik, *Nalogi*, Moscow 1994, p.31; A.Ia.Sukharev ed., *Iuridicheskii entsiklopedicheskii slovar'*, Moscow 1984, p.183; I.I.Kucherov, *Nalogovoe pravo Rossii*, Moscow 2001, pp.17-21.

[2]   *VSND RF i VS RF*, 1992 No.12, item 604.

An OECD report pointed out as follows:

> Russia's tax system has performed very poorly since its creation in 1991 for a number
> of reasons. To start with, it is a cumbersome system. The nominal tax rates are very
> high. There are numerous exemptions for a wide range of favourably treated taxpayers.
> Emergency tax commonly involves draconian penalties, but these penalties are applied
> at the discretion of the officials. The entire system is open to abuse and corruption.
> Regional authorities routinely issue guidelines that contradict centrally issued instructions,
> where the latter exist. In the absence of clear legislation and procedure, tax inspectors
> have tended to act autonomously, leading to a very uneven treatment of taxpayers…
> Not surprisingly, the outcome is a tax system which fails to produce adequate revenue
> to government. Furthermore, it impedes growth, puts off foreign and domestic capital
> and drives investment under ground.[3]

Indeed, at the initial stage, government policy was to make the taxable basis as broad as possible. Various kinds of federal taxes were introduced; the number reached fifty at one stage. In addition, there were seventy regional and local taxes.[4]

The quality of the tax laws introduced in the early 1990s was far from perfect. They were prepared only in several months and amendments had to be contemplated immediately after their enactment and before their taking of effect. Shortage of time, absence of knowledge of international experience in shaping the tax system, and uncertainty of the future course of structural reform of the economy were the primary cause of such defective legislation.[5] Various changes which, between 1992 and 1998, were introduced every year in the tax legislation merely succeeded in solving some partial problems, but failed to address fundamental issues. The system was simply characterised as 'unstable and unpredictable' and gave rise to severe criticism from Russian companies as well as foreign investors.[6]

For most of the time since1991, the system was regulated not only by laws, but by over one thousand subordinate acts, i.e. edicts of the government, instructions, letters, explanations of the tax authorities. Due to the sheer number of these acts, it was difficult to be guided by them in a specific case. Interested parties contested the validity of such subordinate acts in the Constitutional Court and the Supreme Court; in some cases, the courts acknowledged their incompatibility with the law, and even the Constitution.

---

3   *OECD Observer*, No.215, January 1999.
4   Kucherov, *supra*, p.22-23.
5   S.D.Shatalov, *Razvitie nalogovoi sistemy Rossii*, Moscow 2000, p.10.
6   *Ibid.*, p.11.

The lack of stability in the tax regime has affected foreign investors particularly in the first half of the 1990s. In one of the first oil projects in Russian with foreign investment – Polar Lights – the original three taxes increased to 22 with the Russian government's take quadrupling. Moreover, there was even an attempt by the local government to take the foreign investor to court for not paying a mineral reproduction tax from which it was exempted in the original licence.[7]

The need for a comprehensive Tax Code had been acknowledged in Russia for some time. As the market economy developed in Russia, it became obvious that the inadequate tax system was an obstacle to the economic development of the country. Since 1996, several versions of the draft Tax Code were submitted to Parliament by the government. However, since the government proposals affected the interest of powerful lobbying groups, Parliament, under various pretexts, delayed the discussion and the adoption of these drafts.[8]

In the end, the government split the Code in two parts. The draft Tax Code (parts One and Two) went through its first reading in April 1998, but only Part One was adopted in July 1998 and came into force in January 1999. Part One of the Code covers the basic system of taxation, rights and duties of tax payers and other parties such as tax agents, and the power of the tax authorities and the procedure of discharging the duties by them. The enactment of Part Two, which covers specific taxes, took more time. Four chapters of Part Two (individual income tax, unified social tax, value added tax and excise) were adopted in July 2000. In July 2001, the Chapter on profit tax was adopted. Other chapters of Part Two, including chapters on tax on mineral resources and sales tax followed. In the meantime, Part One of the Code has already been amended.[9]

Despite the fact that the draft Tax Code had been somewhat 'watered down' by Parliament and some important provisions and novelties lost and doubtful provisions added in the process, the Code clearly defined the rights and duties of the 'partcipants' in tax relations, and introduced provisions on the process of tax payment and control.[10]

---

7   *The Russia Journal*, June 5, 2000.
8   Shatarov, *supra*, p.14.
9   A good overview of the system is given in A.Taferner, 'Tax Reform – Act II', *European Taxation*, February 2001, pp.48-60.
10 Shatarov, *supra*, p.15.

2   SOURCES OF TAX LAW

The Code provides that tax legislation in Russia comprises the Tax Code and other federal laws enacted in accordance with the Code and furthermore, laws and normative acts of the constituent entities of the Federation as well as the normative acts of the local self-governments (Art.1).

It is worth noting that while the federal laws are required to comply with the Code, such a provision is conspicuously missing for the laws and normative acts of constituent entities of the Federation and local self governments. Considering the fact that regional governments and local self-governments often acted against the federal law, the absence of an accurate provision regulating the relationship between various levels of law may be detrimental.

Concerning the relationship between laws and normative acts enacted by administrative agencies, the Code empowers the federal executive (administrative) agencies and executive agencies of the constituent entities and the local self-governments to enact normative acts on taxation. In addition, the Ministry of Taxes and Levies, Ministry of Finance and State Customs Committee may issue binding orders, instructions and methodical guidance.

The Code expressly provides that these acts may not modify or supplement the law (Art.4). In practice, these agencies often amended or supplemented the laws by way of 'explanations' and other instruments, particularly in relation to the objects of taxation. Although this was against the law even before the enactment of the Code, it is hoped that the new provision would be an effective means of combating such practice.[11]

The Code lists examples of contradictions between the law and subordinate normative acts such as acts adopted by an entity which does not have such a power under the Code, revocation or limitation of rights of tax payers provided by the Code as well as acts which contradict the general principles of the Code. These acts are to be acknowledged as against the Code by court procedure, but the Federal Government and the agencies which adopted such an act, as well as their superior agencies may revoke these acts before the court procedure (Art.6).

However, although the Code provides for the subordination of the normative acts to the Code, the actual remit of various level of the power in enacting these acts is not clear. This will significantly reduce the effect of this provision.

---

11   A.M.Zrdelevskii, *Kommentarii k chasti pervoi nalogovogo kodeksa RF*, Moscow 2000, pp.33-34.

3   TAXES AND LEVIES

The Tax Code covers 'taxes and levies (*sbor*)'. Tax is defined in the Code as a 'mandatory, individual and non-gratuitous payment collected from organisations and individuals in the form of alienating the money which belongs to them for the purpose of financing the activities of the state and/or local governments'. Levies are defined as 'mandatory payments collected from organisations and physical persons which is one of the conditions of the state agencies, local government agencies and other entities as well as officials for performing juridical significant acts for the benefit of payers of levies' (Art.8).

In order to create a tax, the scope of tax payers as well as the essential elements of the given tax have to be determined. These include the object of tax (e.g. profit, assets, income etc.), taxable basis, taxable period, tax rate, methods of calculating tax, methods and terms of tax payment (Art.17).

There are three layers of taxation in Russia; federal, regional, and local. In addition to the federal tax, constituent entities of the Russian Federation as well as local self governments are empowered to create taxes (Constitution Art.132). Taxes and levies established by constituent entities are called 'regional', while those created by local self governments are called 'local' by the Tax Code. The Tax Code provides that federal taxes and levies are created, modified and abolished by the Tax Code. Regional and local taxes and levies are created, modified and abolished by the laws of the constituent entities on taxes and levies and normative legal acts of the local self-governments respectively (Art.3, para.5). Regional and local taxes which are not listed in the Tax Code cannot be created (Art.12, para.5). This is an important step towards certainty and stability in the system.

As late as May 2000, there were 24 federal taxes, 6 regional taxes, and 26 local taxes.[12] The Tax Code is intended to introduce some order to the system of taxation. Part One lists the following taxes at various levels:

(a) Federal Taxes and Levies (Art.13)

    i)   value added tax;
    ii)   excise on specific goods, services, and mineral resources;
    iii)   tax on profits (income) of organisations;
    iv)   capital income tax;
    v)   individual income tax;
    vi)   payment to the state social extra budgetary fund;
    vii)   state fees (*poshilina*);

---

12   *EiZh*, No.21, May 2000.

viii)   customs duties;
ix)   tax on the use of subsoil;
x)   tax on the reproduction of mineral resources;
xi)   tax on the supplementary income from the exploration of hydrocarbon;
xii)   levies on the right to use the objects of stock raising and water with biological resources;
xiii)   forestry tax;
xiv)   ecological tax;
xv)   federal licensing fees.

(b) Regional Taxes and Levies (Art.14)

i)   tax on the assets of organisations;
ii)   tax on immovables;
iii)   road tax;
iv)   transport tax;
v)   sales tax;
vi)   tax on wagering business;
vii)   regional licensing fees.

(c) Local Taxes and Levies (Art.15)

i)   land tax;
ii)   tax on the assets of individuals;
iii)   advertising tax;
iv)   inheritance and gift tax;
v)   local licensing fees.

Until Part Two of the Code came into force, these provisions were not to take effect and instead, equivalent provisions of the 1991 Fundamental Principles of the Taxation System were applicable. Rearrangement of the present taxes was to take place in the meantime. Part Two of the Tax Code failed to be enacted in one piece; in 2000, four chapters of Part Two were enacted first. Some other chapters followed in 2001.

The above list did not necessarily match the relevant chapters of the Tax Code Part Two. For example, the payment to the social extra budgetary funds has been replaced by a unified social tax in Part Two. Chapter 24 on the profit tax of organisations which was enacted in 2001 replaced the income tax of organisations. Capital income tax is likely to be made part of the profit tax and individual income tax.[13] The tax on immovables is to replace the present taxes on assets of organisations and individuals as well as land tax, but this has not taken place yet.

4   BASIC PRINCIPLES AND RULES OF TAXATION

The Code sets out basic principles of taxation which include the following (Art.4):

i)   universality and equality of taxation;

ii)   non-discriminatory nature of taxation (prohibition of applying different rates of tax, providing of privileges based upon the form of ownership, citizenship, or place of location);

iii)   prohibition of taxation which inhibits the realisation by individuals of their constitutional rights;

iv)   prohibition of arbitrary taxation – requirement of 'economic rational' for taxation;

v)   requirement of accuracy and specificity of tax laws;

vi)   interpretation of laws in favour of tax payers in case of irremovable doubt on the interpretation, contradiction, or ambiguity of the tax law.

Russian tax law has not always been fair and non-discriminatory. In the early 1990s, by presidential decrees, some favoured organisations such as the Russian Sports Foundation were exclusively granted tax privileges which amounted to full exemption from taxes, excises, and customs tariff. The result was that these organisations quickly established a monopoly over the importation of alcohol products, cigarettes and cars from abroad and reinforced their influence over the other sectors of the economy. The government lost a significant amount of income until these privileges were finally taken away.[14]

The principle of non-discrimination does not, however, exclude tax privileges or a 'special regime'. Concerning privileges, the Code defines privilege as a preferential treatment of a specific category of tax payers, including full exemption from tax payment. Privileges are available under the Code, but should not have an 'individual character' such as in the case of the above-mentioned Sports Foundation (Art.56). In fact, the Code in its original 1998 version had allowed individual privileges in 'exceptional circumstances', but this paragraph was deleted by the amendment of July 1999.

It is not clear from the Code whether tax privileges should be based upon law or not. The reference to 'legislative acts' in the Code seems to suggest that

---

13   Kucherov, *supra*, p.64.
14   Shatarov, *supra*, p.7.

it does not have to be law, but can also be government edicts and presidential decrees.

The Code also provides for special tax regimes. A special tax regime is defined by the Code as a 'special method of calculation and payment of taxes and levies for a specific period of time'. Special regimes are applicable in cases provided by the Code and other federal laws (Art.18). Special regimes under the Code are simplified procedure of taxation for small businesses, taxation in special economic zones, taxation in closed administrative territorial divisions, and taxation for the enforcement of concession contracts and production sharing agreements. This list is conclusive (Art.18). At present, a special regime of taxation is available to production sharing agreements.

Concerning the stability of the tax regime, the Code provides that legislative acts on taxation which establish a new tax or levy raising the tax rate, increasing the amount of levies, establishing liability or increasing liability for violations of tax law, or by other means worsening the position of tax payers and payers of levies, would not have retrospective effect (Art.5, para.2).

Legislative acts on tax take effect only after 1 month of their official publication and after the end of the first tax period of the tax in question. Federal laws, laws of the constituent entities and acts of the representative bodies of the local self government which amend or supplement the Tax Code by establishing a new tax or levy may not enter into force before the January 1st of the following year, and not before 1 month after its adoption (Art.5, para.1).

5   TAX AGENCY

The agency which is in charge of collecting taxes and levies in Russia is the Ministry of Taxes and Levies (previously, the Federal Tax Services). In cases empowered by law, the State Customs Committee and the State Extra-Budget Fund also exercise the power of tax agencies (Art.30). The Statute of the Ministry is yet to be enacted. The power of the Ministry includes the right to:

i)   request documents which serve as a basis of calculation and payment of taxes and also explanation and supporting documents for the correctness of the calculation and payment of taxes from tax payers and agents;
ii)   conduct tax inspections;
iii)   seize documents which prove the violation of tax laws;
iv)   summon tax payers and agents for questioning in relation to payment of tax or tax inspection;
v)   suspend bank transactions of tax payers and agents and seize their assets in accordance with the procedure set by the Code;

vi)   search the business premises of the tax payers and prepare an inventory of the assets;

vii)   demand tax payers and agent to rectify the violation of tax law and supervise the implementation;

viii)   collect unpaid taxes and levies as well as penalties (*pen'*);

ix)   monitor large expenditure of individuals and their resources;

x)   request from banks documents supporting the entrusted payment of taxes;

xi)   summon witnesses for questioning;

xii)   present petitions for revocation or suspension of license for performing certain kinds of activities;

xiii)   initiate an action at the ordinary court and commercial court for:

> (a) applying punitive sanctions for violation of tax laws;
>
> (b) acknowledging registration of juridical persons and registration of individual entrepreneurs as null and void;
>
> (c) liquidation of organisations regardless of the type of ownership;
>
> (d) collecting of unpaid taxes, levies and corresponding penalties and fines of more than three months of subsidiaries from parent companies in cases where the proceeds from the realisation of products of the subsidiary is paid into the bank account of the parent company or the other way around.

Monitoring of large expenditure by individuals had existed under socialism, but the original 1998 Tax Code did not accommodate this system. On the other hand, it had empowered the tax agency to apply to court for acknowledging a particular transaction of the tax payer to be void and confiscate the proceeds of the transaction for the benefit of the state budget. The tax agency was also empowered to confiscate income from unlawful activities. By the July 1999 amendments, this new system of monitoring was introduced and the latter two provisions were deleted. It was thought that such measures would be better left to law enforcement agencies. On the other hand, under the general provision of the Civil Code, the Ministry is still entitled to initiate an action in court in order to nullify a transaction on the basis of legal order and good morals (Civil Code Art.169).[15]

The purpose of monitoring is to 'establish the compatibility of large expenditure by an individual with his income' (Art.86-1, para.1). Properties whose acquisition is monitored include real estate, means of transportation, shares, treasury and municipal bonds. The monitoring is conducted on the basis of information received from agencies in charge of the registration of such properties as well as notary publics. In fact, these agencies are under an obligation to inform the tax agency of registration within 15 days (Art.86-2).

---

15   Zrdelecskii, *Kommentarii…*, *supra*, p.97.

xiii) (d) as indicated above is potentially a powerful instrument in the hands of the Ministry, but it has to prove that the proceeds of the sale from the daughter/parent company are paid into the account. Besides, tax payers may use another account for this purpose.[16]

Although it is not regarded as a tax agency, the Federal Tax Police is an agency for investigation in the area of tax. It was set up in 1992 as part of the then Federal Tax Service. Its task is to prevent, detect, and investigate violations of tax law which entail criminal or administrative sanctions. At present, according to the Statute on the Federal Agency of Tax Police of 1995, the Tax Police is not subordinate to the tax service (the present Ministry of Tax and Levies), but rather, is an independent agency subordinate direct to the President and is expected to cooperate with the tax agency.[17] The Tax Code lists functions of the tax police including participation in tax inspection upon the request of the Ministry as well as conducting of tax inspection on its initiative when there is sufficient proof of a tax offence (Art.36).

6   THE PROCEDURE

1)   Compulsory Collection of Taxes and Sanctions

In cases of failure to pay tax within the established period, the tax agency is empowered to resort to the compulsory collection procedure. The procedure differs between organisations and individuals.

For organisations, first, the tax agency is to collect the amount by seizing the money in the bank account of the tax payer or tax agent. The decision to seize the money in the account is to be made within 60 days of the day when the tax was due. The actual enforcement takes the form of the tax agency sending a binding instruction to the bank for transferral of the money from the rouble and/or foreign currency account of the tax payer or agent to the government account. In cases where the amount in the account is insufficient or information on the account was unavailable to the tax agency, taxes can be collected from other properties of the tax payer and agent (arts.46 and 47). In such cases, the tax agency adopts the decision and forwards it to the court bailiff for enforcement. The Code provides for the preferential order of properties to be attached.

In contrast, for enforcement *vis à vis* individuals, the above procedure is not available, and the tax agency has to resort to court procedure (Art.48).

---

16   Shatarin, *supra,* p.147.
17   *SZ RF,* 1995 No.51, item 4973.

For a delay in payment of tax, a penalty is charged. The penalty is set at the refinancing rate of the Central Bank and can be collected by the tax agency, together with the unpaid tax by the procedure provided in the Tax Code (Art.75).

Violations of tax law include failures or delays in registering with the tax agency as a tax payer (arts.116 and 117), delays in informing the opening and closing of bank accounts (Art.118), failures to present tax declarations (Art.119), serious violations of rules on accounting income, expenditure and the objects of taxation (Art.120), non-payment of tax by way of understating the taxable basis or other inaccurate calculation of tax (Art.122), unlawful obstruction of officials entering the premises (Art.124), and failures to provide the tax agency with information needed for tax control (Art.126). Banks are held responsible for failures to implement the decisions of the tax agency to suspend banking transactions (Art.134) and to collect taxes and levies (Art.135) as well as for failures to provide information of the financial state of the tax payer (Art.135-1).

Violations of tax law entail sanctions in the form of fines (*shtraf*). Failure to pay tax as a result of understatement of the taxable basis by intention, for example, entails a fine of 40% of the unpaid tax (Art.122, para.1). Sanctions are imposed by court procedure, and not by the tax agency. On the other hand, serious violations of rules on accounting income, expenditure and the objects of taxation results merely in a fine of 5,000 roubles (Art.120, para.1). Sanctions are imposed only when the person was at fault, i.e. has acted on intention or by negligence (arts.106 and 110).

In addition to these sanctions, the Criminal Code provides for penalties for tax evasion (arts.198 and 199).

The harshness of the sanctions under the 1991 Fundamental Principles of the Taxation System led some taxpayers to take the case to the Constitutional Court:

As a result of the tax inspection, joint stock company Bolshevik, Svet and other companies as well as individual entrepreneurs were found liable for violations of the Fundamental Principles of the Taxation System of 1991 by the head of the tax inspectorate and the tax police. The plaintiffs claimed that the sanctions provided by the law were unjustifiably excessive, and that they were applied to the plaintiffs without due observance of procedure, and without establishing fault, which considerably harmed their constitutional rights to free use of property for entrepreneurial activities.

The plaintiffs had been held responsible for violations of tax law and i) had the entire amount of concealed and reduced taxable income confiscated and imposed fine of the same amount, ii) on repeated violations, had a fine of double the amount of the initial fine imposed (the amount could be multiplied by five times, if the act was found to be intentional), iii) had fines for the failure to account taxable incomes at 10% of the unreported income imposed, and iv) had a penalty for the delay in paying tax imposed.

The Constitutional Court found that the law provided for responsibility for different types of violations without properly demarcating them. Responsibilities provided by the Law had failed to take into account the nature or the level of harm on society. The Law contained ambiguous and often mutually indistinguishable concepts. Also, in the majority of provisions on violations, there was no direct requirement of fault as a prerequisite to responsibility. Furthermore, the construction of the provisions allowed an overlapping application of various measures, penalising the taxpayer twice for one and the same act.

The Court concluded that some provisions of the Fundamental Principles of the Taxation System were against the Constitution.[18]

With the amendments to Part One of the Tax Code, sanctions and penalties have now been rationalised and streamlined.

2)   Procedure for Contesting Decisions of the Tax Agency

Taxpayers are entitled to appeal against non-normative acts (decisions) of the tax agency as well as against the act or failure to act on the part of officials of the tax agency, if they consider that their interests have been infringed. Appeal can be made to the superior division (superior official) within the Ministry or to the court. Resort to the former does not exclude the possibility of the latter (arts.137 and 138).

Appeal to court by organisations (companies) and individual entrepreneurs fall within the jurisdiction of the commercial court, while appeal by individuals other than entrepreneurs are handled by the ordinary court.

There is no requirement that appeal should be lodged with the superior body first. In fact, more than 90% of appeals go directly to the court. It is proposed to change the system and alleviate the burden of the court, e.g. by introducing a requirement to first go through an administrative procedure.[19]

Some companies with foreign investment, not to mention fully Russian entities, have successfully contested decisions of the tax agency in the commercial court.

A closed joint stock company, Koka-Kola Bottlera Orel, initiated an action at the commercial court of Orlov province *vis à vis* the tax agency of the district. The tax agency had ordered the company to pay 3,890,893 roubles of VAT and a 35,241 roubles penalty for the delay.

---

18   Decision of the Constitutional Court, July 15, 1999, cited in
j *Nalogovye spory: svornik dokumentov*, second edition, Moscow 2001, pp.228-235.
19   *EiZh*, May 19, 2001.

The decision of the first instance court found part of the order of the tax agency to be void. In the cassation instance, the decision was reversed.

The issue was whether the company was allowed to enter in the tax declaration the amount of VAT paid by the company in the fourth quarter of 1995 as capital contribution when the foreign investor imported materials (sugar), packing cases, and fixed assets. The tax agency did not allow this, and therefore, the declaration by the company was found to be lower than the actual VAT to be paid and the company was ordered to pay the difference plus the penalty.

The Supreme Commercial Court ruled that the amount of VAT paid at the border to the customs office could be deducted when calculating the tax payable to the budget at the time of the realisation of the product, insofar as the materials imported were used for the production and distribution of the product in Russia. This depends on the composition of the imported materials, so the case was referred back to the lower court in order to determine the composition of the imported items.[20]

Normative acts of the tax agency can be appealed to court. Ordinary courts have jurisdiction in such cases.

7   MAJOR FORMS OF TAXES

1)   Corporate Profit Tax

Profit tax was introduced in 1991. There was some confusion when an 'enterprise income tax' was introduced soon afterwards, coexisting with corporate income tax, but before long, the tax on profits of enterprises and organisations became the main direct tax imposed on companies. However, there was some confusion again when Part One of the Tax Code referred to 'income tax on organisations'. Eventually, in July 2001, Chapter 25 on Tax o the Profit of Organisations was added to Part Two of the Tax Code and replaced the 'income tax on organisations'.

(1)   Taxpayers

Payers of profit tax are Russian organisations as well as 'foreign organisations which perform their activities in the Russian Federation through a permanent establishment and/or receive income from sources in the Russian Federation' (Art.246).

---

20   Decision of the Presidium of the Supreme Commercial Court, January 18, 2000, *Nalogovye spory....,* *supra*, pp.93-97.

Regardless of whether or not foreign corporations are liable for profit tax or not, they are required to register as tax payers at the place of their representative office.

(2)   Taxable Base

The object of taxation is the profit of the organisation. For Russian organisations, profit is the received income deducted by cost as determined by the Code, while for foreign organisations with a permanent establishment, it is the income received by the permanent establishment minus the cost incurred by this establishment (Art.247). It should be noted that costs incurred overseas are not deductible.

Not all expenditures deductible in other countries can be deducted in Russia. For example, loan financing costs and insurance costs are deductible only in a limited manner. It is suggested that the taxable base should be made much closer to the actual income earned in the tax year and that all expenditures needed for the production, marketing and sale of goods should be deducted. Full deduction of advertising, insurance, payment of interests, and the cost for the and the cost of training of personnel has been proposed.[21] The Tax Code now has a detailed list of non-deductible costs, which is shorter than before (Art.270).

Depreciation was also a problem. Depreciation was on a straight line basis. In general, it took much longer for fixed assets to be depreciated in Russia than in other countries.[22] The Tax Code provides for straight line as well as other methods of depreciation (Art.259, para.1).

Losses can be carried forward for 10 years. The amount of loss carried forward may no not exceed 30% of the taxable base in any tax year (Art.283, para.2).

(3)   Tax Rate

The maximum profit tax rate used to be 35%, of which 11% went to the federal budget, 19% to the budget of the constituent entities of the Russian Federation, and 5% to the local self governments. In 2001, the rate was significantly reduced. At present, the rate of profit tax is 24%, of which 7,5% goes to the Federal budget, 14,5% to the budget of the constituent entities, and 2% to the local self governments.

---

21 Shatarin, *supra*, p.34.
22 *Ibid.*, p.34.

(4)   Transfer Pricing

According to a Russian commentator, transfer pricing has been actively utilised for a long time by Russian as well as foreign companies. The Tax Code has introduced regulations on transfer pricing for the first time. Reportedly, transfer pricing in Russia does not only have international character, but also 'national' character, since even within the country, an 'off-shore zone' often emerges which enables taxpayers to use different schemes.[23] A provision on the 'principles of determining the price of goods, work or service for the purpose of taxation' provides that the tax agency may examine the appropriateness of the price applied in transactions in the following cases (Art.40, para.2):

i)   transactions between mutually related persons;
ii)   barter transactions;
iii)   foreign trade transactions;
iv)   in cases of deviation of more than 20% from the level of the price applied by the taxpayer in identical products (work, services) within a short period.

The basic criterion for mutually related persons is the capability to exercise direct influence on the conditions or economic results of the activities of the other party.[24] More specifically, the Code provides that if one organisation directly or indirectly has a participating interest exceeding 20%in another organisation, they are mutually related entities (Art.20, para.1). Between individuals, if one individual is subordinate by public position to another person, or there are family relations, they are mutually related.

2)   Value-Added Tax (VAT)

Value-Added Tax is said to be the 'most fundamental and stable' revenue in Russia. In fact, even in the socialist period, there was a similar indirect tax called 'circulation tax', which was also a source of stable revenue for the state.

VAT was introduced by the 1991 Law on VAT; this was replaced by Part Two of the Tax Code. The basic structure of VAT is the same, but the provisions have become clearer.

---

23   *Ibid.,* pp.80-81.
24   Zrdelevskii, *supra,* p.73.

(1)   Taxpayers

Taxpayers are organisations and individual entrepreneurs. Those entities with a turnover of less than one million roubles for the preceding three months are exempted from VAT for twelve months (Art.145). This generous relief is designed to protect small businesses.

Other entities may be acknowledged as a taxpayer in relation to the crossing of the customs border of the Russian Federation (Art. 143). Foreign companies carrying out entrepreneurial activities in Russia are also regarded as taxpayers. Imported goods are subject to import VAT at the border.

(2)   Taxable Base

The basic idea of VAT is to tax the added value created at various stages of production and distribution. The object of VAT is the realisation of goods, services and work in the Russian Federation. Importation of goods into the customs territory of Russia is also covered (Art.146). The place of realisation is regarded to have been in Russia, if the goods were actually in Russia and do not involve dispatching or transportation, or the goods were dispatched or transported from Russia (Art. 147). In cases of work or service, if it is directly related to immovables in Russia, e.g. design and construction of a piece of architecture in Russia, the place of realisation is Russia. If the recipient of the work/services is engaged in entrepreneurial activities in Russia, Russian VAT is imposed (Art.148). These include legal and accounting services and engineering.

The taxable base of VAT is the value of the product, work, or service including excise, but without taxes (Art.154, para.1). The provision on transfer pricing (Art.40) is also applicable here.

(3)   Tax Rates

The general rate of VAT is 20%. Reduced rate of 10% is applied to food products and children's goods.

(4)   Exemptions

There is a list of exemptions from VAT including sale of medical products and providing of medical service (Art.149). Concerning import VAT, 'technological equipment which are to be contributed to the capital of Russian entities are exempted (Art.150). This exemption is considerably narrowed from the previous VAT Law.

(5)   Refunding of VAT

If the outgoing VAT exceeds incoming VAT, the difference is to be refunded to
the taxpayer. The refunding portion can be set-off against the next payment for
three months at the discretion of the tax agency (Art.176).

3)   Excise

Excise is an indirect tax which is imposed on specific goods (*pod-akziznyi tovar*)
as a percentage of the price realised by the producer. It was introduced in 1991,
but its coverage has changed from time to time. Excise is now covered by the
Tax Code Part Two.

(1)   Taxpayers

Taxpayers are organisations and individual entrepreneurs. Those persons who are
acknowledged as taxpayers in relation to the goods crossing the customs border
are also included.

(2)   Goods Subject to Excise

Goods under excise payment include alcoholic beverages, jewellery, furs etc., but
also crude oil, gas condensate as well as natural gas. With the phasing out of tax
on road funds, excise is also imposed on petrol and diesel oil (Art.191).

(3)   Taxable Base

The object of excise is the realisation of excisable goods by the producer within
Russia. In general, excise is not imposed on exported goods. Important exceptions
are mineral resources; oil and gas condensate are excisable at the same rate as
domestic supplies, while for natural gas, the domestic rate is 15%, but the export
rate is 30% (Art.182).
    The price of realisation is determined in accordance with the transfer pricing
provision (Art.40).

(4)   Excise Rate

The rate is determined as an amount in roubles per unit. It varies from 9 rouble
45 kopeck for one litre of champagne to 66 rouble per ton of crude oil (Art.193).

4)   Unified Social Tax

Unified social tax is a novelty introduced by Part Two of the Tax Code (Art.234).
It replaces the payment to extra budgetary funds, i.e. the Pension Fund, Social
Insurance Fund, and Mandatory Medical Insurance Fund. Contributions to the
mandatory work accident insurance are not included and therefore, are still payable
separately.

(1)   Taxpayers

Taxpayers are employers including organisations, individual entrepreneurs as well
as individuals.

(2)   Taxable Base

Object of taxation is determined as 'wages and other remuneration paid by the
employer to the employee on all grounds' (art.236).

(3)   Tax Rate

Tax rate is determined on a regressive basis, starting from a total 35.6% contribution (Art.241).

5)   Individual Income Tax

Individual income tax was introduced in 1991. It is now covered in Part Two of
the Tax Code. The system has undergone significant changes in 2000.

(1)   Taxpayers

Taxpayers are residents of the Russian Federation and non-residents who receive
income from Russian sources. Residents are those who spend more than 183 days
a year in Russia. In most cases, individual income taxes are withheld at the source.
Those taxpayers who are entitled to 'professional deductions' (see below) are
required to submit a tax declaration by April 30 every year.

(2)   Taxable Base

The object of taxation is the world-wide income for residents and Russian sourced income for non-residents (Art.209). The taxable base is all of the income of the tax payer; not only monetary income, but also income received in kind as well as rights of disposal and material benefits (Art.210, para.1). Pensions, payments of compensation, alimony, income of farmers (5 years) and state subsidies, among other payments, are exempted from the taxable base (Art.217).

There are some allowances available. These include 400 roubles per month standard allowance and 300 roubles per month per child. The minimum taxable annual income has been reduced from 50,000 to 20,000 roubles. The current minimum wage is 300 roubles per month.

Deduction of expenses is not generally available for individual income tax, but there are standard deductions, social policy deductions, property deductions and professional deductions. Standard deductions are applicable to those who suffered from the Chernobyl accident and other major accidents, 'heroes of the USSR and RF', and 'participants of the Second World War and other military operations for the defence of the USSR' (Art.218). Social policy deductions include donation to a charity, expenses for the taxpayer's own education, and medical expenses (Art. 219). Property deduction covers income received from the sale of a residential house, flat, *dacha* etc. which has been in the ownership of the taxpayer for less than 5 years and expenditure for the construction or purchase of a house or a flat (Art.220).

As for 'professional deduction', people who are registered as individual entrepreneurs are allowed to deduct the actual costs directly related to the earning of the income provided that these are supported by documents. Those who receive an income from providing service or work based upon civil law contracts are entitled to a deduction of the cost directly related to the carrying out of the service or work. Those who receive royalty payments are also entitled to a deduction of expenses (Art.221).

(3)   Tax Rates

By the latest amendments to the tax law, individual income tax rate was set at 13% flat, instead of the progressive rate which existed earlier. There is a 35% tax rate set for e.g. bank interest exceeding three-quarters of the Central Bank refinancing rate, and 30% for e.g. dividends (Art.224).

8   TAXATION OF FOREIGN COMPANIES

1)   Foreign Companies with a Permanent Establishment in Russia

The Chapter on Profit Tax in Part Two of the Tax Code has some provisions on taxation of foreign organisations. Foreign organisations (companies) which perform entrepreneurial activities in the Russian Federation are taxed on the income received by their activities via a permanent establishment (permanent representation – *postoiannoe predstavitel'stvo*) as well as income from the possession, use, or disposal of the property of the permanent establishment. Costs are deducted.

'Permanent establishment' in this context includes representative offices, divisions, offices, agencies, and other places through which the organisations conduct entrepreneurial activities related to the use of sub-soil and other natural resources, the carrying out of building, assembling, repairing etc. of installations, sale of goods, and providing of other works and services in the Russian Federation (Art.306, para.2). Participation of a foreign company in a consortium is not in itself regarded as a formation of a permanent establishment (*ibid.*, para.6). On the other hand, if a foreign company carries out activities in Russia through a Russian person who represents the interests of this company and concludes or negotiates contracts in the name of this company, this company may be regarded to have a permanent establishment (*ibid.*, para.7).

Foreign organisations with a permanent establishment are taxed at the same rate applicable to Russian organisations (arts.307, para.6, 284, para.1):

> A US company brought an action against the Tax Inspectorate of the City of Ekaterinburg for the revocation of the Inspectorate's order imposing a penalty worth 409,738,800 roubles for lowering the profit for the year 1994.
>
> In this case, the Tax Inspectorate of Ekaterinburg inspected the representative office of the plaintiff US company in the town and ascertained that the representative office, on behalf of the company, sold Hungarian and Yugoslavian medical equipment in the name of the office and generated 120,604,000 roubles of profit, but allegedly failed to fully declare it. In 1996, the Tax Inspectorate ordered the company to pay 409,738,800 roubles, including the undeclared profit, 100% fines and penalty for delay. The tax was calculated on the basis of a 'direct method', i.e. turnover minus cost.
>
> The first instance court and the appellate court acknowledged the claim of the company on the ground that the Tax Inspectorate failed to prove lowering or concealing of the profit, but at the instance of cassation, the court quashed the judgment and dismissed the case. Upon protest, the Supreme Commercial Court quashed the decision of the cassation instance and acknowledged the claim of the plaintiff in 1998.
>
> Referring to the double taxation treaty between Russia and the United States, the Supreme Commercial Court ruled that since the company sold medical equipment through its representative office, in applying the direct method, it is required to deduct the cost

incurred by the company in Russia as well as in the United States. It is also impossible to apply the direct method in the absence of information as to which part of turnover of sale is related to the activities of the company through its representative office in Russia. Therefore, the court ruled that the calculation of profits by the Tax Inspectorate was unlawful.[25]

2)   Foreign Companies without a Permanent Establishment in Russia

Foreign organisations without a permanent establishment in Russia are liable for profit tax on incomes in the Russian Federation including the following (Art.309, para.1):

i)   dividends;

ii)   distribution of profits or assets of organisations, including distribution of the assets at the time of liquidation;

iii)   interests;

iv)   royalties;

v)   income from the sale of shares of a Russian organisation, more than half of whose assets are immovables;

vi)   income from the sale of immovables in the Russian Federation;

vii)   rent;

viii) income from international transportation.

The tax rate for the above is set at 20%, except for dividends received from Russian companies which are taxed at 15%. Interests received from state and municipal bonds are also taxed at 15% (Art.284, paras. 2,3, and 4).

These taxes are withheld at the source.

---

25   Decision of the Presidium of the Supreme Commercial Court, May 12,1998,*VVAS RF* 1998 No.7, pp.60-63).

15

DISPUTE SETTLEMENT – PROCEDURE

1   TERRITORIAL JURISDICTION OF THE COURTS

In the commercial court system, the commercial court of the republics, regions, provinces, cities of federal significance, autonomous provinces and regions handles the case as the first instance court. The basic rule is that the claim has to be presented to the court of the place of the defendant. As an exception, claims against a juridical person which arise from the activities of its subdivision such as a branch or a representative office are to be presented to the court where this subdivision is located (Code of Commercial Court Procedure, hereinafter, 'ComPC', Art.25). A claim arising from an agreement which has a clause on the place of performance can be brought to the court of the place of performance (Art.26). It should be added that parties may agree to a different venue in such cases (Art.30).

There are cases where jurisdiction of a specific venue is mandatory. Insolvency cases are handled by the court of the place of the debtor (Art.28). Cases involving the rights to real property are handled by the court of the location of the disputed property. Cases concerning carriage of goods are handled by the court of the location of the carrier (Art.29).

In the ordinary court system, district courts are, in principle, the courts of first instance, except in cases where higher courts have jurisdiction or the justice of peace has jurisdiction. The latter, *inter alia*, has jurisdiction in minor civil cases where the disputed amount does not exceed 500 times the minimum wage.

The principle that the court of the place of the defendant has jurisdiction is the same in ordinary courts as the commercial court. However, concerning juridical persons, claims can be presented at the location of their bodies, or property (Code of Civil Procedure, hereinafter, 'CivPC', Art.117). It should be noted that by virtue of the Law on the Protection of the Rights of Consumers, consumers may present the claim to the court of their location or the place where the damage was caused (Art.17).[1]

The CivPC provides for disputes in which the plaintiff may select the jurisdiction. For example, claims for damages arising from tortious acts on the life or health of an individual can be brought to the court of the place of the plaintiff or the place where the damage occurred. In cases where the property of an individual or a juridical person was damaged, claims can be brought to the court where the damage occurred (Art.118).

2   COMPOSITION OF THE COURT

At the first instance, in the commercial court, cases are heard by a single judge. As an exception, in bankruptcy cases, the case is heard by three judges. The same applies to cases where the validity of an act of government and local government agencies is contested. Whereas in the socialist period, *gosarbitrazh* heard cases with one arbitrator and the representatives of both parties as a panel as in Western commercial arbitration process, this is no longer the case.

In the civil procedure, the system of people's assessors used to be one of the fundamental principles under socialism. This system was introduced after the October Revolution in lieu of the jury system. It was presumably thought to be inconvenient to have an independent body of laymen to determine the outcome of the case; assessors could be kept under control of the judge. However, things are different now.

In the ComPC, there is no reference to people's assessors. Cases in the first instance are heard by a single judge (Art.14). By the decision of the court, cases can be heard by several judges, but without lay assessors. There is a statute on the experiment of involving assessors in the procedure, but they are invited to take part only when 'specialised knowledge in the area of entrepreneurial and other economic activities is needed for the solution of a specific case'.[2] This is different from the system of lay assessors in the civil procedure where assessors are not required to have any special knowledge.

In contrast, the CivPC, which was amended in 1992 provides that civil cases in the first instance are to be heard either by a single judge or by a judge and two lay assessors (Art 6). Some categories of cases, such as proprietary disputes between individuals up to 30 times the minimum wage, are designated by the Code

---

1   *SZ RF*, 1996 No.3, item 140.
2   Decision of the Plenum of the Supreme Commercial Court, September 5, 1996.

to be heard by a single judge (Arts. 113, 232). Other cases are heard by a single judge, unless either party disagrees (Art.6).

In practice, in the ordinary court, a majority of civil cases in the first instance are heard by a single judge without people's assessors. One of the reasons was that people's assessors were often not active and turned into a 'bystander' in the past. However, the primary reason was financial. Many companies were reluctant in the period of market economy to release employees to perform the duty of a lay assessor. Enormous delay in the civil procedure due to the absence of lay assessors 'spread like an epidemic in the courts of many regions in Russia'. This forced the amendment to the law to do without lay assessors.[3]

3   PARTIES AND OTHER 'PARTICIPANTS' OF THE PROCEDURE

Russian law has concepts of 'participants in the procedure' and 'parties'. The former is broader than the latter in that it encompasses interested parties such as the bankruptcy petitioner as well as third parties who take part in the procedure. Parties are defined in the ComPC as either the plaintiff or defendant. The plaintiff is an organisation or a person who presents the claim for his own interest or for whose interest the claim has been presented, and the defendant is a person (physical or juridical) against whom the claim was presented (Art.34). Naturally, there can be several plaintiffs and defendants. A third party may join the procedure.

In order to exercise their procedural legal capacity by themselves, the parties need to have the capacity to act, i.e. the capacity to perform procedural acts directly. This presupposes not only that they are capable of acquiring rights under substantive law, but also that they are entitled to protection by the court and capable of exercising their rights and performing their duties.[4] Juridical persons acquire this capacity by registration. In the commercial court procedure, this capacity is only acknowledged in juridical persons and licensed individual entrepreneurs, whereas in the civil procedure, such capacity is granted to all physical persons over the age of 18 as well as state enterprises or other entities (CivPC Arts.31 and 32).

Both the ComPC and CivPC provide for the participation of third parties. According to the ComPC, a third party who represents an independent interest in the contested matter is entitled to join at any time before the court renders the judgment. Such a third party is allowed to exercise all the rights of a party, but also bears all the duties attributed to a party (Art.38). A third party who does not

---

3   V.Taranenko ed., *Grazhdanskoe protsessual'noe pravo Rossii*, Moscow 1999, pp.36-37.
4   V.Anokhin, *Arbitrazhnoe protsessual'noe pravo Rossii*, Moscow 1999, pp.148-149.

represent an independent interest may join on the side of either party, provided that the outcome of the case would affect his rights or duties in relation to one of the parties. Such a third party is entitled to exercise the rights of the parties except for major decisions such as the change of the subject matter of the case, change in the amount of claim, withdrawal, acknowledgement of claim, or settlement (Art.39).

The ComPC has an explicit provision which provides that all interested persons are entitled to recourse to court in order to defend their infringed or disputed rights or lawfully protected interests (Art.4). Foreign and international organisations as well as foreign individuals who are performing entrepreneurial activities are granted such rights by the ComCV in the same way as Russian organisations and individuals on a reciprocal basis (Art.210). The CivPC has similar provisions (Arts.3 and 433).

Both codes have a provision on 'inadequate parties'; the court is empowered to replace the initial plaintiff or defendant with the consent of the plaintiff, if it finds that the claim was not presented by the person to whom the right to the claim belongs, or the claim was not addressed to the person who should respond to the claim (ComPC Art.36). This applies in instances where the parties to the procedure were found not to be parties to the disputed matter under substantive law.

There is no provision in either code which enables individuals which does not form a juridical person to sue in the name of the group, such as in the US class action or German *Verbandsklage*. In principle, in such cases, these individuals must sue jointly. However, by some laws, a group of individuals are allowed to sue as a group. For example, the Law on the Protection of Environment provides that a group of individuals may present a claim in order to prevent ecologically harmful activities which cause damage to the health and property of individuals, the economy, and the environment, either to the ordinary court or commercial court (Art.91).[5] Also the Law on the Protection of the Rights of Consumers allows consumer organisations which are not juridical persons to sue on behalf of specific individuals as well as unspecified number of consumers (Art.17, para.3).

Procurators who are a prosecuting agency in criminal procedure also have some role in civil and commercial procedure. Under socialism, procurators were regarded as 'guardians of legality' and were given the power of 'judicial supervision'. They were entitled to participate in the civil procedure at any stage, and if they found the judgment or decision to be against the law, were empowered to appeal or seek supervisory review by superior courts. This system remains in the present civil procedure. In various family cases, the participation of the procur-

---

5   *VSND (RS) i VS (RS)*, 1992, No.10, item 457.

ator is mandatory, but procurators extensively take part in the civil procedure in other areas as well. 'The necessity of taking part in the civil procedure is decided by the procurator'.[6] In the commercial court procedure, the procurator is entitled to bring a case to the commercial court in order to defend the interest of the state and society (Art.40). There are a number of cases where a procurator brought an action to court to annul a contract out of public interest [See chapter 2].

4   PRESENTATION OF THE CLAIM

The claim must be presented to the court of appropriate jurisdiction. Together with the written claim, documents such as the certificate of the payment of state duty should be presented. In the commercial court, a copy of the claim and the attached documents must be sent to other participants in the procedure including the defendant by the plaintiff, whereas in ordinary court, the plaintiff merely has to submit copies to the court for the latter to send them to the relevant people.

According to the ComPC, the court (judge) may refuse to accept the claim in cases on the following grounds (ComPC 107):

i)   the dispute is not within the competence of the commercial court;
ii)   there exists a judgment or decision in force between the same parties on the same matter and on the same grounds or a decision on settlement by the ordinary court or commercial court;
iii)   a dispute between the same parties on the same matter and on the same grounds is pending at the ordinary court, commercial court or arbitration institution;
iv)   there exists an arbitral award in force between the same parties on the same matter and on the same grounds, except in cases where the commercial court refused enforcement of the award, reversed the case to arbitration but the new proceeding proved to be impossible.

These are also the grounds for termination of the procedure (Art.85).

i) not only covers instances where the commercial court does not have jurisdiction, but also where the plaintiff does not have a lawful interest under substantive law to sue, e.g. in cases where the plaintiff was not the real titleholder.[7] However, normally, these circumstances are revealed only after the claim has been accepted by the court, and therefore, in such cases, the court terminates the procedure at the later stage.

---

6   A.Ryzhakov ed., *Postateinyi kommentarii; Grazdanskii Protessual'nyi Kodeks RSFSR*, Moscow 1999, p.108.
7   *Kommentarii...supra*, p.261.

The CivPC lists the existence of an arbitration agreement as a ground for refusal to accept the claim as well as for termination of the procedure (arts.129 and 219), while a corresponding provision is absent in the ComPC. However, this does not mean that despite the existence of an arbitration clause, the commercial court may hear the case. The existence of an arbitration agreement is a ground for leaving the case without consideration (Art.87).

Participants in the procedure, namely the defendant, are entitled to present a response to the claim with documents supporting it to the court (ComPC Art.109). They are also entitled to bring a counter-claim (Art.110). The same applies to ordinary court procedure. In reality, since there is no requirement to present the response before the hearing, it is submitted at the hearing.

5   THE HEARING PROCEDURE

1)   The Preparatory Stage

In both procedures, after the acceptance of the claim by the court (judge), the preparatory stage starts. In the ComPC, this procedure is handled by the judge who accepted the claim. The judge, at this stage, may take the following actions (Art.112):

i)   consider inviting other defendants or third parties to take part in the procedure;

ii)   invite interested parties to the procedure;

iii)   request participants in the procedure as well as organisations and officials to take certain actions, including submission of documents and information which have a bearing on the case;

iv)   check the relevance and permissibility of evidence;

v)   summon witnesses;

vi)   consider appointing an expert;

vii)   send requests for cooperation to other commercial courts;

viii)   summon people who take part in the procedure;

ix)   encourage parties to reach a compromise;

x)   decide on the issue of whether the head of the organisation which takes part in the procedure should be summoned;

xi)   take interim measures.

However, the scope of the preparatory procedure depends on the nature and complexity of the case and the level of preparation of the plaintiff. Not all cases require a full preparatory procedure.[8] In reality, iii) does not take place often, neither does v).

Judges may not pre-empt the formal hearing which is to follow. When considering the relevance and permissibility of evidence, the judge is not allowed to examine the evidence. The judge is not allowed to question the witnesses.[9]

It should be noted that in the commercial court, a settlement can be encouraged at this early stage; however, this seldom happens.

The CivPC lists similar actions to be taken by the judge at this stage, except for the encouragement of a settlement (Art.142). The judge questions the plaintiff on the substance of the claim and asks the plaintiff about the possible argument by the defendant. If necessary, the judge asks the plaintiff to present supplementary evidence. The defendant may be invited to a talk with the judge.[10] Presumably, this is common with the procedure in the commercial court.

2)   Interim Measures

Both in the commercial court and the ordinary court, interim measures are available. These measures are available at any stage of the procedure upon application of the party, provided that the absence of such measures would make the enforcement of the judgment difficult or impossible (Com PC Art.75). The following interim measures are available (Art.76, para.1):

i)   attachment of the defendant's property or monetary instruments;
ii)   prohibition on the defendant from effecting certain actions;
iii)   prohibition on the third party from effecting certain actions which affect the object of dispute;
iv)   suspension of enforcement by ex-parte procedure;
v)   suspension of sale of property in cases where the release of the property from arrest is sought.

The court which handles the case also decides upon interim measures. The court renders a decision in such cases which is subject to appeal. Non-compliance with these measures entails a fine up to 50% of the contested amount (*ibid.*, para.3). It should be added that the defendant may apply to court for a deposit by the plaintiff to cover the possible damage to the defendant by the given measure.

---

8   Anokhin, *supra*, p.292.Taranenko, *supra*, p.226.
9   *Ibid.*, p.292.
10   Taranenko ed., *supra*, p.227.

The CivPC allows interim measures not only upon application by the party, but also ex officio by the court (Art.133). Available interim measures are more or less the same with the ComPC, except that a measure to prohibit third parties from transferring property to the defendant or performing other obligations *vis à vis* the defendant is available (Art.134).

3)   The Hearing

The hearing is the central stage of commercial and civil procedure. Various principles, including those guaranteed by the Constitution apply here. First, there is the principle of openness (*glasnost'*). A closed hearing is only possible in cases provided by the Law on State Secrets and also in cases where the court accepts the petition of the participant referring to the necessity of protecting commercial and other secrets (ComPC Art.9). A closed hearing for the protection of commercial secrets is available only in the commercial court. However, in reality, in order to get through the door to the hearing, one needs to show a power of attorney authorising one to attend the hearing in the ordinary court.

Second, the principle of directness applies. Thus, the ComPC provides that the court must examine all evidence directly (Art.19). The CivPC has a more detailed provision which mandates the court to examine evidence, hear the statement of the parties, witnesses and experts directly (Art.146). As a corollary, the case must be heard by the same court from the beginning. In cases where the composition of the court has changed, the case has to be re-heard from the beginning (ComPC Art.117, CivPC Art.146).

There is also the principle of continuous hearing. In Russia, cases are heard without interruption except for a recess, unless the procedure is suspended. In the commercial court procedure, in exceptional cases, an interval of a maximum of three days is allowed (Art.117). The CivPC prohibits the court from hearing another case before completing the given case (Art.146).

Finally, the Constitution provides that the proceedings shall be conducted by the adversarial system, and with equal rights of the parties (Art.123). This is in contrast to the system under socialism, in which the court played a 'paternalistic role'.

There is a time limit for the procedure. Thus, in the commercial court, the judgment has to be rendered within two months of the day of the presentation of the claim to court, while there is no specific time limit for the preparation stage

(Art.114). According to the 2000 statistics, only in 4,6% of the cases was this time limit unobserved.[11]

In the ordinary court, the preparation stage should not take more than a week after the acceptance of claim, and in principle, within a month of the completion of the preparation stage, the judgment should be rendered (Art.99).

In contrast to the commercial courts, in the ordinary courts, the time limit is not necessarily observed. In 1998, the limit was not observed in 13% of the cases, and in 298,000 cases, the case took more than 3 months, and in 42,000 cases, it took more than a year to have a judgment rendered.[12] The failure to meet the time limit is explained by the caseload of courts which has increased enormously since the mid-1980s. Complicated cases with a large number of plaintiffs such as the MMM financial pyramid scheme case are said to have resulted in the rise in the number of cases which exceeded the statutory time limit for the completion of the case.[13] However, this does not necessarily explain why there is more delay in the ordinary courts than in commercial courts.

In both courts, the actual proceeding is more akin to the Franco-German system than the Anglo-American system in that the court (judge) plays a more active role.

The ComPC does not have detailed provisions on the manner of the hearing. In the absence of detailed provisions, the commercial court is expected to apply the same procedure of hearing *by analogy* to the CivPC.[14]

The CivPC provides that the judge reports at the hearing the substance of the claim, the response of the defendant, circumstances which support the claim and the available evidence (Art.166). Thus, it is not the parties which present the case at the hearing. The judge then asks the plaintiff whether he would like to withdraw the claim, and the defendant whether he would like to accept the claim, and then both parties whether they would prefer to settle the case (Art.166). If the response is in the negative, the court hears the statement of the plaintiff, third party and the defendant and other participants to the procedure (Art.166).

The court examines evidence, hears the statements of the participants to the procedure, the testimony of the witnesses, and the opinion of the experts. According to the CivPC, witnesses must be present at the beginning of the hearing, but are not allowed to be present at the hearing before the testimony and therefore, are instructed to leave the room, and then return separately to give testimony.

Unlike Anglo-American law, the parties do not have a constitutional right to question the witness. In the CivPC, there is a provision on the procedure of

---

11   'Rabota arbitrazhnykh sudov Rossiiskoi Federatsii v 200 godu', [www,akdi.ru/vas/rabota].
12   *RIu*, 1999 No.4, p.60.
13   B.Kondrashov, 'Sluzhba sudebnykh pristavov: stadiia stanovleniia', *ZhRP*, 1999 No.3/4, p.13.
14   Anokhin, *supra*, p.211.

questioning the witness. The judge explains the relevance of the witness to the participants to the procedure and asks the witness to tell everything he or she personally knows about the case. After the testimony, the party who applied for summoning the witness questions the witness followed by others and the judge. The judge may ask questions at any stage (Art.176). The hearing ends with the exchange of opinions between the parties.

4)   Evidence and Testimony

In both procedures, evidence which is produced in court has to be relevant to the case. A novelty in these procedures is that evidence which has been obtained unlawfully is not permitted (ComPC Art.52, CivPC Art.49). In fact, this is a constitutional requirement (Art.50).

Participants in the commercial court procedure may apply to court for obtaining evidence in the possession of others, not limited to the participants, if he does not have the possibility of obtaining it by himself. The possessor of the evidence will be fined at maximum 200 times the minimum wage if he fails to hand over the evidence without a justifiable reason (ComPC 54). Similar provisions are found in the CivPC (Arts. 64 and 69).

The CivPC provides that the representative of a person in a civil or criminal procedure cannot be summoned to give testimony on matters which came to his knowledge in the course of the duty (Art.61), ComPC does not limit the scope of persons who can be summoned as witnesses. However, it is understood that in the commercial court procedure, the same applies.[15] In addition to the codes, there are separate laws which provide for the immunity of members of parliament, 'plenipotentiary for the protection of human rights', and clergy.[16] In reality, witness evidence is seldom used in the commercial court.

Both codes provide for the preservation of evidence. Thus, the ComPC provides that those who have reason to believe that the production of the necessary evidence will become impossible or difficult may apply to the court which accepted their claim for preservation of evidence (Art.71). The CivPC has a similar provision (Art.57). Incidentally, preservation of evidence before the claim is brought can be effected by the notary public.

In contrast with Anglo-American jurisdiction, there are few evidential rules in both procedures. The principle of free evaluation of evidence prevails. Hearsay

---

15   *Kommentarii...*, p.98.
16   *Postateinyi kommentarii...* p.148.

evidence does not seem to be excluded, except that if the witness cannot disclose the source of the information, the statement may not be used as evidence (Art.69).

5)   The Role of the Court at the Hearing

Each party is under an obligation to prove the circumstances which he refers to as the basis of the claim or response (ComPC Art.53). The party which failed to produce information advantageous to him will have to bear the disadvantageous consequence. Because of the active role the court used to play under socialism, the distribution of the burden of proof has not necessarily been clearly determined in Russia.[17] The court does not have an obligation or power to collect evidence on its own initiative, as was the case under socialism.

There are provisions in the substantive law which provide for presumptions. For example, in a dispute involving the performance of obligation, the debtor-entrepreneur is liable, unless he proves that an adequate performance was impossible due to insurmountable circumstances (Civil Code Art.401). Another example is tort liability, in which the fault of the possessor of sources of increased danger to the surroundings is presumed (*ibid.*, Art.1079, para.1)

On the other hand, the ComPC provides that where it is not possible to decide on the case with the evidence at hand, the court is entitled to ask the participants to the procedure to produce supplementary evidence (Art.53). Exercise of this power of the court to 'take all measures for the full clarification of circumstances which have relevance to the case' is regarded more or less as a duty.[18] Although the system is understood to have changed to the adversarial system where the judge is to play a 'passive role', still the intervention of the judge is required on some occasions under this provision. The CivPC has a similar provision. Moreover, the CivPC mandates the court to assist the party in compiling evidence if it is difficult for the party (Art.50).

Under socialism, the right of the parties to dispose of the subject matter of the litigation was not without restriction. The predecessor to the present commercial court, *gosarbitrazh*, had operated under the principle of 'active intervention', since the fulfilment of the state economic plan had precedence over the interest of the parties. In the civil procedure, the court was allowed to exceed the scope of the claim and render a judgment in pursuit of 'objective truth', i.e. if it was necessary for the protection of the rights and lawful interests of state

---

17   *Kommentarii...*, *supra*, P.118.
18   *Ibid.*, p.121; Anokhin, *supra*, p.192.

enterprises, other entities as well as individuals.[19] Even under socialism, this provision had been criticised; there was a view that this should be limited to changes in the amount of the claim.

In contrast, the current system operates on the adversarial principle. As a rule, the commercial court, in accordance with the concept of the passive role of the court, is not granted power to interfere with the power of disposition of the parties or to take initiative in favour of either of the parties, or to exceed the scope of the claim.[20] The above-mentioned provision of the CivPC was slightly modified in 1995 and now provides that the court may exceed the scope of claim if it is necessary for protecting the rights and lawful interest of the plaintiff, as in other cases provided by law (CivPC Art.195). The fact still remains that the court can go beyond the claim of the party. In the ComCV, there is no equivalent to this provision.

A related question is the change to the ground or subject matter of the claim. In the commercial court procedure, the plaintiff may change the ground or subject matter of the claim, change the amount of the claim, or withdraw the claim until the judgment is rendered (Art.37). Subject matter of the claim means the substantive law aspect of the claim, or 'content of the claim', while the ground of the claim means the circumstances on which the claim is based. In the 1992 ComPC, the court was allowed to change the grounds or subject matter of the claim on its own initiative, but this was dropped in the present ComPC. Simultaneous changes to the subject matter and the grounds is not allowed.[21] The CivPC has a similar provision as the above-mentioned provision in the ComPC (Art.34).

6   JUDGMENTS AND DECISIONS

The proceeding of the first instance ends with either a judgment or a decision of the court. When the case has been heard on its merit, the court renders a judgment. At the end of the hearing, after the final words by the parties, the judge (s) retires to the anteroom and prepares the judgment. The judge, after deliberation, may decide to reopen the hearing if he finds it necessary to examine further evidence, or continue clarifying the circumstances relevant to the case (ComPC Art.125). Otherwise, the judge prepares the judgment, returns to the courtroom

---

19   Art.195 before the 1995 amendment. M.Gurvich ed., *Sovetskii grazhdanskii protsess* second edition, Moscow 1975, p.196.
20   Anokhin, *supra*, p.158.
21   Decision of the Plenum of the Supreme Commercial Court, October 31, 1996, No.13, in V.Zhura- kovskii and V.Kalinin, *Kommentarii i primenenie zakonodatel'stva arbitrazhnymi sudami Rossiiskoi Federatsii*, Moscow 2000, p.303.

and announces it (ComPC Art.134). Only in especially complicated cases, can the reasoned judgment wait up to three days, but the concluding part of the judgment has to be announced at the same session which heard the case (Art.134), but in practice, this is the norm. The same applies in ordinary court (CivPC Art.203).

The judgment of the commercial court takes effect after one month of its adoption unless it is appealed, except for judgments of the Supreme Commercial Court, which take effect immediately (ComPC Art. 135). In the civil procedure, the judgment takes effect with the expiration of the period for cassation appeal, i.e. within 10 days of the rendering of the judgment in its final form (CivPC Art.208).

The commercial court renders a decision, instead of a judgment, when the hearing is postponed, suspended, or terminated. The case is suspended in cases, e.g. when a decision of another court, including the Constitutional Court, is pending, or when a party which is a juridical person is being reorganised. The case is terminated on the following grounds (Art.85):

i)   the case does not fall within the competence of the commercial court;
ii)   there exists a judgment in force on a dispute between the same parties on the same subject matter and grounds by the ordinary court or commercial court;
iii)   there exists an arbitral award in force on a dispute between the same parties on the same subject matter and grounds;
iv)   a juridical person participating in the process was liquidated;
v)   the plaintiff withdrew the claim and this has been accepted by the court;
vi)   the parties reached a settlement and this has been confirmed by the court.

In cases where the case has been terminated, the plaintiff may not present a claim to court again on the dispute between the same parties, with the same subject matter and grounds.

The CivPC provides for similar grounds for the termination of the case for ordinary courts (Art.219).

In the commercial court, settlement came to be explicitly allowed for the first time in the 1995 Code. Settlement is allowed at any stage of the procedure, and in fact, it is encouraged. Settlements must be confirmed by the court. According to the decision No.13 of the Plenum of the Supreme Commercial Court, settlement is not permissible if it is against the law or infringes the rights and lawful interests of others, or cannot be enforced in accordance with the agreed conditions.[22]

---

22 *Kommentarii....,* *supra,* p.88.

The plaintiff may withdraw the claim, and the defendant may accept the claim. The court will not accept withdrawal or acceptance, if it is against the law or infringes upon the rights and lawful interests of others (Art.37).

Settlement, withdrawal, and acceptance are regulated in a similar way in the CivPC (Art.34).

7   APPEAL AND SIMILAR PROCEDURES

Russia has a rather peculiar system of appeal in civil and commercial procedure. The system differs in the ordinary court and the commercial court, but the common feature is the extensive possibility of reviewing judgments which have taken force.

In the commercial court, the parties have a right to one appeal. The appeal is lodged with the court of first instance which rendered the judgment in question (Art.146). This does not mean that the commercial court of the first level has a special division on hearing appeals. Appeals are heard by three judges of the first instance court who are members of the relevant trial division. If there is no special court division in the given court, judges of the court hear the appeal. The appeal has to be lodged within a month of the rendering of the original judgment (Art.147).

There are no limits on the ground of appeal. The appellant merely has to specify the reason why he thinks the judgment was wrong and to cite laws and the materials of the case. The right to appeal is not limited to the parties; third parties who took part in the procedure are also granted the right to appeal. New evidence can be examined, but the party has to justify the fact that this evidence could not be produced at the first instance without his fault. The court is not bound by the scope of appeal and may examine the entire judgment (Art.155).

What is unique in the Russian commercial court procedure is first, the cassation procedure. This is different from the appeal procedure. As the name demonstrates, the system was introduced in Russia from France in 1864. However, the system appears to be different from its original institution. The Russian commercial court procedure grants the participants to the first instance procedure the right to lodge a cassation appeal against judgments of the commercial court and decisions of the appellate instance *which have entered into force* (Art.161). In fact, the system was different under the 1992 Code in which cassation appeal was for judgments which *have not taken effect*. In contrast, under the 1995 Code, it is one of the forms of reviewing judgments and decisions which have taken effect together with the supervisory procedure and the procedure for reopening the case upon discovery of new facts. According to a commentator, 'the new system, by taking into account foreign experience, provides for a supplementary guarantee of the rights of those who took part in the procedure'.[23]

Appeal of cassation is to be lodged with the court which rendered the original judgment or decision. The appeal is heard by the federal territorial commercial courts (second level commercial court). There are currently two divisions within the court; the division for disputes arising from civil law and other relations, and the division for disputes arising from administrative law relations.

Appeal of cassation covers only matters of law. The court reviews the original judgments and decisions from the viewpoint of whether substantive and procedure law has been observed (Art.174). The procedure is basically the same as the procedure in the first instance. The cassation court may alter or quash the original judgement or decision in cases where the substantive law was wrongly applied or there was an error in applying procedural law which led to, or may have led to an erroneous judgment (Art.176).

In contrast to the supervisory procedure (see below), the system of cassation does not pose a serious threat to the stability even though it contests the validity of judgments in effect, since appeal of cassation has to be lodged within a month of the contested judgments and decisions taking effect (Art.164).

In 2000, 12,5% of the judgments of the first instance commercial court were appealed, of which 28% were quashed. A further 7,9% were appealed by way of cassation, of which 34% were quashed.[24]

All judgments and decisions of the commercial court which have taken effect are subject to review at the supervisory instance. This is a system that existed in the Tsarist period and was inherited in the Soviet period. The difference with the appeal of cassation is that only a limited scope of officials are allowed to initiate these proceedings. Officials who are entitled to present supervisory 'protests' are: the President of the Supreme Commercial Court and the Procurator General on the judgments and decisions of all commercial courts except those of the Presidium of the Supreme Commercial Court, and the deputies of the above officials on the judgments and decisions of all commercial courts except those of the Supreme Commercial Court (Art.181). Parties to the case are merely entitled to file a petition with these officials to lodge a protest. An appellate procedure or cassation procedure has to precede the petition (Art.185).

Protests by these officials are heard by the Presidium of the Supreme Commercial Court. The Presidium comprises the President of the Court and the deputies as well as the heads of divisions.

---

23 *Ibid.*, p.376.
24 *VVAS RF*, 2001, No.5, pp.13-14.

What is peculiar is that the grounds for supervisory review are almost unlimited, while there is no time limit for lodging protest by the above-mentioned officials. The ground for altering or quashing the original judgment or decision is either unlawfulness or absence of legitimate grounds of the judgment or decision. This system is a serious threat to legal stability. The only restraint on this institution is that the scope of officials who are empowered to lodge protest is very much limited.

On the other hand, it should be noted that under the current system, this is the only way by which a case can be heard by the Supreme Commercial Court. The federal territorial courts are the highest instance the parties can reach. Above this level, remedy is available only by supervisory procedure through a petition filed with the above-listed officials. Judging from the published judgments of the Supreme Commercial Court, the supervisory instance seems to operate more like the system of certiorari in the United States. The time gap between the contested judgment and the supervisory review is not that long.

In 2000, in 14,494 cases, petition was filed for supervisory review in commercial procedure, of which in 584 cases, a protest was lodged and the supervisory proceeding was initiated. In addition, there were 119 cases coming from the Procurator General. In 571 cases, the judgment was quashed.[25] The sheer number of petitions demonstrates that this system is not an extraordinary remedy, but is in fact, a normal remedy system.

For ordinary courts, the system of appeal is slightly different, i.e. it is closer to the former socialist system.

Judgments of the ordinary court can be appealed, in addition to the normal appeal procedure, by way of cassation initiated by the participants to the procedure. Unlike the appeal of cassation in the commercial court, it is lodged against judgments *which have not taken effect*. Thus, it is the third instance review of the judgment of the first instance court. Procurators, regardless of whether they participated in the procedure or not, may lodge a 'protest' against unlawful or groundless judgments. 'Protests' by procurators are treated in a similar way with the appeal of cassation (CivPC Art.282).

Appeals and protests must be lodged within 10 days of the rendering of the original judgment (Art.284). Appeal of cassation and protest are heard by the second instance court, normally, the supreme court of the autonomous republics, territorial, provincial courts, courts of the cities of federal designation, and the courts of the autonomous region (Art.283). At the cassation instance, new evidence

---

25   'Rabota arbitrazhnykh sudakh…', *supra.*

can be examined. 'In the interest of legality', the court may go beyond the scope of appeal or protest and review the entire judgment (Art.294).

Judgments may be quashed, altered, or the case be reversed to the original instance in the following cases (Art.306):

i) erroneous ascertaining legally relevant facts;
ii) insufficient proof of facts relevant to the case;
iii) incompatibility of the conclusion of the court with the facts of the case;
iv) violation or erroneous application of substantive or procedural law.

Against the decision of the court on cassation appeal or protest, no further appeal is allowed; it immediately takes effect (Art.312).

As is the case with the commercial court, judgments and decisions of all ordinary courts which have taken effect can be reviewed by way of supervision. Again, it is not the parties who may initiate the supervisory procedure, but senior judges and procurators, depending on the level of the court, which rendered the original judgment. The parties may only file petition with these officials.

In 1998, the total number of cases where petition for the supervisory review was filed was 31,000.[26] In 380 cases, i.e. in 0.5% of all cases, the original judgment was altered or quashed.[27]

8   COSTS

Court costs comprise state duty and costs related to the hearing of the case, e.g. cost and remuneration of witnesses, experts and interpreters, costs of enforcement. In the judgment, the court also rules on the allocation of the cost (ComCV Art.127). State duty is provided by the Law on State Duty.[28] This Law provides for different rates of state duty for the commercial court and the ordinary court. The amount of state duty depends on the disputed amount. In the commercial court, the highest rate is for disputes the contested amount of which is over one million roubles – 16,600 roubles plus 0.5% of the contested amount over one million roubles. However, there is a ceiling of 1000 times minimum wage. Thus, for a contested amount of two million roubles, the state duty is 66,600 roubles. In contrast, in the ordinary court, the cost for the same contested amount is 1.5% of this amount, i.e. 30,000 roubles.

---

26 *RIu*, 1999 No.8, p.52.
27 *Ibid.*, 1999 No.9, p.53.
28 *SZ RF*

The CivPC provides for exemption of payment of costs in some cases, based upon the financial state of the individual such as employees in labour disputes, spouses in alimony cases, and heirs in cases of the damage to health or death of the breadwinner (Art,80). Although the ComPC does not have a specific provision on exemptions since the parties are basically juridical persons and individual entrepreneurs, in bankruptcy cases, where other individuals may initiate a case, some categories of individuals are exempted from paying the cost.[29] The court may allow deferred payment or payment by instalments (Art.81).

Attorney's fees are not regarded as a cost. This was not an issue in the socialist period when the fees were negligible and often free. The ComPC is silent on this matter. The CivPC has a provision which provides that the court orders the losing party to bear the cost for the assistance of a representative 'within a reasonable scope and by considering specific circumstances' (Art. 91). With the rapid increase of commercial lawyers involved in the procedure at the commercial court, this issue needs to be addressed by the legislature.

9   ENFORCEMENT OF JUDGMENTS

1)   General

Under the planned economy, the enforcement of judgments did not pose a problem. In disputes between state enterprises, voluntary enforcement by the losing party was the norm. The CivPC accommodated some provisions on enforcement, implemented by court bailiffs. The procedure was divided between enforcement on individuals and on state enterprises. The assets of the latter were heavily protected against creditors. On the other hand, since there were virtually no private businesses, no reference was made to enforcement *vis à vis* companies.

In 1997, the new Law on Civil Enforcement Procedure was enacted.[30] This law covers the enforcement of judgments of both the ordinary court and the commercial court, and together with the ComPC and CivPC, it is the basic law on enforcement of civil and commercial judgments. There is also the Law on Bailiffs enacted in 1997.[31]

The new Law on Civil Enforcement Procedure has set out the procedure of enforcement *vis à vis* companies for the first time. Another novelty is that the actual enforcement procedure was transferred from the court to the bailiffs, who

---

29   Anokhin, *supra*, pp.227-233.
30   *SZ RF*, 1997, No.30, item 3590.
31   *SZ RF*, 1997, No.30, item 3591.

form an office which is part of the Ministry of Justice. The underlying idea was that enforcement was not an exercise of judicial power. The court does not actually enforce judgments and decisions; it supervises the process.

Although with the enactment of the new Law, regulation of matters involving enforcement ceased to be an object of the CivPC, provisions of the CivPC on these matters are still valid. According to the joint circular of the Ministry of Justice and the Supreme Court, provisions of the CivPC should be applied, insofar as they do not contradict the new Law.[32]

2)   Enforcement Documents

The Law lists the following documents which serve as a basis of enforcement:

i)   enforcement lists issued by the court on the following grounds;
        a) judgments and decisions adopted by the court,
        b) awards of international arbitration institutions and other arbitration institutions,
        c) judgments of foreign courts and arbitration institutions,
        d) decisions of international organisations concerning the protection of rights and freedom of people.
ii)   enforcement orders by the court;
iii)   notarised agreement for the payment of alimony;
iv)   certificate of the Commission on Labour Disputes;
v)   decisions of government agencies such as the Ministry of Taxes and Levies;
vi)   decisions of government agencies and officials imposing administrative fine;
vii)   decisions of the bailiff.

The party which won the case is entitled to apply for an enforcement list (spisok) to the court or arbitration institution. If the original judgment was rendered by the ordinary court, the application must be made to the ordinary court, while if the judgment was rendered by the commercial court, the application is filed with the commercial court. In the cases where an arbitration institution to which the Provisional Statute on Arbitration Institutions is applicable has rendered an award, the institution has to refer the application for enforcement to the competent commercial court.

The Law on International Commercial Arbitration provides that an arbitral award, regardless of the country where it was rendered, is found to be mandatory and by applying to the competent court, should be enforced (Art.35).[33] Russia

---

32   Ryzhakov and Sergeev, *supra*, p.569.
33   *VSND RF i VS RF*, 1993 No.32, item.1240.

is a signatory to the New York Convention on the Enforcement of Foreign Arbitral Awards. The grounds for refusal of enforcement corresponds to those provided by the Convention. According to the commentary to the Law on Civil Enforcement Procedure, it is the ordinary court, and not the commercial court which has jurisdiction over the enforcement of foreign awards [See chapter 2].[34]

The system of enforcement orders were newly introduced in the CivPC by the 1995 amendment. It represents a facilitated procedure of enforcement. The order is issued by a judge of the ordinary court upon application by a creditor for seizure of money or movables from the debtor. The debtor is informed of the creditor's application and is entitled to respond within 20 days. In the absence of a response from the debtor, or with the acceptance of the claim, the judge issues the enforcement order, which is an enforcement document (CivPC 125-1 – 125-10).

Concerning notarised documents, only those which embody an agreement for payment of alimony qualify as an enforcement document. The CivPC used to allow enforcement on the basis of notarial deeds in general, but this was significantly narrowed in 1995.

3)   Enforcement Procedure

The actual enforcement procedure is handled by bailiffs on the basis of the enforcement documents listed in the Law. The bailiffs used to belong to the court. While there was no serious problem in enforcement until the 1980s, in the 1990s, a backlog started to accumulate, and judgments and decisions were enforced only in 25-35% of the cases which reached the bailiffs. While the caseload of bailiffs increased by 2.5 times between 1994 and 1997, the number of bailiffs remained the same.[35] Since the enactment of the Law on Bailiffs, offices of bailiffs were established from the Federal level to the district level. In 1999, there were 774 bailiff's positions and 11,000 people worked in the bailiff's office.[36]

The report of the Commercial Court of 2000 explicitly refers to the 'low level of qualification on the part of the bailiffs'. This is said to be reflected on the number of appeals against the decisions and acts of the bailiffs submitted to the court on the basis of the Law on Civil Enforcement Procedure (Art.90). There were 14,441 such appeals, of which 36,1% was found to be with grounds. It is not uncommon for bailiffs to return the enforcement list without grounds, on

---

34   T.Andreeva et al., *Kommentarii k federal'nomu zakonu Rossiskoi Federatsii ob ispolitel'nom proizvodstve*, Moscow 1998, p.23.
35   Kondrashov, *supra*, p.13.
36   *Ibid.*, p.18.

grounds not provided by law, or on formal grounds.[37] The bailiff, upon receiving the enforcement documents from the court or the party, within three days, renders a decision to initiate the enforcement proceedings. This decision should not change the judgment of the court, but sometimes, the bailiffs use discretion in interpreting the court's decision, the reason being that these decisions are unclear.

In principle, enforcement documents should be presented for enforcement within a certain period. Thus, judgments and orders of the ordinary court have to be presented within three years, while judgments of the commercial court have to be presented within 6 months. The same applies to the awards of international arbitration institutions and other arbitral institutions (Art.14).

A copy of the decision to initiate the procedure is sent to the creditor, debtor and the court. In order to ensure the effectiveness of the enforcement, upon application of the creditor, at the same time rendering the decision to initiate the proceedings, the bailiff may seize and freeze the assets of the debtor (Art.9).

The entire proceeding of enforcement must be completed within 2 months of the receiving of the enforcement document (Art.13). There is a short period (within a maximum of five days from the decision of the bailiff to initiate the enforcement procedure) in which the debtor is expected to enforce the judgment voluntarily. Expiration of this period is a prerequisite of compulsory enforcement (Art. 44).

The Law lists five measures of compulsory enforcement (Art.45):

i)   seizure of the property of the debtor and its sale;
ii)   seizure of wages, pension, stipend, and other income of the debtor;
iii) seizure of money and other property in possession of a third party;
iv)   retrieval of a property indicated in the enforcement document from the debtor and its transfer to the creditor;
v)   other measures provided by federal laws.

The Law provides for a general procedure of enforcement and then special provisions applicable to enforcement against juridical persons and individuals (chapters 5 and 6) .

In general, the process of seizure of the debtor's property is enforced in three stages; seizure, retrieval, and compulsory realisation (sale).

The Law provides for a certain order in taking possession of the debtor-physical person's property. First, roubles and foreign currency and other valuables, including those in the possession of banks and other financial institutions, will be seized. Cash found in possession of the debtor will also be seized. If there is

---

37   'Rabota arbitrazhnykh sudov....', *supra.*

information that the debtor has money or other valuables in bank accounts or custody, it is frozen. If there is no such information, the bailiff makes an inquiry with the tax agency, which is obliged to supply information within three days. Such information is also supplied to the creditor upon application to the Ministry of Taxes and Levies (Art.46).

It should be noted that banks and other financial institutions are under an obligation, within three days of receiving the enforcement document from either the bailiff or creditor, to enforce the content of the document, i.e. to freeze the account, or, in cases of absence of sufficient money in the account, make an entry in the document to that effect (Art.6). Non-compliance on the part of banks and financial institutions may entail a fine imposed by the court up to 50% of the amount to be seized (Art.86). The bailiff may make inquiries with the banks or tax authorities in search of other accounts of the debtor.[38] Foreign currency is seized only when there is not a sufficient amount of roubles with the debtor.

In cases where the amount of money found is insufficient to fulfil the claim, then, other properties of the debtor will be seized (Art.51). Depending on circumstances of the cases, the bailiff may seize all the assets of the debtor. The creditor does not have to present the list of assets of the debtor to the bailiff; the debtor, upon the request of the bailiff, must submit it. However, locating the assets of the debtor is often difficult (Art.46). One expert suggests applying to the bailiff's office for a search of the debtor's property.[39]

Property which is burdened by security may also be seized, provided that other properties have been seized but proved to be insufficient to cover the debt (Art.49).

In principle, seized properties are sold within two months of the seizure. Except for immovables, properties are sold by specialised organisations on the basis of a commission agreement and other arrangements (Art.54). Immovable property is sold by specialised organisations by auction (*torg*). If the property is not sold within two months, the creditor is entitled to this property (Art.549).

The CivPC has a list of assets which are exempted from seizure; one list covers assets of individuals and the other, assets of enterprises. Those lists have become obsolete and are expected to be deleted in the proposed new CivPC.

The Law provides for the priority order of seizure and sale of properties of juridical persons. First, properties which are not immediately related to production, e.g. securities, deposited money, foreign currency, light vehicles, office furniture, are to be seized. Second, finished products and other property which are not immediately related to production, and not intended to be used directly for production. Finally, immovable objects and raw materials, machine tools, equipment

---

38   *Kommentarii..* p.109.
39   V.Iarkov, 'Obrashchenie vzyskaniia na imushchestvo dolzhnika', *KhiP.* 1998 No.6, p.46.

and other basic means of production are to be seized (Art.59). This is quite different from the previous system under socialism in which basic means of production were totally exempted from enforcement.

The Law also has provisions on the enforcement of non-monetary claims. Particularly important is the enforcement of judgment mandating the debtor to do something or to refrain from doing something.

In cases where the debtor defies enforcement without justifiable grounds, the bailiff may impose fines (maximum 200 times minimum wage for the first time) and apply other measures including administrative sanctions and criminal sanctions to be imposed by relevant bodies (Art.85). If debtor's involvement is not needed for enforcement, the bailiff may arrange it to be enforced by a third party at the expense of the debtor. In such cases, the debtor will be charged three times as much as the cost of enforcement (Art.73).

16

INTERNATIONAL PRIVATE LAW

1   GENERAL

Russia does not have a separate law on international private law equivalent to those found in some jurisdictions such as the UK. Rules on international private law are found in various laws such as the Law on the Status of Foreign Individuals the Family Code, the Merchant Shipping Code, the Law on International Commercial Arbitration and the Code of Civil Procedure. For the status of foreign nationals in Russia, the USSR Statute on the Legal Status of Foreign Individuals in the USSR is still applicable with subsequent amendments.[1] Traditionally, a set of substantive rules on international private law have been accommodated in the Civil Code in Russia. The 1964 Civil Code had a part on the 'legal capacity of foreign nationals and persons without nationality, application of civil law of foreign nations and international treaties'.

The turning point of Russian international private law was the enactment of the Fundamental Principles of Civil Legislation of the USSR in 1990. This Law, which marked a complete departure from the socialist civil law, brought Russian international private law rules closer to internationally accepted rules. Rules contained in this Law 'were characterised by more flexibility and were brought closer to the needs of contemporary international relations as compared with the previous rules', although they were not comprehensive.[2] Part VII of the Law, which accommodated rules on international private law, remained in force even after the collapse of the USSR until Part Three of the Civil Code of the Russian Federation came into force in January 2002.

Part Three of the Civil Code of the Russian Federation was enacted in November 2001. It covers inheritance law and international private law. It is worth noting

---

1   *VVS SSSR*, 1981, No.26, item 836.
2   M.M.Boguslavskii, *Mezhdunarodnoe chastnoe pravo*, third edition, Moscow 1999, p.85.

that the Russian Federation joined the Hague Conference on Private International
Law in December 2001.

2   GENERAL RULES

The Code sets out the general rule on the applicable law as follows (Art.1186):

> Laws, which are applicable to civil law relationships with the participation of foreign
> individuals, juridical persons, or with foreign law elements, including instances where
> the object of civil law is located abroad, are determined on the basis of international
> treaties to which the Russian Federation is a party, the present Code, and other laws
> and custom recognised by the Russian Federation.
>
> If it is impossible to determine the applicable law in accordance with paragraph 1, the
> law of the country with which the civil law relationship with foreign elements is most
> closely connected shall be applied.

In determining the applicable law, legal concepts are to be interpreted in accordance with Russian law (Art.1187, para.1).

The content of the foreign law is determined in accordance with its official
interpretation, practice of application, and the doctrine of the given foreign state.
In order to ascertain the content of foreign law, the court may seek the assistance
of the Ministry of Justice of the Russian Federation. If the content of the foreign
law cannot be ascertained within a reasonable period, Russian law is applied.

Even in the period of socialism, foreign law was applied in Russia by the
predecessor to the present International Commercial Arbitration Court. Now it
is not rare for the Russian commercial court to apply foreign law in transnational
cases:

> A Russian joint stock company initiated an action in the Russian commercial court
> against a German company regarding a contract of lease of a ship. Originally, the
> German company sold the Russian party a ship, which was to be operated by a joint
> venture of both parties. However, this joint venture failed to materialise, and the Russian
> party, which intended to pay for the ship out of the profits from this operation, defaulted.
> Both parties eventually concluded a lease agreement, the German company being the
> lessor and the Russian company, the lessee of the ship. However, this scheme did not
> work. In the claim submitted to the court, the Russian party argued, *inter alia*, that the
> terms of the lease agreement were extremely disadvantageous, and that it was void as
> a predatory transaction under Russian law.
>
>   The court ruled that since the parties had failed to agree on the governing law, the
> law of the country of the lessor, in this case, German law, was applicable by virtue of

the Fundamental Principles of Civil Legislation of 1990, and denied the application of the provision of the Russian Civil Code on predatory transactions.[3]

An important exception to the above which allows the application of foreign law is the mandatory norms of Russian legislation which govern the given relationship regardless of the applicable law as determined by law or by the choice of the parties (Art.1192, para.1).

There are some cases decided by the predecessor to the International Commercial Arbitration Court on this matter. In one case, the provision of the Russian Civil Code which prohibits changes to the length of the limitation period for an action and to the manner of its calculation by mutual consent of the parties was applied, and the agreement was found void.[4] This does not mean, however, that Russian law should always be applied to the limitation period. There was a case where a provision on the limitation period of a foreign law, in this case, Japanese law, which was the law of the country of the seller, was applied under the 1990 Fundamental Principles of Civil Legislation.[5]

In addition to the mandatory provisions of Russian law which are binding on the court, the court may consider mandatory norms of another country which has a close connection with the relationship in question (*ibid.*, para.2).

Another exception to the general rule is public policy. The applicable law determined in accordance with the Code, 'in an exceptional instance', is not applied, if its application apparently contradicts the basis of the legal order (public order) of the Russian Federation. In such cases, if necessary, Russian law is applied (Art.1193).

Restriction of the application of foreign law based upon public policy is common in most jurisdictions. The 1964 Civil Code simply provided that foreign law was not applicable if its application was against the basis of the Soviet system.[6] However, even under the Soviet system, the 'exceptional' nature of this provision was stressed. An example cited in a commentary at that time involved a case where a foreign law allowed racial and gender discrimination in the people's capacity to leave a will.[7]

At the doctrinal level, the exceptional nature of the application of public policy continues to be stressed. A leading specialist of international private law refers

---

3   Obzor sudebno-arbitrazhnoi praktiki razresheniia sporov po delam s uchastiem inostrannykh lits, Informatsionnoe pis'mo VAS RF, February 16, 1998, item 12, *VVS RF* 1998 No.4, pp.50-51.
4   Cases No.139 and No.180, 1988, cited in Bogusulavskii, supra, p.96.
5   International Commercial Arbitration Court ed., *Arbitrazhnaia praktika za 1998 g.*, Moscow 1999, pp.138-140.
6   Art.568 of the 1964 Civil Code.
7   *Kommentarii k grazhdanskome kodekusu RSFSR*, pp.674-675.

to the 'extremely cautious approach to the problem of applying this concept in practice'.[8]

Reflecting this cautious approach, the current provision contains the following paragraph:

> Refusal to apply norms of foreign law may not be justified merely by the difference in the legal, political, or economic systems of the given foreign country with those of the Russian Federation.

Public policy is often quoted by Russian parties in order to prevent the enforcement of foreign arbitral awards against them [see Chapter 2].

3   RENVOI

A novelty in the Civil Code is the provision on renvoi (remission).

In Russia, there always has been a negative attitude towards renvoi. An example is the case decided in the 1960s by the International Arbitration Commission of the USSR Chamber of Commerce:

> An English company Romlus Films Ltd initiated an action at the then Foreign Trade Arbitration Commisison against a Soviet foreign trade organisation. The case involved a right in a film 'Sleeping Beauty'. According to Soviet law, since the contract was concluded in London, English law was applicable. However, the English rules of conflict of laws referred to Soviet law, and therefore, the respondent argued that Soviet law was applicable in this case. The arbitration tribunal rejected this argument and ruled that regardless of the English rules, the application of renvoi was a matter of Soviet law, and that Soviet doctrine and practice, as a rule, did not acknowledge renvoi in foreign trade contracts.[9]

Under the new Civil Code, as a rule, any reference to foreign law is to be regarded as a reference to the substantive law, and not the conflict of law rules of that country, except in cases related to the status of individuals (Art.1190, para.1). The same provision is contained in the Law on International Commercial Arbitration.

---

8   Bogusulavskii, *supra*, p.95.
9   *Ibid.*, pp.91-92.

4   PERSONAL LAW

Part Three of the Civil Code has newly introduced the concept of personal law of individuals and juridical persons. The personal law of individuals is determined by their nationality, not by their domicile. However, if a foreign national resides in Russia, his personal law is Russian law. If this person has dual nationality, one of which is Russian, Russian law is the personal law (Art.1195).

Legal capacity and the capacity to effect juristic acts are determined by the personal law of the given individual (arts.1197 and 1198).

Concerning juridical persons, the personal law is the law of the country where the given juridical person was established. On the basis of the personal law, the following matters concerning juridical persons are determined in accordance with the law of the place of the establishment:

i)   status of the organisation as a juridical person;

ii)   organisational-legal form of the juridical person;

iii)   requirements to the name of the juridical person;

iv)   establishment, reorganisation and liquidation of juridical persons, including succession;

v)   content of the legal capacity of the juridical person;

vi)   manner in which the juridical person obtains rights and assumes obligations;

vii)   internal relations, including relations with the members;

viii) capability of the juridical person to respond to its obligations.

However, juridical persons are not allowed to refer to the restrictions of power imposed on its bodies or representatives in effecting juristic acts, which are not known in the country where the juristic act is effected. This does not apply when it is proved that the opposite party had known or should have known of such restrictions (Art.1202).

5   APPLICABLE LAW IN PROPRIETARY RELATIONS

1)   Ownership Rights and other Real Rights

The general rule is that the content of the ownership rights and other real rights on immovables and movables, and the manner of exercising and defending these rights are determined by the law of the country where the property is located (Art.1205, para.1). The emergence and termination of the ownership rights and other real rights are determined by the law of the country where the given property was located at the time at which the incident which serves as the ground for the emergence or termination of the rights occurred. Regarding these rights that arise from transactions on properties in transit, the law of the consignor's country applies (Art.1296, paras. 1 and 2). Ships and satellites are regarded as immovables; regarding ships and satellites which are subject to registration, the law of the country where they are registered is applicable (Art.1207).

2)   The Form of Juristic Acts

As a general rule, the form of a juristic act is subject to the law of the country where the given juristic act is effected (Art.1209, para.1). On the other hand, the Code provides that insofar as the form required by Russian law is observed, the given juristic act will not be found void for non-compliance with the form.

However, there is an exception. With foreign trade contracts in which one of the parties is a Russian juridical person, the form is determined by Russian law, regardless of the place of the contract. This also applies when one of the parties is an individual entrepreneur registered in Russia (*ibid.*, para.2).

Under socialism, there used to be a requirement that foreign trade contracts must be signed by two designated persons on the Russian side, which was set out in a 1978 edict of the USSR Council of Ministers. Failure to comply with this requirement made the contract void. After the collapse of socialism, it was not clear whether this requirement still existed. There was a serious debate on this issue among the specialists.[10] The current view is that this requirement of two signatures no longer exists; the 1978 Edict is no longer in force.[11] However, several authors point out that nevertheless, such a requirement is still valid if it is provided in the statute of the given Russian organisation. An example of a treasury enterprise which has a statute with such a requirement is cited.[12]

Thus, the only formal requirement to the form of foreign trade contracts now is that such contracts must be made in writing. The Civil Code provides that the failure to comply with this requirement makes a foreign trade contract void (Art.162, para.3). It is unusual for foreign trade contracts themselves to be concluded orally, but in the past, what was at issue was not the validity of the contract per se, but the subsequent amendments to the contract which have not been

---

10   V.P.Zvekov, *Mezhdunarodnoe chastnoe pravo*, Moscow 1999, p.281.
11   O.N.Sadikov, *Kommentarii k Grazhdanskomu Kodeksu Rossiiskoi Federatsii, chasti pervoi*, enlarged edition, Moscow 1999, p.351.
12   Boguslavskii, *supra*, p.204; Zvekov, *supra.*, p.282.

effected in a written form. In the practice of international commercial arbitration in Moscow, such agreements were found void.[13]

The definition of foreign trade activities is given in the Law on the State Regulation of Foreign Trade of 1995.[14] It should be noted that the scope of foreign trade activities extends beyond the trade and covers 'entrepreneurial activities in the area of the exchange of goods, work, services, information, and products of intellectual activities'.

3)   Contracts

(1)   Choice of Applicable Law by the Parties

As a rule, parties are free to choose the governing law of the contract (Art.1210, para.1):

> Parties to a contract may, at the time of the conclusion of the contract, or subsequently, choose by mutual consent, the law which is to be applied to the rights and obligations concerning this contract.

The choice of law by the parties must be either expressly stated, or should be able to be definitely derived from the terms of the contract or the entire circumstances of the case (*ibid.*, para.2). Agreement of the parties on the choice of law after the conclusion of the contract has a retrospective effect, but must not affect the rights of third parties (*ibid.*, para.3). Parties are allowed to choose the law for the entire contract as well as for part of it (*ibid.*, para.4).

Unlike in many other jurisdictions, in Russia, in the absence of an explicit clause, the governing law cannot be assumed from the parties' choice of the venue of dispute settlement. This has been the practice of international commercial arbitration in Russia.[15] The commercial court also takes this approach:

> A Belgian company concluded a contract of supply of equipment to a Russian company. The parties agreed in the contract that all disputes arising from the contract should be subject to the jurisdiction of the Russian commercial court. However, there was no explicit agreement on the governing law.
> The Russian party defaulted, and the Belgian company brought an action in the Russian commercial court for payment. The defendant acknowledged that the company

---

13   Zvekov, *ibid.,* p.283.
14   *SZ RF*, 1995 No.42, item 3923.
15   Boguslavskii, *supra*, p.205.

was at default, but argued that the calculation of the payment should be made under Russian law, since the venue of the court was Russia. The court ruled that the choice of Russia as the venue of dispute settlement did not automatically mean that the relationship between the parties should be subject to Russian law. Absence of the expression of will of the parties means that the choice of the applicable law was left to the court. In such cases, the court is guided by the conflict of law rules of its own law – Russian law. Thus, the court applied the Fundamental Principles of Civil Legislation which was in force at that time and applied Belgian law, which was the law of the seller's country.[16]

(2)   Applicable Law in the Absence of the Agreement of the Parties

In the absence of agreement on the governing law between the parties, the law of the country with which the contract is most closely connected is applied. This means the law of the country where 'the party which performs the act which has the decisive meaning for the contract' is domiciled, or has the basis of business, unless otherwise provided by law, or unless another conclusion emerges from the terms or the content of the contract, or the entire circumstances of the case (Art.1211, paras. 1 and 2).

'The party which performs the act which has the decisive meaning for the contract' varies. The Code has a list of such parties for basic types of contracts (*ibid.*, para.3):

i)   contracts of sale – the seller;
ii)   contracts of gift – the donor;
iii)   contracts of lease – the lessor;
iv)   contracts of unpaid use – the lender;
v)   work contracts – the contractor;
vi)   contracts of carriage – the carrier;
vii)   contracts of freight forwarding – the expeditor;
viii)   contracts of credit – the creditor;
ix)   contracts of financing under assignment of claims – the financial agent;
x)   contracts of bank deposit – the bank;
xi)   contracts of storage – the custodian;
xii)   insurance contracts – the insurer;
xiii)   contracts of mandate – the agent;
xiv)   commission contracts – the commission agent;
xv)   agency contracts – the agent;
xvi)   contracts of commercial concession (franchising) – the party who obtained the right;

---

16   Obzor...., *supra*, item 5.

xvii) contracts of pledge – the pledgor;
xviii) contracts of suretyship – the surety;
ixx)   licensing contracts – the licensor.

As for 'the law of the country with which the contract is most closely connected', the following rules apply (*ibid.*, para.4):

i)   design and construction contracts – the law of the country where the object of the work is located:

ii)   contracts of simple partnership (joint venture contracts) – the law of the country where the basic activities are performed;

iii) contracts concluded on the basis of tender, auction, or in the exchange – the law of the country where the tender or auction took place, or where the exchange is located.

(3)   Consumer Contracts

In cases where a party to a contract is an individual who uses, obtains, or orders movables, or has such an intention for personal, family, or domestic needs, regardless of the chosen law, the mandatory norms of the law of the country where the consumer is domiciled are applied, if i) the conclusion of the contract was preceded by an offer made to the consumer or an advertisement in that country and the consumer performed acts needed for the conclusion of the contract in this country, or ii) the opposite party or the agent of the opposite party received the order of the consumer in this country (Art.1212, para.1).

(4)   Contracts regarding Immovables

In the absence of an agreement on the governing law between the parties, the law of the country which is most closely connected to the contract is applied. Unless otherwise provided by law, or unless another conclusion emerges from the terms or the content of the contract, or the entire circumstances of the case, such a law is deemed to be the law where the given immovable is located (Art.1213, para.1).

Contracts concerning pieces of land, acreage of subsoil resources, divided water resources and other immovables are governed by Russian law. This raises the issue of whether production sharing agreements need to be regulated entirely by Russian law. In the past projects, this was not the case.

(5)   Assignment of Claims

The law applicable to the agreement between the previous and the new creditors is determined in accordance with the above general rules of the choice of law (Art.1216, para.1 and Art.1211, paras. 1 and 2). Problems of the permissibility of assignment, the relationship between the new creditor and the debtor, the presentation of the claim to the debtor, and the appropriate performance by the debtor are governed by the law which is applicable to the claim which is the object of assignment (Art.1216, para.2).

(6)   Interests

Grounds for charging interest, the manner of calculation and the amount of interest for monetary obligations are determined by the law of the country which is applicable to the obligation (Art.1218).

(7)   Matters to be Determined by the Applicable Law

When the law of a particular country has been chosen or determined to be applied to a contract, this law specifically covers the following matters (Art.1215):

i)	interpretation of the contract;
ii)	rights and obligations of the parties;
iii)	performance of the contract;
iv)	outcome of non-performance or inappropriate performance of the contract;
v)	termination of the contract;
vi)	outcome of the voidness of the contract.

4)   Obligations arising from the Causing of Harm (Tort)

To obligations arising from tort, the law of the country in which the tortious act took place, or the circumstances which gave rise to the claim for compensation emerged, is applied. If, as a result of such an act or such circumstances, the damage emerged in another country, the law of that country may be applied, provided that the tortfeasor has foreseen or should have foreseen that the damage would emerge in another country (Art.1219, para.1).

Concerning product liability, in claims for compensation based upon defective products, works and services, the victim may choose from the law of the country where the producer or the seller resides or has the basic place of business, the country where the victim resides, or the country where the work was performed, the service was provided or the product was obtained (Art.1221, para.1).

5)   Unjust Enrichment

The law of the country in which unjust enrichment took place is applicable to obligations based upon unjust enrichment. However, parties may agree to have the *lex fori* applied.

6)   Competition Law

Whether this is a problem of international private law or not is questionable, but there is a provision to the effect that the law of the country whose market was penetrated by unjust competition is applicable, as a rule, to obligations arising from such relations (Art.1222).

INDEX